Anne Barton's essays on Shakespeare and his contemporaries are characterized by their combination of intelligence, humanity and elegance. This book contains two previously unpublished pieces and makes accessible to a wider public of students and scholars essays which have previously been available only in article form, here revised and updated where necessary. In a linked but wide-ranging collection the author addresses such diverse issues as Shakespeare's trust (and mistrust) of language, the puzzle of Falstaff's inability to survive in a genuinely comic world, the unconsummated marriage of Imogen and Posthumus in *Cymbeline*, Shakespeare's debt to Livy and Machiavelli in *Coriolanus*, 'hidden' kings in the Tudor and Stuart history play, comedy and the city, and deer-parks as places of liberation and danger in English drama up to and beyond the Restoration. Professor Barton looks at both major and neglected plays of the period and the ongoing dialogue between them. Taken together the essays reveal a remarkable range of reference and depth of insight, together with an increasing emphasis on historical and social contexts.

ESSAYS, MAINLY SHAKESPEAREAN

ESSAYS, MAINLY
SHAKESPEAREAN

ANNE BARTON

Professor of English, University of Cambridge, and Fellow of Trinity College

Published by the Press Syndicate of the University of Cambridge
The Pitt Building, Trumpington Street, Cambridge CB2 1RP
40 West 20th Street, New York, NY 10011–4211, USA
10 Stamford Road, Oakleigh, Melbourne 3166, Australia

First published 1994

Printed in Great Britain at the University Press, Cambridge

A catalogue record for this book is available from the British Library

Library of Congress cataloguing in publication data
Barton, Anne.
Essays, mainly Shakespearean / Anne Barton.
p.   cm.
Includes bibliographical references and index.
ISBN 0 521 40444 4 (hardback)
1. Shakespeare, William, 1564–1616 – Criticism and interpretation.
2. Shakespeare, William, 1564–1616 – Contemporaries.
3. English drama – History and criticism. I. Title.
PR2976.B34 1994 822.3'3 – dc20   93-25374 CIP

ISBN 0 521 40444 4 hardback

In memoriam
Muriel Clara Bradbrook
1909–1993

Contents

ix

Illustrations

xi

Preface

With one exception, the sixteen essays in this collection were written over a period of some twenty-five years. Two of them, 'Comic London', the 1990 Patrides lecture at the University of York, and 'Wrying but a little', a paper given at the International Shakespeare Conference in Stratford-upon-Avon in 1992, have not been published before. The others have appeared separately, in various periodicals or volumes of essays, often in honour of former teachers and colleagues. Although I have found, in revisiting the work of earlier years, that the combination of responsibility and distance can be disquieting, I am glad that, by reprinting essays written for such friends as C. L. Barber, M. C. Bradbrook, Kenneth Muir, Arthur Colby Sprague and J. P. Stern, I can give my tribute to them a longer life in print.

I have been guided in my selection by the advice of various colleagues and by readers for Cambridge University Press. Some of these have regretted the omission of the introductions to *Hamlet* and *The Tempest* written for the New Penguin Shakespeare, and the wholesale exclusion of those produced for the comedies in *The Riverside Shakespeare*. The ready availability of these, and their address to a more popular audience than most of the essays chosen, explains that decision. Others have missed two pieces on Jonson, 'Harking back to Elizabeth: Ben Jonson and Caroline nostalgia', which appeared in *ELH* 48 (1982), and '*The New Inn* and the problem of Jonson's late style', in *English Literary Renaissance* 9 (1979), as well as the review article, 'The distinctive voice of Massinger', from *The Times Literary Supplement* of 20 May 1977. The first two, however, were absorbed virtually intact into *Ben Jonson, Dramatist*, also published by Cambridge University Press (1984), while the Massinger piece has already been reprinted in Douglas Howard's collection, *Philip Massinger: A Critical Reassessment* (Cambridge, 1985). It has therefore seemed best to include only an outline sketch of my views on Shakespeare's greatest contemporary, in the form of a paper, 'Shakespeare and Jonson', given originally in 1981 at the Second Congress of the Shakespeare Association in Stratford-upon-Avon, and subsequently published as part of its proceedings. Although this essay foreshadows part of the argument later developed in *Ben Jonson, Dramatist*, it is independent of that book as the other Jonson pieces are not.

Not without a few qualms and misgivings, I have allowed myself to be persuaded that '*Love's Labour's Lost*', my earliest article, written when I was still an undergraduate, and published in *Shakespeare Quarterly* 4 (1953) during my final year at Bryn Mawr, ought to form part of this collection. As an essay drawing fresh attention to a play extraordinarily neglected or misrepresented before that date, it does not seem to me negligible. Both its high estimate of the comedy and the particular reading it advances are things in which I still believe. But, however influential it may have been, it is now a period piece, written in a style all too redolent of a youthful passion for Walter Pater. As such, it craves a certain amount of indulgence from readers (myself included) who come to it some forty years later. I have cut the essay somewhat, mainly in order to relieve it of some of its (mostly adjectival) verbiage, but otherwise made no attempt to revise it. Its final paragraph, embarrassing though I now find it, was the germ of what became *Shakespeare and the Idea of the Play*, and I have for that reason allowed it to stand.

Essays, Mainly Shakespearean is divided into two parts. The first is focussed on Shakespeare himself. It begins with my most recent piece, 'Wrying but a little', reflecting my current interest in law and social structure, in patterns of human interaction on and off stage in Renaissance England, and then moves on to the earliest ones included here: '*Love's Labour's Lost*' and 'Shakespeare and the limits of language' (1971). The latter explores a concern (evident throughout the book in various formulations) with what language can and cannot do, both for the characters who must rely upon it and, in more specifically theatrical terms, for the dramatist. The remainder of the first section is devoted to three loosely paired sets of essays: on comedy, on the Roman plays, and on the last plays. In the first group, I consider the immanence of endings in *As You Like It*, *Twelfth Night* and beyond, and Falstaff's struggle to survive when he leaves his proper world of the history plays for the alien one of Shakespearean

comedy. The relation of Renaissance drama to its classical inheritance – a recurring preoccupation of this volume – is especially
marked in the pieces on *Antony and Cleopatra* (1974) and *Coriolanus*
(1985). In the two essays on Shakespeare's last plays which conclude
this section, I explore the changed relationship of verse to speaker,
and the complex interplay of romance convention with the 'real'.

'Enter Mariners wet', the later of these two essays, also addresses
itself to some of the older romances from which Shakespeare drew. In
this respect, it looks forward to the second section of the book,
concerned with the active interrelations between Shakespeare and
his contemporaries: the presence not only of his voice, but those of
Jonson, Massinger, Ford and other dramatists, in an ongoing
dialogue among plays. A considerable number of obscure or minor
works – *Sir Clyomon and Sir Clamydes*, Cartwright's *The Royal Slave*, the
collaborative *Sir John Oldcastle*, or Heywood's delightfully preposterous *The Foure Prentises of London* – feature here. They do so partly out
of a conviction that the major achievements of the period can only be
understood by way of its adjacent, lesser efforts, but also because the
latter (many of them popular in their time) can richly repay
attention when allowed to speak for themselves. There is probably a
link here with my initial essay on *Love's Labour's Lost* and the Paterian
principle that underlay my defence of that (at the time) slighted
comedy. Apart from the great artists, Pater wrote in his essay on
Botticelli, there are some 'who have a distinct faculty of their own by
which they convey to us a peculiar quality of pleasure which we
cannot get elsewhere; and these too have their place in general
culture, and must be interpreted to it by those who have felt their
charm strongly'. That can be as true of individual plays as of their
authors. Heywood's *The Foure Prentises of London* is not *Henry V*, any
more than *Sir Clyomon and Sir Clamydes* is *The Winter's Tale*, but they
deserve to be appreciated for themselves, not simply as a way of
recognizing (as I unfashionably think we should) the intrinsic
superiority of Shakespeare. Critics, Bacon believed, 'are the brushers
of noblemen's clothes'. Many of the works which have received
attentions of this kind from me over the years are very minor gentry
indeed, but I have liked presenting them to other readers looking well
turned-out.

The pairing of essays in Part I (those on comedy, the Roman plays
and last plays) recurs in Part II. Essays 9 and 10, for instance, are both
concerned with disguised kings, while 10 and 11 belong together as

pieces centred on John Ford. The final three are about cities. 'London comedy and the ethos of the city' (1979) meshes with 'Comic London' (1990) and, to some extent, with the wide-ranging essay on 'Parks and Ardens' (1992) which ends the collection. I have not emphasized links of this kind for autobiographical reasons (just as I have avoided a chronological arrangement) but because I hope that putting related essays together will allow different arguments to interact and, without suggesting a monograph in sixteen chapters, provide a sense of continuity. By no means all the connections were apparent at the time of writing: they seem, rather, to have sprung from the gradual discovery of a subject. If this reflects, perhaps, something of what the word 'essay' should mean, it also leaves the writer with a sense (probably illusory) that to have recognized the dimensions of that subject from the start might have benefitted the earlier pieces.

Certainly, I could imagine rewriting any one of these meshed groups, not only consolidating them but developing examples and themes. Only once, however, in the case of 'Nature's piece 'gainst fancy', the essay on *Antony and Cleopatra*, have I actually indulged in a modest amount of recasting. In revising this essay, which began as an Inaugural lecture at Bedford College, I have tried not to stray too far from the spirit of the original – addressed as it was to a general audience; nor have I complicated the analysis at certain points where it would be tempting to re-think 1973 from the vantage point of a further twenty years. Elsewhere in the volume, I have contented myself with corrections only of date, fact, and quotation and with a certain amount of scholarly up-dating in the notes.

In his essay 'Of Bookes', Montaigne offers an apologia for his habits of reading and writing. With disarming but tough-minded modesty, he concedes his casualness of study, selective taste, and large areas of ignorance. 'If one booke seeme tedious unto me', he writes (in Florio's 1603 translation), 'I take another.' Not for him arduous hours among back issues of the *PMLA*. No one these days, myself included, can afford such self-indulgence. Yet there is something to be said for that 'blitheness' which Montaigne seeks to preserve against 'plodding contention', and even (it may be) for his admission that 'hardly could I give others reasons for my discourses, that give none unto my selfe, and am not well satisfied with them'. The cultivation of method in critical practice, as of historical knowledge as an end in itself, has led in some quarters to a neo-scholasticism resembling that which Montaigne was, so learnedly, reacting against. There is at least partial virtue in the humane principles he claimed to follow: 'or if I studie, I onely endeavour to find out the knowledge that teacheth or handleth the knowledge of my selfe, and which may instruct me how to die well, and how to live well'.

It would be presumptuous for someone who belongs to the academy, and who has necessarily been affected by the winds of critical fashion, to insist that her critical essays are a mode of self-enquiry in the manner of Montaigne. It is easy to recognize in the pages that follow certain evolving, general influences: formalist analysis of play-texts, theories of the role of language in imaginative writing, an increasing emphasis on historical and social contexts. If there is any progression apparent in my essays, it is an increasing need for footnotes, the product (in part) of a tendency, recognizably of the moment, to situate texts within a complexly understood moment of time. What I hope begins to happen in the most recent pieces collected here – 'Parks and Ardens' and 'Wrying but a little' – is the emergence of a style of criticism which is open to historical circumstance without losing touch with the general shape as well as the details of plays. It is in this direction that my work in this and later fields is currently moving. Reading back, however, through my pieces on Shakespeare and other dramatists of his period, I have been struck by a long-term insistence upon literature as a source of pleasure and – somewhat in the style of Montaigne – by my habitual use of it to complicate and extend my own understanding. Bacon claimed, in *The Advancement of Learning*, that 'it is the duty and virtue of all knowledge to abridge the infinity of individual experience, as much as the conception of truth will permit, and to remedy the complaint of *vita brevis, ars longa*'. He was not thinking in that passage of poetry or drama, but the statement has always seemed to me, and still does, peculiarly applicable to that special kind of knowledge which imaginative literature can provide.

Acknowledgements

All quotations from Shakespeare have been keyed to *The Riverside Shakespeare*, ed. G. Blakemore Evans *et al.* (Boston, 1974). Unless otherwise indicated, dates given for plays are those suggested in *Annals of English Drama 975–1700*, by Alfred Harbage, rev. S. Schoenbaum (London, 1964).

'*Love's Labour's Lost*', my first publication of any kind, and by far the earliest essay reprinted here, appeared initially in *The Shakespeare Quarterly* IV, 4 (1953); 'Shakespeare and the limits of language' in *Shakespeare Survey 24* (Cambridge University Press, 1971); 'Falstaff and the comic community' in *Shakespeare's Rough Magic: Essays in Memory of C. L. Barber*, ed. P. Erickson and C. Kahn (Associated University Presses, 1985); '*As You Like It* and *Twelfth Night*: Shakespeare's sense of an ending' as chapter 8 of *Shakespearean Comedy*, ed. M. Bradbury and D. Palmer, Stratford-upon-Avon Studies (© Edward Arnold Publishers Ltd, 1972). 'Nature's piece 'gainst fancy': the divided catastrophe in *Antony and Cleopatra*' was published separately in its original form in 1974 as my Bedford College Inaugural lecture. 'Livy, Machiavelli and Shakespeare's *Coriolanus*' first appeared in *Shakespeare Survey 38* (Cambridge University Press, 1985); 'Leontes and the spider: language and speaker in Shakespeare's last plays' in *Shakespeare's Styles: Essays Presented to Kenneth Muir*, ed. P. Edwards, I.-S. Ewbank and G. K. Hunter (Cambridge University Press, 1980); and 'Enter Mariners wet: realism in Shakespeare's last plays' in *Studies in European Realism: Essays in Honour of J. P. Stern*, ed. N. Boyle and M. Swales (Cambridge University Press, 1986).

In Part II of the collection, 'The king disguised: Shakespeare's *Henry V* and the comical history' was published originally in *The Triple Bond: Essays in Honour of Arthur Colby Sprague*, ed. J. Price (Penn

State University Press, 1975), pp. 92–117 (© 1975 by The Pennsylvania State University); 'He that plays the king: Ford's *Perkin Warbeck* and the Stuart history play' in *English Drama: Forms and Development. Essays in Honour of Muriel Clara Bradbrook*, ed. M. Axton and R. Williams (Cambridge University Press, 1977); 'Oxymoron and the structure of Ford's *The Broken Heart*, in *Essays and Studies*, ed. I.-S. Ewbank (John Murray for the English Association, 1980); 'Shakespeare and Jonson' in *Shakespeare, Man of the Theatre*, eds. J. Halio, K. Muir, D. Palmer (Associated University Presses, 1983); 'London comedy and the ethos of the city' in *The London Journal* 4, no. 2 (Longman Group Ltd, 1979); and 'Parks and Ardens' in *Proceedings of the British Academy* 80 (1992).

I am grateful for permissions to reprint granted by the publishers indicated above.

Over and above the indebtedness to individual scholars and friends that I have tried to record in particular essays (and in my Preface), I should like more generally to thank Michael Cordner for not only urging the idea of such a collection upon me, but taking time from his own work to sketch out a possible table of contents. I am also grateful to John Barton, Alison Hennegan, Peter Holland, John Kerrigan, and Jeremy Maule for valuable suggestions and critical advice on the project as a whole.

A grant from Trinity College made it possible for me to employ an indexer, as well as a research assistant to check and correct quotations throughout, in accord with newer and more authoritative editions, and to key the earlier as well as later essays to the Riverside edition of Shakespeare. Nick de Somogyi, who undertook this latter, onerous but less than exciting task, accomplished it with admirable accuracy and intelligence, often going beyond his brief to amend errors of a substantive kind that had escaped my notice. I am deeply grateful to him, to Jonathan Pritchard, who prepared the index, and for the generosity of Trinity College.

PART I

CHAPTER I

'Wrying but a little': marriage, law and sexuality in the plays of Shakespeare

In the second act of *Cymbeline*, Jachimo, emerging stealthily into Imogen's bedchamber, suddenly remembers a fellow-countryman: 'Our Tarquin', who even thus, 'Did softly press the rushes, ere he waken'd / The chastity he wounded' (II.2.12–14). Jachimo does not wake Imogen. He merely records the particulars of her room – its arras, figures, paintings, the adornment of the bed and physical features of its sleeping occupant. Only at the end does he notice Imogen's book, Ovid's *Metamorphoses*, with its page turned down at that point in the tale of Tereus 'Where Philomele gave up' (II.2.45). Of no conceivable use to him in the incriminating account destined for the ears of Posthumus Leonatus, this culminating detail is far more than an ironic comment on Imogen's choice, on this of all nights, of the Tereus/Philomel story as something with which to read herself asleep. It focusses attention on the blurred and contradictory nature of the sexual signals given out by this bedroom, and Jachimo's activities in it, as a whole.

That his voyeuristic intrusion upon the unconscious Imogen constitutes a symbolic rape is obvious. But what kind of rape? Tarquin's victim Lucrece, in all versions of the legend, was a wife whose marriage with Collatine had been consummated some time before. Tereus violated a virgin. Imogen's position is far less clear. Shakespeare sends his heroine to sleep in a chamber where (as Jachimo reveals when he returns to Italy) the heady spectacle, in the arras, of Cleopatra acquiring yet another Roman lover on the river Cydnus seems implicitly rebuked by the chimney-piece on the south wall: 'Chaste Dian bathing'. Ethereal 'golden cherubins' suspended in the fretwork of the roof exist in a similarly uneasy relationship with the pair of blind cupids in the fireplace, each leaning on a hymeneal torch (II.4.82, 88). Imogen herself reminds Jachimo of Venus ('Cytherea'), but she is also a 'fresh lily, / And whiter than the

3

sheets' (II.2.14, 15–16). Lilies are flowers linked with marriage,
through their association with the goddess Juno, who wears a diadem
of them in Jonson's wedding masque *Hymenaei* (1606). They connote
motherhood as well, because they sprang from the milk that spilled
from Juno's breast when the infant Hercules, laid there in secret, was
taken away. Rather less cheerfully, Rabbinic commentators discovered their origins in the tears of Eve when she realized, after the
expulsion from Eden, that she was pregnant.[1] But lilies also, of course,
symbolize the unsullied purity of the Virgin Mary in countless
representations of the Annunciation, an idea exploited by Cranmer
at the end of *Henry VIII*, when he prophesies of the infant Queen
Elizabeth that 'yet a virgin, / A most un-spotted lily shall she pass /
To th' ground, and all the world shall mourn her' (v.3.60–3).

Imogen's bracelet, the 'manacle of love' (I.I.122) her husband
gave her when they parted, slides with surprising ease from her arm:
'As slippery', Jachimo notes in an arrestingly oblique comparison,
'as the Gordian knot was hard!' (II.2.34). The Gordian knot, whose
intricacies could be severed by violence, but never untied, had
become an emblem of Christian marriage. 'Come faire *Emelia* the
preeste is gon', Polidor says in *The Taming of A Shrew* (?1589):

> And at the church your father and the reste,
> Do stay to see our marriadge rites performde,
> And knit in sight of heaven this *Gordian* knot,
> That teeth of fretting time may nere untwist.[2]

But it could also be used, as it is (for instance) in *The Duchess of Malfi*
(1614) or in the manuscript play *Tom a Lincoln*, now available in a
Malone Society reprint, and very close to *Cymbeline* in date, of an
unsolemnized *de praesenti* handfast in a chamber.[3]

Finally, Jachimo's discovery of the 'mole cinque-spotted' under
Imogen's breast is 'a voucher, / Stronger than ever law could make'
that 'I have pick'd the lock, and ta'en / The treasure of her honor'
(II.2.38–42). Imogen and Posthumus, as we are informed at the start,
are 'married' (I.I.18). That word has a very precise significance in

---

[1] Ernst and Johanna Lehner, *The Folklore and Symbolism of Flowers, Plants and Trees* (New York, 1960), pp. 32–3.

[2] Anon, *The Taming of A Shrew*, in *Narrative and Dramatic Sources of Shakespeare's Plays*, ed. Geoffrey Bullough, 1 (London, 1957), scene xiv, p. 98, lines 71–5.

[3] John Webster, *The Duchess of Malfi*, ed. John Russell Brown (London, 1964), 1.1.480. *Tom A Lincoln*, prep. G. R. Proudfoot (Oxford, 1992), p. 82, line 3023.

Shakespeare, although not always for his contemporaries. When Don Pedro, at the end of *Much Ado About Nothing*, misuses it after the handfast that officially betroths Beatrice and Benedick – 'How dost thou, Benedick the married man?' – he is instantly corrected: 'I do *purpose* to marry', Benedick replies (v.4.99, 105). 'Treasure', on the other hand, frequently refers in the period to a maiden's physical virginity. Laertes uses it in this sense when expressing concern for Ophelia's loss of 'honor' should she believe Hamlet's vows, and 'your chaste treasure open / To his unmast'red importunity' (1.3.29, 31–2). Conjoined, as it is by Jachimo, with the notion of picking a lock, 'treasure' in *Cymbeline* suggests an illicit penetration of the hymen. At the same time, it transforms Posthumus' bracelet into a very particular kind of manacle: a chastity belt cunningly pried open by someone other than the husband who, after the wedding night, made his wife put it on.

After several decades of critical squabbling, the exact nature and implications of the precontracts in *Measure For Measure* – Claudio's with Juliet, Angelo's with Mariana and, one might add, Lucio's with Kate Keepdown – at last seem clear, even if the question of just what the Duke is doing with them remains no less problematic than before. That this should be the case is primarily thanks to the social historians: to the continuing investigation of spousal and related matrimonial and sexual litigation, as preserved in the still largely uncatalogued, archival records of ecclesiastical courts all over early modern England, which has been undertaken by Ralph Houlbrooke, Martin Ingram, G. R. Quaife, R. G. Emmison, Charles Donahue, Jr, and others. Like the particular case histories assembled in Lawrence Stone's *Broken Lives* and *Uncertain Unions* (although these are mainly post-Restoration) this work demonstrates the complexity of the relationship in the period not only between theology and canon law, but in the vexed relation of the latter to civil law, to its own interpretation in the church courts, and (finally) to actual social behaviour.[4] Much of the latter clearly was swayed by popular

---

[4] See, in particular: Charles Donahue, Jr, 'The canon law on the formation of marriage and social practice in the later Middle Ages', *The Journal of Family History* 8 (1983), 144–58; F. G. Emmison, *Elizabethan Life: Morals and the Church Courts* (Chelmsford, 1973); John R. Gillis, *For Better, For Worse: A Political and Social History of British Marriage 1600 to the Present* (1985); Ralph Houlbrooke, 'The making of marriage in mid-Tudor England: evidence from the records of matrimonial contract litigation', *The Journal of Family History* 10 (1985), 339–51, *Church Courts and the People During the English Reformation* (Oxford, 1979) and *The English Family 1450–1700*, chs. 4 and 5 (London, 1984); Martin Ingram, *Church Courts, Sex and*

tradition: unsanctioned beliefs given licence by the fact that even distinguished canon lawyers like Henry Swinburne, let alone individual church courts, often failed to agree among themselves about points that may to us seem nice, but were in practice consequential.

They managed things better in Catholic Europe – at least after the Council of Trent in 1563 had ruled that clandestine marriages and *de praesenti* contracts no longer constituted valid matrimony. The situation in England remained ambiguous, and this despite the partial success of the church courts in discouraging unsolemnized precontracts by increasingly finding, in such cases, against the plaintiffs. The ambiguities of English matrimonial law were productive of a good deal of real-life heartache. Not surprisingly, they also found their way into contemporary drama, to an extent, and with a seriousness and richness of effect that (despite recent work by Margaret Ranald, David Bevington, Ann Jennalie Cook and others) has yet to be fully grasped.[5] Indeed Swinburne's treatise *Of Spousals or Matrimonial Contracts*, composed shortly after 1600, often reads, despite its formidable legal phraseology, like a collection of scenarii. Many of its illustrative imbroglios actually turn up in the drama of the period. With others, like the case of that unhappy King of Cyprus who found he had married by proxy the wrong princess of Milan, and that she was every bit as furious as he once she had learned about the mistake (plucking the 'Nuptial Ring from her Finger' and hurling it into the fire, 'swearing and protesting with many Damnable

---

Marriage in England 1570–1640 (Cambridge, 1987); Alan Macfarlane, *Marriage and Love in England 1300–1840* (Oxford, 1986); G. R. Quaife, *Wanton Wenches and Wayward Wives: Peasants and Illicit Sex in Early Seventeenth-Century England* (London, 1979); R. M. Smith, 'Marriage processes in the English past: some continuities', in *The World We Have Gained: Histories of Population and Social Structure*, ed. Lloyd Bonfield, Richard M. Smith and Keith Wrightson (Oxford, 1986). Also Lawrence Stone's *Road to Divorce: England 1530–1987* (Oxford, 1990) and its companion volumes, *Uncertain Unions: Marriage in England 1660–1753* (Oxford, 1992) and *Broken Lives* (Oxford, 1993). For the fullest and most persuasive account of the situation in *Measure For Measure*, see Karl Wentersdorf, 'The marriage contracts in *Measure For Measure*: a reconsideration', *Shakespeare Survey 32* (1979), 129–44.

Among older works, George Elliott Howard's monumental three-volume *A History of Matrimonial Institutions* (London, 1904), the two volumes of John Cordy Jeaffreson's *Brides and Bridals* (London, 1872), and Chilton Latham Powell's *English Domestic Relations* (New York, 1917) remain invaluable.

[5] David Bevington, *Action is Eloquence: Shakespeare's Language of Gesture* (London, 1984); Ann Jennalie Cook, *Making A Match: Courtship in Shakespeare and his Society* (Princeton, 1991); Margaret Loftus Ranald, '"As marriage binds and blood breaks": English marriage and Shakespeare', *Shakespeare Quarterly 30* (1979), 68–81 and *Shakespeare and his Social Context* (New York, 1987).

Execrations' that she would never acknowledge the King of Cyprus for her husband, but would 'presently marry another Man') one can only regret that no one, apparently, thought to write the play.[6]

Because Shakespeare is Shakespeare, far more attention has been paid to the questions raised by the precontracts in *Measure For Measure* than to those surrounding (for instance) the analogous situation of Jane Russell in Middleton and Rowley's *A Fair Quarrel* (1617), let alone that of Radagon and Ariadne in the anonymous *Thracian Wonder* (1599), a play that hovers tantalizingly in the background of both *Cymbeline* and *The Winter's Tale*. There are plays – Wilkins' *The Miseries of Enforced Marriage* of 1606, William Sampson's *The Vow-Breaker* of 1625 (almost certainly a re-doing of the lost Henslowe property *Black Bateman of the North* of 1598),[7] or Ford's less polemical *The Broken Heart* (1629) – in which the intricacies and contradictions of contemporary marriage law have always been too central for readers to ignore. Recent scholarship may have heightened awareness of such questions in Shakespeare. Yet there remain within the canon a surprising number of points at which troth-plights have been ignored, or their emotional and theatrical subtleties gone unrecognized. In the case of *Cymbeline*, we misunderstand the central human relationship of an entire play by not being sufficiently alert, as Shakespeare's audience was, to the diverse ways by which, in early modern England, one could set up, legalize (and sometimes enforce or destroy) a marriage.

Because the ecclesiastical records for Stratford-upon Avon during Shakespeare's lifetime are incomplete – they extend, as E. R. C. Brinkworth has established, with gaps, from 1590 to 1608, with a single session reported in 1616[8] – it is impossible to know if Shakespeare's patently rushed marriage to Anne Hathaway in 1582 was the result of insistence by a church court to which the bride's pregnancy had been reported that their precontract must be solemnized without delay. Let alone whether they were threatened (as not infrequently happened in such cases) with public penance or a fine for anticipating their marriage. We don't, for that matter, know if they had any extenuating precontract. What is clear is that

---

[6] Henry Swinburne, *A Treatise of Spousals, or Matrimonial Contracts* (London, 1686), pp. 65–77.

[7] The case is argued persuasively by Kathleen Tillotson in 'William Sampson's *Vow-Breaker* (1626) and the lost Henslowe play *Black Batman of the North*', *Modern Language Review* 35 (1940), 377–8.

[8] E. R. C. Brinkworth, *Shakespeare and the Bawdy Court of Stratford* (London, 1972), p. 117.

for the young Shakespeare to obtain his special licence, dispensing with the normal threefold calling of the banns, two substantial citizens of Stratford, Fulke Sandells and John Rychardson, were obliged to enter into a bond for the not inconsiderable sum of £40 that neither bride nor groom had a potentially disabling precontract with anyone else: in effect, that the sort of 'lawful let' by a disappointed partner which costs Master Gallipot, in the sub-plot of Middleton and Dekker's *The Roaring Girl* (1608), such anguish, not to mention cash, wasn't (so far as the guarantors knew) ever going to rear its head.[9]

This was far from being Shakespeare's only brush with the complexities of matrimonial law. In 1610, he gave evidence in London in the Mountjoy/Belott case: a dispute over financial arrangements made at a handfasting he seems himself to have witnessed.[10] His death in 1616 may have been hastened by the impact of public scandal when Thomas Quiney, to whom his daughter Judith was betrothed, was accused and then, after the Shakespeare marriage had been celebrated, actually convicted in the local church court of having got one Margaret Wheeler with child. In March Margaret died in childbirth and, shortly thereafter, Shakespeare changed his will, in ways that reflect a lack of trust in Quiney.[11] Interestingly, the overseer of that will, Thomas Russell, had himself been guilty of a spousal irregularity, neatly illustrative of the gap between English canon and civil law. In 1600 Russell entered into a precontract before witnesses with Anne Digges, a widow. They moved in together, while the lawyers worked out an arrangement whereby Anne's son by her previous union agreed to reimburse his mother for the annuity she would forfeit by re-marriage, in exchange for her releasing his inheritance before he reached twenty-four. As soon as it had all been agreed, late in 1603, Thomas and Anne got married, in the carefully chosen obscurity of a church about twenty miles from Stratford. Clearly, their only reason for delaying the ceremony was that civil law, which controlled matters of inheritance and property, paradoxically refused to recognize as legal any union not solemnized openly in church. As soon as Anne Digges gave her

[9] Samuel Schoenbaum, *William Shakespeare: A Documentary Life* (Oxford, 1975), pp. 62–5.
[10] Samuel Schoenbaum, *William Shakespeare: Records and Images*, 2 vols. (London, 1981), II, pp. 20–9.
[11] Brinkworth, *Shakespeare and the Bawdy Court*, pp. 78–84; Schoenbaum, *Documentary Life*, pp. 233–41.

hand again to Thomas Russell, this time in Rushock church, before a priest, and according to the service set down in *The Book of Common Prayer*, she lost her annuity. Yet as far as canon law was concerned, she and Russell had been husband and wife – although of course they shouldn't have been cohabiting – ever since the precontract of 1600.[12]

'Husband' and 'wife' were not words used idly in such a context. Shakespeare's Richard II is not, as it might seem, being culpably redundant when he speaks of his 'married wife' (v.1.73), nor should Autolycus necessarily be supposed to mean 'widow' or 'woman' generally when he confesses to having 'married a tinker's wife' (iv.3.97). The Old Testament, as both canon lawyers and divines were continually pointing out, was full of contracted couples who were so designated – as when Jacob (as William Perkins noted) 'speaking of *Rahel* who was onely betrothed unto him, said to *Laban*, "*Give me my wife*"'.[13] The most august example of all was the Virgin Mary, 'betroathed to Joseph', as Swinburne remarks, 'but neither solemnly married with him, nor secretly known by him, at the Conception of Christ; and yet nevertheless termed Wife in the Holy Scriptures'.[14] Shakespeare's grandfather was perfectly correct when, in a legal document of 1550, he described his daughter Agnes as 'now the wife of Thomas Stringer', even though the two did not actually marry until three months later.[15] Thomas and Agnes themselves were less correct, because they were clearly living together at the time, on the basis of their precontract. Like Anne Digges, however, she was a widow, and the courts tended to be less perturbed about their sexual misdemeanours than about those of spinsters, partly because they were less likely to leave a child upon the parish.

Behind the customary use of 'husband' and 'wife' to describe couples affianced on a *de praesenti* basis – and of the word 'adultery' to describe the carnal coupling of either with a third person – lay more than just the authority of Scripture, backed up by Augustine, Gregory, Chrysostom, Origen, etc. Canon lawyers and divines in England, whether Catholic or Protestant, including Puritans, found

---

[12] William Empson first drew attention to the relevance of the Russell case in *The Structure of Complex Words* (London, 1951; 3rd edn 1979), p. 286. For a full account, see Arthur Scouten, 'An historical approach to *Measure For Measure*', *Philological Quarterly* 54 (1975), 69–70.

[13] William Perkins, 'Of Christian oeconomie, or household government', in *The Works of that Famous and Worthy Minister of Christ in the Universitie of Cambridge, Mr. William Perkins*, 3 vols. (Cambridge 1616–18), iii, p. 672.   [14] Swinburne, *Treatise of Spousals*, p. 14.

[15] First pointed out by Halliwell-Phillips. See John Semple Smart, *Shakespeare, Truth and Tradition* (London, 1928), p. 78.

it uniformly difficult to relinquish the idea that mutual consent between a man and woman was the essential part of marriage, that it alone made them man and wife in the sight of God. Thomas Watson, the last Catholic bishop of Lincoln, went so far as to claim in 1558, in *The Seven Sacraments of Christ's Church*, that a couple might do everything they were supposed to do in terms of parental consent, plus a proper church ceremony with nuptial mass and priestly blessing and yet, though of course they could not forsake one another or take other partners,

> they be not husband and wyfe nor maried before god, and that is because they did not wyll and consent in their hartes so to be when they sayde the wordes of matrymonie. And therefore yf these two persones do use carnall companye together, then the partie which did not consent doth commyt fornication and sinneth deadlie in so doynge the duetie of mariage, as longe as he continueth in the same wyll and mynde that he had when he was insured, be it the man or the woman.[16]

A powerful warning, not least to parents who pressured their children into repugnant marriages, it made perfect sense in England even among those who did not, like Watson, regard matrimony as a sacrament. It helps to explain why the entirely rational legislation introduced under Henry VIII in 1540, making it impossible to overthrow a solemnized and consummated marriage by proving a previous un-solemnized, unconsummated *de praesenti* contract, lasted barely nine years before being overthrown in the reign of Edward VI. Even Swinburne, long after the Council of Trent, was certain that the repeal of this law in England had been right because 'a present and perfect Consent... alone maketh Matrimony, without either Publick Solemnization or Carnal Copulation; for neither is the one, nor the other of the *Essence* of Matrimony, but *Consent* only'.[17]

Shakespeare required no formal legal training to make a creative and highly individual use of things that for him and his audience were matters of common knowledge. Certainly he tended from the start to elaborate contractual material only hinted at in his sources, or to invent it when it was not there. In *The Taming of the Shrew*, for instance, his careful discriminations between Kate and Petruchio's *de praesenti* handfast in the presence of her father and two witnesses,

---

[16] Thomas Watson, *The Seven Sacraments of Christ's Church* (London, 1558), fo. clxxvii.
[17] Swinburne, *Treatise of Spousals*, p. 14.

followed (after banns have been called) by a properly solemnized church marriage; another *de praesenti* contract in a chamber, that of Bianca and the disguised Tranio, to be legitimized this time by a scrivener and clergyman as well as the two fathers, and finally that clandestine marriage in church, by an old priest willing to proceed without banns, which unites Bianca and Lucentio, are nowhere to be found in Gascoigne's *Supposes*. He evinces the same kind of scrupulosity in *Twelfth Night* when distinguishing Olivia's 'contract of eternal bond of love' (v.1.156), complete with clergyman and exchange of rings, in a private chapel, from her actual marriage (and that of Viola and Orsino) at the end.

In play after play, Shakespeare evokes the specifics of marriage contracts and solemnizations along familiar contemporary lines, regardless of whether the setting is Catholic, Protestant, or pre-Christian.[18] The early church, of course, had essentially taken over Roman law on betrothal and marriage (although not on divorce), something of which the canonists were entirely aware. In Shakespeare's time, moreover, as in Chaucer's, the classical world was widely believed, on the basis of works such as Ovid's *Heroides*, to have entertained basically the same distinction between private contracts and public weddings as contemporary English society. Both Chaucer and Dante regarded Dido as Aeneas' lawful wife, as a result of their contract and its consummation in the cave, even though Virgil's own attitude is carefully ambiguous.[19] The comedies of Plautus are full of betrothals, although most of these are effected, in accord with New Comedy conventions, in the absence of the girl. There was material available too in Horace and Cicero, Juvenal and Pliny. Ovid's tale of

---

[18] In *Titus Andronicus*, Shakespeare's first classical play, where Tamora's sons actually do what Cloten only imagines doing in *Cymbeline* – killing a woman's husband before her eyes, and then raping her in the presence of his corpse – all the Andronici, with the significant exception of Titus himself, regard the troth-plight of Bassianus and Lavinia as legally and morally binding. Saturninus, however, although careful to betroth himself publicly to Tamora before his own wedding in the Pantheon, finds it both convenient and possible (like Titus, if for different reasons) to ignore his brother's precontract.

[19] See the excellent essay by Henry Ansgar Kelly, 'Clandestine marriage and Chaucer's "Troilus"', in *Viator* 4 (1973), 434–57. For Ovid's *Heroides* as a fifth-form grammar school text, used for the study of letter-writing, and Erasmus' particular recommendation of the Acontius/Cydippe epistles, see T. W. Baldwin, *William Shakspere's Small Latine & Lesse Greeke*, 2 vols. (Urbana, 1944), II, p. 239. Carol Gesner, in *Shakespeare and the Greek Romance* (Lexington, 1970) notes a number of parallels between the lovers in *Cymbeline* and in the *Aethiopica* of Heliodorus, including the fact that 'both pairs are married, but in each case the consummation of their union has been with-held' (102). She believes, however, that Imogen and Posthumus only have 'a handfasting', not a clandestine marriage.

Plate 1   A handfast, 'till death us do part', emblem no. 87 in Gabriel Rollenhagen,
Nucleus Emblematum (Arnheim, 1611).

Acontius and Cydippe is worth pausing over briefly, not only because
it was standard fifth-form reading in the grammar schools, recommended by Erasmus in his *Modus Conscribendi Epistolas* as an especially
chaste text, but because it demonstrates just how provocatively
pagan and Christian ideas on the subject could meet.

Cydippe was the girl who went on holiday to Delos and, while she was admiring the porticoes and statues in the temple, picked up an apple – always an ill-advised thing to do, whether you are Paris, Atalanta, or Adam and Eve. Cydippe's real mistake, however, was to read aloud the words inscribed on it: 'I swear by the sanctuary of Diana that I will wed Acontius.' She had inadvertently made what Swinburne would almost certainly rule, having regard purely to its grammar, was a narrowly admissible *de praesenti* contract. He would have let her off, though, on the grounds that she did not *mean* the words she spoke, and also because the element of '*Jeast* or *Sport*' involved rendered 'such wanton words... not at all obligatory in so serious a matter as is Matrimony'.[20] Unfortunately, the goddess was of a different mind. Although Cydippe later complained bitterly to the young man, in terms that would have wrung the heart of Bishop Watson, that her pledge had been purely verbal and unwilled, she found that every time she approached the hymeneal altars to marry someone else, she was struck down by a burning fever. In the end, she and her family gave in and she married Acontius.

Improbably moralized by medieval commentators on Ovid into an allegory about virtuous betrothals, the story turns up in Chapman's comedy *Sir Giles Goosecap* (1602) as a benevolent stratagem by which Momford tries to trick his niece Eugenia into marriage with Clarence, his friend. The promise is contained in a letter, not an apple, and Eugenia signs her name rather than reading it aloud, but the parallel strikes her at once: 'Why, thus did false Acontius snare Cydippe.'[21] As, however, she is half in love with Clarence anyway, her uncle's threat of a church court – the play's equivalent of Diana – doesn't need to be implemented. Eugenia capitulates. Both she and Cydippe were considerably more fortunate than Ann Boote, the fair maid of Clifton in Sampson's *The Vow-Breaker*. Ann rashly asked, in making her *de praesenti* contract, that she might 'ever / From heaven, and goodnes rest a cast-away, / If e're I give this hand to any one / But my sweet *Bateman*'.[22] Then she broke the promise and married someone wealthier, with the result that (as

---

[20] Swinburne, *Treatise of Spousals*, p. 105.

[21] George Chapman, *Sir Giles Goosecap, Knight* in *The Plays of George Chapman*, ed. Thomas Marc Parrott, 2 vols. (New York, 1914), II, p. 647 (IV.1.205).

[22] William Sampson, *The Vow-Breaker, or The Faire Maide of Clifton* I.1.45–8, in W. Bang, gen. ed., n.s., H. de Vocht, gen. ed. *Materialien zur kunde des älteren englischen Dramas* (1914), p. 10.

soon as she had been safely delivered of her first child – a nice point)
she was haled off by the ghost of her initial troth-plight husband
straight to Hell. The tragedy is based on a ballad, and Sampson is as
coyly insistent as Autolycus that every bit of it is true.

The closest Shakespeare ever came to writing this kind of domestic
play – and it isn't very close – was in *The Merry Wives of Windsor*. The
fate of Ann Boote, however, is by no means irrelevant to Fenton's
final statement about his clandestine marriage to Anne Page:

> The truth is, she and I (long since contracted)
> Are now so sure that nothing can dissolve us.
> Th' offense is holy that she hath committed,
> And this deceit loses the name of craft,
> Of disobedience, or unduteous title,
> Since therein she doth evitate and shun
> A thousand irreligious cursed hours
> Which forced marriage would have brought upon her. (v.5.223–30)

Fenton prevaricates slightly, though understandably, over 'long
since contracted'. It is clear, though modern directors tend not to
notice, that in the fourth scene of Act III, before Shallow nervously
orders Mistress Quickly to 'break their talk' (21–2), Fenton and
Anne, who have retreated to a little distance ('hark you hither'),
make a hasty but binding pledge. Because Page subsequently drives
Fenton away (ironically, with the words 'I told you, sir, my daughter
is dispos'd of' [70]), the young man is forced to hand Mistress Quickly
the betrothal ring with which the contract ought to have been
concluded, and ask her to give it 'tonight' to 'my sweet Nan'
(99–100). That, according to Elizabethan practice, is the ring Anne
will remove from her right hand as she stands before the accommodating vicar of Windsor church at a very un-canonical time of
night in order that her husband can replace it on her left. The
'irreligious cursed hours' she thus avoids have less to do with the
horrors of being stuck for life with either Slender or Doctor Caius
than with the sufferings of Ann Boote – or of Clare Harcop in *The
Miseries of Enforced Marriage*, who actually chooses what she regards
as the lesser sin of suicide in order to free her troth-plight husband
from adultery in his enforced marriage to someone else.

Precontracts in Shakespeare are not, of course, invariably solemn
and irrevocable matters, any more than they were in real life. Men
and women sceptical about divine retribution often took advantage

of a lack of witnesses to cut themselves loose from a bond they no longer wished to honour. The church courts were sadly familiar with such cases, most but by no means all of them initiated by the woman. We don't know, in *Henry V*, what kind of 'troth-plight' (II.1.17–19) Nym had with the widowed Mistress Quickly before she married Ancient Pistol, but she suffers no apparent pangs of conscience, and Pistol certainly frightens Nym out of pressing any legal claim. Touchstone also does this with William in *As You Like It*. William's single appearance at the beginning of Act v gives Oliver and Celia time to contract themselves. But it is also a carefully planted clue as to how Touchstone – who has already hoped that Oliver Martext will not marry him 'well', because he wants 'a good excuse... hereafter to leave my wife' (III.3.93–4) – may try in future to terminate a wedding voyage destined after only two months, as Jaques predicts, to run aground. Audrey, of course, denies William's claim to a precontract, but then people frequently did.

Lysander, in the opening scene of *A Midsummer Night's Dream*, suggests, without accusing him directly, that a contractual agreement may exist between Demetrius and Helena. Theseus too – who apparently occupies, like the Duke and his deputies in *Measure For Measure*, a position equivalent to the head of jurisdiction in a church court – has heard rumours of the kind, and meant to interrogate Demetrius about it 'but, being over-full of self affairs, / My mind did lose it' (II.1.113–14). At the end of the scene, he takes both Egeus and Demetrius off with him, for 'private schooling', and because he needs to 'confer with you / Of something nearly that concerns yourselves' (116, 125–6). This is likely to strike us as a dramatist's conveniently vague excuse for getting both Egeus and Demetrius out of the way so that Lysander and Hermia can agree that the course of true love never did run smooth, and plan an elopement. Shakespeare's audience is more likely to have recognized an imminent and (as subsequent events reveal) unavailing interrogation of Demetrius about the existence of a precontract. It is useless for Helena to complain that before Demetrius spotted Hermia he 'hail'd down oaths that he was only mine' (1.21.243), even though what she evokes here is one of the most common *de praesenti* formulae – as in Claudio's 'Lady, as you are mine, I am yours' (II.1.308) when he betroths himself publicly to Hero in Act II of *Much Ado About Nothing*. Not until Oberon and love-in-idleness have done their work is Demetrius willing to confess to Theseus that he lied about his relationship

with Helena: 'To her, my lord, / *Was* I betrothed ere I saw Hermia'
(IV.1.172).

This belated admission affects the way we see the end of the play,
as does the recognition, in the last scene of *Love's Labour's Lost*, that
what the Princess of France finally offers Navarre, in exchange for the
'world-without-end bargain' (v.2.789) of the *de praesenti* contract he
had hoped to cement, is a less binding but in legal terms still definable
handfast of the conditional *de futuro* kind. She promises him, 'by this
virgin palm now kissing thine', that at the expiration of a year, if his
love has survived her stipulated 'frosts and fasts, hard lodging and
thin weeds', 'I will be thine' (v.2.806, 801, 807). Otherwise, the
contract lapses: 'Neither intitled in the other's heart' (812). Linked
on the one hand with the kind of romance troth-plight that Neronis,
the king of Denmark's daughter, makes in the old *Historie of Clyomon
and Clamydes* (1570) – that she will wed Clamydes if he can kill a
particularly troublesome flying serpent with an appetite for virgins
– it is enmeshed on the other in those unromantic technicalities by
which marriages were made conditional upon monetary payments or
the transfer of a piece of land. Indeed, it can be read as a sort of
obverse of that little academic fabliau that Swinburne uses to
illustrate an unenforceable conditional contract: another wealthy if
less princely student distracted from his books by female charms, who
escaped marriage to the simple maid whose 'poor and base kindred'
arranged to surprise them in bed, and so 'force him to marry her, and
maintain them' by employing the plausible but legally invalid
formula that his tutor despatched by special post: '*If she shall live
honestly*', or 'not do with another as she had done with him'.
(According to Swinburne, the undergraduate 'escaped joyfully,
thanked his Tutor heartily and thence forward applyed his Study
more diligently'.)[23]

Bertram's situation in *All's Well That Ends Well*, as Margaret
Ranald and others have pointed out, is complicated by the fact that
he is both a minor and a royal ward.[24] When the King announces
that he is prepared to bestow both title and wealth upon Helena,
Bertram is deprived of one of the strongest legal arguments a ward
could employ to escape an unwelcome marriage: that of gross
inequality, or 'disparagement'. Forced into a public handfast

[23] Swinburne, *Treatise of Spousals*, p. 144.
[24] Ranald, 'The betrothals of *All's Well That Ends Well*', *Huntington Library Quarterly* 26 (1973),
179–92.

followed immediately by marriage, his only recourse now is to flee abroad in the hope that desertion and non-consummation may finally procure him an annulment. Meanwhile, he enters into a conditional *de futuro* contract with Diana of a highly irregular, although not unique, kind (there is a parallel in Heywood's *The English Traveller*, 1625), promising to marry her once his present wife is dead.

When Helena re-appears, possessed of Bertram's ring, and carrying his child, he is initially shocked into denying her negative self-description: 'the shadow of a wife...the name and not the thing'. 'Both, both', he protests, 'O, pardon' (v.3.307–8). Ann Jennalie Cook claims that for her this acceptance without proof 'fully legitimizes her marital position' and 'unreservedly ratifies their bond'.[25] But what Helena makes Bertram do here is return to Act II and re-enact their original betrothal. When she asks, using the familiar formula, 'Will you be mine now you are doubly won?' (v.3.314), the acceptance she elicits is better, certainly, than Bertram's original and ungracious 'I take her hand' (II.3.176), but still not the bonding she craves. Bertram's 'If she, my liege, can make me know this clearly, / I'll love her dearly, ever, ever dearly' (v.3.315–16), is only a conditional *de futuro* agreement – as Helena recognizes. Editors misunderstand her last words: 'If it appear not plain and prove untrue, / Deadly divorce step between me and you!' (317–18). Helena does not mean 'divorcing death', the usual gloss. She is invoking 'divorce', the kind of legal separation that ended the Essex marriage in 1613, on grounds of non-consummation. This is what a still-suspicious Bertram has asked to know 'clearly' – that it *was* Helena in the bed. Taken together with the King's tentative 'All yet seems well' (333), it ambiguates as opposed to strengthening the ending.

In *The Winter's Tale*, Florizel reveals in speaking of 'that nuptial, which / We two have sworn shall come' (IV.3.50–1), that he and Perdita have already entered into a private contract before the scene of the sheepshearing. When a more formal betrothal, blessed by the Old Shepherd, and in the presence of witnesses, is rudely interrupted, the couple still have that earlier 'oath' (IV.4.491) to fall back on. Florizel finally admits in Sicily that they are not 'married', but he insists on the 'contract' (v.1.204–5), although without describing

[25] Cook, *Making A Match*, p. 228.

Perdita, as Claudio had Juliet, as 'my wife'. He makes it plain, moreover, just as Ferdinand (with a little prompting from Prospero) will do in *The Tempest*, that 'my desires / Run not before mine honor, nor my lusts / Burn hotter than my faith' (IV.3.33–5) – something Leontes is particularly concerned to establish before promising to be their advocate. This union (unlike the one in *Measure For Measure*) remains unconsummated. Indeed, even if they had not, at least according to Autolycus, both become woefully sea-sick, the opportunity provided by the voyage from Bohemia to Sicily was not one that this scrupulous pair would be inclined to seize.

The contracts between Perdita and Florizel, however, are far more straightforward than another series in the play. The opening description of Polixenes' and Leontes' loves – how even at a distance they 'shook hands' and 'embrac'd', with 'interchange of gifts, letters, loving embassies' (I.1.28–31) – suggests a male bonding conceived in terms close to those of a traditional betrothal. Hard on its heels comes Leontes' tetchy memory of his own youthful handfast with Hermione:

> Three crabbed months had sour'd themselves to death,
> Ere I could make thee open thy white hand,
> And clap thyself my love; then didst thou utter,
> 'I am yours for ever.' (I.2.101–5)   .

This is the contracting that Leontes sees re-enacted, his own role in it usurped by Polixenes, when Hermione gives her hand in friendship to their suddenly malleable guest. He cannot hear their words as they talk apart, any more than Shallow and Slender could with Fenton and Anne Page. He can only interpret what he thinks he sees. Betrothal, wedding and consummation rush together as the formal handfast slides, in Leontes' imagination, into 'paddling palms and pinching fingers', and then into the confident and easy sexual codes of married lovers: Hermione offering herself, arousing Polixenes' desire, 'with the boldness of a wife / To her allowing husband' (I.2.115, 183–5).

This spurious new contract, the cause of two deaths, and Leontes' sixteen-year loss of his friend, his counsellor Camillo, his infant daughter, and his queen, has to be cancelled. For that more is needed than penitence and a merely implied reinstatement of the original bond. As in *All's Well That Ends Well*, the original handfasting is re-run. Paulina, by whose sole permission Leontes had vowed to take a second wife, presides at the end over a third betrothal: 'Nay, present your hand. / When she was young, you woo'd her; now, in age, / Is she become the suitor?' (v.3.107–9). The fact that Hermione never speaks to Leontes in the final scene has often seemed disturbing. But then, like Euripides' Alcestis, returning from the dead to another guilty husband, what *could* she possibly say? What she does offer Leontes, before they embrace, is both easier and more important than words. Once again the Emperor of Russia's daughter takes the hand of the Sicilian king. The contract this time is initiated by her. It is also made (as it was not before) in perfect silence. That, as Swinburne explains, in a spousal context like the one provided for it by Paulina, is sufficient. Indeed, even 'where no words at all be uttered, neither by the Parties, nor by any third Person, may Spousals or Matrimony be contracted by Signs only'.[26] Hermione's voiceless hand – tendered and accepted – seals a promise for the future, and a full consent.

Dr Johnson's strictures against 'the folly of the fiction' in *Cymbeline*, 'the absurdity of the conduct, the confusion of the names and manners of different times, and the impossibility of the events in any system of life',[27] have long since been displaced by an appreciation of the play's extraordinary (if for some critics perversely self-conscious) artistry. It may be what John Lyly called a 'mingle-mangle', but the mixture no longer seems careless. Among what are now the recognized contradictions and conundrums of the play – the Cloten/ Posthumus relationship; Cymbeline's abrupt concession at the end over Roman tribute; the masque of Jupiter; and the soothsayer who goes into reverse – not the least puzzling is the nature of the union between Posthumus and the woman who, at the beginning of Act I, looks like England's future queen.

Although Swinburne remarks that 'Our Temporal lawyers... do usually confound these terms of *Espousals and Marriage*, using them *promiscue*, or one for another', in the drama of the period the two are clearly distinguished.[28] Exceptions – the Duchess of Malfi's 'I have heard lawyers say, a contract in a chamber / *Per verba de presenti* is absolute marriage', or the jilted Scudmore's 'She is contracted, sir – nay, married / Unto another man, though it want form', in Nathan

---

[26] Swinburne, *Treatise of Spousals*, pp. 204–6.
[27] Quoted by Horace Howard Furness in the Preface to his New Variorum edition of *Cymbeline* (London, 1913), p. v.   [28] Swinburne, *Treatise of Spousals*, p. 2.

Field's *A Woman is a Weathercock* of 1609 – actually prove the rule:
these characters are straining to make a precontract seem all-
sufficient in a way that, thanks to church and other legal pressures in
England, it increasingly was not.[29] When Posthumus promises in Act
I to 'remain / The loyall'st husband that did e'er plight troth'
(1.1.95–6), the word 'husband' – like 'wife' when applied to Imogen
– could indicate that they have only a precontract. 'Wedded', on
the other hand, in the seventh line of the play, and the First
Gentleman's statement that Posthumus has 'married her' (1.1.18)
make an apparently unequivocal case for a union both solemnized
and consummated. The situation doesn't stay unequivocal for long.

In the second scene of Act I, this wedded couple – the husband
banished, she newly released from prison – snatch a farewell.
Curiously, their parting exchange of love-tokens (the bracelet and
Imogen's mother's ring) seems to belong to an earlier stage of the
relationship: a symbolic betrothal coming, as in *All's Well That Ends
Well* and *The Winter's Tale*, after the marriage rather than before.
Rings, customarily though not always given by the man, constituted
such powerful evidence of a contract that often, in the church courts,
nothing else was required.[30] It is futile for Lady Anne to protest that
'To take is not to give' (1.2.202), after she has allowed the future
Richard III to slip a ring on her finger. She has done both, as
Richard knows when he describes her in the next moment as both
wooed and won. Imogen's ring looks like a spousal gift: like Portia's
to Bassanio, Fenton's to Anne Page, or the cannily refused jewel that
Olivia sends after Cesario, under the pretence that Orsino has tried
to force it on her. Indeed, in *Loose Fantasies*, the extraordinary
autobiographical romance Sir Kenelm Digby began to write in 1628,
Theagenes and Stelliana (alias Digby and Venetia Stanley) exchange
exactly the *Cymbeline* tokens, a bracelet and a diamond ring, as
spousal pledges before Theagenes is despatched for three years to the
Continent by his disapproving family.[31] Even the anxieties of Imogen
and Posthumus about keeping faith when they are parted seem more

[29] Webster, *The Duchess of Malfi* 1.1.478–9; Field, *A Woman is a Weathercock*, ed. W. Carew
Hazlitt (London, 1875), II.1. The clown Rusticano, in *Tom A Lincoln*, is characteristically
confused, as well as premature, when he describes his master as 'married' at lines 2986–7.
It is clear that Anglitera and the Red Rose Knight will formally solemnize their
precontract, in Arthur's court, after the end of the play.

[30] See Peter Rushton, 'The testament of gifts: marriage tokens and disputed contracts in
north-east England, 1560–1630', *Folk Life* 24 (1985–6), 25–31.

[31] Kenelm Digby, *Loose Fantasies*, ed. Vittorio Gabrieli (Rome, 1968), p. 43.

appropriate to a contracted couple like Bateman and Ann Boote, or Shakespeare's Troilus and Cressida, than to a man and woman newly wed.

When Posthumus arrives in Rome, 'this matter of marrying his king's daughter' (1.4.14) has already reached Philario and the others. Yet, strangely, no one in the wager scene itself (including Posthumus) ever uses that word, or even as in Boccaccio and *Frederyke of Jennen*, Shakespeare's sources for this part of the play, the less definitive 'husband' or 'wife'. Again, time seems to run backwards as the contention between Posthumus and the Frenchman at Orleans some time before, when he was by his own admission but 'a young traveller' (1.4.43–4), is not only re-played with Jachimo but re-played using the same courtly terminology: 'your mistress', 'lady', or Posthumus' curious claim that he is Imogen's 'adorer, not her friend' (1.4.68–9). The Variorum notes are copious on 'friend', the difficulty stemming, of course, from its ambiguity as an a-sexual designation, our own usage, or a specifically sexual term – as when Claudio, in *Measure For Measure*, gets 'his friend with child' (1.4.29) or Juliet after her wedding night describes Romeo, in an ascending order, as 'love, lord, ay, husband, friend!' (III.5.43). In *The Winter's Tale*, it was this sexual meaning which, for Leontes, disastrously replaced the other as Hermione, giving her hand to Polixenes, remembered that this was how she once acquired 'a royal husband', and now 'for some while a friend' (1.2.107–8). It is impossible to tell, however, in the *Cymbeline* passage, in which sense Posthumus intends 'friend', or whether that 'title' (in a legal sense) by which he affirms Imogen to be his own (1.4.88) is any different now from what it was in Orleans.

Meanwhile, back in Britain, no one behaves as though this union is impossible to undo. The king has earlier accused his daughter of intending to contaminate the royal line: thou '*wouldst* have made my throne / A seat for baseness' (1.1.141–2) – not that she already has. The queen muses, in soliloquy, about Imogen's 'hand-fast' (1.5.78), not marriage, 'to her lord', and Cloten tells her, 'For / The contract you pretend with that base wretch, ... / It is no contract, none': merely a 'self-figur'd knot', of the kind allowable to 'meaner parties', but not to her, given 'the consequence o'th'crown' (II.3.113–21). 'Self-figur'd' certainly suggests unsolemnized: a private contract of the sort Hamlet apparently has with Ophelia but which cannot in Imogen's case any more than his bind the heir to a throne. Imogen starts back from Cloten's 'Good morrow, fairest: sister, your sweet

hand' in the third scene of Act II as though from an adder;
responding at all to his vow of love only because she knows her
Swinburne: 'that you shall not say I yield being silent' (94). And the
second lord, speaking of 'that horrid act / Of the divorce he'ld
make', prays the heavens to 'keep unshak'd' the temple of Imogen's
'fair mind' as though the danger of her being pressured (like
Ophelia) by her father to renege was very real (II.1.61–4). Finally,
Jachimo tells her that he has lied about Posthumus only 'to know if
your *affiance* / Were deeply rooted' (1.6.163–4).

Like 'adultery', 'divorce' was a word equally applicable to
betrothal and matrimony.[32] Polixenes uses it to break up the contract
between Florizel and Perdita in Bohemia: 'Mark your divorce,
young sir' (IV.4.417). The divided jurisdiction of civil and canon law,
however, meant that it was something relatively easy to accomplish
in the case of betrothal – as plays like *The Miseries of Enforced Marriage*
and *The Vow-Breaker*, not to mention testimony in the church courts,
make plain – and diabolically difficult before 1753 in that of
marriage. Arbella Stuart was, like Imogen, in line for the British
throne. When she secretly married William Seymour (who also had
royal blood), James locked them both up in The Tower, where
Arbella eventually died. But he did not try to effect a legal divorce.
The case of Lady Catherine Grey, an even more powerful claimant,
was complicated by the fact that both the priest who officiated and
the witnesses were too terrified of Queen Elizabeth to come forward,
with the result that the clandestine marriage of 1563 could never be
proved. It had certainly been consummated, because Catherine
produced two children, but Elizabeth (and her Privy Council)
annulled it as undemonstrable, turning the children into bastards.

Victorian and early twentieth-century readers loved Imogen: 'the
immortal godhead of womanhood', as Algernon Charles Swinburne
put it, Granville-Barker's 'paragon of chastity, faith, fidelity', or
even 'a home-maker', 'the companion Shakespeare wanted all his
life, a composite of what was lacking in his wife and mistresses'.[33]

---

[32] See Swinburne, *Treatise of Spousals*, p. 196, and Perkins, 'The order of the causes of salvation
and damnation': 'This sin is called adulterie: and God hath inflicted by his word the same
punishment upon them, which commit this sinne, after they be betrothed, as he doth upon
such as are already married' (*Works*, 1, p. 59).

[33] Algernon Charles Swinburne, 'Third period: tragic and romantic', in his *A Study of
Shakespeare* (London, 1880), pp. 153–4; Harley Granville-Barker, 'Cymbeline', *Prefaces to
Shakespeare*, 2nd series, II (London, 1930), p. 329. Also George W. Gerwig, *Shakespeare's
Ideals of Womanhood* (East Aurora, N.Y., 1929) and Robert Kemp, 'En relisant *Cymbeline*', *Le*

Posthumus' anguished account, in the soliloquy that ends Act II, of his wife's sexual refusals troubled these critics not at all:

> Me of my lawful pleasure she restrain'd,
> And pray'd me oft forbearance; did it with
> A pudency so rosy the sweet view on't
> Might well have warm'd old Saturn; that I thought her
> As chaste as unsunn'd snow. (II.5.9–13)

Indeed, her marital reluctances fitted nicely into the encomium. Later readers have been less impressed. Gradually, a chastely ideal Imogen has been replaced by the wife who continually pleads a headache; the paragon by a woman, at once titillating and frigid, who may even have teased Posthumus physically, without surrendering her virginity – in which case, no wonder he becomes murderous.[34]

Attempts have sometimes been made to exonerate Imogen by claiming that what she represents is a specifically Puritan ideal of restraint in marriage.[35] There seems, however, to be no difference between Catholic writers such as William Harrington and Puritans like Gouge on the issue of intercourse being refused, by either wedded partner, when requested by the other. Harrington goes so far as to say that although in late pregnancy, or during menstruation,

man and wife ought not to meddle fleshly together and if they do he or she which is occasion and the provoker therof doth sin greatly. But the other which doth obey doth not sin. For the one must answer the other in that behalf at all seasons when he or she doth require.[36]

Lust and 'beastliness', certainly, are to be avoided in married love – but so is abstinence, except when enforced by separation, the forbidden periods or (very briefly) by mutual agreement during a time of fasting or prayer. Not only do all Protestant, including Puritan, writers agree on this, it is striking that the various English

Temps (28–29 March 1942), 3, cited, with many similar assessments of Imogen, in *Cymbeline*, comp. Henry E. Jacobs (The Garland Shakespeare Bibliographies) (London, 1982).

34 See, for instance, John P. Cutts, *Rich and Strange: A Study of Shakespeare's Last Plays* (Washington State, 1968), pp. 39–48; David M. Bergeron, 'Sexuality in *Cymbeline*', *Essays in Literature* 10 (1983), 159–168; J. S. Lawry, '"Perishing root and increasing vine" in *Cymbeline*', *Shakespeare Studies* 12 (1979), 179–93; Carol Thomas Neely, *Broken Nuptials in Shakespeare's Plays* (London, 1985), p. 181; and Harry Zuger, 'Shakespeare's posthumus and the wager: from delusion to enlightenment', *Shakespeare Jahrbuch* [*Weimar*] 112 (1976), 133–42.

35 As by Juliet Dusinberre, *Shakespeare and the Nature of Women* (London, 1975), pp. 118–19. Contrast the subtle account of Patrick Collinson, 'The Protestant family', in his *The Birthpangs of Protestant England* (London, 1988), pp. 60–93.

36 William Harrington, *Commendations of Matrimony* (London, 1528), sig. diiv; William Gouge, *Of Domesticall Duties* (London, 1622), Part II, Treatise 2, pp. 221–4.

plagiarists of Heinrich Bullinger's enormously influential *Golden Book of Christian Matrimonie*, first translated in 1543, steadily strengthen his condemnation of voluntary abstinence as an evil.[37]

There is no reason to doubt the veracity of Posthumus' recollection. Yet it accords ill with the passionate, impulsive Imogen whose first response to the news that her husband is physically present, at Milford Haven, is to wish for a horse with wings. Editors, however, have ignored another difficulty a few lines later in the same soliloquy. In Posthumus' fevered imagination, Jachimo, the 'full-acorn'd boar', mounting Imogen 'found no opposition / But what he look'd for should oppose and she / Should from encounter guard' (II.5.16–19). Just what is meant here by 'opposition'? It does not seem to be an abstraction – his wife's honour, for instance – nor a vague allusion to the vagina. 'Opposition', surely, is a specific reference to the hymen. One must remember that in the Italian scenes Posthumus has never spoken of himself as married, and that Jachimo and the others do not disclose to him their knowledge that he is. There is no reason why Posthumus should not assume that Jachimo assailed Imogen thinking her still a virgin. More startling is the implication that he himself knows that she was.

Later, in the dream-vision, Jupiter says of Posthumus that 'in our temple was he married' (v.4.106). It seems an odd place to pick. In Beaumont's *Masque of the Inner Temple and Gray's Inn*, performed at court in February 1613, following the marriage of Princess Elizabeth, elaborate excuses have to be made, given Jupiter's reputation, for involving him at all: 'What hath he to do with Nuptiall rights?', Iris asks. Nothing, Mercury agrees, but it was laid down long ago that for the marriage of Thames and Rhine, of much concern to 'his generall government', he would trespass just this once upon Juno's preserve.[38] For 'Jupiter' in Beaumont, read James I, but it seems unlikely (despite the ingenious arguments of Leah Marcus) that the Thunderer in *Cymbeline* is a Stuart king.[39] The ghosts of the Leonati accuse him too embarrassingly of having fallen out with Juno, 'That thy

---

[37] See Kathleen M. Davies, 'Continuity and change in literary advice on marriage', in *Marriage and Society: Studies in the Social History of Marriage*, ed. R. B. Outhwaite (London, 1981), p. 74.

[38] Francis Beaumont, *The Masque of the Inner Temple and Gray's Inn*, in *A Book of Masques: in Honour of Allardyce Nicoll* (Cambridge, 1967), pp. 135–6.

[39] Leah S. Marcus, '*Cymbeline* and the unease of topicality', in *The Historical Renaissance: New Essays on Tudor and Stuart Literature and Culture*, ed. Heather Dubrow and Richard Strier (London, 1988), pp. 134–68.

adulteries / Rates and revenges' (v.4.33–4). Queen Anne, of course, was still alive and although this play does not seem to have been performed at court before 1634, the allusion would still have been extremely tactless.

Shakespeare could easily have staged, in *Cymbeline*, a Roman marriage ceremony like the one his friend Ben Jonson had re-created in *Hymenaei*: a procession to Juno's altar complete with Hymen, the *auspices* who handfasted the couple, youths bearing various symbolic objects, pages and musicians, as well as the groom and his bride – the latter attired simply in white, with a garland, a woollen girdle and fleece, and her hair 'flowing and loose, sprinkled with grey'.[40] Indeed, in *The Two Noble Kinsmen* a few years later, he did produce his own highly theatrical version, the bride in that case with a wheaten garland and, as the stage direction says, 'encompass'd' in her hair, 'her tresses... hanging' (1.1.SD). About the actual wedding of Imogen and Posthumus, at some indeterminate time shortly before *Cymbeline* begins, we are told only that it occurred under the auspices of Jupiter, and that her father and the court have only just found out. Given the circumstances, it must have been furtive and irregular. This might explain Pisanio's curious reference, in the woods of Wales, to Imogen's 'laborsome and dainty trims wherein / You made great Juno angry' (III.5.164–5). Considering that Imogen stands before him obscured in 'a riding-suit, no costlier than would fit / A franklin's huswife' (III.2.76–7), the memory would seem to demand more than the usual editorial explanation: Juno's disapproval of finery likely to attract her lecherous spouse. Imogen's servant may well be recalling the courtly attire, with hair bound-up and intricately arranged, in which his mistress stole her clandestine marriage, in the wrong garb and venue, omitting the public ceremonies and proper rites.

A clandestine marriage in the early seventeenth century was one legally valid in terms of property – inheritance, a dowry and the rest – but which broke canon law by lacking public announcement (the banns, or a valid licence), solemnization in the correct parish church, and (where applicable) parental consent.[41] If sexual intercourse

---

[40] Ben Jonson, *Hymenaei*, in *Ben Jonson: The Complete Masques*, ed. Stephen Orgel (London, 1969), p. 77.

[41] See Martin Ingram, 'The reform of popular culture? Sex and marriage in early modern England', in *Popular Culture in Early Seventeenth Century England*, ed. Barry Reay (London, 1985), pp. 143–5; Kelly, 'Clandestine marriage and Chaucer's "Troilus"'; Stone, *Road To Divorce*, pp. 96–108, and *Uncertain Unions*, pp. 22–9. Also Gouge, *Of Domesticall Duties*, p. 205.

purely on the basis of a precontract, although forbidden and punishable by the church authorities, was fairly widely practised – only 'a small sin' Erasmus calls it –[42] the consummation of a clandestine marriage was scarcely a sin at all, and certainly had not been regarded as such by the Shakespeare who wrote *Romeo and Juliet* and *The Merry Wives of Windsor*. One should remember, however, not only the fulminations of writers like Gouge and Perkins against the sin of bypassing a parental blessing, but the efforts being made by the English church at this time to stamp out both unsolemnized precontracts and clandestine marriages.[43] The canons of 1604 had tightened the laws on licences issued without banns, forbidden marriage without parental consent for children under twenty-one, and required parental consent (except in the case of widows) for all couples regardless of age. Marriages which contravened these regulations were still valid – the church not being able to bring itself to weaken the fundamental principle of free consent – but they had become much more reprehensible. At the same time, persistent, if so far abortive, Puritan legislation in Parliament was attempting to make adultery a capital offence and clamp down even on minor irregularities. Such a bill was put forward again in 1604. Shakespeare may or may not have been sensitive to such things. His late work, for whatever reason, displays a changed and markedly less permissive attitude towards irregular sexual unions.

There can be no question of his continued celebration, not merely acceptance, of female desire. It is there in the frankness with which Miranda offers herself to Ferdinand, in the portrayal of Hermione, and in the Perdita who wants Florizel, 'quick, and in mine arms' (IV.4.132). Imogen reflects it too, not only in her anguished recollection of her husband's body in Act IV, but when, at the end, she holds that body against her own: 'Why did you throw your wedded lady from you? / Think that you are upon a rock, and now / Throw me again' (v.5.261–3). What is new in these late plays is their abhorrence of sexuality that is in any way illicit – not only that of

---

[42] Desiderius Erasmus, 'Conjugium', in *Colloquia. Opera omnia*, 9 vols. (Basel, 1540), I, p. 596.

[43] In his essay in the collection *Marriage and Society*, ed. Outhwaite, Ingram remarks that 'in the late sixteenth and early seventeenth centuries…the church courts increasingly brought prosecutions for incontinence before solemnization even when the couple concerned had, before proceedings commenced, already got married in church or clearly intended to do so' (54). For the new strictures of the canons of 1604, see *Constitutions and Canons Ecclesiastical 1604*, facs. ed. H. A. Wilson (Oxford, 1923), Q3ᵛ. Also Gouge on the nullity of marriages solemnized without parental consent, *Of Domesticall Duties*, Pt II, Treat. 5, pp. 446–9, and Perkins, 'Of Christian oeconomie', Ch. 8, p. 685.

incest and the brothel in *Pericles*, or the kind of cohabitation on a precontract which *Measure For Measure* had treated with such a fruitfully ambiguous mixture of tolerance and reproof, but even the consummation of a clandestine marriage. In *The Tempest*, Prospero introduces a betrothal masque presided over by Juno with a warning to Ferdinand that if he breaks Miranda's

> virgin-knot before
> All sanctimonious ceremonies may
> With full and holy rite be minist'red,
> No sweet aspersion shall the heavens let fall
> To make this contract grow; but barren hate,
> Sour-ey'd disdain, and discord shall bestrew
> The union of your bed with weeds so loathly
> That you shall hate it both. Therefore take heed,
> As Hymen's lamps shall light you.   (iv.1.15–23)

Hymen's lamps, a 'full and holy rite', are exactly what the smuggled union of Imogen and Posthumus did not have.

Posthumus both is and is not correct when he describes as 'lawful' those pleasures which Imogen has denied him. Permitted under civil law, they were not – strictly speaking – under canon. ''Tis set down so in heaven, but not in earth', Isabella told Angelo in *Measure For Measure* (ii.4.50), and her words seemed to stretch out beyond their immediate context to embrace that whole, agonized dispute between divine and earthly ordinances, ideals whether of love or justice, and the compromises human beings make, upon which that comedy turns. There is a sense in which Shakespeare in *Cymbeline* re-creates the legal and moral contradictions of *Measure For Measure*, but with the hiddenness and reticence, the refusal to clarify enigmas, characteristic of his late work. There is in all these plays (including *Henry VIII*) a near obsession with the status and solemnization of marriage contracts. Equally distinctive is the impulse, particularly apparent in *Cymbeline*, to explore the psychological awkwardness and pain created by suspended, uncertain and vulnerable kinds of spousal agreement or marriage.

If there is anything we can know about the lost *Cardenio*, performed at court in 1612 and 1613, it is that Shakespeare, in his part of it, must have gone straight to the heart of Cervantes' story about betrothals and illicit sexuality, the difficulty of knowing at what point a marriage has irrevocably taken place. In *Don Quixote*, the story of Cardenio and Luscinda is that of lovers, too punctilious to enter into a private troth-plight until their respective fathers have agreed to the match, who then face the problem of deciding what to claim in this respect in the moment that she is publicly forced to give her hand to Fernando. Entwined with it are the miseries of Dorotea, who has avoided simple rape by Fernando only by agreeing to a private contract, witnessed by a statue of the Virgin and her maid, which then costs her a great deal of trouble (some of it endured in boy's disguise) to get him to acknowledge. Having gravitated to this story, Shakespeare could not but have made the plot draw on some of the same uncertainties as *Cymbeline*. It is a measure of the degree to which attitudes shifted after the Restoration that, in Theobald's *The Double Falsehood* (1728), said to be based on *Cardenio*, the problem of private spousals (now largely alien to the audience) has been suppressed.

As heir to the throne of Britain, a woman still hoping to be forgiven by the king for her marriage with his erstwhile ward, Imogen might well share something of Shakespeare's own apparent anxiety now about the consummation of unions celebrated with maimed, imperfect rites and without a father's blessing. It was not unknown for participants in such nuptials to re-do them more ceremonially later on – as in the case of Leicester's clandestine marriage to the widowed Countess of Essex in 1578 – in the proper, and newly acquiescent presence of parents and kin. A sense that her irregular union ought, for the time, to remain physically incomplete would not, however, necessitate the exclusion of Posthumus from Imogen's bedchamber, or even from considerable intimacy with her person. Social historians are discovering more and more about the (to us) somewhat bizarre practice of bundling: the custom which allowed contracted couples in the period to spend the night together, sometimes actually in bed, and to engage in a good deal of sexual play so long as actual intercourse did not occur. Rather surprisingly, very few pregnancies seem to have resulted.[44] This is usually described as a lower and middle-class phenomenon, but there is much to suggest that even among the aristocracy similar familiarities could be allowed. In Digby's *Loose Fantasies*, Theagenes, allowed into Stelliana's chamber by her maids, 'who had no cause to doubt he would do the least thing that might be displeasing to her', slips into bed beside his lady and feasts his eyes on her belly, thighs, and the nipples of her breasts: 'of so pure a colour, and admirable shape'.[45] When she wakes, and his

---

[44] See Stone's *Road to Divorce*, pp. 61–3, and the cases of *Bentley v. Bentley*, *Harris v. Lingard*, and *Ryder v. Jones* in *Uncertain Unions*.   [45] Digby, *Loose Fantasies*, pp. 114–18.

attentions become too dangerous, Stelliana springs out of bed, manifesting a good deal of rosy pudency, and sings to him until she manages to cool him down. There is no reason why Posthumus needed to consummate his marriage in order to know about the mole cinque-spotted under Imogen's breast.

An understanding of the technicalities of contractual and matri-monial law in Shakespeare's day can affect our response to *Cymbeline* as a whole not only by rescuing Imogen herself from charges of prudery, while also making sense of the conflicting signals given out by the decor of her bedchamber, and the shifting definitions of her union with Posthumus. It also makes a great difference to the way we see Posthumus himself. This is partly because his murderous fury against women generally and his wife in particular becomes more excusable if Imogen is a virgin and what Posthumus has endured in listening to Jachimo is an account of another man's triumph in the very room where he himself maintained a difficult 'forbearance'. But there is another thing to say.

When Pisanio has, as Posthumus thinks, killed Imogen and sent him that horrible travesty of a love-token – the blood-stained cloth – as proof, his response is unlike that of any other cuckolded husband in the drama of the time.

> You married ones,
> If each of you should take this course, how many
> Must murther wives much better than themselves
> For wrying but a little! (v.1.2–5)

At this point, Posthumus thinks Imogen is both dead and guilty of what must, for him, be a peculiarly shaming adultery. The late plays are very hard on sexual irregularity. Yet he can now describe her sin as only one of the 'little faults' (v.1.12); what he has committed, a great one. There are many husbands in Renaissance drama who (like Othello) brutally kill their wives for adultery, whether falsely suspected or true. Frankford, in *A Women Killed with Kindness* (1603), who merely breaks Anne's heart, and Jane Shore's wronged husband in Heywood's *Edward IV* (1599), are unusual for the loving forgiveness and support they offer guilty and dying wives, but neither seeks to extenuate what still seems to him the appalling gravity of the woman's crime.

Kenelm Digby, himself unusual, was far ahead of his time in his attitude to Venetia Stanley and the lovers everyone knew she had

had before they married. 'I will go further in controlling the fond imaginations of the world concerning women's honour', he wrote:

for they are deceived that place it only in chastity, since they are capable of worse corruptions, and that there are innumerable vices incident to them, as well as to men, that are far more to be condemned than the breach of this frozen virtue. But...carrying much difficulty with it in that sex, and being of most importance for them to preserve for men's interests, we have drawn it into this consequence without their consent; whereas if the mind be not otherwise tainted, it is no greater a fault in them than in men.[46]

Aware that chastity is something men impose on women 'without their consent', and 'for men's interests', Digby is surprisingly generous. Yet it is clear that his tolerance extended only to pre-marital relations. Once she became his wife, he expected absolute fidelity from Venetia while often (as he would remember with anguish after her death) philandering himself.[47]

Neither Posthumus nor we understand how deeply he does love Imogen until his remorse carries him not only to seek his own death, but completely to overturn the double standard.[48] Shaw re-wrote the fifth act of *Cymbeline* in order to make it clear that Imogen, although irrevocably married to Posthumus, could never forgive him. But the play itself suggests that her forgiveness was easy compared with the one Posthumus has already achieved, and even extends in the final moments to Jachimo. When Imogen kneels to receive her father's blessing, that blessing must represent, even if Posthumus does not kneel beside her, a bestowal of consent upon this strangely tested marriage. Certainly it is more than a quirk of the dialogue that, a moment later, Cymbeline calls him 'son-in-law' (v.5.421). Amid the various feasts and sacrifices promised, after the play is over, more will be solemnized, and consummated, than just a British and Roman peace.

---

[46] *Loose Fantasies*, pp. 144–5.

[47] 'A new Digby letter-book: "In praise of Venetia"', ed. Vittorio Gabrieli, *The National Library of Wales Journal* 9 (1956), 440–62, at p. 448.

[48] The material assembled in Keith Thomas, 'The double standard', *Journal of the History of Ideas* 20, (1959), 195–216, makes Posthumus' forgiveness seem all the more remarkable. Cf. Thomas's 'The Puritans and Adultery: the Act of 1650 reconsidered' in *Puritans and Revolutionaries: Essays in Seventeenth-Century History Presented to Christopher Hill*, ed. Donald Pennington and Keith Thomas (Oxford, 1978), pp. 257–82.

CHAPTER 2

Love's Labour's Lost (1953)

In a sense the play has ended; an epilogue has been spoken by
Berowne and that haunting and beautiful kingdom created by the
marriage of reality with illusion destroyed, seemingly beyond recall.
In the person of Marcade, the world outside the circuit of the park
has at last broken through the gates, involving the characters in its
sorrows and grim actualities; the plague-houses and desolate retreats,
the mourning cities and courts of that vaster country overshadowing
the tents and towers of Navarre. Yet before the final dissolution of
that minute and once isolated kingdom of the play, when some of the
characters seem already to have disappeared and the others are
preparing sadly to journey into the realms beyond the walls of the
royal close, there is granted suddenly a little moment of grace. In the
waning afternoon, all the people of the comedy return to the stage
and stand quietly together to hear the song which 'the two learned
men have compiled in praise of the Owl and the Cuckoo', a song into
which the whole of that now-vanished world of *Love's Labour's Lost*
seems to have passed, its brilliance, its loveliness and laughter
gathered together for the last time in a single strain of music.

> When daisies pied, and violets blue,
> And lady-smocks all silver-white,
> And cuckoo-buds of yellow hue
> Do paint the meadows with delight... (v.2.894–7)

It is the landscape of the royal park that lies outstretched before us,
a little world of thickets and smooth lawns, meadows and wooded
hills. In the foreground, their appearance and speech as decorative
and charming as the setting in which they have met to solemnize their
vows of asceticism and study, stand four young men, Berowne,
Dumain, Longaville, and that ruler of Navarre whose slender
kingdom of foresters and dairy-maids, courtiers, pedants, and fools

31

seems bounded by the park and its single, rustic village. Mannered and artificial, reflecting an Elizabethan delight in patterned and intricate language, Navarre's lines at the beginning of the play are nevertheless curiously urgent and intense.

> Let fame, that all hunt after in their lives,
> Live regist'red upon our brazen tombs,
> And then grace us in the disgrace of death;
> When spite of cormorant devouring Time,
> Th' endeavor of this present breath may buy
> That honor which shall bate his scythe's keen edge,
> And make us heirs of all eternity.   (I.I.I–7)

With the King's first words, a shadow darkens for a moment the delicate dream landscape of the park. Touched by this shadow, affected by its reality, the four central characters of *Love's Labour's Lost* enter the world of the play.

Fantastic and contrived as they are, those absurd vows to which the four friends commit themselves in the initial scene spring from a recognition of the tragic brevity and impermanence of life that is peculiarly Renaissance. For many people in the sixteenth century, the world was no longer the mere shadow of a greater Reality, the imperfect image of that City of God whose towers and golden spires had dominated the universe of the Middle Ages. While the thought of Death was acquiring a new poignancy in its contrast with man's increasing sense of the value and loveliness of life in this world, Immortality tended to become, for Renaissance minds, a vague and even a somewhat dubious gift unless it could be connected in some way with the earth itself, and the affairs of human life there. Thus there arose among the humanist writers of Italy that intense and sometimes anguished longing, voiced by Navarre at the beginning of *Love's Labour's Lost*, to attain ' an immortality of glory, survival in the minds of men by the record of great deeds or of intellectual excellence...'[1] At the very heart of the plan for an Academe lies the reality of Death, the Renaissance desire to inherit, through remarkable devotion to learning, an eternity of Fame, and thus to ensure some continuity of personal existence, however slight, against the ravages of 'cormorant devouring Time'.

It is obvious, however, from the very beginning of the play, that the

---

[1] Nesca Robb, *Neoplatonism of the Italian Renaissance* (London, 1935), p. 45.

Academe and the idea of immortality which it embodies must fail. Less remote and docile than Dumain and Longaville, the brilliant and sensitive Berowne first realizes how unnatural the vows are, how seriously they trespass, despite their three-year limit, against the normal laws of life. The paradox of the Academe and the reason why its failure is not only understandable but necessary lie in the fact that this elaborate scheme which intends to enhance life and extend it through Fame even beyond the boundaries of the grave would, if successfully carried out, result in its limitation and, ultimately, complete denial. In their very attempt to retain hold upon life, the King and his companions, as Berowne alone understands, are cutting themselves off from it, from love, and the beauty of women, from all those sensuous pleasures of the world which have prompted the establishment of the Academe in the first place by making the 'too much loved earth more lovely',[2] and the thought of its loss in Death so grim.

Long before the appearance of those two amusing but sobering characters, Holofernes and Nathaniel, Berowne has seen the barrenness of learning that is divorced from life, the tragedy of those industrious men of science who find a name for every star in the western skies and yet 'have no more profit of their shining nights / Than those that walk and wot not what they are' (I.I.90–1). Even in the first scene of the play, before his love for Rosaline has made his perception deeper and more sensitive, Berowne realizes that the only way to deal with the reality of Death and Time is to accept it, to experience as much of life as possible while the opportunity is given. Implicit in his earliest lines is the knowledge, related to the first group of the 'Sonnets', that 'we cannot cross the cause why we were born', and although he agrees at last to take the oath, it is through him that we first sense the conviction expressed by the play as a whole that this idea of intellectual glory is an essentially sterile one, that the price exacted is too great to pay for a fame and a memory on earth that will soon be lost in Time.

It was one of Walter Pater's most famous dictums that 'All art constantly aspires towards the condition of music.'[3] In his essay on 'Shakespeare's English Kings' he asserted more particularly that 'into the unity of a choric song the perfect drama ever tends to return,

---

[2] Sir Philip Sidney, *An Apology for Poetry*, ed. Geoffrey Shepherd (Manchester, 1973), p. 100.
[3] Walter Pater, 'The School of Giorgione', in *The Renaissance* (London, 1900), p. 135.

its intellectual scope deepened, complicated, enlarged, but still with
an unmistakable singleness, or identity, in its impression on the
mind'.[4] Such a unity is evident throughout *Love's Labour's Lost*, and,
indeed, the quality of the whole is very much that of a musical
composition, an inexorable movement forward, the appearance and
reappearance in the fabric of the play of certain important themes,
forcing the harmony into a series of coherent resolutions consistent
with each other and with the drama as a whole. Berowne has scarcely
finished speaking before his assertion that 'every man with his affects
is born, / Not by might mast'red, but by special grace' (1.1.151–2) is
echoed in the structure of the comedy itself, with the entrance of
Constable Dull and the reluctant Costard, the first to disobey the
edicts of the new Academe.

The episode which follows is significant of the trend of future
action. As the King reads Armado's convoluted accusation and
Costard tries feebly to avert impending doom by making Navarre
laugh, it becomes obvious how much enchantment the play holds for
the ear, how subtly it combines highly individual idioms of speech.
Love's Labour's Lost is a play of many voices, and much of its beauty
stems from the sheer music of their rise and fall, the exploitation of
their differences of quality and tone, accent and complication. Here
in the first scene, the frank simplicity of Dull, the awed monosyllables
of Costard, are placed by Shakespeare in relationship with the
studied sentences of Longaville, the fantastic style of Armado, and
the more attractive elegance of Berowne, and the whole episode given
the quality of a polyphonic composition. The Costard scene has,
however, a more serious purpose in the play: one virtually identical
with that fulfilled by a scene in *Measure For Measure*. In the later
comedy, Angelo appears in the opening scene of the second act in a
role analogous to Navarre's in *Love's Labour's Lost*, and the old
counsellor Escalus in one similar to Berowne's. The scheme of justice
which Angelo would enforce in Vienna is as inflexible, as ignorant of
the nature of human beings as Navarre's Academe, and it is
challenged by Escalus. Not, however, until the sudden entrance of
Constable Elbow, an Austrian cousin of Dull's, and Pompey, who
can be compared to Costard, does it become obvious how impractical
the system is, how helpless its high-minded idealism when forced to

---

[4] 'Shakespeare's English kings', in *Appreciations, With an Essay on Style* (London, 1901), pp.
203–4.

deal with real individuals, their private standards of morality and human weaknesses. The fate of Angelo's justice is settled even before he himself has sinned against it, in the process of that riotous contention between Elbow, Froth, and Pompey, and in the same way, Navarre's Academe has failed before he and his friends are actually forsworn, from the moment that the intensely individual figures of Costard and Dull appear in their respective roles as transgressor and upholder. Among the lower social levels of the park, life itself destroys the King's scheme almost in the moment of its foundation.

Walter Pater found *Love's Labour's Lost* charming in its changing 'series of pictorial groups, in which the same figures reappear, in different combinations but on the same background ',[5] a composition, for him, like that of some ancient tapestry, studied, and not a little fantastic. The grouping of the characters into scenes would appear, however, to have been dictated by a purpose more serious than the mere creation of such patterns; it is one of the ways in which Shakespeare maintains the balance of the play world between the artificial and the real, and indicates the final outcome of the comedy.

There are, of course, huge differences in Shakespeare's realization of the people who walk and speak together within the limits of the royal park. From the virtually indistinguishable figures of Dumain and Longaville, never much more than fashionable voices, the scale of reality rises gradually towards Berowne, in whom the conjunction of a certain remote and fantastic quality with the realism which first recognized the flaws in the Academe reflects the comedy as a whole, and reaches its apogee in the substantiality and prosaic charm of Constable Dull, who could never in any sense be accused of affecting an elegant pose. Again and again, characters from different levels along this scale are grouped into scenes in a manner that helps to maintain the delicate balance of the play world; thus, in the first scene, against the implausible idea of the Academe and the sophisticated dialogue of Berowne and Longaville, Costard and the bewildered Dull are employed in much the same way that the mocking voice of the cuckoo is in the glowing spring landscape of the closing song, to keep the play in touch with a more familiar world, as well as to indicate the ultimate victory of reality over artifice and illusion.

---

[5] '*Love's Labour's Lost*', in *Appreciations*, p. 163.

As the first act ends, this theme is repeated again, and the inevitability of future events made more clear with the abandonment of the edicts of the Academe by the very individual who was responsible for the deliverance of Costard into the righteous hands of Dull: the intense and serious Armado. The grave figure of the Spanish traveller is one of the most enigmatic to appear in *Love's Labour's Lost*, and his sudden love for Jaquenetta the strangest of the five romances which develop within the park. Like Berowne, Armado is playing a part, but in his case it is far more difficult to separate the actor from the man underneath, and the pose itself is more complex than the fashionable role of Berowne. Even in his soliloquies, Armado seems to be acting to some invisible audience, and it is only in one moment at the end of the play that we are granted a glimpse of the man without the mask.

Romantic and proud, intensely imaginative, he has retreated into illusion much farther than Berowne, creating a world of his own within the world of the park: a world peopled with heroes of the past, Samson and Hercules, Hector and the knights of Spain. Somehow, it is among these long-dead heroes that Armado really exists, rather than among the people of the play, and his bizarre language, so strange and artificial when placed beside the homely speech of Costard, was created for that remote, imaginative environment and possesses there a peculiar beauty and aptness of its own. A character with some of the isolation of Jaques, always separated from the gibes and chatter of Moth, he falls in love with Jaquenetta without accepting her as the country-wench she is, but creates a little drama about the object of his passion in which his is the central role, and Jaquenetta appears in any likeness that he pleases, Delilah or Deianira. The illusion in which Armado lives has its own charm, but as the play progresses it becomes evident that this illusion is not strong enough to withstand the pressure of reality and must in the end be destroyed.

With the arrival of the Princess of France and her companions a new stage in the development of *Love's Labour's Lost* has been reached, and a theme not heard before begins slowly to rise in the musical structure of the play. Before the arrival of the ladies, it has been made clear that the Academe must fail, and it is no surprise when in the opening scene of the second act we find each of the four friends stealing back alone after the initial meeting to learn the name of his love from the obliging Boyet. As life itself breaks swiftly through the scholarship of the court, the vitality of the play increases; the Academe is kept constantly before us, the reasons for its failure elaborated and made more plain, but at the same time, while the world of the royal park becomes more and more delightful, while masque and pageantry flower within its confines, it becomes obvious that more than the Academe will be destroyed by the entrance of the ladies. Not only its scholarship, but the entire world of the play, the balance of artifice and reality of which it was formed, must also be demolished by forces from without.

The Princess and her little retinue represent the first penetration of the park by the normal world beyond, a world composed of different and colder elements than the fairy-tale environment within. Through them, in some sense, the voice of reality speaks, and although they seem to fit perfectly into the landscape of the park, indulge in highly formal, elaborate skirmishes of wit with each other and with the men, they are detached from this world in a way that none of its original inhabitants are. The contrived and fashionable poses which they adopt are less serious, more playful than those of the other characters, and they are conscious all the time, as even Berowne is not, that these attitudes are merely poses. With them into the park they bring past time and a disturbing reminder of the world outside, and from them come the first objective criticisms which pass beyond the scheme of the Academe to attack the men who have formed it. Maria, remembering Longaville as she saw him once before in Normandy, points out for the first time in the play the danger of attitudes which develop without regard for the feelings of others, of wit that exercises itself thoughtlessly upon all.

In the wit of the ladies themselves, an uncompromising logic cuts through the pleasant webs of artifice, the courtly jests and elaborations in the humour of the men, and emerges victorious with an unfailing regularity. Unlike the women, the King and his companions play, not with facts themselves, but with words, with nice phrases and antithetical statements, and when their embroidered language itself has been attacked, their courteous offers disdained as mere euphemisms, they retire discomfited. Even Berowne is defeated when he approaches Rosaline with his graceful conceits.

BEROWNE: Lady, I will commend you to mine own heart.
ROSALINE: Pray you, do my commendations——I would be glad to see it.
BEROWNE: I would you heard it groan.
ROSALINE: Is the fool sick?

BEROWNE: Sick at the heart.
ROSALINE: Alack, let it blood.
BEROWNE: Would that do it good?
ROSALINE: My physic says 'ay.'   (II.1.180–8)

Witty as Berowne, as agile of mind, Rosaline attacks his conventional protestations with a wit based on realism, a ridicule springing from her consciousness of the absurdity of artifice. That Berowne could be expressing a real passion in these terms never enters her mind; he is merely mocking her, and she defends herself in the most effective way she can.

Berowne, however, like the King, Dumain, and Longaville, is suddenly and genuinely in love. The academe has been demolished and now, in the fourth act, Shakespeare introduces, in the characters of Holofernes and Nathaniel, reminders of what such a scheme might have led to, examples of the sterility of learning that is unrelated to life. As usual, Dull, surely the most delightful of that illustrious Shakespearean series of dim-witted but officious representatives of constabulary law, appears with them as the realistic element in the scene, the voice of the cuckoo which mocks, unconsciously, the intricate speech of the two pedants. Bewildered as usual, Dull shows here a quality of stubbornness we had not expected, maintaining stolidly against the fantastic perorations of Holofernes and Nathaniel that the deer killed by the Princess was 'not a haud credo, 'twas a pricket' (IV.2.12). It is one of the nicest of his infrequent appearances, matched only by that little scene later in the play in which, utterly stupefied by the conversation which he has endured from Holofernes and Nathaniel at dinner, he sits mute and quiescent through all the arrangements for the pageant of the Nine Worthies, only at the very last, when roused by another character, entering the dialogue at all to offer a personal performance upon the tabor, a talent as engaging and unexpected in Dull as song is in the Justice Silence of 2 *Henry IV*.

Unlike Dull, the schoolmaster and the curate are in some sense mere types, elements of a satire, but Shakespeare is after all not writing a treatise; the two have a charm of their own, and their interminable quibblings a faint and grotesque beauty. On a lower, less refined level, they reflect the love of words themselves that is visible throughout the play, revelling, not like Armado in the romance of the past, but in Latin verbs and bits of forgotten erudition, spare and abstract. As Moth says, 'They have been at a great feast of languages and stol'n the scraps', (V.1.36) and in their conversation the wisdom of ages past appears in a strangely mutilated form, the life drained from it, curiously haphazard and remote.

When in the third scene of Act iv, Berowne appears alone on the stage, it becomes plain that his love for Rosaline is becoming increasingly intense. Although he seems at first only to be adopting another pose, that of melancholy lover, he is slowly becoming, as the play progresses, a more convincing and attractive figure, and his love more deeply grounded.

By heaven, I do love, and it hath taught me to rhyme and to be mallicholy; and here is part of my rhyme, and here my mallicholy. Well, she hath one a' my sonnets already: the clown bore it, the fool sent it, and the lady hath it: sweet clown, sweeter fool, sweetest lady! (iv.3.12–16)

Often, by way of ornament and convention the Elizabethans conveyed genuine emotion. Berowne's love for Rosaline is as painful as Astrophil's for Stella, his longing as real as that of the unknown Elizabethan lover in Nicholas Hillyarde's strangest and most haunting miniature who stands in the attitude of a familiar poetic conceit, gaunt and dishevelled, against a background of flames.

The episode which follows Berowne's introductory soliloquy is the first of three scenes in *Love's Labour's Lost* which possess the quality of a play within the play, formal in construction, always beautifully handled. Here, above the whole scene, Berowne acts as spectator and as Chorus, establishing the play atmosphere in his various asides, crying out upon the entrance of Longaville, 'Why, he comes in like a perjure, wearing papers' (iv.3.46), or in a more general affirmation,

'All hid, all hid,' an old infant play.
Like a demigod here sit I in the sky,
And wretched fools' secrets heedfully o'er-eye. (iv.3.76–8)

Throughout *Love's Labour's Lost*, games or plays are symbols of unreality. Here, both are employed to render the convenient but obvious device of having each of the four lovers appear alone upon the stage, read aloud the poem addressed to his lady, and step aside for the advance of the next one, not only acceptable, but delightful. In this heightened environment, a level of unreality beyond that of the comedy as a whole, the multiple discoveries are convincing, and the songs and sonnets read by the lovers the testimonies of a passion that is not to be questioned.

Through the comments of Berowne, the scene is still, however, kept in touch with reality. From his rocketing line upon the entrance of the

King, 'Shot, by heaven!' (IV.3.22), to the moment when he steps from his concealment in all the splendour of outraged virtue, Berowne's role is again analogous to that of the cuckoo in the closing song, mocking the lovers 'enamling with pied flowers their thoughts of gold',[6] maintaining the balance of the play. When he actually appears among his shamefaced friends to chide them for this 'scene of fool'ry' (IV.3.161), the play within the play ends, as the spectator becomes actor, and we return, with his beautifully sanctimonious sermon, to the more usual level.

Then, only a few lines after the close of the play scene, another and even more effective climax is built up. Costard appears with Berowne's own sonnet written to Rosaline, and suddenly the verse rises into magnificence. 'Guilty, my lord, guilty! I confess, I confess' (IV.3.210). Berowne's speech attains a power and a radiance new in the comedy: an utterance still fastidious, still choice, but less self-conscious, as he sums up for Navarre, Dumain, and Longaville all that Shakespeare has been saying long before, in the Costard scene, in the fall from grace of Don Armado.

> Sweet lords, sweet lovers, O let us embrace!
> As true we are as flesh and blood can be.
> The sea will ebb and flow, heaven show his face;
> Young blood doth not obey an old decree.
> We cannot cross the cause why we were born;
> Therefore of all hands must be we forsworn.   (IV.3.210–15)

Following these lines, there is a deliberate slackening of intensity, and the scene descends for a moment into an artificial duel of wits among the King, Berowne, and Longaville, on a somewhat hackneyed conceit. Berowne's toying with the various meanings of dark and light is as contrived as anything we have heard from him earlier in the play, but from these lines the scene suddenly rises to a lyrical height in his speech justifying the breaking of the vows, 'Have at you then, affection's men-at-arms' (IV.3.286). Finally and completely, the Academe has crumbled, and it is Berowne, as is proper, who sums up all that the play has been saying up to this point in his peroration upon earthly love.

'Other slow arts entirely keep the brain; / And therefore, finding

---

[6] 'Astrophil and Stella', 3, in *The Poems of Sir Philip Sidney*, ed. W. A. Ringler (Oxford, 1962), p. 166.

barren practicers, / Scarce show a harvest of their heavy toil' (IV.3.321–3). Holofernes and Nathaniel are indirectly brought before us, the symbols of learning divorced from life, and having thus disposed of scholarship, Berowne passes on to speak of Love itself, and the task of justifying his own perjury and that of his three friends. His customary eloquence and delicacy of language transfigured and made splendid, sincerity is perfectly blended with the surviving mannerism. 'And when Love speaks, the voice of all the gods / Make heaven drowsy with the harmony' (IV.3.341–2). After these lines, the speech loses something of its beauty, but its intensity remains and fires the King, Dumain, and Longaville. The actions flares up suddenly in great, vibrant lines; 'Shall we resolve to woo these girls of France?' (IV.3.368) 'Saint Cupid, then! and, soldiers, to the field' (363), and in a whirlwind of vitality and excitement the scene moves towards its close. 'For revels, dances, masks, and merry hours / Forerun fair Love, strewing her way with flowers' (376–7). Yet the scene ends quietly, with two thoughtful, foreboding lines which are prophetic of what is to come in the next act. As though he turned back for a second, musingly, in the act of going off with the others, Berowne, as Chorus, remarks more to himself and that deserted little glade which was the scene of the play within the play than to his retreating friends, 'Light wenches may prove plagues to men forsworn; / If so, our copper buys no better treasure' (382–3), lines which despite their apparent gaiety are curiously disturbing.

With the beginning of that long, last act, a turning point in the action of the play has been reached. The Academe defeated by life itself on all levels of the park, one might expect that *Love's Labour's Lost* would move now into an untroubled close. But as we have in some sense been told by the title, and by the comments of the ladies, such an ending is, in this case, impossible. From the Academe theme the play turns now to the destruction of the half-real world within the royal park, a destruction which, in the actual moment in which it is accomplished, is unexpected and shocking, and yet has been prepared for and justified by previous events. As we enter the fifth act, shadows begin to fall across the play world. Life within the park, its brilliance and laughter, mounts higher and higher, yet it is the winter stanzas of the closing song that this act suggests, and a new darkness, a strange intensity forces the harmony of the play into unforeseen resolutions. Vanished now are the untroubled meadows of spring, and the landscape acquires a realism that is somehow a little harsh.

When icicles hang by the wall,
　And Dick the shepherd blows his nail,
And Tom bears logs into the hall,
　And milk comes frozen home in pail;
When blood is nipp'd and ways be foul...　　　(v.2.912–16)

With Act v, the thought of Death enters the park. The play opened, of course, under the shadow of death, the great motivation of the Academe, but after that opening speech of Navarre's, it vanished altogether, never appearing again even in the imagery of the play until the entrance of the ladies. Significantly, it is they, the intruders from outside, who first, in Act iii, bring death into the park itself. In this act, the Princess kills a deer, but in the lines in which the hunt is spoken of, those of Holofernes and the Princess herself, the animal's death is carefully robbed of any disturbing reality. After Holofernes has told us how 'The preyful Princess pierc'd and prick'd a pretty pleasing pricket,' (iv.1.56) the fate of the deer is as unreal as the wooded landscape over which it ran. It might just as well have sprung to its feet and gambolled off when the forester's back was turned.

Not until Act v does the death image become real and disturbing, and even here, until the final entrance of Marcade, it is allowed to appear only in the imagery, or else in the recollection by some character of a time and a place beyond the scope of the play itself: the country of France where Katherine's sister died of her melancholy and longing, or that forgotten antiquity in which the bones of Hector were laid to rest. Appearing thus softened, kept in the background of the comedy, it is nevertheless a curiously troubling image, and as it rises slowly through the fabric of the play, the key of the entire final movement is altered. In the masque scene, Berowne, half-serious about his love and that of the King, Dumain, and Longaville, cries to the ladies,

Write 'Lord have mercy on us' on those three:
They are infected, in their hearts it lies;
They have the plague, and caught it of your eyes.
These lords are visited; you are not free,
For the Lord's tokens on you I do see.　　　(v.2.419–23)

and while the image is playfully treated still, it is surely a curious and grotesque figure, this marriage of love, the symbol throughout the comedy of life itself, with death. One cannot imagine such an image appearing earlier in the play, before the outside world, the echoes of its great plague bells sounding through desolate streets, the lugubrious cries of the watchmen marking the doors of the infected houses, began to filter obscurely through the little kingdom of the park.

It is the tremendous reality of death which will destroy the illusory world of Navarre as thoroughly as the gentler forces of life destroyed the Academe and the artificial scheme it represented, earlier in the play. At the very beginning of the fifth act, it is made apparent why this must happen, why it is necessary for the world of the comedy, despite its beauty and grace, to be demolished. The Princess and her gentlewomen have been discussing the favours and the promises showered upon them by the King and his courtiers, laughing and mocking one another gently. Suddenly, the atmosphere of the entire scene is altered with a single, curious comment, a kind of overheard aside, made by Katherine, upon the real nature of Love. Rosaline turns to her, and as she remembers past time and a tragedy for which the god of Love was responsible then, the scene suddenly becomes filled with the presence of death.

> ROSALINE: You'll ne'er be friends with him, 'a kill'd your sister.
> KATHERINE: He made her melancholy, sad, and heavy,
> And so she died. Had she been light, like you,
> Of such a merry, nimble, stirring spirit,
> She might 'a' been a grandam ere she died.
> And so may you; for a light heart lives long. (v.2.13–18)

Against such a memory of the reality of love, the Princess and her three companions place the fantastic protestations of Navarre, Berowne, Dumain, and Longaville. As we have seen, their love is genuine; it has made the character of Berowne immeasurably more attractive, caused him no little anguish of spirit, created that great speech of his at the end of Act IV. Beneath the delicate language, the elegance and the gaiety, lies a real passion, but the women from the world outside, where love has been coupled for them with death, see only artifice and pose. The artificiality which has become natural to the four friends and the environment in which they live holds them from the accomplishment of their desire, for the ladies, hearing from Boyet of the masque in which their lovers intend to declare themselves, are unable to perceive in the scheme anything but attempted mockery, and in defending themselves, frustrate the serious purpose of the entertainment.

> They do it but in mockery merriment,
> And mock for mock is only my intent...
> There's no such sport as sport by sport o'erthrown,
> To make theirs ours and ours none but our own;
> So shall we stay, mocking intended game,
> And they, well mock'd, depart away with shame.
>
> (v.2.139–40; 153–6)

In this masque scene, the second of the plays within the play, the part of audience and commentator is played by Boyet. As usual, the men are completely defeated by the ladies, the delicate fabric of their wit and artifice destroyed by the realistic humour of opponents who play with facts, not merely with words. Berowne, approaching the supposed Rosaline with a courteous request, 'White-handed mistress, one sweet word with thee', is mercilessly rebuffed by the Princess – 'Honey, and milk, and sugar, there is three' – and the masque itself ruined by the satiric comments of Boyet who, unlike Berowne in the earlier play scene, actually insinuates himself into the unreal world of the entertainment, and upsets it.

Even when the exposure is complete and the men have asked pardon from their loves, the women think only that they have defeated a mocking jest directed against them, not that they have prevented their lovers from expressing a genuine passion. For the first time, Berowne reaches simplicity and humbleness in his love; his declaration to Rosaline at the end of the masque is touching and sincere, but for her, this passion is still unbelievable, a momentary affectation, and she continues to mock her lover and the sentiments he expresses.

> BEROWNE: I am a fool, and full of poverty.
> ROSALINE: But that you take what doth to you belong,
>   It were a fault to snatch words from my tongue.
> BEROWNE: O, I am yours, and all that I possess!
> ROSALINE: All the fool mine?
>
> (v.2.380–4)

More sensitive, gifted with a deeper perception of reality than his companions, Berowne seems to guess what is wrong, and he forswears 'Taffata phrases, silken terms precise, / Three pil'd hyperboles, spruce affection, / Figures pedantical...,' (v.2.406–7) at least to Rosaline, but the rejection itself is somewhat artificial, and he remains afterwards with more than 'a trick / Of the old rage' (v.2.416).

The masque has failed, and Berowne's more direct attempt to announce to the ladies the purpose behind the performance and detect in them an answering passion has been turned away by the unbelieving Princess. At this point, Costard enters to announce that Holofernes and Nathaniel, Moth and Armado are at hand to present the pageant of the Nine Worthies, and the third and last of the plays within the play begins. As we enter this play scene, the vitality and force of the comedy reaches it apogee, but in its laughter there rings now a discordant note that we have not heard before. The actors themselves are, after all, no less sincere than Bottom and his troupe in *A Midsummer Night's Dream*, and they are a great deal more sensitive and easy to hurt. They are real people whose intentions are of the very best, their loyalty to their King unquestioned, and although their performance is unintentionally humorous, one would expect the audience to behave with something of the sympathy and forbearance exhibited by Duke Theseus and the Athenians.

The only civil members of the audience in *Love's Labour's Lost*, however, are the ladies. The Princess cannot resist one sarcasm upon the entrance of Armado, but it is addressed quietly to Berowne, before the play itself begins, while Armado is engrossed with the King and obviously does not hear. Thereafter, every one of her comments to the players is one of interest or pity: 'Great thanks, great Pompey', 'Alas, poor Machabeus, how hath he been baited', 'Speak, brave Hector, we are much delighted.' (v.2.557; 631; 665) The players have only the Princess to appeal to in the storm of hilarity which assails them, and it is only she, realistic as she is, who understands that a play is an illusion, that it is to be taken as such and respected in some sense for itself, regardless of its quality. Like Theseus in *A Midsummer Night's Dream*, she realizes that 'the best in this kind are but shadows; and the worst are no worse, if imagination amend them',[7] and when she addresses the players she is wise and sensitive enough to do so not by their own names, which she has read on the playbill, but by the names of those whom they portray, thus helping them to sustain that illusion which is the very heart of a play.

In contrast to that of the Princess, the behaviour of the men is incredibly unattractive, particularly that of Berowne. It is difficult to believe that this is the same man who spoke so eloquently a short time ago about the soft and sensible feelings of love, and promised

---

[7] *A Midsummer Night's Dream* v.1.211–12.

Rosaline to mend his ways. Costard manages to finish his part before
the deluge, and Nathaniel, although unkindly treated, is not
personally humiliated. Only with the appearance of Holofernes as
Judas Maccabaeus and Armado as Hector is the full force of the
ridicule released, and it is precisely with these two characters that the
infliction of abuse must be most painful. Costard, after all, is a mere
fool; he takes part in the baiting of the others with no compunction
at all, and Nathaniel throughout the comedy has been little more
than a foil for Holofernes, but the village pedagogue is a more
sensitive soul.

Holofernes has his own sense of the apt and the beautiful which,
though perverse, is meaningful enough for him, and it is painful to see
him stand here on the smooth grass of the lawn, his whole subjective
world under merciless attack, a storm of personal epithets exploding
about him.

> DUMAIN: The head of a bodkin.
> BEROWNE: A death's face in a ring
> LONGAVILLE: The face of an old Roman coin, scarce seen.
> BOYET: The pommel of Caesar's falchion.
> DUMAIN: The carv'd-bone face on a flask.
> BEROWNE: Saint George's half-cheek in a brooch.   (v.2.611–16)

The laughter is unattractive, wild, and somehow discordant, made
curiously harsh by the introduction of Berowne's 'death's face', and
it has little resemblance to the laughter which we have heard in the
play before this, delicate, sophisticated, sometimes hearty, but never
really unkind. When Holofernes cries at the last, 'This is not
generous, not gentle, not humble', (v.2.629) he becomes a figure of
real dignity and stature, restrained and courteous in the face of the
most appalling incivility.

Meanwhile, around the pedagogue and his little audience the
afternoon has been waning slowly into evening, long shadows falling
horizontally across the lawn, and Boyet calls after the retreating
Holofernes in a strangely haunting line, 'A light for Monsieur Judas!
It grows dark, he may stumble' (v.2.630). A kind of wildness grips all
the men, and though Dumain says in a weird and prophetic line,
'Though my mocks come home by me, I will now be merry' (635),
Armado faces a jeering throng even before he has begun to speak. Of
all the players, Armado is the one for whom we have the most
sympathy. He is a member of the court itself, has had some reason to
pride himself upon the King's favour, and has been good enough to

arrange the pageant in the first place. The people represented in it are those who inhabit that strange world of his fancy, and one knows that his anguish is not alone for his personal humiliation, but for that of the long-dead hero he portrays, when he cries, 'The sweet war-man is dead and rotten, sweet chucks, beat not the bones of the buried. When he breathed, he was a man' (v.2.660). A little grotesque, as Armado's sentences always are, the line is nevertheless infinitely moving in its summoning up of great spaces of time, its ironic relation to the idea of immortality through fame expressed in the opening speech of the comedy. Not since the reference to Katherine's sister have we had such a powerful and disturbing image of death brought before us, death real and inescapable although still related to a world and a time beyond the play itself.

In the remaining moments of the play scene, the hilarity rises to its climax, a climax becoming increasingly harsh. During the altercation between Costard and Armado which results from Berowne's in-genious but unattractive trick, images of death begin to hammer through the fabric of the play. The painfulness of the scene grows as Armado, poor, but immensely proud, is finally shamed and humbled before all the other characters. For the first time in the play, the mask falls from Armado's face, and the man beneath it is revealed, his romanticism, his touching personal pride, the agony for him of the confession that in his poverty he wears no shirt beneath his doublet. Still acting, he tries feebly to pass off this lack as some mysterious and romantic penance, but the other characters know the truth; Armado knows they do, and the knowledge is intensely humiliating. The role he has played throughout *Love's Labour's Lost* is destroyed for others as well as for himself, and he stands miserably among the jeers of Dumain and Boyet while the little personal world which he has built up around himself so carefully shatters at his feet.

The other people in the play are so concerned with Armado's predicament that no one notices that someone, in a sense Something has joined them. His entrance unremarked by any of the other characters, materializing silently from those shadows which now lie deep along the landscape of the royal park, the Messenger has entered the play world.

> MARCADE: I am sorry, madam, for the news I bring
> Is heavy in my tongue. The King your father –
> PRINCESS: Dead, for my life!
> MARCADE: Even so: my tale is told. (v.2.718–20)

There is perhaps nothing like this moment in the whole range of Elizabethan drama. In the space of four lines the entire world of the play, its delicate balance of reality and illusion, all the hilarity and overwhelming life of its last scene has been swept away and destroyed, as Death itself actually enters the park, for the first time, in the person of Marcade. Only in one Elizabethan madrigal, Orlando Gibbons' 'What Is Our Life?' is there a change of harmony and mood almost as swift and great as this one, and it occurs under precisely the same circumstances, the sudden appearance among the images of life in Ralegh's lyric of 'the graves that hide us from the searching Sun'[8], the memory of the inescapable and tremendous reality of Death.

Clumsy, as one always is in the presence of sudden grief, the King can think of nothing to say but to ask the Princess 'How fares your Majesty?' (726) a question to which she, from the depths of her sorrow and bewilderment, gives no reply, but prepares with the dignity characteristic of her to leave for France. Now, the men come forward uncertainly, and first the King and then Berowne, clinging still to a world no longer existing, attempt to express their love in terms which had been appropriate to that world, terms at first still incomprehensible to the women and then, at last, understood, but not altogether trusted.

As vows had begun the play, so vows end it. The King is assigned as his symbol of reality a 'forlorn and naked hermitage' (795) without the walls of the royal park, in the real world itself, in which he must try for a twelvemonth if this love conceived in the sunlit landscape of Navarre can persist in the colder light of actuality. For Dumain and Longaville, those shadowy figures, penances more vague but of a similar duration are assigned, and then at last, Berowne, shaken and moved to the depths of his being, enquires from Rosaline, who has been standing a little apart from the others, lost in thought,

> Studies my lady? Mistress, look on me,
> Behold the window of my heart, mine eye,
> What humble suit attends thy answer there.
> Impose some service on me for thy love.   (v.2.837–40)

Slowly, speaking with great care, Rosaline answers, and in the strangest and most grotesque of the penances, Berowne is condemned to haunt the hospitals and plague-houses of the world outside the park, to exercise his wit upon the 'speechless sick', (851) and try the

---

[8] 'What is our life?', in *The Poems of Sir Walter Ralegh*, ed. Agnes Latham (London, 1951), p. 52.

power of his past role, the old breeziness that had no concern for the feelings of others, that humiliated Armado in the play scene, the careless mocks of the old world, upon the ailing and the dying. 'A jest's prosperity lies in the ear / Of him that hears it, never in the tongue / Of him that makes it' (v.2.861–3). It was this that Berowne was unconscious of when he led the unthinking merriment of the play scene just past. Yet, at the end of the year, love's labours will be won for Berowne, and he will receive Rosaline's love, not in the half real world of the park, but in the actuality outside its walls. Thus the play which began with a paradox, that of the Academe, closes with one as well. Only through the acceptance of the reality of Death are life and love in their fullest sense made possible.

The world of the play past has now become vague and unreal, and it is not distressing that Berowne, in a little speech that is really a kind of epilogue, should refer to all the action before the entrance of Marcade, the people who took part in that action and the kingdom they inhabited and in a sense created, as having been only the elements of a play. It is a play outside which the characters now stand, bewildered, a little lost in the sudden glare of actuality, looking back upon that world of mingled artifice and reality a trifle wistfully before they separate in the vaster realm beyond the royal park. Through *Love's Labour's Lost*, the play has been a symbol of illusion, of delightful unreality, the masque of the Muscovites, or the pageant of the Nine Worthies, and now it becomes apparent that there was a further level of illusion above that of the plays within the play. The world of that illusion has enchanted us; it has been possessed of a haunting beauty, the clear loveliness of those landscapes in the closing song, but Shakespeare insists that it cannot take the place of reality itself, and should not be made to. Always, beyond the frost-etched countryside of the pastoral winter, like the background of some Flemish Book of Hours, lies the reality of the greasy kitchen-maid and her pot, a reality which must sooner or later break through and destroy the charm of the artificial.

For us, however, knowing how Shakespeare's later work developed, and how the play image itself took on another meaning for him, there is a strange poignancy in this closing moment, with its confident assertion of the concrete reality of the world into which the characters are about to journey, the necessity for them to adjust themselves to that reality. Later, in *As You Like It* and *Hamlet* Shakespeare would begin to think of the play as the symbol, not of illusion, but of the world itself and its actuality, in *Macbeth* and *King Lear* as the symbol of the futility and tragic nature of that actuality, that 'great stage of fools'. Yet he must always have kept in mind the image as it had appeared years before in the early comedy of *Love's Labour's Lost*, for returning to it at the very last, he joined that earlier idea of the play as illusion with its later meaning as a symbol of the real world, and so created the final play image of *The Tempest* in which illusion and reality have become one and the same, and there is no longer any distinction possible between them. The world itself into which Berowne and his companions travel to seek out reality will become for Shakespeare at the last merely another stage, a play briefly enacted,

> And like the baseless fabric of this vision,
> The cloud-capp'd tow'rs, the gorgeous palaces,
> The solemn temples, the great globe itself,
> Yea, all which it inherit, shall dissolve,
> And, like this insubstantial pageant faded,
> Leave not a rack behind. We are such stuff
> As dreams are made on; and our little life
> Is rounded with a sleep.[9]

[9] *The Tempest* IV.1.151–8.

CHAPTER 3

Shakespeare and the limits of language
(1971)

> It's strange that words are so inadequate.
> And yet we go on trying to compel them to our service
> Though all words fail us, even falsify our meaning.[1]

These lines, from an early version of the last scene of T. S. Eliot's play *The Elder Statesman*, express an attitude towards language characteristic of our own moment of historical time. We live in a period marked by its profound mistrust of words. How this distrust has arisen, and what the role may have been of the mass media and of the revolution in philosophy instituted by Wittgenstein in producing it, is not my concern here. I would merely suggest that when Eliot, in another work, described his own craft of poetry as 'a raid on the inarticulate / with shabby equipment always deteriorating',[2] he spoke not merely for himself as an artist but for a modern society which has become obsessed with the limitations and inadequacies of speech.

Certainly the contemporary theatre reflects this obsession. For Beckett, for Pinter, for Albee and Ionesco, dialogue has become not so much a medium of understanding, the means through which human beings reveal themselves to one another, as a measure of the hopelessness of any attempt to communicate. Words measure the gap between individuals: they do not bridge it. Every man is an island in a sense slightly different from the one John Donne had in mind, but this fact is no longer a source of suspect spiritual pride. In it, we find our own particular despair. The characters of *Waiting for Godot*, of Pinter's two plays *Landscape* and *Silence*, of *Who's Afraid of Virginia Woolf?* or of Ionesco's *Exit the King* talk and talk and talk. At the end of it all, language arrives at self-contradiction. It is there to reinforce

---

[1] From a typescript of the play, in the possession of John Barton. Eliot retained only the first of these lines.   [2] T. S. Eliot, *Four Quartets* (London, 1944), p. 22.

and make more poignant a human isolation which cannot even be regarded as tragic.

Arguably, this way of handling dramatic dialogue, a style in which the unsaid looms larger than what is actually spoken, in which characters talk at but not really to one another, stems from the plays of Chekhov. It is there at least, in the pathetic cross-purposes, the endless but futile discussions among people placed in the attitudes of conversation whose words and thoughts never meet, that modern dramatists (or many of them) have found the source of a technique. This technique seems strikingly un-Shakespearean. In her book *Themes and Conventions of Elizabethan Tragedy*, M. C. Bradbrook has emphasized that a faith in words was characteristic of Shakespeare and his contemporaries:

The essential structure of Elizabethan drama lies not in the narrative or the characters but in the words. The greatest poets are also the greatest dramatists. Through their unique interest in word play and word patterns of all kinds the Elizabethans were especially fitted to build their drama on words.[3]

It would seem, then, that we stand today at an opposite extreme from the Elizabethans with respect to the trust we are willing to place in words. This, indeed, is one of the points made by George Steiner in the introduction to his collection of essays, *Language and Silence*. According to him, Shakespeare is divided from us now less by questions of the so-called Elizabethan world picture, Tudor orthodoxy or religious and moral conservatism, than by his unfaltering belief in language: a belief which we, in the twentieth century, can no longer share.[4]

The plays of Shakespeare do indeed stand as the most complete testimony there has ever been to the efficacy of language, to what words can make. They deny and refute the reductivist attitude towards language and the imagination later promulgated by Hobbes, an attitude from which much modern thinking derives. Nevertheless, they are concerned at times to criticize the means of their own success. Certainly the word in Shakespeare is not allowed an unexamined triumph. At the heart of his drama lies an ambiguity of attitude towards the transformations effected by language which links him, surprisingly, with the outlook characteristic of our own theatre. Although his plays celebrate words, exploit their capacities

---

[3] Cambridge, 1960, p. 5.   [4] London, 1967, pp. 44–5.

fully, they also include and foreshadow something of the twentieth-century distrust. I should like to look at some of the plays in which linguistic doubt seems most important. I shall be concerned in all of them with questions of the relationship between words and deeds, between speech and silence, and with the adequacy (or otherwise) of verbal formulation to the events and emotions upon which it operates. Even for the dramatist who depended most heavily upon it, there were certain limits to language. Shakespeare confronted these limits squarely. They are never, in fact, far away from his tragic vision of life, nor from his understanding of his own art.

It may be useful to begin by considering an Elizabethan play which does not recognize these limits: a play which actually embodies the attitude towards language which Steiner would attribute to Shake-speare. In Marlowe's *Tamburlaine*, words can do almost anything:

> Brother Cosroe, I find myself aggrieved
> Yet insufficient to express the same,
> For it requires a great and thund'ring speech:
> Good brother, tell the cause unto my lords;
> I know you have a better wit than I.[5]

This is the weak and contemptible King Mycetes, in the opening moment of part I. The very first lines of *Tamburlaine* indicate that this is a play in which an inability to command words will be identified with political failure. Mycetes cannot express himself adequately, and we are asked to accept this fact as evidence of his unfitness to rule. He himself recognizes the importance of eloquence. Feebly, he asks his brother to make the speech the king himself should make. He sends Theridamas out to capture Tamburlaine with the significant judgement: 'thy words are swords' (1.1.74). But Theridamas is no match, linguistically, for Tamburlaine. After about five minutes of rhetoric he and his thousand horse belong to Tamburlaine and no longer to Mycetes. That this purely verbal winning over of Mycetes' captain got Marlowe out of the awkwardness of a staged battle is true. The important thing is the degree to which victory in these linguistic terms is characteristic of the play generally. It seems right and proper that Tamburlaine's conquest, offstage, of Bajazeth and his army should be represented by Zenocrate's purely verbal triumph over Bajazeth's queen.

[5] *Tamburlaine the Great*, ed. J. S. Cunningham (Manchester, 1981). *Part I*, 1.1.1–5.

Tamburlaine himself may be a brute, a beast, a murderer. The fact remains that before the verbal splendour of

> Now walk the angels on the walls of heaven,
> As sentinels to warn th' immortal souls
> To entertain divine Zenocrate (Part Two, II.4.15–17)

or the promise that 'Thorough the streets, with troops of conquered kings / I'll ride in golden armour like the sun' (Part Two, IV.3.114–15), the antipathy towards the speaker which we ought to feel simply collapses. As readers, or members of a theatre audience, we are scarcely more successful than Theridamas or Zenocrate at resisting the appeal of Tamburlaine's rhetoric. If we were, there would be no play. Over and over again Marlowe persuades us that words are self-sufficient: not the servants of reality, but reality's masters. So, when Tamburlaine betrays Cosroe, he does so, as it seems, purely because of the effect upon him of a verbal formula: 'Your majesty shall shortly have your wish, / And ride in triumph through Persepolis'. This is what one of Cosroe's followers, most unfortunately, says to his master. Tamburlaine overhears him and the results are fatal:

> And ride in triumph through Persepolis!
> Is it not brave to be a king, Techelles?
> Usumcasane and Theridamas,
> Is it not passing brave to be a king,
> And ride in triumph through Persepolis?   (II.5.50–4)

Words, the emotional force of a chance phrase, generate a real and consequential political ambition. And one feels, I think, that had the name only been different – had it been Leeds (say) or Slough that was offered as the scene of triumph, instead of that polysyllabic splendour Persepolis, the streets might have been paved with diamonds and Cosroe would still have been safe, the course of history different.

In the special context of this play, Tamburlaine is absolutely right when he refuses to accept the crown of Persia as the shamefaced gift of Mycetes, who has been trying in his terror to bury it on the field of battle. A crown accepted in such a hugger-mugger fashion, with no onlookers and no opportunity for a great and thundering speech, would be a crown devalued, indeed meaningless.

> Nature, that framed us of four elements
> Warring within our breasts for regiment,
> Doth teach us all to have aspiring minds:

Our souls whose faculties can comprehend
The wondrous architecture of the world
And measure every wand'ring planet's course,
Still climbing after knowledge infinite
And always moving as the restless spheres,
Wills us to wear ourselves and never rest
Until we reach the ripest fruit of all,
That perfect bliss and sole felicity,
The sweet fruition of an earthly crown.   (II.7.18–29)

These are the words with which Tamburlaine eventually consents to become king of Persia. As he speaks them, the crown itself – that circlet of mock-gold which is a mere stage property, the embarrassing object Mycetes tried to conceal – becomes what Tamburlaine says it is. It alters its identity, grows great before our eyes. Words do not simply interpret events and emotions. They *create* reality in the act of defining it. There has never perhaps been a play which so greatly magnified the power of language. It is true that at the end Death cannot be persuaded away by rhetoric. Tamburlaine may talk about setting black streamers in the firmament to signify the slaughter of the gods. His words have no power to bring back Zenocrate, or avert his own fate. In the course of the action they have, however, been able to do virtually everything else: to conquer kingdoms, persuade enemies and even to turn the whole world and its moral values upside-down.

That scene in which Tamburlaine and Mycetes stand on the field of battle with the crown of Persia suspended between them can usefully be compared with the deposition scene in Shakespeare's *Richard II*. Here again is a situation in which one claimant to the crown is a master of language, of words in all their shapes and colours, while the other is basically matter-of-fact. But the balance of political power here lies with the silent Bolingbroke, not with Richard's verbal dexterity. It is the weak king in Shakespeare who insists upon inventing a rite, a ceremony which may invest the crown, and the transference of royal power, with meaning. Richard, not Bolingbroke, gropes towards the invention of a litany, fumbles for words which will make this moment of time significant. Bolingbroke submits up to a point –

Here, cousin, seize the crown;
Here, cousin,
On this side my hand, and on that side thine.
Now is this golden crown like a deep well

That owes two buckets, filling one another,
The emptier ever dancing in the air,
The other down, unseen, and full of water:
That bucket down and full of tears am I,
Drinking my griefs, whilst you mount up on high... (IV.1.181–9)

– but his submission is oddly qualified. Bolingbroke is willing to participate in the game to the extent of reaching out his hand, silently, at Richard's request, to seize the crown. Verbally, he will not co-operate at all. 'I thought you had been willing to resign': this blunt enquiry is all the response he will vouchsafe to Richard's imaginative enactment of the situation, and it serves to tear through and destroy the validity of metaphor.

Essentially, the situation here is the reverse of the one in *Tamburlaine*. Shakespeare's man of power, Bolingbroke, simply does not believe in the transforming power of language. Terse, impersonal and reticent, he trusts to cold fact, avoids eloquence. Not for nothing does Richard call him the 'silent king' (IV.1.290). It is Bolingbroke's defeated rival who indulges in dazzling word-games, only to find that language breaks against a reality which it is powerless to alter. After his return from Ireland, Richard's chief activity is that of attempting to change the nature of things as they are by means of words. His success is doubtful. Certainly he plays with words in a vacuum as Tamburlaine had not. The world in this play is very far from being the docile servant of Richard's imagination, springing to life at his touch. Rather, he is checked at every turn, made to feel the difference between words and those unalterable facts – like the stone walls of his prison – against which imagination breaks.

On the surface, no two Shakespearean characters could seem more dissimilar than Richard and Falstaff. And yet I would suggest that it is through Falstaff that the attitude towards language associated with Richard is extended into the two parts of *Henry IV*. After all, Falstaff's one aim, his tireless activity, is to transform the facts of a world of time and harsh reality into more attractive entities. The distinguishing feature of his wit is its extraordinary ability to make things look like something they are not, to re-create reality in Falstaffian terms:

Let not us that are squires of the night's body be call'd thieves of the day's beauty. Let us be Diana's foresters, gentlemen of the shade, minions of the moon, and let men say we be men of good government, being govern'd, as the sea is, by our noble and chaste mistress the moon, under whose countenance we steal. (I.2.24–9)

As an example of how to avoid the plain and consequential word 'thief', how to employ language to metamorphose fact, this speech from *1 Henry IV* could hardly be bettered. It is a kind of transformation at which Falstaff is an adept. He tries it again, with remarkable success, in his account of what really happened at Gadshill. Just as the Prince and Poins think they have him trapped at last, Falstaff metamorphoses things as they really were on that occasion into a fictional encounter between a true prince in disguise and a valiant but extremely discerning lion. To this conjuring trick with words, they have no effective rejoinder.

A little later, in the Boar's Head Tavern play scene, Falstaff employs the same technique, but this time the sense of strain is evident and disturbing. By the sheer force of wit, he tries to alter the disreputable facts of his own character and appearance, to pass himself off as 'sweet Jack Falstaff, kind Jack Falstaff, true Jack Falstaff, valiant Jack Falstaff' (II.4.475–6). But not for nothing is Hal Bolingbroke's son. The Prince is no more taken in by Falstaff's rhetoric here than his father had been by Richard's poetry, or by old Gaunt's persuasions that a man may sweeten the rigours of banishment through the exercise of imagination. Just as fast as Falstaff transforms things into what they are not, Hal turns them back again. 'This chair', Falstaff announces, 'shall be my state, this dagger my sceptre, and this cushion my crown.' But the Prince will have none of it. 'Thy state is taken for a join'd-stool, thy golden sceptre for a leaden dagger, and thy precious rich crown for a pitiful bald crown' (II.4.378–82). The man of fact announces firmly that he is not fooled, that reality resists linguistic metamorphosis. Hal's own attitude is typified by his final response to Falstaff's elaborate pleas that he should not be turned away in the golden time to come: 'I do. I will', four bare, stripped monosyllables that are precisely equivalent to fact.

In the end Falstaff, like King Richard, is defeated. Or at least on one level he is. There is a sense in which both these characters do indeed create something of value out of words, taking with them into oblivion more sympathy than we can accord to their victorious opposites. The fact remains that they are losers, and losers in precisely those areas of life where Tamburlaine, whose linguistic attitudes they share, had been triumphant. It is tempting to believe that Shakespeare recognized and deliberately reminded his audience of the gulf dividing his tragical histories from Marlowe's *Tamburlaine* when he allowed Henry V, the night before Agincourt, to encounter Ancient Pistol. The two men can barely communicate. Pistol, for the most part, spouts verse. Henry's laconic replies are couched in prose. 'As good a gentleman as the Emperor', as he puts it, Pistol creates an imaginary sovereignty for himself by linguistic means. He is Shakespeare's mischievous parody of Tamburlaine: gorgeous, assertive, an ego magnified. With Pistol, the high, astounding terms of Marlowe's hero appear once again on the stage, but they break and become absurd in a world which refuses to accommodate itself now to Pistol's overblown imagination. Impersonal, terse and matter-of-fact, Henry himself seems almost colourless beside Pistol, but his is the sovereignty in which we believe. Pistol, like Falstaff, is only a king in jest: a character composing lines for himself in a play of his own devising. When Henry leaves Pistol, still secure in his cocoon of grandiloquence, and moves on to encounter Williams and Bates, the last of three linked Shakespearean meetings comes to its end. Richard and Bolingbroke, Falstaff and Prince Hal, Pistol and Henry V. One meeting was tragic, one comic, and one a mixture of both, but in all of them the issues were fundamentally the same. Imagination against fact, words against political realism, the personal against the unmoving mask of kingship. Our sympathies may be drawn towards the former qualities; it is the latter which win out. Not until *Antony and Cleopatra* will King Richard, and with him Falstaff (even in a sense, Ancient Pistol) at last come out on top.

The history play was by no means the only dramatic form in which Shakespeare explored the relation between speech and silence, imagination and fact. *Love's Labour's Lost* stands out among the comedies as a play overtly about language, filled with verbal games, with parody and word patterns, firing off its linguistic rockets in all directions. Yet this, paradoxically, is a play which ends with the defeat of the word. After Berowne and his companions have painfully forsworn 'Taffata phrases, silken terms precise' (v.2.406), after they have admitted that the language of love has become so contaminated that it can no longer exact belief, they face an impasse. Words have got them into their dilemma, but words are incapable of getting them out again. Only through an acceptance of silence, that year of residence in a forlorn and naked hermitage, can the King, Dumain and Longaville persuade the women that their love is genuine and not merely an idle game. As for Berowne, the penance enforced upon

him by Rosaline, to 'jest a twelvemonth in an hospital' will be, in
effect, a demonstration of the way language breaks before the reality
of pain and death (v.2.871).

Although *Love's Labour's Lost* is the most striking example of a
Shakespearean comedy concerned to examine the nature of its own
medium, it is by no means the only one. Touchstone and Feste,
Elbow, Dogberry and Lavatch are all corrupters of words. Their
mistakings are in some cases wilful, in others involuntary, but all of
them – the wise fools and the dull – use puns, quibbles and plain
misunderstanding to open a rift between words and the things they
signify. 'To see this age!', Feste says admiringly to Viola in *Twelfth
Night*. 'A sentence is but a chev'ril glove to a good wit. How quickly
the wrong side may be turn'd outward ... words are grown so false, I
am loath to prove reason with them' (III.1.11–25). He is, of course,
only half serious. In general, the positive side of language is
uppermost in the comedies, *Love's Labour's Lost* excepted. It is in the
tragedies (as one might expect) that words are exposed to a scrutiny
not only intense but, in the case of *King Lear*, distinctly unfriendly.

This scepticism becomes apparent in the first scene of the play:

> Sir, I love you more than words can wield the matter,
> Dearer than eyesight, space, and liberty,
> Beyond what can be valued, rich or rare,
> No less than life, with grace, health, beauty, honor;
> As much as child e'er lov'd, or father found;
> A love that makes breath poor, and speech unable:
> Beyond all manner of so much I love you.   (1.1.55–61)

This is how Goneril fawns on her father. She insists that language is
inadequate to express the depth of her love. Where her predecessor in
the old anonymous play of *King Leir* had offered, melodramatically,
to kill herself at once if her father wished, to leap into the sea or marry
a slave if this would please him, Shakespeare's Goneril contents
herself with saying, at some length, that she can't say how much she
loves the king.

Something very like Goneril's technique here is familiar from
Elizabethan sonnet sequences. The lover's assertion, carried through
fourteen carefully wrought lines, that the worth of the beloved passes
the power of language to express is a common enough device. Sidney
could spend a whole sonnet informing his reader that nothing but the
simple naming of Stella was worthwhile. Drayton, in the twenty-
eighth Sonnet of *Idea*, asserted that his lady's graces were more than

'my wond'ring utterance can unfold', but promptly went on to unfold them. It is, after all, a stock rhetorical device, like the claims made by Greek and Latin orators in their court pleas: 'I could not begin to describe to you this man's iniquities' – followed inevitably by several thousand words describing them in detail. Goneril's graceful, fluent protestation of the inadequacy of language belongs to a recognized literary tradition. And her sister Regan underscores it.

One begins to see something of the true and agonizing nature of Cordelia's problem. 'What shall Cordelia speak? Love, and be silent', is her response to Goneril (1.1.62). 'My love's / More ponderous than my tongue', she says when Regan has finished speaking (1.1.77–8). The irony lies in the fact that both these broken statements only echo what her sisters have so fulsomely been saying: 'I love you more than word can wield the matter.' In Cordelia's case, the declaration of the inadequacy of language happens to express a true state of feeling. Her love for her father does indeed make her breath poor and speech unable; it is not a mere rhetorical flourish. But how can one tell the difference between sincerity and pretence, especially when both employ the same disclaimers? Cordelia's sisters have usurped, falsely, her own genuine excuse. All she can do at this point is to state plainly what they have offered with embellishments, conscious that this plainness must appear ungracious. Their professions have contaminated the truth of her own situation. When Cordelia says, 'Unhappy that I am, I cannot heave / My heart into my mouth', she is being honest (1.1.91–2). But she has already been anticipated in this very protestation by Goneril. For her at the beginning of the tragedy, as for the lovers at the end of *Love's Labour's Lost*, actions provide the only test. Words have lost all significance. 'And your large speeches may your deeds approve, / That good effects may spring from words of love', as Kent says bitterly when he has heard the love-trial through (1.1.184–5).

Winifred Nowottny has pointed out that Lear himself is a character who must consistently 'use language not as the adequate register of his experience, but as evidence that his experience is beyond language's scope'.[6] This judgement seems to me true, and also applicable to other characters besides Lear. Over and over again, in the vital moments of the play, it is stated explicitly that language has failed. In scene 4 of Act II, Lear is about to exchange the comforts of

---

[6] In 'Some aspects of the style of *King Lear*', *Shakespeare Survey 13* (1960), p. 53.

Gloucester's house for the heath and the storm. He speaks what will be his last words to Goneril and Regan in the play:

> No, you unnatural hags,
> I will have such revenges on you both
> That all the world shall – I will do such things –
> What they are yet I know not, but they shall be
> The terrors of the earth!   (II.4.278–82)

The breaks in his utterance here, the disjointed phrases, are not due entirely to climbing sorrow and the madness it portends. The fact is that the old king cannot find words adequate to his anger, cannot give his intentions a linguistic shape that is worthy of them. There is no vocabulary for what he feels. There will not be one in scene 7 of Act IV either, when he wakes to find himself clad in fresh garments, and tended by Cordelia. 'I know not', he falters, 'what to say' (53). The words he does find in the scene are so slow, so halting and simple as almost to constitute a language invented on the spot; full of monosyllables and terms so stripped and bare that they seem talismanic: 'You do me wrong to take me out o' th' grave' (44). Not even in the world of this play can such a line be regarded as normal speech. Nor is Cordelia much more articulate here than she had been during the love trial at the beginning, or in scene 3 of this same act, when Kent received an account of her behaviour at hearing of her father's misfortunes. 'Made she no verbal question?' Kent asked the gentleman giving the report, and he was told:

> Faith, once or twice she heav'd the name of "father"
> Pantingly forth, as if it press'd her heart;
> Cried, 'Sisters, sisters! Shame of ladies, sisters!
> Kent! father! sisters! What, i' th' storm? i' th' night?'(IV.3.25–8)

Once again it is a broken, a dislocated speech that is offered. All Cordelia can do is to repeat proper and generic names, tangible things which weigh like coins in the hand, without verbs to link them, without sentence structure.

Edgar too discovers the limits of language:

> O gods! Who is't can say, "I am at the worst?"
> I am worse than e'er I was...
> And worse I may be yet: the worst is not
> So long as we can say, "This is the worst".   (IV.1.25–8)

This is what he says in the moment that he recognizes his father coming towards him, blind and poorly led. He returns to the idea later on in the act, in the midst of the encounter between Gloucester and the mad Lear. Of Lear's appearance in this scene, one of Cordelia's attendants says that it is 'A sight most pitiful in the meanest wretch, / Past speaking of in a king' (IV.6.204–5). Witness to the appalling interchange between his blind father and Lear, Edgar says simply: 'I would not take this from report; it is, / And my heart breaks at it' (IV.6.141–2). Once again, events have outrun language, have rendered it inadequate. Situations overwhelm words.

'It is': to those two words, the barest possible indication of existence, much of what happens in *King Lear* must be reduced. So, at the end, Albany will be unable to find a word that can describe Goneril accurately. 'Thou worse than any name', he calls her (v.3.157). Not, I think, by accident are repeated words so characteristic of this tragedy. The last two acts are filled with frenzied repetitions, some of them hammered upon as many as six times in the course of a single line: 'Kill', 'Now', 'Howl', 'Never', the monosyllable 'No'. One comes to feel that these words are being broken on the anvil in an effort to determine whether or not there is anything inside. It is a common psychological experience that if you look at or repeat a single word long enough, concentrate upon it in isolation, it ceases to be a familiar part of speech. Instead, it will take on a bizarre, essentially mysterious quality of its own, like a word in some arcane and alien tongue. Something of this kind happens as a result of the *Lear* repetitions. If only one could crack these words: words of relationship, of basic existence, simple verbs, perhaps they would reveal a new and elemental set of terms within big enough to cope. So, Lear's five-times-repeated 'Never' in the last scene is like an assault on the irrevocable nature of death, an assault in which the word itself seems to crack and bend under the strain.

Caroline Spurgeon has stated that the dominant image of *King Lear* is that of a body on the rack: stretched and twisted, wrenched in agony.[7] This is something which happens to words in the play, as well as to characters. Language itself is tormented and broken. It is uttered much of the time by people who confess themselves to be incapable of expressing what they feel, who are halting and dumb before the enormity of occurrences. It is true that Oswald and Cornwall, Goneril and Regan display a certain kind of linguistic efficiency. But it is oddly lifeless. Language in this tragedy is really

[7] *Shakespeare's Imagery and What it Tells Us* (Cambridge, 1935), p. 339.

fluent, is various and highly coloured, only on the lips of madmen or of fools. They are the custodians of verbal excellence, but the nature of their office gives one pause.

Edgar in his role as Bedlam beggar, Lear in his insanity and the Fool (who is partially deranged) all make an assault upon the normal conventions of language. A near neighbourhood to nonsense is characteristic of all three. When, in their heightened state of consciousness, they are most eloquent, they are also only one step away from entire incomprehensibility. The Fool takes refuge in scraps from forgotten ballads – 'Whoop Jug! I love thee' – and in riddles which have no point. He deals in chaotic prophecy, or in aphorisms which can be understood only if you reverse all the terms in them. As poor Tom, Edgar's speech is voluble, copious and unstructured. His sentences move forward by fits and starts, following remote chains of association, connections dimly grasped in a dark, devil-haunted world. Like the Fool, he is a truth-teller, but it is a truth continually lapsing into gibberish. Lear too, fantastically crowned with flowers, invents a kind of wild language with which to penetrate the veil of appearances. Both he and Edgar rely heavily on mere sounds in their utterance: they imitate the wind blowing through the hawthorn, the whistling of an arrow, hunting horns, the wordless babble of an infant, or inarticulate cries. Their most terrifying generalizations about the gods, or human life, are likely to trail off in some such fashion. They are fond, too – and this is something they share with the Fool – of nonsense words: 'Fie, foh, and fum', 'nonny', 'alow'. Non-words of this kind are a familiar feature of ballad refrains and nursery rhymes. Used, however, as a substitute for normal speech, as the place towards which language tends when hard-pressed, they become sinister and disturbing. They remind us that structured language, as opposed to the simple capacity to make a noise, not only distinguishes the rational human being from the idiot. It also separates man from the other members of the animal kingdom. In *King Lear*, this distinction between man and beast is of vital importance precisely because it comes so close to being lost.

I am not trying to suggest that in the end *Lear* leaves us with the conviction that man is on a level with the beast. This is a dark tragedy, but not quite that dark. Although one may feel that a distinction made as much as it is in terms of man's capacity for complex and excruciating suffering, suffering out-reaching that of the animal, is a distinction dearly bought. The failure or distortion of language evident throughout the play is, however, linked closely with its discussion of man's relation to the animal: his equivalence or superiority. These are inter-locking strands in the tragedy, and they are anything but cheering. Truth and love in this world are tongue-tied and silent. The glib and the verbally adroit, the Edmunds, Oswalds and Regans, are deeply suspect. Only madness and folly are truly articulate, and their speech hovers continually on the edge of the meaningless, the place where words dissolve into pure noise or inarticulate cries. At the very end, entering with Cordelia dead in his arms, Lear will find that the howl of an animal is the only possible response to the situation. As for the gods, so often invoked, accused and questioned in this tragedy, their usual response is silence. When they do speak at all, they do so in the form of thunder: an undistinguishable blur of sound which will not resolve itself into words, let alone into doctrine.

If *Richard II* is a play whose protagonist tries desperately to transform fact through linguistic means, and *King Lear* a tragedy in which words seem to undergo a general attack, *Coriolanus* by contrast presents a Roman world of rhetoric and persuasion in which the hero alone resists the value placed on verbal formulations. To a surprising extent, the tragedy of Coriolanus is worked out in terms of the hero's attitude towards words. A hatred not merely of flattery but even of a just recital of his own exploits is absolutely characteristic of this man. Cominius speaks more truly than he knows when he tells Coriolanus after the surrender of Corioli that 'if I should tell thee o'er this thy day's work, / Thou't not believe thy deeds' (1.9.1–2). Later, Coriolanus will insist upon leaving the Senate until the oration in praise of his valour has ended:

> Oft,
> When blows have made me stay, I fled from words...
> I had rather have one scratch my head i' th' sun
> When the alarum were struck than idly sit
> To hear my nothings monster'd. (II.2.71–7)

This word *monster'd* means something more than just 'exaggerated'. It suggests distortion, a grotesque and degrading alteration. And here, in truth, lies the heart of the matter. Essentially, Coriolanus fears and despises words. They are, for him, serviceable commodities, but notably inferior to the deeds and actions they describe. The terrible consideration is that, even so, they should be able to violate the integrity of events. You transform facts by speaking of them, and this Coriolanus simply cannot bear. Action is simple while it is taking place, while the sword strikes, while the body of the enemy is still toppling to the earth. It is only afterwards that moments of this kind become complicated and uncertain. That they should do so is the direct result of their subjection to words, the fact that events live only by way of verbal description. In a very real sense, language assaults the purity of action.

Hence the ghastly appropriateness of the means by which Coriolanus is destroyed. The consulship of Rome, which his mother and his friends desire for him, is an office which must not only be won by words, it places these words in a relation to actions past which is calculated to outrage Coriolanus' very nature. 'It then remains / That you do speak to the people' (II.2.134–5). The man who could not bear to hear his friends violate his exploits by speaking of them must now consent to carry out the desecration himself, before a crowd of people he despises. From this point on, the people of Rome are characterized almost obsessively as 'voices'. 'Sir', says Sicinius, 'the people / Must have their voices' (II.2.139–40). The word comes to hammer through the play: 'If he do require our voices, we ought not to deny him … if he show us his wounds and tell us his deeds, we are to put our tongues into those wounds and speak for them' (II.3.1–7). Talkers and not doers like Coriolanus, the people of Rome place their trust in words over deeds. A voice cannot wield a sword, does not fight off invading Volscians. The exile of Coriolanus is made even bitterer by the fact that it constitutes a victory of language over action. By the 'voice of slaves', the hero is 'hoop'd out of Rome' (IV.5.77–8).

In the end, words destroy this man utterly. Back in Corioli, Aufidius has only to use language to distort what actually happened in the scene between Coriolanus and the women and his purpose is achieved:

at his nurse's tears
He whin'd and roar'd away your victory,
That pages blush'd at him, and men of heart
Look'd wond'ring each at others.   (v.6.96–9)

It is an extreme example of the violation of action – here, of that eloquent moment of silence in which Coriolanus had taken Volumnia's hand – by dishonest speech. Reality is monstered by language in the way Coriolanus most fears and detests. Predictably, he revolts, and is hacked down by the swords of the conspirators. Afterwards, Aufidius repents. But there is a terrible irony in the words he speaks over the body of his fallen enemy: 'Yet he shall have a noble memory' (v.6.153). Language in the end, stories, elegies and accounts, are to be the keepers of Coriolanus' fame: indeed of all of Coriolanus that survives. He detested the praises of his friends, the monstering of action by words. He is now given over utterly into the power of language.

Beyond *Coriolanus* lies the world of the last plays. Unlike M. M. Mahood, whose book *Shakespeare's Word-Play* I have otherwise found extremely illuminating, I cannot see the final romances as embodying a renewed faith in words after the scepticism of the tragedies. If anything, they seem to me to foreshadow, at a number of points, those techniques with dialogue employed by the post-Chekhov theatre. In Act IV of *Pericles*, Marina walks on the sea-beach with Leonine, a murderer. This is what they say to one another in the moments before Leonine tries to kill his companion.

> MARINA: Is this wind westerly that blows?
> LEONINE: South-west.
> MARINA: When I was born, the wind was north.
> LEONINE: Was't so?
> MARINA: My father, as nurse says, did never fear,
>   But cried "Good seamen!" to the sailors, galling
>   His kingly hands haling ropes,
>   And clasping to the mast, endur'd a sea
>   That almost burst the deck.
> LEONINE: When was this?
> MARINA: When I was born.
>   Never was waves nor wind more violent,
>   And from the ladder-tackle washes off
>   A canvas-climber. 'Ha!' says one 'wolt out?'
>   And with a dropping industry they skip
>   From [stem] to stern. The boatswain whistles, and
>   The master calls, and trebles their confusion.
> LEONINE: Come say your prayers.
> MARINA: What mean you?   (IV.1.50–66)

These two people may be placed, formally in the attitude of conversation. Until Leonine draws out his dagger with unmistakable intent, neither one is really listening to the other. Arbitrarily sealed off in separate worlds, they talk at but not really to each other.

It is true that there are a number of examples in the early and mature comedies of characters like Feste and Touchstone, Dogberry and Elbow who either wilfully or out of ignorance misunderstand one another. Anger could transport Hotspur into a frenzy which baffled Northumberland's attempt to talk to him. Mistaken identity, concealed facts in the intrigue, can also produce dialogue at cross-purposes in these earlier plays as it does in the first meeting between Olivia and Sebastian in *Twelfth Night*, or in the terrible mis-understanding in *The Comedy of Errors* when Antipholus of Syracuse tries to make love to a woman who, for her part, believes that he is already married to her own sister.

Leonine and Marina labour under no delusion born from mistaken identity. Neither one is hysterical, nor are they trying to overwhelm each other through any linguistic sleight of hand. They are simply not listening to any voice but the one which sounds within their own minds. Although parallels can be suggested from earlier plays, dubious verbal encounters such as the one involving Margaret and Suffolk at the end of *1 Henry VI* (v.3.72–109), the special quality of the last plays as a group and, particularly, the simplification of character upon which Shakespeare was now insisting lends to these linguistic mis-meetings a new and more central significance. Words define the gap between individuals; they do not bridge it. Certainly Marina stumbles through most of her scenes, up to the point of her recognition of King Pericles, as a creature apart for whom the speech of her associates registers dimly, if at all.

BAWD: Pray you come hither awhile. You have fortunes coming upon you. Mark me: you must seem to do that fearfully which you commit willingly, despise profit where you have most gain. To weep that you live as ye do makes pity in your lovers; seldom but that pity begets you a good opinion, and that opinion a mere profit.

MARINA: I understand you not.   (IV.2.115–22)

From the moment of her first appearance, bearing flowers to strew a grave, and speaking a lament which takes no cognisance of the other characters on the stage, Marina is a figure strangely sealed off from other people.

At the end of *Pericles*, when Marina at last finds her father, this sealed-off quality moves into the centre of the stage, becoming the subject of action as well as a feature of dialogue. King Pericles, as Helicanus says, has not spoken to anyone for three months. Even more radically than his daughter, he has cut himself off from that

world of speech which binds human beings together. On board the
Tyrian galley, father and child deal for a time in obliquities and
broken language:

> PERICLES: My fortunes – parentage – good parentage –
> To equal mine – was it not thus? What say you?
> MARINA: I said, my lord, if you did know my parentage,
> You would not do me violence.
> PERICLES: I do think so. Pray you turn your eyes upon me.
> You are like something that – What country[-woman]?
> Here of these [shores]?
> MARINA: No, nor of any [shores],
> Yet I was mortally brought forth, and am
> No other than I appear.
> PERICLES: I am great with woe, and shall deliver weeping…
> Where do you live?
> MARINA: Where I am but a stranger.   (v.1.97–114)

Question and answer circle like hawks about a quarry around the
hidden, essential fact of their relationship to each other. Once this
fact is out, Marina and Pericles leave their respective private worlds
for an entire mutual awareness. Words and eyes meet as they have
not done before in this play. The enormous emotional force of this
recognition scene seems to depend upon our sense of release, of giddy
joy, at the re-establishment of communication, a vindication that had
come to seem impossible, of words.

In subsequent plays, the barriers dissolve less easily. In *The
Tempest*, in fact, they never disappear. At the end as at the beginning,
characters remain isolated. They are disposed about the stage singly,
like Prospero or Caliban, or else in strangely inviolable groups. When
Prospero taught Caliban language, the only profit his pupil gained
was the ability to curse his master. Obviously, this is an extreme and
distorted view of the value of speech. Yet it remains true of this play
as a whole that words catch up and express the separateness of
characters more than any mutual understanding. This isolation
persists up to the very end. The eyes of Prospero and Antonio, of
Miranda and Sebastian, Gonzalo and Ariel, Ferdinand and Caliban
will never meet: neither on the island, nor back in Naples, or Milan.
These are parallels which require infinity to conjoin them. The play
itself offers us nothing closer to infinity than Prospero himself and a
magic which he rejects at the end as rough and insufficient. This
distrust of dialogue in *The Tempest*, the insistence upon the difficulty

of communication, foreshadows the techniques of the modern theatre. Not even Prospero, the magician-dramatist who orders this play-world, can bring about a true coherence of minds. He stands among characters sealed off in private worlds of experience, worlds which language is powerless to unite. It seems at least possible that *The Tempest* was Shakespeare's last non-collaborative play because in it he had reached a point in his investigation of the capabilities of words beyond which he found it difficult to proceed.

CHAPTER 4

Falstaff and the comic community (1985)

For a long time now, *The Merry Wives of Windsor* has seemed to exist uncomfortably apart from the rest of Shakespeare's comedies. Like *King John* among the English histories, it is a play few want to consider either as part of a sequence – in this case, Shakespeare's development as an artist in comedy from *The Comedy of Errors* through *Measure For Measure* – or on its own, for the qualities and achievements that are particular to it. The situation is made worse by a feeling that, irrespective of whether Shakespeare wrote *The Merry Wives of Windsor* before, during, or after *2 Henry IV*, the comedy itself constitutes a betrayal of Falstaff even worse than the one inflicted by Henry V. Prince Hal, after all, was committed from the beginning to turning away 'that huge bombard of sack, that stuff'd cloak-bag of guts, that roasted Manningtree ox with the pudding in his belly, that reverent Vice, that grey Iniquity, that father ruffian, that vanity in years' (*1 Henry IV* 11.4.451–4), as soon as he became king. He had, as we have come to accept, no real choice. It is harder to explain why Shakespeare should have attacked his own great comic creation, quite gratuitously, by allowing Falstaff to be humiliated at the hands of an unremarkable, small-town society: deceived by housewives, mocked and tormented by children, and outwitted for all his linguistic dexterity, by men who make 'fritters of English' (v.5.143).

Queen Elizabeth I can be made to shoulder some of the blame. If, as Charles Gildon reported in 1710, she really was so imperceptive as to commission a comedy about Falstaff in love, and so unreasonable as to exact completion of the work within a fortnight, Shakespeare might well have been driven to desperate shifts. (Such as hastily reworking a lost Henslowe farce, with Falstaff imperfectly assimilated to the role of the original Italian *pedante* figure.)[1] In fact, the

---

[1] See the article by O. J. Campbell, 'The Italianate background of *The Merry Wives of Windsor*', *University of Michigan Publications in Language and Literature* 8 (1932), 81–117.

credentials of Gildon's story are no better than those of that other, early eighteenth-century legend which insists that the young Shakespeare pilfered venison from Charlecote Park. The first anecdote has gained far more credence than the second only because, unlike the somewhat disconcerting image of Shakespeare as a Warwickshire poacher, Queen Elizabeth's supposed highhandedness can be made to serve certain critical and emotional needs. Even if true, however, Gildon's account of the circumstances under which *The Merry Wives of Windsor* was written fails to resolve the chief problem posed by the play. Falstaff is one of the most memorable embodiments of a comic type stretching back to Aristophanes. But Shakespeare seems to have found it possible to realize this character fully only within the context of English history, and not within that of comedy, his expected and proper domain.

The Falstaff of *The Merry Wives of Windsor* is not, of course, in love. If that was what Elizabeth demanded, she was not obeyed. In effect, Falstaff treats Alice Ford and Margaret Page as he treats Mistress Quickly in *2 Henry IV*. His sexual adventurism, including the promise of marriage at some indefinite future date, is fundamentally an attempt by him to raise cash. In Eastcheap this works brilliantly; in Windsor it does not. Falstaff descends upon this little, bourgeois society in much the same way that he fastens upon the rural Gloucestershire of Justice Shallow. He is a predatory intruder from a more sophisticated world, a visitor who means to ingratiate himself and then bleed the environment that gives him temporary shelter. But where Gloucestershire is unsuspecting and acquiescent, Windsor not only resists but unites to dismember the outsider. The problem (pace Bradley) would seem to be not so much that Falstaff is an altered character in *The Merry Wives of Windsor* as that Windsor is, by nature, a place he does not understand and in which he cannot thrive. Although Fenton is accused of having 'kept company with the wild Prince and Poins' (III.2.72–3), and Falstaff is joined at Windsor by several characters – Shallow, Mistress Quickly, Pistol, Bardolph, and Nym – who also share his life in *1* and *2 Henry IV*, or *Henry V*, the world here is unequivocally comic, not historical. And the norms of Shakespearean comedy are even more destructive to Falstaffian values than the Lord Chief Justice, the grinning honours of Shrewsbury, or the cold blood of Prince John.

C. L. Barber excluded *The Merry Wives of Windsor* from his brilliant account of Falstaff as Carnival, the festive lord of the histories who

must be defeated when he seeks to set up his holiday licence on an
everyday basis. Subsequent writers have often found this omission
puzzling, arguing that *The Merry Wives of Windsor* is surely a festive
comedy in precisely Barber's terms: a play in which the entire community finally bands together to sacrifice an ageing fertility god in
preparation for a seasonal return to order and normality.[2] Barber's
instincts, characteristically, were right. *The Merry Wives of Windsor* is
not properly or primarily a festive comedy. Its ritual patterns, where
they exist at all, lie deep below the surface and cannot be made to
control the movement and atmosphere of the play. Whether his hand
was forced by Elizabeth, or because the experiment interested him for
its own sake, what Shakespeare created in *The Merry Wives of Windsor*
was a painful confrontation between an immemorial kind of comic
hero and his own form of comedy – a form that had already declared
its basic, and daring, independence from characters of this type.

Associated more or less specifically, at various points, with both the
braggart soldier and the parasite of New Comedy, with the Vice, the
Prodigal Son, the Fool, and the Lord of Misrule, Falstaff can lay
claim to an intricate and venerable family tree. His most authentic,
as well as earliest surviving, theatrical ancestors appear in the
comedies of Aristophanes. Dicaeopolis in *The Archarnians*, the
Sausage-Seller in *The Knights*, the 'reformed' Philocleon in *The
Wasps*, Trygaeus in *Peace*, and Peithetaerus in *The Birds* all share
certain characteristics with each other and, up to a point, with
Falstaff. Shameless self-seekers, men significantly past their youth
who are nonetheless inordinate eaters, drinkers, and wenchers, their
shrewdness and imaginative mastery of words makes them highly
successful deceivers.[3] A law unto themselves, insidiously attractive,
they behave outrageously and manage to get away with it. The
relation of these figures to society, very recognizably the fifth-
century BC Athens of Aristophanes, is complex. They exploit the
community ruthlessly, for their own ends, but their unbridled

---

[2] Northrop Frye seems to have been the first to isolate the ritual and folk patterns of *The Merry
Wives of Windsor* in 'The argument of comedy' in *English Institute Essays, 1948*, ed. D. A.
Robertson, Jr (New York, 1949), pp. 58–73. Attempts to treat the play as a festive comedy
in C. L. Barber's terms have been made by Jeanne Addison Roberts, '*The Merry Wives of
Windsor* as a Hallowe'en Play', *Shakespeare Survey 25* (1972), 107–12 and by J. A. Bryant, Jr
'Falstaff and the Renewal of Windsor', *PMLA* 89, no. 1 (1974), 296–301.

[3] I am indebted to Cedric Whitman's book, *Aristophanes and the Comic Hero* (Cambridge, 1964)
for my treatment of Aristophanes.

individualism has an odd way of embracing attitudes that, in fact, this community would do well to accept – and sometimes does accept in the end. These comic heroes detest war and ideals of military glory. They are healthily sceptical of the pretensions and promises of politicians, and their own unabashed physicality makes them insist on recognizing and celebrating man's links with nonhuman creation. Monstrous egotists and opportunists, they are enemies of society but also its raffish saviours.

Aristophanes's finely held balance between the comic individualist and the community, which both suffers and benefits at his hands, was the product of a unique moment of historical and dramatic time. It begins to dissolve in his own late plays, written after the renewal of the war with Sparta in 413 BC, and in Greek New Comedy and its Roman imitations it vanishes almost entirely. In general, as comedy narrowed its focus to concentrate upon relationships within a particular family or neighbourhood, and the boy-gets-girl plot replaced the old, civic concerns, the Aristophanic hero tended to become peripheral. In Plautus and Terence, he has declined socially, no longer his own master, but somebody's parasite or clever slave. He remains his old inventive and sensual self, and he can act as the engine of plot, but his is no longer the dominant viewpoint of the play.

The one apparent exception, among the plays that have survived, is Periplectomenus, the next-door neighbour of Pyrgopolynices in Plautus' comedy (based on the lost *Alazon* of Menander), the *Miles Gloriosus*, or *Swaggering Soldier*. Periplectomenus is very much a gentleman and free agent. White-haired and well over fifty, an eminently consolable and wealthy widower, he insists that he has just as much right to revel, feast, and dance as a young man. His life is based upon an ideal of untrammelled personal liberty, which is why he has no intention of marrying again (although he can produce a ravishing courtesan within minutes when one is required) and he displays not the slightest interest in producing children of his own, or in family ties. Without making a business of it, as Volpone does, Periplectomenus cheerfully encourages friends and relatives who hope to inherit his estate to lavish gifts and expensive feasts on him. Pleusicles, a young Athenian visitor anxious to rescue his concubine from the clutches of the braggart soldier, is grateful for Periplecto-menus' highly efficient help, but is also puzzled that a man of his age should want to meddle in such matters. This is why Periplectomenus pauses to expound his philosophy of life.[4] Although he is a *bon viveur* of far greater acceptability and restraint than Aristophanes' Philocleon – last seen in *The Wasps* as a drunken and manic dancer engaged in a kind of Lobster Quadrille with some creatures that have crawled out of the sea – Periplectomenus is still a sufficiently isolated and atypical member of New Comedy society to need to explain himself.

When, in about 1552, Nicholas Udall set himself to acclimatize Periplectomenus within the sixteenth-century London of *Rafe Royster Doyster*, a free adaptation of Terence's *Eunuchus* and Plautus' *Miles Gloriosus*, he found his task complicated by an intervening, and probably quite independent, late medieval manifestation of the type. As a concealed emissary from Hell, concerned to win souls for his master's kingdom, the Vice can only pretend to share the life of the community that he invigorates and corrupts. It says a good deal for the power and universality of the Aristophanic hero that he should not only have sprung up again in the apparently inimical soil of morality drama, but that he should turn so rapidly into its star attraction. Vital, engaging, irreverent, a homeless haunter of taverns and disparager of virtue and the ordered life, the Vice tended to seduce theatre audiences as well as his victims in the play. Although he manages, like Periplectomenus, to elude moral judgement, Mathew Merygreeke in *Rafe Royster Doyster* bears the imprint of the Vice as well as that of his forebears in classical comedy.

As the Vice frequently did, Mathew Merygreeke first 'entreth singing', and proceeds to establish immediate contact with the audience. A middle-aged form of human grasshopper, as he winningly explains, he has no fixed establishment of his own: 'My lyving lieth heere and there, of Gods grace' (1.1.15).[5] His list of the various good companions at whose expense he subsists – Lewis Loytrer, Watkin Waster, Davy Diceplayer, Nichol Neverthrives, Tom Titivile, and so on – conjures up for an instant the punitive and repressive world of the moralities. But *Rafe Royster Doyster* is not a play of this kind: its classical roots run too deep. Royster Doyster himself, Udall's version of Pyrgopolynices, and Merygreeke's chief quarry, is 'such a foole ... as no man for good pastime would forgoe or

---

[4] Plautus, *The Swaggering Soldier*, in *The Pot of Gold and Other Plays*, trans. E. F. Watling (Harmondsworth, 1965), pp. 177–81.

[5] Nicholas Udall, *Rafe Royster Doyster*, in *Tudor Plays: An Anthology of Early English Drama*, ed. Edmund Creeth (New York, 1966).

misse' (v.5.19–20). Merygreeke attaches himself to the braggart because this is his current source of dinner, but he encourages him in his absurdities and in his misguided suit to the rich widow Christian Custance for a different reason: sheer, amoral delight in eliciting the arrogance and folly of a man far less intelligent and self-aware than himself.

Christian Custance is a character for whom there are no equivalents in classical comedy. A widow of unblemished chastity, but also of high spirits, she governs her household in the most unexceptionable manner while awaiting the return of her fiancé, the London merchant Gawyn Goodlucke, from sea. Significantly, Merygreeke is obliged to come to an understanding with this sensible and intelligent woman in Act IV if he is to carry his 'pastance' with Royster Doyster any further. At the end, Christian Custance, Goodlucke, and their mutual friend Tristram Trusty cheerfully carry Merygreeke off to dinner with them. They even agree, at his request, to include Royster Doyster on the grounds that 'he woulde make us al laugh' (v.5.17). Udall was obviously influenced here by the resolution of Terence's *Eunuchus*, his subsidiary source, in which the humiliated braggart Thraso is similarly invited to share the victors' feast at the urging of his parasite Gnatho, who admits disarmingly that 'all I'm doing is primarily in my own interest'.[6] But the little society centred upon Christian Custance's house has no intention, unlike Phaedria, Thais, and Chaerea in Terence, of quietly fleecing the braggart they pretend to accept. Only Merygreeke, it is understood, will continue to do that. The others tolerate Royster Doyster purely for his comic value – a reaction that serves to link them with Merygreeke himself, an acknowledged eccentric who nonetheless has his place within a community whose norms of behaviour he does not share, but is wise enough to respect.

Udall's decision to locate *Rafe Royster Doyster* quite specifically in London turned out to be prophetic. Athens had been the breeding ground of the Aristophanic hero, and in Elizabethan and Jacobean comedy the City remained the natural home of characters of this kind. It was also the habitat of the prodigal, a related but distinct dramatic type. Unlike the Aristophanic hero, the prodigal is young. He is a man caught by the dramatist in what is essentially a passing phase, sowing a crop of wild oats before setting his feet safely, like his

[6] Terence, *The Eunuch*, in *The Brothers and Other Plays*, trans. with an intro. by Betty Radice (Harmondsworth, 1965), p. 81.

New Testament prototype, on the road home. A few late sixteenth-
and seventeenth-century prodigals – Penniboy Junior, for instance,
in Jonson's *The Staple of News*, (1626) the apprentice Quicksilver in
Eastward Ho! (1605), Young Lionel in Heywood's *The English
Traveller*, (1625) or Flowerdale Junior in the anonymous *London
Prodigall* (1604) – actually come to regret and repent of their wicked
ways. A larger, and more subversive, group is formed by clever
wastrels who recognize that they have come to the end of this
particular stage of life, and briskly set about to recoup their losses –
usually by means of a rich marriage. Palpably undeserved good
fortune greets the three prodigals in Haughton's *Englishmen For My
Money* (1598), Middleton's Wit-Good in *A Trick to Catch the Old One*
(1605), Stephen in Rowley's *A New Wonder, A Woman Never Vexed*
(1625), and Spendall in Cooke's *The City Gallant* (1611), among a
host of others. In many cases, it is precisely the wildness and
irresponsibility of the prodigal that renders him sexually attractive to
the woman, often a young widow, who rescues him from financial
and social ruin. Fletcher's witty comedy *The Scornful Lady* (1613) even
transforms the defeated usurer Morecraft into a tavern-haunter and
spendthrift at the end. Judging from the spectacular success of his
escaped victim Loveless, this is the kind of behaviour that pays.
Cutting Morecraft, as this formerly sober man of business is now
called, elects to follow Philocleon's path in *The Wasps*. What becomes
of him, Fletcher does not say. Loveless himself, however, like most
young prodigals in comedy, has prudently acquired a household and
an established place in society.

Although the Falstaff of the histories has occasional impulses to
'give over this life', to 'purge and leave sack, and live cleanly as a
nobleman should do' (*1 H IV* 1.2.95, v.4.164–5), his resolutions never
come to anything. A man well on in years, his fecklessness is not the
youthful phase of the ordinary prodigal, but an engrained attitude, as
integral a part of his self and way of living as that of Udall's
Merygreeke. Improvident and unregenerate to the end, he will
finally die in *Henry V* in an upstairs room of that London tavern,
which, for so many years, has been his nearest approximation to a
home. Singularly devoid of family in the literal sense, Falstaff does
have relatives scattered throughout the comedy of Shakespeare's
contemporaries, as well as in some of Shakespeare's own, later plays.
He is kin to Jonson's Captain Bobadill, Simplicity in Robert Wilson's
two-part play *The Three Ladies of London* and *The Three Lords and Three*

Ladies of London (1588), or (most extreme of all) 'cogging Cocle-demoy' in Marston's *The Dutch Courtesan* (1604), the gentleman who stubbornly refuses to live like one, and who persecutes the tavern-keeper Mulligrub even to the foot of the gallows for being guilty of two cardinal sins against the comic spirit: parsimony and adulterating his wine. Some of these characters are more clever and have more worldly success than others. All are men of mature years with a settled habit of exploiting the community on whose fringes they exist. Yet in most of them there lingers some vestige of the old Aristophanic duality of purpose. Even Wilson's Simplicity, probably the most clownlike and least intelligent of the entire group, can take time off from a life of ballad-mongering, begging, and petty thievery to identify Fraud and Dissimulation unerringly for what they are, when his betters are blind. The outrageously scatological and dangerous Cocledemoy makes even Freevill uneasy, but he blows through society nonetheless with some of the disruptive but purifying power of the mistral. Cocledemoy does not, as he points out, 'bite' the poor or honest (III.2.33–43).[7] It is difficult for any theatre audience to quarrel with his view that the Mulligrubs of the world are fair game.

Francis Beaumont clearly knew that he could rely on his audience's long-term familiarity with characters of this type when he created Charles Merrythought in *The Knight of the Burning Pestle* (1607?). A brilliant distillation and parody of that whole line of engaging scoundrels which runs from Udall's Merygreeke through Falstaff and long past Beaumont's own time into Restoration comedy, Merry-thought, as his horrible wife complains, is 'an old man, and thou canst not work, and thou hast not forty shillings left, and thou eatest good meat and drinkest good drink, and laughest' (1.361–3).[8] As his slender stock of cash diminishes, Merrythought sings even more gaily. The welcome departure of his wife allows him to fill his house near London Bridge with musicians and revellers of a like mind with himself. Equally unperturbed by reports that his son Jasper has stolen the merchant Venturewell's daughter, and then by the arrival of a coffin supposedly containing the remains of the young man himself, Merrythought carries irresponsibility and hedonistic self-interest to

---

[7] John Marston, *The Dutch Courtesan*, ed. M. L. Wine, Regents Renaissance Drama Series (London, 1965).

[8] Francis Beaumont, *The Knight of the Burning Pestle*, ed. Sheldon P. Zitner, Revels Series (Manchester, 1984).

what Beaumont knew was the breaking point. Even here, however, in
what is essentially theatrical parody, the two faces of the Aristophanic
hero remain visible. Merrythought counsels the son he is sending out
into the world to 'Be a good husband, that is, wear ordinary clothes,
eat the best meat, and drink the best drink; be merry and give to the
poor and, believe me, thou has no end of thy goods' (1.405–7). At the
end, he interrupts his nonstop carousal just long enough to trick
Venturewell into countenancing the marriage of Jasper and Luce.
George and Nell, Beaumont's citizen 'spectators', regard Merrythought as a disgrace to the community. So he is, but he is also one
of its prime assets.

Between 1580 and 1642, hundreds of comedies appeared that were
set in contemporary London. In their interweaving of social and
topographical realism with fantasy, they were the true heirs of Greek
Old Comedy. Some dramatists, notably Jonson and Middleton,
made a special study of London life, but after 1600 virtually every
significant writer of comedy produced at least one play dealing with
the City. The glaring exception, of course, was Shakespeare.
Although London was the place in which he lived and worked, and
although he was perfectly prepared to resurrect a much older City in
the English histories, London comedy was a genre he eschewed.
Vienna, in *Measure For Measure*, sometimes looks suspiciously
familiar, but almost invariably Shakespearean comedy kept at least
the English Channel between itself and the urban life of its audience.
Only once did Shakespeare even approach London, and then he
compromised by settling at the safe distance of Windsor. Even so, *The
Merry Wives of Windsor* comes closer than any of his other plays in its
plot and social structure to the City comedies written by his
contemporaries.

If, as many scholars now believe, *The Merry Wives of Windsor* was
written in 1597, it must have followed hard upon *The Merchant of
Venice*, another comedy with pronounced middle-class interests.
Shakespeare's Venice is emphatically not London, and Belmont is
not genuinely discoverable on any map. Distance and a carefully
cultivated foreign atmosphere almost, but not quite, conceal the fact
that Bassanio is the usual prodigal: a well-born young man who has
squandered his own inheritance and now seeks to re-establish himself
in the manner that was to become virtually obligatory in Jacobean
City comedy – a rich marriage. Just like his successors in Middleton

and Fletcher, Bassanio depends for success upon a loan from the City. But here, the paradigm breaks. Bassanio does not go directly to the usurer, but to a merchant friend. It is the magnanimous businessman Antonio, not the prodigal himself, who falls into Shylock's clutches, and he is delivered by means – the generosity and intelligence of Portia – which link the play more closely with *As You Like It* than with the amoral stratagems of London comedy.

Despite its small-town setting, *The Merry Wives of Windsor* displays affinities with City comedy more precise than those of *The Merchant of Venice*. Young Fenton is a prodigal, a man of 'riots past' and 'wild societies' whose estate 'being gall'd with my expense' craves replenishing (III.4.4–10). Although we believe Fenton, as we believe Bassanio, when he declares that he has learned to love his intended bride for herself, and not simply for her wealth, it matters that Anne Page, unlike Portia, is a citizen's daughter and of a lower social rank than her suitor. In objecting to Fenton because, among other deficiencies, he is 'too great of birth' (III.4.4), Anne Page's father displays the wariness of an English middle class accustomed by this time, both in real life and (increasingly) in comedy, to the sexual manoeuvres and depredations of an impoverished aristocracy. Sir Roger Otley, the Lord Mayor of London, adopts a similar attitude in Dekker's *The Shoemaker's Holiday* (1599) when the young Earl of Lincoln – another prodigal – seeks the hand of his daughter Rose.

Courtiers and gentry who tried to repair their fortunes by marrying the daughters of wealthy citizens were, however, nothing like as troublesome as those who focussed their attentions on the City's wives. The frequency in London comedy of adultery between the spouses of tired businessmen and certain impecunious but lively members of the upper classes seeking access to the citizen's well-stocked coffers by way of his wife's bed suggests a measure of social truth behind what rapidly became a comic fixture. Fallace and Fastidious Brisk in Jonson's *Every Man Out of His Humour* (1599), the Jeweller's Wife and her knight in Middleton's *The Phoenix* (1604), the middle-class wives and their gallants in *The Roaring Girl* (Middleton and Dekker 1608) or *Westward Ho!* (Dekker and Webster 1604) are only a few examples. The seducers are not always successful, but their appeal lies invariably in a combination of social superiority and finesse with a sexual vitality, born of leisure and high feeding, supposedly greater than that of husbands who dissipate their energies in the counting house, or the Exchange.

Although a close analogue for Falstaff's relation with the disguised Ford, and for his concealment in the basket of washing, has been identified in Ser Giovanni Fiorentino's *Il Pecorone*, the general concerns and the plot of *The Merry Wives of Windsor* possess a marked and prophetic affinity with those of Jacobean City comedy. Shakespeare deliberately minimized the Fenton/Anne Page courtship and pushed it into the background, not infrequently the fate of young lovers in these plays. Attention is centred instead on a fabliau situation involving marital jealousy and sexual intrigue, a pattern most uncharacteristic of Shakespearean comedy, however familiar it was to become in London plays. But Mistress Ford and Mistress Page are not like the usual run of London wives – Mistress Allwit in *A Chaste Maid in Cheapside* (1611), Mistress Justiniano, Judith Honeysuckle, and Mabel Wafer in *Westward Ho!*, or Mistress Gallipot, Mistress Tiltyard, and Mistress Openwork in *The Roaring Girl* – women who finally preserve their virtue, if they do so at all, by accident, or for reasons that are calculating and self-interested.

However atypical their place of residence, relatively mature years, and married state, the wives of Windsor are, in fact, heroines of Shakespearean comedy: predictably frank, spirited, intelligent, and loving. Margaret Page may attempt to marry her daughter off behind Page's back to Caius rather than to Slender, and Alice Ford is not above tormenting her husband for his lack of faith in her. It is clear nonetheless that even if Falstaff were a far more seductive and glamorous would-be adulterer than he is, and had not made the mistake of composing two identical love letters, he would fare no better with these women than Rafe Royster Doyster did at the hands of Christian Custance. Like her, and unlike most of the City wives in later comedy, they are honestly and fully self-aware. Their faith and loyalty remain engaged to the men they have married, and they are not dissatisfied with the bourgeois community to which they belong.

Mistress Ford's exasperated question – 'What tempest, I trow, threw this whale (with so many tuns of oil in his belly) ashore at Windsor?' (II.1.64–5) – is one that Shakespeare, tantalizingly, refuses to answer. We never know what drove Falstaff and his entourage to set up their quarters at the Garter Inn. As far as Falstaff is concerned, it was a mistake. Falstaff in Windsor *is* a stranded leviathan, a man hopelessly out of his element, beached and floundering. Verbally, he remains able to run rings around everyone else. Windsor, indeed, seems to be filled with people engaged in a losing battle with the subtleties of the English language. For Dr Caius and (probably) Parson Evans, it is not their native tongue. Shallow, Slender, and Simple have only a restricted vocabulary on which to draw: Mistress Quickly, Pistol, Bardolph, Nym, and the Host are colourful, but their speech is so idiosyncratic, mistaken, and perverse as to render them frequently unintelligible. The Fords and the Pages are more adept. None of them, however, has anything like Falstaff's gift of metaphor and phrasing, his ability to use words creatively, whether to deceive, persuade, or simply to fix and illuminate his own experience. The man who can transform even the ignominy of being dumped into the Thames, along with the dirty linen, by the brilliance of his description ('to be compass'd like a good bilbo in the circumference of a peck...' [III.5. passim]), is perfectly recognizable as the verbal conjurer who makes language serve him so well at Eastcheap, Shrewsbury, and in Gloucestershire. At Windsor, no one advances an alternative idiom as powerful as those which challenge him in the histories by way of Hotspur, Prince Hal, Henry IV, or the Lord Chief Justice. Yet the main function of Falstaff's verbal dexterity, brilliant though it is, in this comedy, is to chronicle defeat.

Falstaff fares as badly as he does in *The Merry Wives of Windsor* partly because the Shakespearean heroine is a phenomenon not dreamed of in his philosophy. There are no women at all in Justice Shallow's Gloucestershire establishment. Even the cook, William, is male. Eastcheap confronts Falstaff only with Mistress Quickly and Doll Tearsheet the whore, neither of them morally scrupulous or very bright. It is Falstaff's fatal mistake to believe that, however respectable they appear on the surface, Alice Ford and Margaret Page are at bottom creatures of this kind. Sitting at Page's table, Falstaff is cunning enough to pay lip service to bourgeois proprieties: he 'would not swear; [prais'd] women's modesty; and gave such orderly and well-behav'd reproof to all uncomeliness, that I would have sworn his disposition would have gone to the truth of his words' (II.1.57–61). All the time, however, he was convinced that Mistress Ford and Mistress Page were regarding him with secret lust. Cynicism about women's virtue is common to characters of Falstaff's general type (indeed, it is a defining feature of the Vice), but it runs counter to the values of Shakespearean comedy. In Windsor, as in Arden, Belmont, Milan, Rousillion, and Navarre, the women are the chief custodians of these values. When Falstaff misprizes and attacks them, he is broken.

Critics have often complained that the imbroglio with which *The Merry Wives of Windsor* begins, concerned with Falstaff's depredations in Shallow's Gloucestershire deer-park, and Slender's rifled pockets and broken head, seems oddly purposeless. The quarrel simply evaporates, despite Shallow's original threats that he would make a Star Chamber matter of it. In fact, Shakespeare shows Falstaff handling these outraged fellow visitors to Windsor with magnificent effrontery and aplomb. Slender, as he craftily demonstrates, was too drunk to know whether he was robbed by Pistol, Bardolph, or Nym. The accusation collapses. Shallow's demand that the violence done to his lodge, his men, and his venison 'shall be answer'd' Falstaff deals with immaculately in his own terms: 'I will answer it straight: I have done all this. That is now answer'd' (1.1.114–16). As with his splendid reply to Simple, later ('Marry... the very same man that beguil'd Master Slender of his chain cozen'd him of it' [iv.5.36–8]), it wrenches a true cause the false way in the characteristic Falstaffian manner. The fat knight enters the comedy in excellent form and, apart from his chronic ailment, that incurable 'consumption of the purse' (*2 H IV* 1.2.236–7) which plagues him wherever he goes, apparently in control of his situation.

Theft, however, is something that Windsor takes far more lightly than it does sexual immorality. Even the Host of the Garter, whose position in the community is interestingly ambiguous, adopts a strict line when he believes that Falstaff is entertaining a 'fat woman' in his rented room: 'Let her descend, bully, let her descend; my chambers are honorable. Fie, privacy? fie!' (iv.5.21–3). It is an attitude very unlike that of the management at the Boar's Head in Eastcheap. Moreover, the air of Windsor seems to have had a transforming effect upon Falstaff's companions, Pistol and Nym. They have no qualms about picking pockets, but they will not be accessories to a seduction. Pistol indignantly repudiates the role of 'Sir Pandarus of Troy', while Nym astonishingly announces that he means to 'keep the havior of reputation' (1.3.75,78). Dining with the Pages, Falstaff only pretended to share their moral standards. Pistol and Nym actually put what seem to be their newly discovered principles into practice: neither one will carry Falstaff's love letters. Indeed, so concerned are they to preserve the personal honour one would never have credited them with possessing that they proceed to warn Master Ford and Master Page of Falstaff's adulterous designs. At the end, Pistol in the role of Hobgoblin will participate in the Herne the Hunter play through which Falstaff is unmasked and shamed. He has, as it seems, become a bona fide member of the community at Windsor.

Mistress Quickly presents even more of a problem. Falstaff appears not to remember or recognize her at all. Readers of the comedy tend to find that she both is, and she is not, the woman of Eastcheap. She has no scruples about accepting bribes from several of Anne Page's suitors at once, and deluding each that he is the favoured man. As an onlooker at young William Page's Latin lesson, Mistress Quickly displays exactly the combined ignorance, naiveté, and unknowing instinct for the bawdy characteristic of her in London. But like Pistol and Nym, she has yielded to the values of Windsor. The Mistress Quickly who has Doll Tearsheet for a friend, and can eagerly summon her to bed with Falstaff at the Boar's Head, is transformed in this play into someone shocked by sexual irregularity ('Jinny's case'): 'Fie on her! never name her, child, if she be a whore' (IV.1.62–3). In London, the Hostess is Falstaff's doormat, to be walked over and cajoled into lending him money she will never see again. At Windsor, by contrast, she gulls Falstaff. Her ability to do so seems dependent in large part upon her stricter moral attitude, and the fact that her employment as an emissary by Mistress Ford and Mistress Page – in which she only pretends to fulfil the function rejected by Pistol and Nym, and is even witty enough to invent, for Falstaff's benefit, a Mistress Ford beaten black and blue by her outraged husband – aligns her with the eponymous heroines of the comedy.

In its characteristic movement 'through release to clarification', as C. L. Barber defined it, Shakespearean comedy often depends upon the agency of one or more intruders from a different world. *The Comedy of Errors, The Taming of the Shrew, Love's Labour's Lost, Much Ado About Nothing,* and *Twelfth Night* all begin with the arrival in a settled community of strangers whose presence will radically alter that community's allegiances and normal way of life. Although, initially, the newcomers cause a certain amount of disruption, and even pain, the society that assimilates them by the end of the play is invariably happier and more firmly based than the one which existed at the beginning. This is partly because it has freed itself from various weaknesses and affectations, especially in the area of sexual relationships, and also because the strangers have precipitated one or more marriages that we welcome and believe to be good.

The Merry Wives of Windsor presents a highly individual variation on this basic pattern. Most successful productions of the play within recent years have been comparatively realistic in style, stressing the particularity and completeness of the play's picture of contemporary, small-town life. This seems right. Windsor itself, as a corporate entity, is the true protagonist of the comedy, not Falstaff, the shadowy young lovers, or even the merry wives themselves, who uphold its values so well. This is why seemingly irrelevant details, such as young William's grapple with Latin grammar, Mistress Quickly's itemization of her household responsibilities, or Slender's exercise of his prerogative as a 'distinguished' visitor to give the town's children a 'playing-day' (IV.1.9), are in fact central. Children, adolescents, mature married couples, bachelor members of the professional classes, servants, and postmaster's boys: only the very old are excluded from the panorama of life at Windsor. It seems significant that unlike any other heroine in Shakespearean comedy (except Marina in *Pericles* and Perdita in *The Winter's Tale*, where the circumstances are very special), Anne Page is actually provided with a mother. This is very much a family play.

The community at Windsor has its flaws and delusions, notably the way the Pages try to dispose of their daughter in marriage, and the causeless jealousy of Ford, but at heart it is sound, stable, and remarkably well defined. It undergoes far less of a change between Acts I and V than do Illyria, Ephesus, Padua, Messina, or Navarre. Most important of all, it represents the polar opposite of Falstaff's Eastcheap world, which is one of rootless individuals, separated from their family contexts and sometimes, like Prince Hal, in active rebellion against them. The Boar's Head, as Hal rather unkindly puts it, is Falstaff's customary sty, and the place from which he gathers strength (*2 H IV* II.2.146-7). Although Falstaff, in the histories, does encounter a community and family structure of sorts when he goes to Gloucestershire, it is made more manageable for him by the absence of women. Much of it impinges upon him only obliquely, in glancing references to the home circumstances of the luckless recruits, Davy's friendship with William Visor of Woncot, or in the gossip and reminiscences of the two old men. Shallow's orchard, in any case, is only a temporary, if highly strategic, retreat. The London tavern is Falstaff's real home and it, by definition, is the place of irresponsibility, an artificial society whose components are in a continual state of flux. The drinkers at the Boar's Head come and go, many of them anonymously. The drawers, such as Francis, are young apprentices, uprooted from their own home backgrounds, whereas Doll Tearsheet's alleged kinship with Falstaff, as Hal points out, is spurious: 'even such kin as the parish heckfers are to the town bull' (II.2.157–8).

Mistress Quickly is married in *1 Henry IV*, and apparently widowed in its sequel. Whatever impelled her to move from London to Windsor, she clearly does so as a single woman. She might well be expected to gravitate to the Garter Inn, in some approximation to her old position at the Boar's Head. Instead, she turns up along with Jack Rugby as servant to Dr Caius, Windsor's physician. In this more domestic capacity, as she says, 'I keep his house; and I wash, wring, brew, bake, scour, dress meat and drink, make the beds, and do all myself' (1.4.95–7). Her shift from public to private employment – and her new pride in her 'great charge' – matters. Although the Garter Inn is an establishment more respectable than the Boar's Head, it is nonetheless a slightly suspect and dangerous enclave in the centre of Windsor. This is because its function, in large part, is to harbour outsiders, transients who may benefit but who also may harm the community on the edges of which they exist.

As it happens, it is one of Windsor's strengths as a society that it is remarkably inclusive and willing to absorb foreign elements. Neither Sir Hugh Evans, its parson and schoolmaster, nor its local doctor, Caius, are indigenous to the place – as their accents continually declare. But, whenever it was that they arrived, they have become fully accepted and indeed leading members of the community. Mistress Quickly, on a humbler level, appears to have acclimatized herself equally successfully, and Pistol seems, at least for a time, to be following in her footsteps. There are limits, however, to what this society is willing to embrace, particularly when its provenance is the Inn. As Page's favoured suitor for the hand of Anne, Slender (together with his servant Simple and his uncle Shallow) is an innocuous and welcome visitor. Falstaff, and those other dimly glimpsed strangers who also book rooms at the Garter, some of them pursuing mysterious business at Court, are another matter. Whether or not Fenton actually lodges at the Garter during his visits to Windsor is unclear; he is, however, closely associated with its host.

A cheerful, exuberant figure, the 'ranting' and 'merry' Host of the Garter (II.1.189, 207) possesses a linguistic extravagance that serves to link him significantly with Falstaff, his paying guest. Far more comprehensible verbally than Pistol, he is nonetheless given to larding his discourse with references to cavaleiros and bully-rooks, Ethiopians, Anthropophaginians, Ephesians, and Bohemian-Tartars. Often, he sounds remarkably like Dekker's Simon Eyre, and indeed he is (like Eyre) a shrewd man of business who is also a trickster and *bon viveur*. His motives in deceiving Caius and Evans as to the place of their potentially fatal encounter are far more benevolent than those of Sir Toby Belch in stage managing the duel between Caesario and Sir Andrew Aguecheek in *Twelfth Night*. Toby's doubledealing is chastized by Sebastian, Viola's twin. The Host, far less deservedly, incurs the ire of both Caius and Evans, the two touchy men he has prevented (at the expense of a modicum of their social dignity) from trying to kill one another without cause. Because Windsor's doctor and its parson abruptly join forces in a revenge action against the 'mad host' (III.1.112), he finds himself, at the end, missing three of his best horses. This part of the plot is puzzlingly sketchy and incomplete, but it looks very much as though Shakespeare were insisting upon a certain distrust, and even resentment, of the freewheeling comic innkeeper: a man whose allegiances, by temperament, as well as by the nature of his trade, are more fluid and dangerous than those of the solid citizens of the town.

Significantly, the Host is not present in Windsor Great Park in Act v, when the community bands together to humiliate Falstaff, the interloper who spurns marriage and an establishment, and makes taverns and inns his home. As it happens, Fenton requires the Host's services elsewhere, arranging his clandestine union with Anne Page. It is interesting, however, that he should not apparently have been invited to join the Page family, the Fords, Shallow, Slender, Caius, Evans, Pistol, Mistress Quickly, and the children of Windsor around the blasted oak. Equally telling is the fact that it should be the Host to whom Fenton appeals after all the young man's attempts to obtain Anne Page with her parent's consent – the method approved of in Windsor – have failed. As a kind of stationmaster, whose professional duty it is to meet incoming and departing trains, the Host has tolerated and even enjoyed Falstaff, turning a tolerant eye on his faults, and relieving the drain on his finances by providing his follower, Bardolph, with employment at the Garter. Fenton, however, is the man who will recompense the Host for his stolen horses (doubtless out of Anne Page's dowry), and through whom he will be associated with the winning side at the end of the play.

For all his greed and riot, his selfishness and occasional brutality,

Falstaff does function in the histories as a truth-teller, a man who presents a genuinely alternative point of view. Among people half-crazed (as Hotspur is) by the thirst for honour and personal glory, cold, unfeeling politicians such as Prince John and, to some extent, Hal himself, joyless officers of the law, and monstrous egotists such as Worcester and Northumberland who shelter (as Falstaff does not) behind an affectation of high principle, Shakespeare's sensual pacifist comes to operate to some extent like his remote ancestor, the Aristophanic hero. He qualifies and questions certain limiting and dangerous assumptions that society is prone to make, without forgetting for a moment that he himself is a rogue. It is true that, unlike Dicaeopolis, Trygaeus, and Peithetaerus, the Falstaff of the Henry IV and V plays ultimately loses. His voice is silenced – but silenced at a cost. A whole dimension of life and personal relationship, of a frequently squalid but nonetheless vital kind, disappears with him at the end of *2 Henry IV*. To banish Falstaff may not be quite, as he prophesied himself, to 'banish all the world' (*1 H IV*. ii.4.480), but it is certainly to impoverish it, and to allow various doubtful ideals, whether of military conquest and splendour, contempt for the flesh and its pleasures, or what the Lord Chief Justice calls 'gravity' – and Falstaff, 'gravy' (*2 H IV* i.2.161) – to flourish unchecked.

In *The Merry Wives of Windsor*, on the other hand, Falstaff never functions in this way. That Ford should finally be enlightened as to the folly of suspecting a good and chaste wife of trying to cuckold him is obviously a good thing. Falstaff's role, however, in bringing this about is inadvertent. Indeed, the discovery is one that runs counter not only to his own personal wishes in the matter but, more importantly, to his characteristic attitudes and ways of thinking. The fact is, that although Windsor is certainly not perfect, its faults are not of a kind which render it vulnerable to Falstaff's particular kind of dissent. It is young Fenton, the former prodigal, who emerges at the end to remind Windsor of certain youthful impulses and prerogatives that it was in danger of forgetting, redressing an imperilled balance by restoring the community to its own best self. He needs the help of the Host, at last, to accomplish this, but his own future will not lie in inns or taverns. Fenton's deceit, as he says tellingly, 'loses the name of craft', because it has been committed genuinely in the interests of love, and because it honours that ideal of true, as opposed to 'forced marriage' (v.5.226, 230) upon which life in Windsor – and in Shakespearean comedy generally – relies. Both Fenton and Falstaff go home from Windsor Park to Page's house to 'laugh this sport o'er by a country fire' with the others (v.5.242). Fenton, however, is not only a victor but a man who has won a wife and acceptance in a comic community whose values he has not only respected but actually helped to keep in repair. Falstaff, by contrast, the failed hero of a different kind of comedy, will have no option tomorrow but to move on.

Shakespeare never again allowed Falstaff, or characters generically like him, to occupy the central place in a comedy. They do, however, reappear from time to time in firmly subsidiary roles. Falstaff had no genuine predecessors in the comedies Shakespeare wrote before *The Merry Wives of Windsor*, but Sir Toby Belch later, in *Twelfth Night*, Lucio in *Measure For Measure*, Parolles in *All's Well That Ends Well*, and Autolycus in *The Winter's Tale* are recognizably his kin. All but Autolycus are defeated. Sir Toby's precarious middle-aged existence as a bachelor reveller and a parasite, fraudulently filling his pockets by encouraging foolish suitors in their addresses to his niece, comes to an abrupt end when Olivia accepts Sebastian as her husband, leaving Toby with little more than a painful head injury and his own hasty and equivocal marriage to Maria. Parolles, another parasite and professional cynic about women's virtue, is repudiated by his patron after being exposed and shamed by the captains. He plummets ignominiously from the position of gentleman and supposed military expert to that of allowed fool, glad to accept a penny from his old enemy Lafew, and stripped of pretensions: 'Simply the thing I am / Shall make me live' (*All's well* IV.3.333–4). As for Lucio the 'fantastic', a lapsed gentleman who, like Marston's Cocledemoy, tends to reduce human love to its grossest and most physical terms ('filling a bottle with a tun-dish', 'a game of tick-tack', and so on (*Measure* III.2.172, I.2.190–1), he narrowly escapes whipping and hanging at the Duke's orders, only to be condemned to what he regards as an equally savage fate: enforced marriage to his own whore.

After this unbroken succession of failures in the later comedies, the success of Autolycus in *The Winter's Tale* comes as a distinct surprise. Autolycus, who in his time has 'compass'd a motion of the Prodigal Son' (IV.3.96–7) in both the literal and the metaphorical sense, was 'litter'd under Mercury' (IV.3.25). Indeed, his name is that of Odysseus' grandfather, a son of Mercury and accomplished thief, which provides Autolycus with an ancestry of deviousness even older and more distinguished than the one Falstaff can claim. A former courtier and companion of Prince Florizel's, he has been undone (as he freely confesses) by whores and dice, whipped out of court, and now 'haunts wakes, fairs, and bear-baitings' (IV.3.102) in various guises, including that adopted by Wilson's character Simplicity: a ballad-singer. Almost as tuneful as Beaumont's Merrythought, Autolycus (like Udall's Merygreeke) enters the play singing. He alludes, rather bewilderingly, to having 'married a tinker's wife' (IV.3.97), but fornication, petty thievery, and quarts of ale appear to dominate his unorthodox and peripatetic existence.

Irrepressibly cheerful, with respect both to this life and whatever may await him in the next ('For the life to come, I sleep out the thought of it', IV.3.30), Autolycus is a predatory intruder into a less sophisticated society, just as Falstaff was in Gloucestershire and Windsor. He is like him, too, in being a strayed member of a higher social class, a coward, and a master of language. Pastoral Bohemia, whether in the form of the Clown who pities him and loses all his money for his pains, or the shepherds and shepherdesses who buy his counterfeit jewellery and believe his ballads are true (while having their pockets deftly picked) is helpless in his hands. He even manages to deceive Camillo and his former master Florizel. The most extraordinary thing about Autolycus, however, is that he manages to do all these things and escape unscathed. At the end of the play, he has even managed to worm his way back into court under the patronage of those new-made gentlemen the Old Shepherd and the Clown, without having the slightest intention (as even they can see) of mending his ways.

It would be difficult to see Autolycus as a comic hero who probes and questions, however unsystematically, the illusions and weak places of the society he exploits. Rural Bohemia, even more unequivocally than Windsor, is a fresh and honest locale. Indeed, as has often been observed, the knavery of Autolycus redeems it from the danger of seeming sentimentalized and overly innocent, a pastoral paradise too good to be true. He has, however, a function even more positive. Without intending to do so, Camillo and Florizel place their destinies, and that of Perdita, in his hands. Autolycus agrees to exchange his shabby garments with those of the runaway prince, sees exactly what capital he could make out of his knowledge of Florizel's elopement, and then, through a weird, backward logic of his own, declines to act:

I understand the business, I hear it. To have an open ear, a quick eye, and a nimble hand, is necessary for a cutpurse; a good nose is requisite also, to smell out work for th'other senses. I see this is the time that the unjust man doth thrive. What an exchange has this been, without boot! What a boot is here, with this exchange! Sure the gods do this year connive at us, and we may do any thing extempore. The Prince himself is about a piece of iniquity: stealing away from his father with his clog at his heels. If I thought it were a piece of honesty to acquaint the King withal, I would not do't. I hold it the more knavery to conceal it; and therein am I constant to my profession.

(IV.4.670–83)

Here, as from a great distance, there seems to sound an echo of the convoluted but triumphant reasoning of Falstaff on the field of Shrewsbury, arguing that 'to die is to be a counterfeit, for he is but the counterfeit of a man who hath not the life of a man; but to counterfeit dying, when a man thereby liveth, is to be no counterfeit, but the true and perfect image of life indeed' (*1 Henry IV* v.4.115–19). Autolycus makes the concept of 'knavery', as Falstaff did that of 'counterfeiting', redefine itself and undergo a sea-change. A few minutes later, acting on an imperfectly rationalized impulse, he tricks the Old Shepherd and the Clown out of appealing to Polixenes and decoys them instead aboard Florizel's ship. And so the all-important farthel, and the truth about Perdita's origins, reach Sicily and King Leontes. Autolycus, the disreputable outcast from respectable society, the sensualist and thief, is the agent of the happy ending: the man who victimizes but also redeems and restores the social order. It is far more than Falstaff managed to do, even in the histories. That Autolycus should succeed where all of his Shakespearean predecessors, even the greatest, failed, testifies not so much to his own brilliance and sagacity as to the gulf which separates Shakespeare's early and mature comedies from the last plays.

CHAPTER 5

As *You Like It* and *Twelfth Night*:
Shakespeare's 'sense of an ending' (1972)

I

Henri Focillon has argued that the word *classicism*, rightly understood, has nothing to do with academicism nor even necessarily
with our formal legacy from Greece and Rome. Correctly, it refers to
a condition of poise: 'a brief, perfectly balanced instant of complete
possession of forms' occurring at certain crucial moments in artistic
styles which may otherwise have nothing in common.

Classicism consists of the greatest propriety of the parts one to the other. It
is stability, security, following upon experimental unrest. It confers, so to
speak, a solidity on the unstable aspects of experimentation (because of
which it is also, in its way, a renunciation) ... But classicism is not the result
of a conformist attitude. On the contrary, it has been created out of one final,
ultimate experiment, the audacity and vitality of which it has never lost ...
Classicism: a brief, perfectly balanced instant of complete possession of
forms; not a slow and monotonous application of 'rules', but a pure, quick
delight, like the ἀκμή of the Greeks, so delicate that the pointer of the scale
scarcely trembles. I look at this scale not to see whether the pointer will
presently dip down again, or even come to a moment of absolute rest. I look
at it instead to see, within the miracle of that hesitant immobility, the slight,
inappreciable tremor that indicates life.[1]

Focillon was writing about the visual arts, but there is surely a
classicism of the kind he describes in literary styles as well. Dramatists
too may achieve a 'perfectly balanced instant of complete possession
of forms', the very stillness of which will, in the next moment, seem to
imply limitation and invite its own destruction.

    As You Like It is, in Focillon's sense, Shakespeare's classical comedy.
It confers solidity upon the dazzling experimentation of eight

---

[1] Henri Focillon, *The Life of Forms in Art*, 2nd edn, trans. C. B. Hogan and George Kubler
(New York, 1948), pp. 11–12.

91

comedies written before it, stands as the fullest and most stable realization of Shakespearean comic form.[2] Critics, aware now of the 'social' nature of the comedies, of their complex structure of silently juxtaposed scenes, tend to take this form more seriously than they once did. C. L. Barber and Northrop Frye in particular have argued for the essential unity of Shakespearean comedy in ways that reach far beyond shared plot devices, or the old spotting of resemblances among the clowns and witty heroines of different plays. It has become possible to agree that the comedies, from *The Two Gentlemen of Verona* and *The Comedy of Errors* to *Twelfth Night*, are plays concerned primarily with transformation, with the clarification and renewal attained, paradoxically, through a submission to some kind of disorder, whether festive or not. We have learned to notice as typically Shakespearean the way characters move between two contrasted locales – one of them heightened and more spacious than the other – and we regard that 'new society' which makes its way back to the normal world at the end of the play as a subtler and more consequential achievement than older critics did.

The exceptionally full participation of *As You Like It* in this (after all) startlingly innovatory comic form built up through preceding plays is obvious. The comedy opposes its two environments, Arden and the court of Duke Frederick, with particular clarity and richness. This greenwood, even more strikingly than the ones in *The Two Gentlemen of Verona* and *A Midsummer Night's Dream*, is a place where people yield themselves for a time to the extraordinary, and emerge transformed. Realism is interwoven with romance, truth to life with certain fairy-tale conventions frankly exploited as such. To a greater extent than Julia and Portia, Rosaline and Beatrice before her, Rosalind in her boy's disguise is the central consciousness of it all: a heroine both involved and dispassionate who seems largely responsible for the structure of that new social order which leaves Arden so hopefully at the end. Most important of all, *As You Like It* tests against each other a great variety of love relationships and possible attitudes towards experience, by means of a technique of contrast and parallel which Shakespeare may have learned originally from Lyly, but which he had refined in the course of writing his earlier comedies to the point where it could, here, actually take the place of plot.

---

[2] I am assuming that *The Merry Wives of Windsor* preceded *As You Like It*.

Except as a convenient excuse for getting characters into Arden, and out again at the end, intrigue scarcely seems to matter in this play. *As You Like It* derives much of its classical stability and poise from the fact that its plot barely exists. The comedy moves forward, not through a complex story line of the kind Shakespeare had spun out in *The Comedy of Errors,* or in the Hero/Claudio plot of *Much Ado About Nothing*, but simply through shifts in the grouping of characters. Their verbal encounters, their varying assessments of each other assume the status of events in this pastoral landscape where the gifts of Fortune are bestowed so equally as to throw a new and searching light on what people really are. Shakespeare's customary generosity to his characters, his reluctance to legislate, his faith in romantic love and in the ability of human beings to transform their own natures make *As You Like It* a richer and far more dramatic play than Jonson's *Every Man Out of His Humour* (1599). These two comedies, written perhaps in the same year, are nevertheless alike in their subordination of plot in the traditional sense to an intricate structure of meetings between characters, a concentration upon attitudes rather than action. The normal functions of plot are fulfilled almost entirely by form and, in both cases, a curious stillness at the heart of the play is the result.

Shakespeare had once before composed a comedy singularly devoid of intrigue. *Love's Labour's Lost,* too, unfolds principally by way of echo and antithesis, through thematic juxtapositions suggesting relationships and judgements which Shakespeare often does not care to make explicit in his text. There is a sense in which the only thing that 'happens' in *Love's Labour's Lost,* after the arrival in Navarre of the Princess and her ladies in Act II, is the death of the King of France as reported in the fifth act by Mercade. Yet the effect produced by this second event, geographically distant though it is, is nothing less than the annihilation of the entire world of the comedy. In the moments following the entrance of Mercade, the sheltered, un-eventful and thoughtlessly cruel life of the royal park comes in retrospect to seem not only frivolous but unnatural and false. The comedy turns and rends its own former preoccupation with words and attitudes as opposed to actions. Sadly, Navarre and his companions prepare to leave their retreat for an altogether less comfortable, if ultimately more rewarding, world in which things happen and death and time cannot be sidestepped. Only by deeds as opposed to vows, by dearly-bought and tangible 'deserts' (v.2.805), can love's labours, grossly misconceived by the men for most of the play, at last be won.

The plotlessness of *As You Like It* is not like this. In no sense does it represent a criticism of the characters who flee into Arden, nor of the life they lead there. Although it will be necessary for most of them to return to an urban civilization at the end, to leave the greenwood, this return does not imply a rejection of the values of the forest. They have not been idle, nor is death a fact which the inhabitants of Arden have ever tried, fraudulently, to evade. *Love's Labour's Lost* is extreme in the suddenness with which it introduces its reminder of mortality in Act v. Yet it is surely significant that all but two of the comedies Shakespeare wrote before *As You Like It* achieve their comic catharsis by way of some kind of confrontation with the idea of death. *The Comedy of Errors* unfolds feverishly under the shadow of the fate threatening old Aegeon at the setting of the sun. It achieves recognition and pardon in the last act after a virtual massing of images of destruction, many of them clustered around the skeletal figure of Pinch, that 'mere anatomy...a living dead man' (v.1.239–42). *The Two Gentlemen of Verona* seems to disintegrate, never really to recover, when it introduces the murderous attack of the outlaws and Proteus' attempted rape in Act v. In *A Midsummer Night's Dream*, the death sentence which sends the lovers into the forest is caught up and forcibly transmuted into laughter by the Pyramus and Thisbe interlude at the end. Bottom and his friends may render the tragedy ridiculous; they remind us all the same that this is the way Hermia's story might in all seriousness have ended: with blood and deprivation. As it is, Lysander's dismissal of Pyramus, 'He is dead, he is nothing' rings disturbingly in the ear (v.1.308–9). *Much Ado About Nothing* goes so far as apparently to kill and ceremonially inter Hero before a comic resolution can be reached. Antonio must be rescued, narrowly, from Shylock's knife before *The Merchant of Venice* can permit a consummation of the marriages made at Belmont. Only *The Taming of the Shrew* and *The Merry Wives of Windsor* are devoid of any genuinely dark tones, and this perhaps is one reason why critics have persistently felt that these plays are closer to farce than to true comedy.

Even as Shakespearean tragedy usually makes some delusive gesture towards a happy ending just before the catastrophe, providing us with a tantalizing glimpse of Lear re-united with Cordelia, Antony successful, or Hamlet reprieved, so the comedies tend to win through to their happy endings by way of some kind of victory over the opposite possibility. In doing so, they assure the theatre audience that the facts of the world as it is have not been forgotten. Like the moment of false hope which animates the fourth acts of tragedy, the encounter with death which precedes the comedy resolution demonstrates a saving awareness that this story might well have ended differently. Comedy pauses to look disaster squarely in the face, but is still able to proceed honestly towards a conclusion flattering to our optimism. The manoeuvre is designed to shore up the happy ending, to allow us to surrender ourselves, at least temporarily, to a pleasing fiction.

II

In all the comedies which Shakespeare wrote before *As You Like It* (*The Taming of the Shrew* and *The Merry Wives of Windsor* excepted) this emphasis upon death towards the end of the play is strident and momentarily disorientating. The effect produced is not unlike the one achieved by Nicolas Poussin in the earlier of his two paintings on the theme 'Et in Arcadia ego'. In the version at Chatsworth (Plate 2), painted about 1630, two shepherds and a shepherdess discover, in a pastoral landscape, a tomb which is the spokesman of death: 'I am here, even in Arcadia.' Poussin was influenced at the time by Titian (and also, as Erwin Panofsky has pointed out, by Guercino's treatment of the same subject[3]), but it is not simply an interest in Baroque diagonals which governs the rush of the three figures towards the sarcophagus. The movement contains within itself a sense of recoil: of sudden horror and dismay. Neither emotionally nor in terms of the composition do the two shepherds and the girl accept the object before them. They react against it with gestures full of disorder. Some twenty years after the Chatsworth *Et in Arcadia ego*, Poussin returned to the subject. The painting he produced, now in the Louvre (Plate 3), is classical both in terms of specific stylistic indebtedness and, more importantly, in the sense of Focillon's definition. It stands in something of the same relationship to the

---

[3] Erwin Panofsky, '*Et in Arcadia ego*: Poussin and the elegiac tradition', in *Meaning in the Visual Arts* (New York, 1955), pp. 295–320.

Plate 2 'Et in Arcadia ego', by Nicholas Poussin. The first version, in the Devonshire Collection, Chatsworth.

Chatsworth painting as does *As You Like It* to Shakespeare's earlier comedies. Here, the tomb stands solidly and uncompromisingly in the midst of a sunlit landscape. The words carved on it now seem to emanate both from Death personified and from the regret of the dead man himself that he too once lived in Arcadia but does so no longer.

Plate 3 'Et in Arcadia ego', by Nicholas Poussin. The second version, in the Louvre.

The three shepherds and the shepherdess grouped about the monument are serious, but they are in no way discomposed by this reminder of their own mortality which they have come upon so suddenly in the midst of the Golden World, in no way frightened or thrown off balance. Indeed, they have contrived to use the rectangular mass of the tomb in the centre of the composition as a kind of support, or focal point, for the achieved harmony of their own attitudes and gestures. They have made it part of their own order, accommodated it perfectly within a pattern of line and movement which both emotionally and technically has been able to accept this potentially awkward fact of death and even to build upon it.

In *As You Like It* too, death is something faced steadily and with due consideration, but it has almost no power whatever over the balance, the poise of a comedy which has quietly assimilated this factor from the start. A comparison between *As You Like It* and its source, Thomas Lodge's *Rosalynde* (1590), reveals Shakespeare's desire at almost every point to mitigate the violence inherent in the original story. Lodge had moved from one explosive moment of time, one crisis, to another. Shakespeare refused to do this. In his re-working of the tale, Charles the wrestler injures the old man's sons but does not kill them, and he himself is not killed. The episode of the robbers in *Rosalynde*, their attempt to abduct the heroine and her companion, is omitted and so is the battle at the end in which Lodge's usurping prince had been defeated and slain. Instead, Shakespeare's Duke Frederick is peacefully converted to goodness through the agency of an old religious man palpably invented for that purpose. The protracted scenes of enmity and struggle between Lodge's hero and his elder brother are made perfunctory, almost abstract, in the comedy. It is true that both Rosalind and Orlando incur a threat of death early in the comedy, but this threat is in both cases a transparent device for sending them into the forest rather than a possibility seriously explored. The wrestling match, Oliver's intention to burn the lodging where Orlando lies, the spite of Duke Frederick, are all treated in the manner of fairy-tale. Not for an instant do they endanger the comic tone. Lodge had described his hero's rescue of his unworthy brother in rousing and basically realistic terms. Shakespeare distances it into the most static and heraldic of pictures: an emblem of lioness and serpent sketched at secondhand. Old Adam may imagine that he is going to die in Arden for lack of food; Orlando rushes into the banquet with drawn sword. These images are no sooner presented than they are corrected. The crisis was false. Calmly, even a little mockingly, the play rights itself. It assimilates the intrusion. Harmonious, balanced, and tonally even, *As You Like It* harbours a stillness at the centre which no turn of the plot, apparently, can affect.

Although a consciousness that 'men have died from time to time, and worms have eaten them' (IV.1.106–7), that human life is 'but a flower' (V.3.28) is spread throughout the comedy, this consciousness is never allowed to sharpen into a dramatic or even into a genuine emotional climax. Reminders of mortality flicker everywhere through the language of the play. Most of the characters seem to carry with them, as visibly as the shepherds painted by Poussin, an awareness of death and time. Rosalind's high spirits, Orlando's love, Duke Senior's contentment in adversity, and Touchstone's wit all flower out of it. Yet when the melancholy Jaques, in his meditation on the wounded deer, his delighted account of Touchstone's platitudes – 'from hour to hour, we ripe and ripe, / And then from hour to hour, we rot and rot' (II.7.26–7) – or in his dismal chronology of the ages of man, tries to argue that life must necessarily be trivial and pointless because it ends in the grave, his attitude is amended or put aside. It is as important to the classical equilibrium of the play that Jaques' pessimism should be qualified in this fashion, firmly displaced from the centre of the composition, as it is that the violence built into the story as Lodge had told it should be smoothed away.

In his encounters with the Duke and Touchstone, with Orlando and (above all) with Rosalind, Jaques fares badly. He stumbles from one discomfiture to another. Only in the closing moments of the play when Shakespeare, without warning, allows him to speak the valediction of the entire comedy does his voice go uncontradicted. Formally, in a speech which considerations of rank ought to have assigned to Duke Senior, and symbolism to the god Hymen, Jaques estimates the futures and, by the way, the basic natures of all the other main characters. He puts the seal on the weddings, sets in motion the dance he himself declines to join. As he does so, he becomes something that he was not when he wished for a suit of motley, when he destroyed the harmony of Amiens' song, begged Orlando to rail with him against the world, or when he sentimentalized over the herd-abandoned deer. A figure of sudden dignity, his judgements are both generous and just. Although his decision to seek out Duke Frederick, separating himself firmly from that new society embodied in the dance, may be regretted, it cannot really be criticized. Moreover, his absence from the dance sets up reverberations, asks questions more disturbing than any that were roused earlier by his twice-told tales of transience and decay. This new attitude towards Jaques is important in determining the character of *As You Like It* at its ending. It represents, in Focillon's terms, that 'slight, inappreciable tremor' within the immobility of the classical moment, a tremor which guarantees the vitality of the moment itself but which also prefigures its imminent destruction.

III

It is notoriously difficult for endings in fiction not to seem false.[4] They are likely to declare their own artificiality, reminding us that although plays and novels necessarily reach a more or less tidy conclusion, real events and relationships do not. For Fortinbras, the death of Prince Hamlet was a beginning; even for Horatio, it is only an event occurring near the middle of another play. This continuum, this extension of the story into an infinity of contiguous persons and episodes is something that Shakespeare, in shaping his fifth act, was forced to indicate only slightly, or to ignore. To a certain extent, tragedy as a form aids the dramatist in overcoming the problem of conclusions. Although tragedy endings abbreviate and distort reality, they can nonetheless afford to suggest a finality which the chronicle history for instance cannot, precisely because we recognize in the death of the tragic protagonist an image of our own future extinction. Every member of the theatre audience feels that he stands, like Hamlet or Othello, in the centre of his play, surrounded by minor characters who for their part are equally convinced of their centrality in a performance which is both the same as ours and different. An objective awareness that the play will continue without us does not conflict with our private sense that it stops as soon as we cease to be a part of it. In terms of the individual consciousness, tragedy fifth acts are true.

Artistic forms which dismiss their characters into happiness, often through the solemnization or promise of marriage, are far more problematic. Such endings are not real conclusions, even in the

---

[4] I am indebted here, and indeed throughout this essay, to Frank Kermode's discussion of the problem of beginnings and endings in fiction in *The Sense of an Ending: Studies in the Theory of Fiction* (Oxford, 1967).

qualified sense that tragic obsequies are. They are a kind of arbitrary arrest. By means of art, the flux of life has been stilled. Satiety, death, the erosion of personality by time have all been denied or else indefinitely postponed in order that an ephemeral moment of happiness may pose as a permanent state. Fairy-tale accepts and indeed flaunts this implausibility. Formulaic concluding sentences like the familiar 'And so they all lived happily ever after', the more evasive 'And for all I know, they are reigning there yet', or 'If they have not left off their merry-making, they must be at it still' are really signal-flares of impossibility. They are the appropriate finish for stories about beggars who become kings, benevolent frog-princes who rescue maidens in distress, or sea-nymphs who keep open house for mistreated younger sons in halls of crystal drowned forty fathoms deep. Fairy-tales are like Christian allegories of salvation, in that both ask the reader to accept on faith the idea of an eternity of bliss which is deliberately at odds with the way of the world as we know it. As such, they stand at a remove from those comic forms which are determined both to gratify our longing for a golden world and to realize it in what, for lack of a better phrase, one must call 'realistic terms'.

Anthony Trollope, adept though he was at happy endings designed to please his feminine readers, was too honest an artist not to question them. At the end of *Barchester Towers*, he complained wryly of the difficulty of composing last chapters that were both cheerful and genuinely satisfying:

Promises of two children and superhuman happiness are of no avail, nor assurance of extreme respectability carried to an age far exceeding that usually allotted to mortals... I can only say that if some critic, who thoroughly knows his work, and has laboured on it till experience has made him perfect, will write the last fifty pages of a novel in the way they should be written, I, for one, will in future do my best to copy the example. Guided by my own lights only, I confess that I despair of success.[5]

If comedy endings pose problems for the novelist, they are even more tricky for the dramatist who, deprived as he is of the novelist's weapons of digression and objective comment, wishes to leave us with the image of a world transfigured but to make it credible as fairy-tales are not. Shakespeare's handling of the end of *As You Like It* is masterful in the way it welds together realism and romance. The play

---

[5] Anthony Trollope, *Barchester Towers*, 2 vols. (Oxford, 1953), II, pp. 251–2.

releases its audience cheered and consoled, conscious of having participated briefly in an existence which, although heightened and more harmonious than its own, cannot be dismissed as a mere 'improbable fiction'.

It is important to the ending of *As You Like It* that Arden has never, unlike the wood in *A Midsummer Night's Dream*, been presented as magical. This is not quite an ordinary Warwickshire forest. References to palm trees and lionesses, to Duke Senior and his followers as reincarnations of 'the old Robin Hood of England', men who 'fleet the time carelessly, as they did in the golden world' (1.1.116–19), ensure that this is to some extent Arcadia. It is, however, an Arcadia touched by the older, pre-Virgilian tradition: a place where the seasons alter, where the wind can be cold and the underbrush tangled, where food is hard to come by and Corin's master is of churlish disposition. Touchstone's initial reaction to the forest: 'Ay, now am I in Arden, the more fool I. When I was at home, I was in a better place' (11.4.16–17) is exactly that of the disgruntled traveller arriving, after much effort, at Venice in the rain.

Essentially Arden is enchanted only in the sense that it is a place where, miraculously, Fortune does not oppress Nature. In the forest, people are free to be themselves as they are not in the court of Duke Frederick. There, Le Beau needs to adopt a foppish false countenance in public and can only whisper nervously to Orlando, when he finds him alone, of that 'better world than this' in which it might be possible to drop the mask and to 'desire more love and knowledge of you' (1.2.285). Although Le Beau himself never reaches it, Arden is indeed this 'better world'. The freedom it offers, however, is not unlimited and dizzying like that of fairy-tale. At the end of the comedy as at the beginning, William will be a clod and Audrey awkward and ill-favoured. Frogs remain frogs and ugly ducklings stay ugly; they do not change into princes or into swans. The changes which do occur in characters like Rosalind and Orlando, Duke Senior, Phebe, Celia and even Oliver, are really self-discoveries, a deepening and development of personality. For the most part, these people earn their own happy endings. Their destinies are not imposed upon them arbitrarily, as they are upon Hermia and Lysander, Helena and Demetrius, by a supernatural world.

Four pairs of lovers marry at the end of *As You Like It*, a number so great that Jaques can pretend to fear another Flood is toward, as they range themselves two by two. Four weddings agreed upon in the final scene of a comedy is daring, a test of audience credulity. In his previous plays, Shakespeare had never attempted more than three (leaving aside the deferred nuptials of *Love's Labour's Lost*), and he preferred to space them through the course of the comedy. The conclusion of *As You Like It* veers towards the implausible in asking us to accept four marriages, two lightning conversions, and the inexplicable appearance of the god Hymen among the cast of characters. At the same time it insists that although fairy-tale elements are undeniably present here, as indeed they have been in varying intensities through the play, this ending still presents an image of reality. The classicism of the comedy declares itself both in the assurance with which it exacts belief for improbabilities so considerable, and in the unprecedented generosity and inclusiveness of the society which finally emerges from Arden. The cynicism of Touchstone, the unseemly postures of Audrey, may disturb the symmetry of the dance at the end. No society, not even this one, is perfect. Nevertheless, the fact that the fool and the goat-girl can form part of the pattern testifies to the flexibility of the new social order, its ability to accommodate deviation. More than any of its predecessors, *As You Like It* demonstrates Shakespeare's faith in comedy resolutions. It is a triumph of form.

Of the characters whom one would expect to find in the final scene, only two do not participate in the dance. Adam is too old to take part in the establishment of the new order. Quietly, he has vanished from the play. His absence defines one kind of limitation admitted by the comic society. Jaques, who is present when the revels begin, but refuses either to join or to watch them, defines another that is more important. Unlike Shylock or Don John, this man has never menaced the lives or happiness of other characters in the play. His exile at the end is voluntary, a reasoned decision against which the Duke protests in vain: it is not in any sense a punishment or ritual casting out. That 'better world' created in Arden which prepares now to reinvigorate the court would gladly assimilate Jaques, if only he were willing. The fact that he is not willing suggests that there are certain kinds of experience after all, certain questions, which lie outside the scope of the happy ending, generous and convincing though that is.

Jaques' pessimism has hitherto been blunted by characters who, although fully aware themselves of the facts of death and time, have wisely refused to be crippled by such knowledge. His despair has functioned as a useful test of Rosalind and Orlando's sanity and sense of proportion. A seeming threat to the classical equilibrium of the comedy, Jaques has in fact provided it with needful opportunities to demonstrate its own strength and poise. His withdrawal at the end impoverishes the comic society about to leave Arden. Like a ship which has suddenly jettisoned its ballast, the play no longer rides quite evenly in the waves. Jaques' departure does more than simply imply that 'there is a world elsewhere'. It accentuates that slight inclination towards fantasy already present in this final scene, a tendency signalized by the abrupt entrance of Jaques de Boys, his extraordinary account of Duke Frederick's conversion, and by Hymen's affirmation of something we should all wistfully like to believe: that the gods themselves delight in happy endings:

> Then is there mirth in heaven,
> When earthly things made even
> Atone together.   (v.4.108–10)

A tremor appears in the balance of the comedy.

Yet the balance holds. It would be wrong to over-stress the fairy-tale elements in the conclusion, even as it would be inaccurate to see its joyousness as impaired by Jaques' decision to seek a kind of experience unavailable within the comic dance. Essentially *As You Like It* remains whole and complete at its ending, displaying only a flicker of qualification and unease. In associating Jaques' self-banishment with the dreamlike figure of the old religious man, the fabulous quality of Duke Frederick's decision to embrace an ascetic life, Shakespeare deliberately minimizes its impact. Although he may choose to separate himself from the comic society, Jaques remains within a heightened world. The journey he is about to undertake will not conduct him to a reality serving, by its contrast, to diminish and render fictional the world centred upon Rosalind, Orlando and Duke Senior. Such a distinction would destroy the play's classical poise. The moment of classical stasis must always, however, be brief. In *Twelfth Night*, the next of the comedies, the fragmentation only hinted at in the last scene of *As You Like It* became actual, as Shakespeare began to unbuild his own comic form at its point of greatest vulnerability: the ending.

IV

All of *Twelfth Night*, up to the final scene, takes place in a heightened world. There is no contrasting environment, no Athens or Duke Frederick's court, to set against Illyria. Messaline, the place from which Viola and Sebastian have come, is even more shadowy than Syracuse in *The Comedy of Errors*, or those wars from which Don Pedro, Claudio and Benedick find release in Messina. Messaline has no character whatever, and certainly no claim to be regarded as that normal world to which characters have so often returned at the end of a Shakespearean comedy. Illyria itself, on the other hand, has a very distinct character and declares it from the opening moments of the play. The sea-captain, appealed to by Viola for information about the country in which she has so unexpectedly arrived, might just as well have said to her what the Cheshire Cat says to Alice: 'They're all mad here.' Even before the unsettling appearance of twin Cesarios, both the ruler of Illyria and his reluctant mistress have manoeuvred themselves into unbalanced states of mind. They are surrounded, moreover, by characters even madder than they: Sir Toby Belch, Sir Andrew Aguecheek, or Feste, the man whose profession is folly. Malvolio in his dark room may seem to present the play's most extreme image of insanity, yet Olivia can confess that 'I am as mad as he, / If sad and merry madness equal be' (III.4.14–15). Sebastian, bewildered by Olivia's passionate claims upon him, will earnestly debate the question of his own sanity. Antonio, already bewitched as he sees it by Sebastian, is accused of madness by Orsino's officer when he tries to explain his situation.

The eruption onto the stage of identical twins is calculated to make people distrust the evidence of their own senses. *The Comedy of Errors*, which plays the same game of mistaken identity in a doubled form, had also made use of images of madness. Yet the lunacy of *Twelfth Night* is both more widespread and more various. It is part of the whole atmosphere of the Feast of Fools suggested by the play's title, not simply a product of the failure to understand that there are two Cesarios and not just one. For Elizabethans this title would have stirred immemorial and continuing associations with a period of time in which normal rules were suspended, in which the world turned ritually upside down, allowing the plain man to become king and pleasure to transform itself into a species of obligation. Certainly the spirit of holiday reigns in Illyria, particularly in the household of the

mourning Olivia. The countess herself may disapprove from a distance of the nightly chaos presided over by Sir Toby: only Malvolio
tries in earnest to repress it. As soon as he does so, he places himself
in danger. He becomes the churl at the banquet, the sobersides at the
carnival. The revellers, forgetting their own private dissensions, recognize him at once for the common enemy and hunt him from their
midst. As feasters, men living in a celebratory world that, temporarily
at least, is larger than life, they instinctively protect themselves
against the niggard who refuses to yield himself to the extraordinary.

As members of the *Twelfth Night* audience, we too are sharers in the
extraordinary, a fact which perhaps explains why Malvolio has
found tender-hearted apologists in the study but very few sympa-
thizers in the playhouse. His humiliation at the hands of Feste,
Maria, Fabian and Sir Toby removes a threat to our own
equilibrium, to the holiday mood induced by the comedy in its early
stages. We make common cause with Sir Toby and the Fool against
Malvolio because we do not want him to spoil fun which in a sense is
ours as well as that of characters actually on the stage. By means of
laughter, we too cast Malvolio out. As soon as the steward has pieced
together the meaning of the mock letter to his own satisfaction, as
soon as he has swallowed the bait, he ceases to be a threat. Yellow-
stockinged and cross-gartered, trying to produce some rusty approximation to a smile, Malvolio has become part of precisely that
heightened world of play-acting, revelry and lack of control which he
so despised. Festivity has made him its unwilling prey. Thereafter, it
will do with him what it likes, until the moment of awakening.

This moment of awakening is in some ways the most distinctive
feature of *Twelfth Night*. Sir Toby is the first to scent the morning air.
At the end of Act IV, he is wishing that 'we were well rid of this
knavery', that some means of releasing Malvolio 'conveniently'
might be devised before the mood of holiday inconsequence breaks
(IV.2.67–8). Act V displays a marked harshening of tone. It begins by
massing together images of death in a fashion that harks back to
Shakespeare's preferred comic practice in the plays written before *As
You Like It*. In this respect, as in its renewed emphasis on plot, *Twelfth
Night* breaks away from the classicism of its predecessor. Orsino,
confronting Antonio in his fetters, remembers that when last he saw
this face 'it was besmear'd / As black as Vulcan in the smoke of war'
(V.1.52–3). To the grim realities of combat and mutilation now
recalled there is added the agony of Antonio's account of his friend's

treachery. The appearance of Olivia only makes matters worse. Orsino, half-crazed with jealousy of Cesario, threatens publicly to 'kill what I love' (v.i.119):

> Him will I tear out of that cruel eye,
> Where he sits crowned in his master's spite.
> Come, boy, with me, my thoughts are ripe in mischief.
> I'll sacrifice the lamb that I do love,
> To spite a raven's heart within a dove. (v.i.127–31)

The situation is further complicated by the priest's confirmation of Olivia's marriage, a marriage so recent that since its solemnization 'my watch hath told me, toward my grave / I have travell'd but two hours' (v.i.162–3). Between sincere and passionate affirmation on the one side and, on the other, equally sincere and passionate denial, the deadlock is complete. Only Sebastian can untangle this knot. The next character to enter is not, however, Sebastian but the wretched Sir Andrew Aguecheek. He comes, surprisingly, as the victim of real violence:

> For the love of God, a surgeon! Send one presently to Sir Toby... H'as broke my head across, and has given Sir Toby a bloody coxcomb too. For the love of God, your help! I had rather than forty pound I were at home.
>
> (v.i.175–8)

Sebastian has levelled precisely those inequalities upon which Sir Toby battened. Predator and prey have been used alike despite the considerable difference in their swordsmanship and general efficiency. And indeed something more than a pair of coxcombs has been broken.

Surgeons, after all, belong to a sober reality of sickness and disease outside the limits of festivity. This, at least, ought to be their territory. Feste's reply to Sir Toby's question, 'didst see Dick surgeon, sot?', is less than consoling: 'O, he's drunk, Sir Toby, an hour agone; his eyes were set at eight i' th' morning' (v.i.197–9). Sir Toby himself has hitherto turned day into night and night into day. He has argued in Falstaffian terms that 'to be up after midnight and to go to bed then is early; so that to go to bed after midnight is to go to bed betimes' (II.3.7–9). For the reveller, the only meaningful chronicity is the one Prince Hal attributed to Falstaff, one in which hours are 'cups of sack, and minutes capons, and clocks the tongues of bawds, and dials the signs of leaping houses' (*1 Henry IV*, 1.2.6–12). Bleeding and in pain, forced to recognize another and harsher kind of time, Sir Toby demands the services of the surgeon, only to discover that this functionary, like himself in happier state, has sat up all night revelling and is now blissfully asleep in just those daylight hours when he is wanted. It is bad enough to be jolted unceremoniously into reality, but even more bitter to find that the surgeon you urgently require is still, in an unregenerate fashion, disporting himself at the carnival. Condemned to suffer pain without relief, Sir Toby gives vent to the uncharacteristic utterance, 'I hate a drunken rogue' (v.1.201).

In the next moment, he turns savagely on Sir Andrew's well-meant offer of assistance and companionship in misery. 'Will you help? – an ass-head and a coxcomb and a knave, a thin-fac'd knave, a gull!' (v.1.206–7). Only a moment before, Sir Andrew had wished for 'forty pound' that he was safely at home again. It was the genuine accent of the reveller for whom the party has suddenly become poisonous, who wishes now that he had never set out from the familiar, homely world to the masked ball; the man for whom day breaks after a night of abandon and fruitless pursuit of profit in a garish and essentially shaming way. On top of all this comes the sudden treachery, the revelation in his true colours of a supposed friend. Sir Andrew does not reply to Sir Toby's abuse. He simply vanishes, never to reappear in the comedy. Sir Toby leaves the stage too, not to be seen again. Subsequently it will be revealed that he has married Maria, as a recompense for her plot against the steward. For him, as for Sir Andrew creeping back to his depleted lands, holiday has been paid for in ways that have real-life consequences.

At precisely this point, as the two broken revellers are being helped away in a state of debility and antagonism, Shakespeare exchanges prose for verse and radically alters the mood of the scene. He allows Sebastian, that comedy resolution personified, at last to confront his twin sister, to assure Olivia of his faith, to renew his friendship with Antonio and to enlighten Orsino. There will be a happy ending. It is, however, a happy ending of an extraordinarily schematized and 'playlike' kind. Viola has already had virtual proof, in Act III, that her brother has survived the wreck. They have been separated for only three months. Yet the two of them put each other through a formal, intensely conventional question and answer test that comes straight out of Greek New Comedy:

VIOLA: My father had a mole upon his brow.
SEBASTIAN: And so had mine.

VIOLA: And died that day when Viola from her birth
  Had numb'red thirteen years.
SEBASTIAN: O, that record is lively in my soul!
  He finished indeed his mortal act
  That day that made my sister thirteen years.   (V.I.202–8)

This recognition scene is intensely moving. Its emotional force and purity derive, however, from consonances that are recognizably fictional. In the theatre, the fact that an audience will always be more struck by the *dissimilarity* in appearance of the actors playing Viola and Sebastian than by that marvellous identity hailed so ecstatically by the other characters, also serves to drive a wedge between fact and literary invention. We are dealing here, Shakespeare seems to announce, with a heightened, an essentially implausible world.

For Olivia and Sebastian, Viola and Orsino, this heightened world perpetuates itself. For them, there will be no return from holiday, no need to leave Illyria. Yet the little society which they form at the end of the play is far more fragmentary and insubstantial than the one that had been consolidated in Arden. The final pairings-off are perfunctory. Olivia accepts Sebastian for himself. Orsino, rather more surprisingly, accepts a Viola he has never seen as a woman. Rosalind had returned in her own guise as a girl at the end of *As You Like It*, uniting Ganymede with the lady Orlando loved first at Duke Frederick's court. Considering the abruptness of Orsino's resolve to substitute Viola for Olivia in his affections, an unknown Viola only guessed at beneath her 'masculine usurp'd attire' (V.I.250), Shakespeare might well have done something similar here. Instead, he treats this joining of hands summarily, and turns away at once to the very different issue of Malvolio.

In the final act of *Twelfth Night*, a world of revelry, of comic festivity, fights a kind of desperate rearguard action against the cold light of day. It survives only in part, and then by insisting upon an exclusiveness that is poles apart from the various and crowded dance at the end of *As You Like It*. Viola and Orsino, Olivia and Sebastian may no longer be deluded, yet it is still Illyria in which they live: an improbable world of hair's-breadth rescues at sea, romantic disguises, idealistic friendships and sudden, irrational loves. This is not quite the country behind the North Wind, but it approaches those latitudes. The two romantic couples stand on the far side of a line dividing fiction from something we recognize as our own reality, and

the society they epitomize is too small to initiate a dance.[6] Of the
other main characters, no fewer than four are conspicuous by their
absence. Maria, Sir Toby and Sir Andrew are not present to witness
the revelations and accords of the closing moments. Malvolio intrudes
upon them briefly, but entirely uncomprehendingly. Like Sir Toby
and Sir Andrew, he comes as a figure of violence and leaves
unreconciled, meditating a futile revenge. For him too, the dream is
over and the moment of awakening bitter. Jaques had walked with
dignity out of the new society; Malvolio in effect is flung.

There is only one character who can restore some sense of unity to
Twelfth Night at its ending, mediating between the world of the
romantic lovers and our own world, which is (or is about to be) that
of the chastened Sir Andrew, the sobered Belch and the unbending
Malvolio. In a sense, he has been doing just this all along in
preparation for some such ultimate necessity. Throughout *Twelfth
Night*, Feste has served as commentator and Chorus, mocking the
extravagance of Orsino, the wasteful idealism of Olivia's grief,
Viola's poor showing as a man. He has joined in the revels of Sir Toby
and Sir Andrew while remaining essentially apart from them, aware
of their limitations. Most important of all, he has kept us continually
aware of the realities of death and time: that 'pleasure will be paid,
one time or another' (II.4.70–1), that 'beauty's a flower' (I.5.52) and
youth 'a stuff will not endure' (II.3.52). Two contradictory kinds of
time have run parallel through the comedy, diverging only at its end.
One is the time of holiday and of fiction, measureless and essentially
beneficent, to which Viola trusts when she remains passive and
permits the happy ending to work itself out with no positive assistance
from her (II.2.40–1). The other time is remorseless and strictly
counted. Although even Viola and Orsino catch glimpses of it, its
chief spokesman has been Feste.

At the very end of *Twelfth Night* these two attitudes towards time
distinguish two groups of characters, dividing a world of fiction from
one of fact. The audience leaving the theatre faces its own jolt into
reality, into the stern time of a world beyond holiday, but at least it
is given Feste and not Malvolio as its guide. Left alone on the stage,
Feste sings his song about the ages of man, a song which draws its

---

[6] It consists, in fact, only of themselves and the minor figure Fabian. There is no place for this
Antonio, as there was for his namesake in the love/friendship resolution of *The Merchant of
Venice*. In John Barton's 1969 Stratford production of *Twelfth Night*, Antonio made his exit
alone at the end, in a direction different from that taken by the lovers.

material from the same source as Jaques' pessimistic catalogue. This time, there will be no attempt at qualification or correction. Yet the song itself is curiously consoling. It leads us gently and in a way that is aesthetically satisfying from the golden world to the age of iron which is our own. A triumph of art, it builds a bridge over the rift which has opened in the comedy at its conclusion.

Feste is tolerant as Jaques, on the whole, was not. He does not attempt to judge, or even to reason. He simply states fact. The child is allowed his fancies: a foolish thing is but a toy. When he grows up he pays for them, or else discovers that the self-deceptions in which he is tempted to take refuge are easily penetrated by the world. Marriage ultimately becomes tedious, and so do the infidelities to which it drives a man. The reality of wind and rain wins out, the monotony of the everyday. The passing of time is painful, may even seem unendurable, but there is nothing for it but resignation, the wise acceptance of the Fool. All holidays come to an end; all revels wind down at last. Only by the special dispensation of art can some people, Viola and Orsino, Olivia and Sebastian, be left in Illyria. For the rest of us, the play is done; fiction yields to fact, and we return to normality along with Sir Toby and Maria, Sir Andrew and Malvolio.

v

Endings, Frank Kermode has stated, are most satisfactory when they are not negative, in the sense of representing a mere absence of continuation, but instead 'frankly transfigure the events in which they were immanent'.[7] He cites *Anna Karenina*. Shakespeare's comedies before *Twelfth Night* are also works of art in which a retrospective view from the final scene is encouraged, and alters our understanding of the play as a whole. Essentially teleological, as *Volpone* and *The Alchemist* are not, their fifth-act marriages and revelations are designed to carry far more weight than Jonson's ultimate exposures of roguery or deflation of peccant humours. The fact that Volpone ends in prison, that Doll and Subtle flee over the back wall, or that Young Kno'well marries Bridget Kitely, constitutes in each case a tidy rounding-off of plot, a convenient place for the comedy to stop. These endings do not illuminate earlier scenes in the way that Marcade's announcement both elucidates and transforms the entire previous development of *Love's Labour's Lost*, or the

[7] Kermode, *The Sense of an Ending*, p. 175.

harmonies of *As You Like It* at its conclusion transfigure the 'broken music' (1.2.141–2) of the wrestling match at Duke Frederick's court. Even *The Taming of the Shrew* and *The Merry Wives of Windsor*, although in some respects standing apart from the other comedies, still ask to be considered afresh in the light of Katharine's final position, and of the accords worked out in Windsor Park.

Only with *Twelfth Night* did Shakespeare, apparently, lose faith in endings of this kind. The consequences of that divided fifth act, of admitting the fictional nature of the comic society, are manifest both in the ironically titled *All's Well That Ends Well* and in *Measure For Measure*. Even less than *Twelfth Night* can these be described as plays whose conclusions 'transfigure the events in which they were immanent'. Instead, realism collides painfully with romance. The world as it is submits at the end, with a calculated artificiality, to the laws of comic form. In doing so, it belittles those laws. There is no question in these comedies of some characters being excluded from the final scene, as they were in *Twelfth Night*. Everyone participates in the resolutions of *All's Well That Ends Well* and *Measure For Measure*, such as they are. These resolutions, however, float free and unattached above the comedies they supposedly crown. As admitted fairy-tale endings, they do not pretend to shadow reality. They are not even consonant with the previous development of the two plays, nor with the nature and personalities of the characters involved. It is hard not to see both these endings as confessions of the inadequacy of comedy resolutions. Certainly they stand at a remove from the damaged but poignant harmonies of *Twelfth Night*, let alone from the artistic balance and optimism of *As You Like It* in its fifth act. After *Measure For Measure* Shakespeare abandoned comedy. When he did return to the form in *Pericles*, some years later, he made it perfectly clear that he was now writing fairy-stories. The last plays as a group flaunt their own impossibilities and theatrical contrivance. They announce at the very beginning that they are only plays and insist throughout upon revealing the wires which make the puppets move. The marvellous restorations and discoveries which conclude *Pericles*, *Cymbeline* and *The Winter's Tale* are perfectly in accord with their nature as old tales: dreams before daylight, a dance of shadows. Only the emotions generated are, miraculously, real. Out of this readjustment of form Shakespeare seems to have drawn for a little while – up to the point of *The Tempest* and the incomplete symmetries of its fifth act – a renewed faith in comedy endings.

CHAPTER 6

'Nature's piece 'gainst fancy': the divided catastrophe in *Antony and Cleopatra* (1974/1992)

When Ajax, in Sophocles' play, announces that from now on he will humble himself before the gods he once disdained, that he is going down to the sea to cleanse himself of blood and to bury Hector's unlucky sword, it seems for a moment that there will be no tragedy. The hero's words, however, were ambiguous. When he reaches the sea, Ajax buries the sword of Hector in his own heart. Abruptly, the rejoicings of the Chorus turn to lamentation. Tecmessa discovers and shrouds her husband's body. Teucer, Ajax' half-brother, points bitterly to the ineluctable nature of divine will. The tragic movement of the play appears, at this point, to have completed itself: there has been a reversal, a discovery, and whatever Aristotle really meant by *catharsis*, the audience would seem to have been offered the experience or something like it – to have participated in, and perhaps been changed by, pity and fear. It seems perverse that Sophocles should extend his tragedy for almost four hundred lines beyond this apparently climactic moment. Why, when we could have ended with Ajax' heroic death and the valedictions of Teucer and the Chorus, should he insist upon a long, unpredictable final movement occupied entirely by the struggle between Teucer, Menelaus, Agamemnon and Odysseus over the issue of whether Ajax' body should be properly buried, or left above ground to rot?

Dissatisfaction with the last section of the *Ajax* was registered even in antiquity. The scholiast commenting on 1121 (where Teucer and Menelaus launch into twenty-two lines of stichomythic bickering) complained that 'this kind of quibbling is inappropriate to tragedy', and then went on to protest that although Sophocles apparently wanted to prolong his play after the death of Ajax, 'his artistic judgement failed and he dissipated the tragic emotion' ('epekteinai to drama thelesas epsukhreusato kai eluse to tragikon pathos').[1] The question of just *why* Sophocles might have wished to extend the action in this way the scholiast did not address. It has, however, been an issue of considerable concern to later commentators on the tragedy – some of them respectful of what has come to be called the 'diptych' structure of the *Ajax*, others considerably less admiring.[2]

Of the seven complete Sophoclean tragedies which survive, no fewer than three are 'diptychs' or, to put it another way, possess a divided catastrophe. The *Trachiniae* concentrates for three-quarters of its length upon Deianira, the neglected and aging wife of Heracles. When her son tells her that the 'love-charm' she sent her husband has destroyed him, she says farewell to the household things which symbolized her marriage, and then kills herself with a sword. Her body is displayed to the horrified Chorus of Trachinian women, and an ending seems imminent. Instead, the tragedy lurches forward again as Heracles himself, a character hitherto present only in name, suddenly arrives in Trachis to die. It is true that the hero's return to Trachis, after accomplishing his labours, has been predicated from the beginning. But it is also true that the last movement of the play, wholly taken up with Heracles, dismisses and diminishes Deianira in a way for which neither its previous development nor its title have left the audience prepared. The same actor must originally have played both Heracles and Deianira, but theatrical exigency, while explaining why they never meet, cannot account for the fact that she suddenly becomes important to him (and to everyone else) only as the agent of his fate. Heracles is not even interested in the revelation that his wife was innocent, deceived by the centaur, and that she now is dead.

The *Antigone* has, on the whole, been more lavishly admired than either the *Ajax* or the *Trachiniae*. It too, however, arrives at a tragic culmination only to press on beyond it. Antigone, who gives her name to the tragedy, and dominates most of it, is sent to her death by Sophocles with full tragic honours. Then, almost slightingly, he forgets her to focus on Creon – a man who has appeared previously as an oppressor courting his own ruin, but scarcely as a tragic

---

[1] Quoted in Malcolm Heath, *The Poetics of Greek Tragedy* (London, 1987), p. 204.

[2] The term 'diptych' for these Sophoclean plays was probably invented (see A. J. A. Waldock, *Sophocles the Dramatist*, Cambridge, 1951, p. 50) by T. B. L. Webster, *An Introduction to Sophocles* (Oxford, 1936), pp. 102–3. Also C. M. Bowra, *Sophoclean Tragedy* (Oxford, 1944), p. 116, G. M. Kirkwood, *A Study of Sophoclean Drama* (Ithaca, 1958, repr. 1967), pp. 42–54, and R. P. Winnington-Ingram, *Sophocles: An Interpretation* (Cambridge, 1979).

protagonist whose destruction could carry an entire, concluding section of the play. Sophocles even frustrates expectation by refusing to bring Antigone's body on stage at the end, to join those of Creon's wife and the son who dies, we are told, embracing her corpse. It is as though he feared that, by allowing her to take what would seem to be her logical place in this final tableau of death, he might blur the double, the essentially divided nature of this catastrophe.

No one (and most certainly not Sophocles) constructs plays in this fashion out of carelessness or ineptitude.[3] The risks are too obvious, the danger of anti-climax too great. It would seem more profitable to enquire into the possible rewards of a procedure so apparently wayward, so determined to defeat an audience's normal expectation that tragic action will culminate – as it does in Sophocles' *Oedipus Tyrannos* – in a single, unmistakable catastrophe in which subsidiary disasters (like Jocasta's suicide) resemble the moons which circle around Jupiter: co-existent satellites, not planets in their own right. A dramatist, I believe, is likely to experiment with a divided catastrophe when he wants, for some reason, to alter the way his audience has been responding to the experience of the play. It is a means of forcing reappraisal, a radical change of viewpoint at just that penultimate moment when an audience's complacency is likely to be greatest: when it is tempted to feel superior or even dismissive because it thinks there is little or nothing left for it to discover and understand.

It is important here to distinguish between the use, in Greek tragedy, of the divided catastrophe and of the *deus ex machina*. When the deified Heracles descends to break the human deadlock at the end of Sophocles' *Philoctetes*, or Apollo forcibly prevents arson and murder at the end of Euripides' *Orestes*, the action seems to have been halted and then, quite arbitrarily, reversed. Endings of this kind can be highly effective, but they are also likely to be ostentatiously fictional, parading (especially in the hands of Euripides) their own falsehood. The *deus ex machina* works characteristically to establish a gap between the story as it has traditionally been told and the more dispiriting, untidy, but also more convincing truth suggested by the rest of the play. A coda rather than an organic final movement, this sudden intrusion of the supernatural paradoxically reinforces the first, and

---

[3] A number of plays by Euripides, notably the *Hecabe* and the *Hippolytus* also utilize a 'diptych' or even (as in the case of the *Heracles*, possibly a response to Sophocles' *Ajax*) a 'triptych' structure.

psychologically realistic, conclusion, one articulating unresolvable human muddle and mess. So, the divine intervention of Heracles at the end of the *Philoctetes* highlights how realistically impossible it is for Philoctetes, after the years of pain on the island, to agree to go to Troy with Odysseus and the Atridae who betrayed him, even though that refusal means he will never be healed. In summarily marrying off the crazed Electra to Pylades at the end of the *Orestes*, and Hermione to the man who has just been trying to kill her, Euripides plumbs the abyss between emotional truth and what in the *Heracles* the protagonist calls the 'poets' wretched lies' ('aoidon oide dustenoi logoi').[4]

Both the *deus ex machina* and the divided catastrophe are ways of grappling with the immemorial problem of endings in fiction: with Kermode's insistence that endings are truly satisfactory only when they 'frankly transfigure the events in which they were immanent'.[5] The transfiguration achieved by the *deus ex machina* usually acknowledges itself to be spurious: a conclusion in which nothing is genuinely concluded. The divided catastrophe, on the other hand, imposes a new angle of vision, a change of emphasis which, while it need not conflict with the previous development of the tragedy, modifies our understanding of that development from a point beyond it in time. In its unpredictability and raggedness, moreover, it reflects life as it is normally experienced in a world where events invariably straggle on beyond the point that art would regard as climactic.

Because, for all their apparent disjunctiveness, endings of this kind rise out of and qualify an entire and particular dramatic context, no two divided catastrophes are exactly alike. In *Antigone*, the apparent rationality of allowing public considerations to take precedence over private is suddenly, and radically, undermined. Deianira's private catastrophe in the *Trachiniae*, by contrast, her sexual anguish and grief, is not only superseded but re-focussed by the agony of Heracles as he proceeds towards the fire that will re-locate her as only a small (if fatal) thread in the total web of his life, while transforming him to a god. In the case of the *Ajax*, Sophocles obviously wanted his audience to respond fully and emotionally to Ajax himself as a great, almost superhuman figure. The play is a unique example of what

[4] Euripides, *Heracles*, trans. William Arrowsmith, *The Complete Greek Tragedies*, ed. David Grene and Richmond Lattimore, 4 vols. (Chicago, 1953–9), III, line 1346. For the Greek text, see the Loeb *Euripides*, trans. Arthur S. Way (London, 1912), III, line 1346.

[5] Frank Kermode, *The Sense of an Ending: Studies in the Theory of Fiction* (Oxford, 1967), p. 175.

E. R. Dodds would call a shame-culture as opposed to a guilt-culture tragedy.[6] Ajax himself never regrets the fact that, purely out of wounded pride, he has attempted treacherously to murder all the other Greek leaders. He is sorry only that he failed. So dominant is Ajax through most of the play, so engrossing and persuasive as a tragic hero, that we accept his selfishness and passionate individualism, even as we accept behaviour on the part of heroes in the *Iliad* which, in a different context, would seem outrageous. There is no rival standard – or at least not until the second catastrophe, when Odysseus suddenly emerges as a kind of counter-hero. The man whose behaviour in the opening moments was embarrassingly pusillanimous, who quailed at the idea of approaching Ajax' tent even under the protection of Athena, stands firm now against both Agamemnon and Menalaus. Odysseus continues to insist until he wins that the body of Ajax, his own bitterest enemy, must be honourably interred. His reasons are not those of Teucer, nor are they ones that Ajax himself could have stomached, or even understood. What Odysseus sees is that no man is an island. The predicament of being human is common to us all, the potential for tragedy universal, the end the same. Ajax must be buried, whatever his sins, because (as Odysseus says) 'I too shall come to that necessity.'[7] Agamemnon misinterprets this as blatant self-interest, but the selfishness of Odysseus is really a form of generosity. Sophocles poises it against the heroic individualism of Ajax in the first catastrophe, not in order to denigrate or cancel out that catastrophe, but to modify our earlier understanding of it. There are other kinds of heroism, other ways of regarding the self and one's relationship to others. In the light of Odysseus' behaviour in the second catastrophe, Ajax becomes in retrospect a glorious anachronism: an epic hero whose attitudes we perceive as limited, without for a moment ceasing to recognize that they were great.

As a structural form, the divided catastrophe is distinctly rare if by no means unknown in sixteenth- and seventeenth-century tragedy. Corneille created in the last act of *Horace* (1640) a situation in some ways resembling that of the *Ajax*. Valère, Sabine, and the father of Horace argue at length before Tulle about what should be done with

---

[6] E. R. Dodds, *The Greeks and the Irrational* (Boston, 1951, repr. 1957), pp. 28–50.

[7] Sophocles, *Ajax*, trans. John Moore, *The Complete Greek Tragedies*, (Chicago, 1959), II, line 1365.

the hero who, at the end of Act IV, tarnished his day of glory by murdering Camille. Corneille himself felt impelled to apologize for this debate in the *Examen* of 1660. Camille's death

fait une action double, par le second péril où tombe Horace après être sorti du premier. L'unité de péril d'un héros dans la tragédie fait l'unité d'action; et quand il en est garanti, la pièce est finie, si ce n'est que la sortie même de ce péril l'engage si nécessairement dans un autre que la liaison et la continuité des deux n'en fasse qu'une action; ce qui n'arrive point ici, où Horace revient triomphant, sans aucun besoin de tuer sa soeur, ni même de parler à elle; et l'action serait suffisamment terminée à sa victoire.[8]

In fact, *Horace* would be a much lesser (if neo-classically more decorous) work had Corneille not allowed a man – Valère – at last to say some of the things about patriotism and glory that the women have been expressing all along, and then created a wholly new perspective on Horace himself and his actions by way of the king. Naked self-interest determines that the man who has made Tulle 'maître de deux États' should be adjudged, despite what he recognizes to be a crime 'énorme, inexcusable', to be 'au-dessus des lois'.[9]

English dramatists availing themselves of the divided catastrophe were less embarrassed by theory than Corneille. Marlowe, in *Edward II* (1592), craftily leads his audience to believe that Gaveston's death and the king's reaction to it will be climactic – and then presses on to Edward's shoddy and immediate replacement of his dead minion by Young Spencer, and the king's protracted and ignominious dying. In *The Duke of Milan* (1621) Massinger completes one half of the tragic action in Act IV and then explores its consequences in Act V. With the introduction there of a wholly new character (Francisco's wronged sister Eugenia) it suddenly becomes apparent that the destruction of Marcelia was only a means to an end, not (as it seemed previously) an end in itself. Even more striking are the diptych structures employed by Ford in *The Broken Heart* (1626) and Webster in *The Duchess of Malfi* (1613). Ford alters what had seemed to be the settled perspective of the entire play and even the meaning of its title by continuing beyond the deaths of Ithocles and Orgilus to the unexpected and cunningly delayed love-suicide of Calantha – a princess we have been led to regard as a kind of Fortinbras or

---

[8] Corneille, *Examen D'Horace*, in *Horace*, ed. Peter H. Nurse (Walton-on-Thames, 1963), p. 139.   [9] *Horace*, v.3.1740–54.

Malcolm, restoring order to the shattered state, not as the last and, in a sense, the most important of its tragic victims. Webster, even more daringly, after conducting the Duchess to death in Act IV, devotes a long fifth act to demonstrating how the world festers and becomes poisonous: good and evil tumbled together and equally impotent, once she has ceased to exist. The theatre audience, not merely Bosola, is forced into a new understanding of what the Duchess was and signified after the tragic climax (as it seemed at the time) has taken place.

Antony and Cleopatra appeared originally in the First Folio without act and scene divisions. This omission, as A. C. Bradley remarked, is of no particular consequence.[10] The tragedy divides logically and inevitably into five acts. Within this overall structure, Shakespeare has created a divided catastrophe, split between Acts IV and V. Antony's crushing defeat at Actium comes in Act III. In Act IV, scenes 4 through 8, there is for him a moment of respite. Not only does he seem temporarily to regain his lost heroic identity, he moves towards a reconciliation within himself of the warring values of Rome and Egypt. May it not be possible after all to be a soldier, a brilliant practitioner of 'the royal occupation' (IV.4.17) during the day, and still return to feast and sleep with Cleopatra in the night? Scenes 7 and 8 in particular are scenes in which Shakespeare almost persuades us that there will be no tragedy. Caesar is beaten back. Antony discovers that he can be 'himself... but stirr'd by Cleopatra' (I.1.42–3). That formula for the reconciliation of opposites which rang so false when it appeared in the first scene, here becomes almost true. And, for reasons buried deep in an audience's psychology, and in the play, we want terribly to believe it. After all, beneath the surface of this tragedy lies one of the great Renaissance wish-dreams: that of exchange and union, not merely harmony, between the masculine and feminine principles.

Shakespeare's use of the Heracles/Omphale myth – Antony tricked out in Cleopatra's tires and mantles while she wore his sword Philippan – has all too often been seen through the cold eyes of Octavius, as an indication of Antony's degradation. He 'is not more manlike / Than Cleopatra; nor the queen of Ptolemy / More womanly than he' (I.4.5–7). This essentially comic image of a transvestite Antony has for many readers epitomized the destruction

---

[10] A. C. Bradley, '*Antony and Cleopatra*', in *Oxford Lectures on Poetry* (London, 1909), p. 299.

of his masculinity at the hands of Cleopatra. Almost nothing in this play, however, up to the point of the final scene, is easy to judge. Certainly the simplistic view of Octavius needs to be balanced against other, more complicated Renaissance attitudes. In both versions of *Arcadia*, Philip Sidney treated Pyrocles' disguise as a woman as educative, if perilous: a prelude to emotional maturity. Even Artegall's shaming captivity in female dress in the castle of Spenser's Radigund was an oddly necessary part of his quest, preparation for his eventual and tempering union with Britomart, a woman who finds it natural to set out in search of her future husband wearing full armour and disguised as a man. Shakespeare may or may not have been aware of the iconographical tradition of synthesis, the blurring of identity between Venus and Mars, about which Edgar Wind writes in *Pagan Mysteries in the Renaissance*.[11] He was, however, the author of 'The Phoenix and Turtle'.

The heroic Antony of past time, the one recollected by Octavius, Pompey, Philo and Demetrius, was intensely male. On one level, it is bad that Cleopatra has made him womanish. On another, his Egyptian bondage asks to be read as an attempt to regain the kind of wholeness, that primal sexual unity, about which Aristophanes is half joking, half serious, in Plato's *Symposium*. Certainly there is something both unattractive and maimed about the exclusively masculine world of Rome in this play. It emerges in that distasteful all-male party on board Pompey's galley in Act II – a party which may ripen towards an Alexandrian revel, but never gets there – as it does in the public and chilly ostentation of Caesar's affection for his sister. Octavia, it seems, is the only woman in Rome and, unlike Portia and Calphurnia, Virgilia and Volumnia, she exists chiefly in order to be manoeuvred and pushed about by the men.

Cleopatra is as quintessentially female as the younger Antony seems to have been male. Left alone among women and eunuchs after Antony's departure, she finds that life is scarcely worth living. Yet she does try, in the second half of the play, to become a kind of epic, warrior maiden. She is not exactly cut out to be Britomart. When she tries to function as Antony's male body servant in Act IV, she merely succeeds in putting his armour on back to front. She must have looked preposterous wearing his sword. Although at Actium she announces that she will appear 'for a man' (III.7.18), it is as a fearful

[11] Edgar Wind, *Pagan Mysteries in the Renaissance* (London, 1958), pp. 81–96.

woman that, when the battle is joined, she runs away. It is important, nonetheless, that she should at least have tried to participate in Antony's masculine world – as Octavia never could, and Fulvia did in the wrong way – that he should feel that one of her rebukes to him for military delay 'might have well becom'd the best of men' (III.7.26). Like Desdemona in Cyprus, Cleopatra seems for a moment to reconcile opposites, to become Antony's 'fair warrior' (*Othello* II.1.182).

This moment of harmony is brief. As so often in the fourth acts of Shakespeare's tragedies, a door swings open to reveal the possibility of a happy ending, only to be slammed shut. What is unique about *Antony and Cleopatra* is that this door closes where it opened – in Act IV – not, as in the other tragedies, in Act V. In scene 12 of the penultimate act, Antony loses the third and final battle. This time, there can be no recovery. He also loses all conviction of his own identity, let alone any belief that the values of masculine Rome and feminine Egypt might, after all, be united and reconciled. Only the false report of her death restores Cleopatra for him as a person. His own identity, from the first scene of the play a persistent source of question and debate for other characters, now becomes for Antony himself as cloudlike and indistinct 'as water is in water' (IV.4.14). For him, as for Sophocles' Ajax, the way to self-definition, to recovery of the man that was, seems to lie through heroic suicide. Unlike Ajax, however, Antony bungles his death. The greatest soldier of the world proves to be less efficient than Eros, a former slave. Antony fails to kill himself cleanly, and no one will respond to his requests for a terminating blow. Decretas simply steals his sword and carries it to Caesar in the hope of promotion. After receiving the equivocal news that his serpent of old Nile has again demonstrated what Enobarbus called her remarkable 'celerity in dying' (1.2.144) – and reviving again at a propitious moment – the dying Antony must be hauled up to her, slowly and unceremoniously, because Cleopatra is too frightened to leave her monument. He finds it almost impossible to persuade the queen, caught up in a tirade against Fortune and Octavius, actually to attend to his last words. The advice he gives her, to trust Proculeius, is characteristically misguided. After a last attempt (which, under the circumstances, seems more pathetic than convincing) to re-establish his heroic identity as 'the greatest prince o'th'world...a Roman, by a Roman / Valiantly vanquish'd' (IV.15.54, 57–8), he expires in his destroyer's arms.

This is not, by comparison with that of Ajax, a glorious, or even a very controlled end. It does, however, distinctly feel like an end, in ways that go beyond Antony's individual death. This is already a long play, and one that seems to hanker after conclusion. The entire tragedy, after all, has been focussed on Antony far more than Cleopatra. He has been the character standing, like his ancestor Heracles, at the cross-roads, with an important decision to make. The journeying has been his, while she remained in Egypt, and these journeys have not been simply geographical, but the forays of a divided mind. Rome or Egypt, virtue or vice, the active life or one of pleasure, the Antony of the past or the sybarite of the present: between these antinomies his mind has swung, and the movement has to a large extent been the movement of the play. Now that he is dead, the world seems almost as vacant and still as Cleopatra imagines: a 'dull world, which in thy absence is / No better than a sty' (IV.15.61–2). There is room for tragic obsequy – 'The crown o' th' earth doth melt' (63), 'O, wither'd is the garland of the war' (64) – but surely not for tragic continuation. It is true that Cleopatra herself remains to be accounted for, but that conclusion appears to be foregone:

> We'll bury him; and then, what's brave, what's noble,
> Let's do't after the high Roman fashion,
> And make death proud to take us. Come, away,
> This case of that huge spirit now is cold.
> Ah, women, women! Come, we have no friend
> But resolution, and the briefest end.   (IV.15.86–91)

No matter how well one knows the play, it is hard not to be seduced at this point into believing in that 'briefest end'. Surely Cleopatra will send out on the spot for a commodity of asps and follow Antony without delay. Shakespeare does nothing to prepare his audience for a second catastrophe, sharply divided from the first, which will occupy an entire fifth act and more than four hundred lines of the tragedy.

Both historically and in Shakespeare's main source, Plutarch's *Life of Marcus Antonius*, Cleopatra's death was divided from Antony's by a significant gap of time. Drama, however, is an art of temporal compression. The Shakespeare who took the liberties he did with the chronology of Holinshed and Hall, and had already collapsed ten years of Plutarch into the playing time of *Antony and Cleopatra*, was scarcely going to worry about this kind of trivial inaccuracy. Nothing prevented him from sending the lovers to death within minutes of each other, and in the same final scene, as he had already done in *Romeo and Juliet* and *Othello*. This was the structure Dryden adopted later in *All For Love* (1677), where Cleopatra sinks lifeless into the arms of an Antony who has ceased to be only a short time before. In Thomas May's *Tragedy of Cleopatra, Queen of Egypt* (1626), as in Sir Charles Sedley's *Antony and Cleopatra* (1677), the deaths of the two protagonists are again contained within Act v, May's Cleopatra dying four short scenes after Antony's off-stage death, Sedley's after less than a hundred lines. Not only did these plays reject Shakespeare's divided catastrophe; in all three Antony's body is on stage, in full view of the audience, as Cleopatra unhesitatingly prepares for and accomplishes her own suicide. As for Cinthio, Jodelle, Garnier and Daniel, all of whom wrote tragedies on the subject before Shakespeare, none of them anticipated his use of the divided catastrophe.

Cinthio's *Cleopatra*, published in 1583 but acted in the 1540s, opens after Actium. It concentrates on Cleopatra, although the Prologue promises that some attention will be paid to Antony as well. In fact, the latter's appearances are confined to three scenes, and he encounters his mistress in only one of them – the first of Act II – at which point he is already dying. The rest of the play concerns Cleopatra's preparations for her own death, preparations which cannot occupy much time, because the queen finally expires of a broken heart while conducting the funeral rites over Antony's as yet unburied corpse. Jodelle's *Cléopâtre Captive*, first presented in 1552, published in 1574, addresses itself even more narrowly to the last day of its heroine's life. Antonie, véry recently dead, appears only at the beginning, as a singularly vindictive Senecan ghost. He yearns for his lady's company in the underworld, not to couch with her on flowers, or even walk hand in hand, but simply because he wants her to suffer hellish torments too. It comes as something of a surprise, after so ferociously moral an opening, to discover that Antonie's temptress is presented quite sympathetically: queenly and proud, honourable, and still deeply in love. When, after completing her lover's obsequies, she manages to outwit Caesar and kill herself (off-stage), and Proculeius rhapsodizes about the reunion of the pair in death, it is difficult not to feel, remembering the savageries of the ghostly Antonie, that the queen is in for a shock.

Garnier's *Antonie* appeared in 1578 and was translated by the Countess of Pembroke in 1590. Like Cinthio's play, it opens after Actium, with Antonie's downfall assured and the lovers estranged. They appear together only in the last scene, when Antonie is already dead. Cléopâtre, an honest and tender-hearted woman, apparently wills herself to die, and collapses over his corpse. Samuel Daniel's closet drama *Cleopatra* was conceived as a companion piece to the Countess of Pembroke's translation. Shakespeare must have known this play, initially published in 1594, then in a slightly revised form in 1599, as a number of specific parallels, additions or alterations to the story Plutarch told, attest. It seems, indeed, to have been Daniel who suggested to Shakespeare that Cleopatra was ageing and worried about it, and also that her death scene re-created the glory of Cydnus. Of more importance, however, is a connection which seems to have gone unnoticed. Something relatively simple and verbally explicit in Daniel, it becomes in Shakespeare both more generalized and diffuse, and infinitely complex: an underlying assumption conveyed not through direct statement but by structural, visual and metaphoric means.

Daniel's Cleopatra makes, in her opening soliloquy, a unique confession. She has been loved during her life by so many men that 'I to stay on Love had never leisure.'[12] Antony was different from these other men because he loved the autumn of her beauty, when she was no longer what she had been. During his lifetime, she took this love for granted, failing to distinguish it from that of a Caesar or a Pompey. Now that Antony is dead, she sees it truly and, for the first time in her life, she herself genuinely loves.

> Now I protest I do, now am I taught
> In death to love, in life that knew not how...
> For which in more then death, I stand thy debter,
> Which I will pay thee with so true a minde,
> (Casting up all these deepe accompts of mine)
> That both our soules, and all the world shall find
> All recknings cleer'd, betwixt my love and thine.[13]

This motive for suicide runs parallel through Daniel's play with Cleopatra's horror of being led in Caesar's triumph: indeed, they

[12] Samuel Daniel, *The Tragedie of Cleopatra* in G. Bullough, ed., *Narrative and Dramatic Sources of Shakespeare*, v (London), v.i.162.   [13] Daniel, 1.1.153–4, 182–6.

cannot be separated. When the Nuntius enters to describe her last moments: how Honour scorning Life led forth 'Bright Immortalitie in shining armour', he puns significantly on the words *part* and *touch*:

> she performs that part
> That hath so great a part of glorie wonne.
> And so receives the deadly poys'ning touch;
> That touch that tride the gold of her love, pure,
> And hath confirm'd her honour to be such,
> As must a wonder to all worlds endure.[14]

The acting imagery here – and there is a good deal more of it in the Nuntius account – obviously caught Shakespeare's imagination. But so did Daniel's association of the poisonous touch of the asp with the touchstone that distinguishes true gold. Daniel's Cleopatra alters her attitude towards Antony after she has lost him. In her own death, she sets out to transform their story: in effect, to do the impossible, and re-make past time. It is true that Daniel could not do a great deal with this idea. He was hampered, for one thing, by his obligatory French Senecanism. Shakespeare, on the other hand, exploited it fully. Daniel's play, indeed, is likely to have been the factor that impelled him towards the one use, in all his tragedies, of the divided catastrophe.

All four of these previous dramatizations of the Antony and Cleopatra story pick that story up late in its development. They tend to concentrate on Cleopatra at the expense of Antony, and they are chary of showing the lovers together. All dignify Cleopatra herself, for reasons that have something to do with neo-classical decorum, smoothing away the trivial or discreditable features of her character as outlined by Plutarch. She becomes, even in Daniel, a simple and straightforward woman, a great queen who ought (certainly) to have restrained her passions, but whose loyalty to Antony is beyond question. Lies do not come easily to these Cleopatras. Garnier is the only dramatist of the four who allows her to send the false report of her death to Antony, and he goes out of his way to explain and excuse it. When it comes, moreover, to the point of her suicide, there is nothing but compassion and respect. This last response almost seems inherent in the story. Even Plutarch, for whom Cleopatra represented

[14] Daniel, v.2.1562–3, 1592–7.

'the last and extreamest mischiefe of all other' that befell Antony, had respected her grief and 'her noble minde and corage' at the last.[15] Cleopatra would not seem a particularly likely candidate for inclusion in Chaucer's *Legend of Good Women*, but hers is the first story the poet tells. He makes it clear, moreover, that she stands beside Alcestis and Philomela, Ariadne, Hypermnestra and Lucrece solely because of the way she kept faith with Antony in her death. Even Spenser could be grudgingly respectful. Although he consigns Egypt's queen to the dungeon of Lucifera's House of Pride in Book I of *The Faerie Queene*, his description of 'high-minded Cleopatra that with stroke / of Aspes sting herselfe did stoutly kill' is at least half admiring.[16]

As a result of their sympathetic treatment of Cleopatra, all four tragedies are to some extent morally ambiguous. Certainly it becomes difficult to reconcile the attitude adopted toward her, and in particular toward her suicide, with the official commentary on the story provided by the prologues to these plays, or by those innumerable Choruses of depressed Egyptians concerned to point out that the wages of lust are death, not to mention a great deal of public misery. Even Dryden later, although he did without this kind of choric commentary, and rashly sub-titled his play 'The World Well Lost', was careful to declare in the preface that, for him, the principal appeal of the subject lay in 'the excellency of the Moral'.[17] It is not easy, in the face of *All For Love* itself, to see exactly what he means.

By transferring this moral ambiguity to Antony and Cleopatra themselves, Shakespeare greatly complicated and enriched the situation dramatized by his predecessors. As characters, his protagonists become singularly hard to assess or know. Part of this opacity springs from the fact that she has nothing even resembling a soliloquy until the last scene of the play, and that Antony is not much more forthcoming about his innermost feelings and intentions. Such reticence contrasts sharply not only with the inveterate mental unburdenings indulged in by the protagonists in Daniel or Garnier, but with Shakespeare's own, earlier tragic practice. Emrys Jones has argued that the construction of *Antony and Cleopatra* – the wasteful, drifting movement of all those short scenes – reflects the haphazard

[15] Plutarch, *The Life of Marcus Antonius*, in Bullough, pp. 273, 317.
[16] Edmund Spenser, *The Faerie Queene*, ed. A. C. Hamilton (London, 1977), 1.5.50.
[17] John Dryden, *All For Love*, in *The Works of John Dryden*, XIII, ed. G. R. Guffey, M. E. Novack, A. Roper (Berkeley, 1984), p. 10.

nature of phenomenal experience, that it seems more like the life process itself than like formal tragedy.[18] Certainly this effect is one that Shakespeare reinforces through his handling of the protagonists. With Romeo and Juliet before, with Othello and Desdemona, even with Macbeth and his wife, evaluation of the two individuals concerned had been possible, as well as encouraged. With Cleopatra and Antony, on the other hand, it simply cannot be managed. Our place of vantage is essentially that of Charmian or Enobarbus: people sufficiently close to their social superiors to witness informal and often undignified behaviour, without participating in motive and reflection like the confidants in Garnier or Jodelle. It is true that we see more of the picture, in range if not in depth, than these attendant characters. They cannot move, as we can, from Rome to Egypt and back again within an instant, nor are they party to all the scenes. Our perspective upon the affairs of Antony and his mistress is far wider than theirs, but this very breadth makes judgement more difficult, instead of less.

Other characters continually try to describe Shakespeare's Cleopatra and Antony, to fix their essential qualities in words. This impulse generates a number of the great, set speeches of the play: Enobarbus' evocation of Cleopatra at Cydnus, or Caesar's account of Antony crossing the Alps, like a lean stag inured to privation. It also makes itself felt in less obvious ways. Because of the constant shifting of scene, the protagonists are continually being discussed by bewildered rivals or subordinates while they themselves are absent, whether in Athens, Egypt, Alexandria, or Rome. The results of this unremitting attempt at evaluation are bewildering. In the course of the tragedy, Antony is called 'the noble Antony', the 'courteous Antony', the 'firm Roman', 'Mars', a 'mine of bounty', the 'triple pillar of the world', 'the demi-Atlas of this earth', the 'lord of lords, of infinite virtue', the 'crown o'th'earth' and 'the garland of the war'. These are only a few of the celebratory epithets. He is also 'poor Antony', a 'libertine', 'the abstract of all faults that all men follow', a 'gorgon', a 'sworder', an 'old ruffian', a 'doting mallard', the 'ne'er lust-wearied Antony', and 'a strumpet's fool'. There is no progression among these epithets, no sense of alteration in Antony's character during the play as there is, for instance, with Macbeth. Macbeth begins his tragedy as 'worthy Macbeth', and ends it as 'this

---

[18] Emrys Jones, *Scenic Form in Shakespeare* (Oxford, 1971), p. 275.

dead butcher', and if neither description seems wholly accurate at the time it is offered, still the space between them marks a tragic evolution. Antony, by contrast, is all the contradictory things that people say he is more or less simultaneously. Nor is there any neat division of the celebratory and the pejorative between Antony's friends and Antony's enemies. Enobarbus and Octavius are alike in acknowledging both sides of the moon: the bright as well as the dark.

Cleopatra's situation is similar. She is 'great Egypt', 'dearest queen', a 'rare Egyptian', a 'triumphant lady', 'Thetis', 'this great fairy', 'day o' the world', 'nightingale', 'eastern star', a 'most sovereign creature', a 'lass unparalleled' – but also a 'foul Egyptian', the 'false soul of Egypt', a 'witch', a 'gipsy', a 'strumpet', a 'whore', a 'trull', 'salt Cleopatra', a 'boggler', a 'morsel cold upon dead Caesar's trencher', Antony's 'Egyptian dish', the 'ribaudred nag of Egypt', and 'a cow in June'. It is possible to feel that language used so indiscriminately to describe a single person becomes meaningless and self-defeating, that it would be better to adopt Antony's method when he described a different serpent of old Nile to the drunken Lepidus. 'What manner o' thing is your crocodile?' And Antony replies:

It is shap'd, sir, like itself, and it is as broad as it hath breadth: it is just so high as it is, and moves with its own organs. It lives by that which nourisheth it, and the elements once out of it, it transmigrates.   (II.7.42–5)

It is of its own colour too, and the tears of it – like Cleopatra's – are wet.

The uncertainty is made all the more great by the fact that all the other characters in the play are – for Shakespeare – unusually monolithic. Enobarbus surprises somewhat in his death, but up to that point there is no temptation to depart from the general consensus that he is 'good Enobarb', 'strong Enobarb', a soldier and a blunt, honest man. Even Cleopatra can see that Octavia is 'patient'. For everyone else, Caesar's sister is also holy, modest, still and obedient. When Cleopatra, in her jealous rage, tries to add a few spurious qualities, to make out that her rival must also be dull of tongue and dwarvish, the falsehood is immediately recognizable, as it is when Caesar announces smugly that he has got rid of Lepidus because the latter had grown 'too cruel'. For Caesar himself, the epithets are again remarkably consistent: 'scarce-bearded Caesar', 'the young man', 'blossoming Caesar', 'the novice', the 'young Roman boy'.

Such references to his youth and rising star may be made in scorn or envy, but there is no real ambivalence about his character, regardless of whether it is held to be admirable or not.

When it comes to the vital task of assessing one another, Cleopatra and Antony seem as uncertain as everyone else. After she learns of Antony's Roman marriage, the queen tries to arrive at a stable judgement, only to fail:

> Let him for ever go – let him not, Charmian –
> Though he be painted one way like a Gorgon,
> The other way's a Mars. (ii.5.115–17)

This Janus-faced image of Antony derives from Elizabethan perspectives, pictures in which the identity of the object represented changed according to the angle from which it was viewed. Cleopatra finds that she must put up with two contradictory but equally real Antonys: on the one hand a Mars, 'a god in love to whom I am confin'd' (Sonnet 110), on the other an uncouth Gorgon with a heart of stone. Antony too wavers continually up to the point of his suicide in his estimation of Cleopatra. Is she his 'most sweet queen', or a 'triple-turn'd whore'? He can never be sure of her, only of his own irrational fascination, and even that has its unpredictable ebbs and flows. He loses faith again and again, mildly at the end of Act i, violently after Actium and when he catches her with Caesar's messenger in Act iii, catastrophically in Act iv. Cleopatra rules his life, but he remains uncertain as to just who she is. A man does not react with the hysteria of Antony at the mere sight of a messenger kissing his lady's hand unless he has hidden doubts.

We too have doubts. At the beginning of the play, Antony tells Cleopatra that his love is beyond reckoning, vaster than heaven and earth. A few minutes later, he is seeking ways to break off from 'this enchanting queen'. What really was in his mind when he agreed so readily to marry Octavia? Is he telling the truth when he assures Caesar's sister that 'I have not kept my square, but that to come / Shall all be done by th' rule' (ii.3.6–7)? Or a moment later, when he admits that 'I' th' East my pleasure lies' (41)? Cleopatra's behaviour is even more ambiguous. What was she intending to do in that scene with Thidias in Act iii, when she agrees smoothly that she has never loved Antony, but merely been forced into being his paramour? Was Caesar right to think that she could be bribed to murder her lover? Again, is she betraying Caesar, or Antony, in the quarrel with

Seleucus in Act v when, after so many protestations of her intent to follow Antony in death, we find her, a boggler to the last, trying to conceal the true amount of her treasure from Octavius?

These are questions which elude resolution. Continually, the play directs one back to Cleopatra's perspective picture, to the monster who is also a Mars. With these two people, moreover, the same quality tends to evoke contradictory descriptions, to become a virtue or a vice depending on the position of the viewer, or the particular moment of time. So, Cleopatra's infinite variety, the quality that holds Antony captive in Egypt for so long, both is and is not the same as her deplorable tendency to tell lies. Enobarbus himself, that shrewd and cynical commentator, cannot distinguish between her charm and her deceit at a number of crucial moments in the play. Nor, alas, can he separate Antony's extravagance, that culpable waste about which Caesar is so censorious, from Antony's bounty: that godlike generosity of spirit which makes Antony send Enobarbus' treasure after him when he defects to Caesar, and breaks the soldier's heart. Antony's behaviour, as Philo complains in the opening scene, 'o'er-flows the measure', but the very phrase reminds us that when the Nile does exactly this, it showers goodness and prosperity on everyone around. Caesar's 'bounty', on the other hand, on the one occasion when the word is associated with him (v.2.43), is a meaningless abstraction – a politic lie invented by Proculeius in the hope of deceiving Cleopatra. Antony's bounty is very different. A protean and mercurial thing, it is as stunning and unnecessary as the spontaneous leaps of the dolphin, and as difficult to restrain or assess. The worst things about Cleopatra and her lover are also, maddeningly, the best.

Like the vagabond flag of Caesar's image, *Antony and Cleopatra*, up to the point of its final scene, has seemed to go 'to and back, lackeying the varying tide, / To rot itself with motion' (1.4.45-7). This restlessness is not only that of shifting places – Alexandria to Rome, to Misenum, to Athens, to Parthia, to Rome again, to Egypt – but also the flickering of the perspective picture, as Mars dissolves into the Gorgon, and then again becomes Mars. By the end of Act iv, we long for stasis, for the movement to stop. But it refuses to do so. Most of Act v is taken up with Cleopatra's hesitation and delay. Indeed, all of its dramatic tension derives from the uncertainty as to whether, despite her protestations, she will keep her word and follow Antony in death. And, oddly enough, in a way for which there is no parallel elsewhere in Shakespeare, an audience *wants* Cleopatra to die. It is a reaction that flies in the face of normal tragic convention. Most of the suspense generated in the fifth act of *Hamlet* springs from an undefined hope that somehow the prince will manage to kill Claudius and escape alive. In *Othello*, there is the tantalizing possibility, raised specifically in the 'brothel' scene, when the Moor finally accuses Desdemona directly, that he will recognize her innocence before it is too late or, in *Romeo and Juliet*, that Juliet will wake before Romeo takes the poison. Only in *Antony and Cleopatra* do we long for a protagonist who has not, like Macbeth, been villainous to decide to die, and do so.

This unconventional desire was precisely what Shakespeare set out, by way of the divided catastrophe, to elicit. In gratifying it, he also modifies our feeling about the entire previous development of the tragedy. As Cleopatra wavers and procrastinates, we see that there can be only one way of putting doubt and ambiguity to rest. This love story has fluctuated continually between the sublime and the ridiculous, the tragic and comic. It has been impossible to decide which of the two sets of perspective images was the right one, or to reach any compromise between them. Only if Cleopatra keeps faith with Antony now and dies can the flux of the play be stilled, and their love claim value. The act itself is indeed one that 'shackles accidents and bolts up change' (v.2.6), and not merely in the sense that it will free Cleopatra herself from mutability and time. More importantly, it will transform the past, re-make it in terms more far-reaching than anything envisaged by Daniel's Cleopatra. The vagabond flag will come to rest, leaving the triple-turned whore a lass unparalleled, the Gorgon an immutable (if injudicious) Mars. It may even be possible to adumbrate a reconciliation between masculine Rome and feminine Egypt more lasting than the one so fleetingly achieved in Act IV – one which will diminish Caesar forever by comparison.

Caesar, of course, is the enemy. He needs to get a living Cleopatra back to Italy because, as he says, 'her life in Rome / Would be eternal in our triumph' (v.1.65–6). If only he can do this, he will fix the qualities of the story forever in his own terms, which are those of the strumpet and the Gorgon, not the lass unparalleled and the Mars. Cleopatra will dwindle into a parody queen in the epic pageant of his own imperial greatness, and Antony become the brother-in-arms who deserted his superior for a royal trull, and got what he deserved.

This threat makes it imperative not only that Cleopatra should die, but that she should die in the way she does – ostentatiously, as a tragedy queen. The achievement is not easy. At last, Cleopatra makes up her mind. Despite her apparent duplicity with Seleucus, her anxious enquiries as to Caesar's intentions, and her own fear of physical pain, she does finally recognize and repudiate Octavius' plan: 'He words me, girls, he words me, that I should not be noble to myself' (v.2.191–2). She understands what will happen in Rome:

> the quick comedians
> Extemporally will stage us, and present
> Our Alexandrian revels. Antony
> Shall be brought drunken forth, and I shall see
> Some squeaking Cleopatra boy my greatness
> I' th' posture of a whore.   (v.2.216–21)

If she does not die well, this is the way her story, and Antony's, will be told for all of time to come. The puppeteers, the ballad-makers and comedians will cheapen and impoverish a love which was flawed at best, but never merely absurd.

Appropriately, the last obstacle Cleopatra faces on her way to death is Comedy, personified by that ribald and garrulous country-man who brings her the asps, concealed in his basket of figs. Patiently, the woman who once haled a messenger about the stage by the hair for intruding on her with unwelcome tidings, listens and even responds to the clown's slanders about women: to a kind of sexual innuendo that threatens to diminish the whole basis of love tragedy. When he cautions her that the worm is not worth feeding, she asks humorously, 'Will it eat me?' (v.2.271), bringing together and reconciling in death two warring images of herself from earlier in the play: the positive one in which she was 'a morsel for a monarch' (1.4.31), but also Antony's savage description of her as mere broken meats, 'A morsel cold upon / Dead Caesar's trencher' (III.116–17). When she finally persuades the clown to depart – and the woman committed to tragedy has to ask comedy to leave no fewer than four times – we feel that precisely because she has walked through the fire of ridicule, the thing she most dreads, and potentially the thing most deadly for her, she has earned the right to say, 'Give me my robe, put on my crown, I have / Immortal longings in me (v.2.280–1). And she does so at once. Comedy flowers into tragedy, without a break or a mediating pause.

'Immortal' was one of the words the clown stumbled over most absurdly: 'I would not be the party that should desire you to touch [the worm]', he cautioned, 'for his biting is immortal; those that do die of it do seldom or never recover' (v.2.245–8). It must take courage for Cleopatra to use that word 'immortal' again, so differently, within the space of only a few lines. She succeeds, however, in winning it back as part of the vocabulary of tragedy. Indeed, she even imposes, in retrospect, a truth upon the clown's blunder. The biting of this particular asp will indeed be 'immortal': the cause of Cleopatra's, and through her of Antony's undying fame.

Cleopatra dies as a tragedy queen, even her crown instantly adjusted by Charmian, just before her own death, because it threatens to seem 'awry'. In doing so, she not only redeems the bungled and clumsy nature of Antony's death in Act IV, catching it up and transforming it within her own flawless farewell, but crystallizes and stills all the earlier and more ambiguous tableaux of the play: Cydnus, her appearance throned in gold as the goddess Isis, even the dubious spectacle presented to the Roman messenger in the opening scene. This is a divided catastrophe of a very special kind. Not only does it alter the way we feel about the previous development of the tragedy, hushing our doubts about Cleopatra's faith, it clarifies something about historical process. There does, after all, seem to have been something about this death, as the story was perpetuated in time, that made it impossible not only for Plutarch, but for Cinthio and Jodelle, Garnier and Daniel (not to mention Chaucer and Spenser) to condemn her entirely, whatever the overall moral pattern of the work in which she appeared.

Shakespeare's second catastrophe helps to explain this phenomenon. It demonstrates how the ending of this story transfigures its earlier, more suspect stages, the modification of feeling which it imposes upon readers or audiences repeating and re-enacting what has happened within historical time. In the play itself, we watch as Octavius acquiesces to Cleopatra's tragedy, consents indeed to become its Fortinbras. No parody queen will be led in triumph before a hooting mob; there will be no bawdy Roman ballads, no comic puppet-shows presenting and coarsening the revels of Alexandria. Instead,

> She shall be buried by her Antony;
> No grave upon the earth shall clip in it
> A pair so famous...

> ...Our army shall
> In solemn show attend this funeral,
> And then to Rome. Come, Dolabella, see
> High order in this great solemnity.   (v.2.358–60, 363–6)

Because Cleopatra has left him no real choice, Caesar consents to become a supporting actor in her tragedy. Indeed, his order that the Roman army should, 'in solemn show', attend her funeral extends and develops the spectacle she has contrived.

It has sometimes been suggested that Cleopatra is necessarily diminished by ending her life as histrionically as she does, assuming costume and a role, gathering Iras and Charmian as minor players around her, and confronting Caesar and his soldiers when they break in upon her with a contrived and formal tableau of death. That is surely to misunderstand. When he remembered Cleopatra at Cydnus, Enobarbus said that the sight 'beggar'd all description'. As she lay in her pavilion, she o'er-pictured 'that Venus where we see / The fancy outwork nature' (II.2.200–1). The living Cleopatra surpassed a picture of Venus in which art itself had outdone reality. Cleopatra herself develops this favourite Renaissance paradox when she tells Dolabella, shortly before her death, about the mythical Antony of her dreams: 'His legs bestrid the ocean, his rear'd arm / Crested the world' (v.2.82–3). Asked if there 'was or might be such a man / As this I dreamt of', Dolabella answers literally: 'Gentle madam, no'. And Cleopatra flashes out:

> You lie up to the hearing of the gods!
> But if there be or ever were one such,
> It's past the size of dreaming. Nature wants stuff
> To vie strange forms with fancy, yet t'imagine
> An Antony were nature's piece 'gainst fancy,
> Condemning shadows quite.   (v.2.95–100)

An Elizabethan cliché, the conceit of an art more realistic than reality itself, acquires in the second catastrophe of *Antony and Cleopatra* a special meaning. Cleopatra here bestows upon Antony an heroic identity so colossal, but also in a sense so true – after all, those kingdoms dropping like plates, unregarded, from his pockets summon up the careless Antony we have always known – that it will defeat Time. She is also working towards her own death scene, a fictional masterpiece of another kind, out-classing the normal fictions of tragedy by also being real. In this death, reality will borrow the techniques of art as a means of fighting back against oblivion.

Moreover, it will be victorious. Hitherto, all the images of stasis offered by a tragedy yearning towards rest have been either distasteful, like Caesar himself and his 'universal peace' spread through a silent world from which everything remarkable has departed, or else fragile: 'the swan's down feather, / That stands upon the swell at the full of tide, / And neither way inclines' (III.2.48–50). In the very next moment, that tide will ebb. It is Cleopatra, no longer the moon's votaress but 'marble constant', who finally arrests the eddying of the vagabond flag, and gives to the swan's down feather an immutable poise. She does so by creating a tableau, still and contemplative in *living* art, which transfigures the events in which it was immanent in a way that Sophocles might have understood.

CHAPTER 7

Livy, Machiavelli and Shakespeare's
Coriolanus (1985)

In Book 7 of his great history of Rome, from her foundation to the time of Augustus, Titus Livius recounts, with a certain admixture of scepticism, the story of Marcus Curtius. In the year 362 BC, a chasm suddenly opened in the middle of the Forum. The soothsayers, when consulted, declared that only a ritual sacrifice of the thing 'wherein the most puissance and greatnes of the people of Rome consisted' could close the fissure and 'make the state of Rome to remain sure for ever'.[1] Much discussion followed, but no one could determine what that precious thing might be. Then Marcus Curtius, described in Philemon Holland's Elizabethan translation of Livy as 'a right hardie knight and martiall yong gentleman', 'rebuked them therfore, because they doubted whether the Romanes had any earthly thing better than armour and valor'. Armed at all points, he mounted a horse 'as richly trapped and set out as possiblie he could devise', and – like Hotspur at Shrewsbury – 'leapt into destruction' (*2 Henry IV*, 1.3.33). The gulf closed.

In the Rome of Marcus Curtius, a century after the time of Coriolanus, it is by no means obvious that valour is 'the chiefest virtue', the one to which the city still owes her greatness. Times have changed. The Romans need to be reminded, by the gods and by the heroic action of one 'martial yong gentleman', that formerly, as Plutarch asserts in his 'Life of Coriolanus', 'valliantnes was honoured in Rome above all other vertues: which they called *Virtus*, by the name of vertue selfe, as including in the generall name, all other speciall vertues besides. So that *Virtus* in the Latin, was asmuche as valliantnes.'[2] This passage, in North's translation, caught Shake-

---

[1] *The Romane Historie Written by T. Livius of Padua*, trans. Philemon Holland (1600), book 7, pp. 252–3.

[2] *Plutarch's Lives of the Noble Grecians and Romanes*, trans. Sir Thomas North (1579), in *Narrative and Dramatic Sources of Shakespeare*, ed. Geoffrey Bullough, 8 vols. (London, 1957–75), v, p. 506.

speare's eye. But the version of it that he introduced into Act II, scene 2 of *Coriolanus* is qualified and uncertain. 'It is held', Cominius says as he begins his formal oration in the Capitol in praise of Coriolanus,

> That valor is the chiefest virtue, and
> Most dignifies the haver; if it be,
> The man I speak of cannot in the world
> Be singly counterpois'd.   (II.2.83–7)

'If', as Touchstone points out in *As You Like It*, is a word with curious properties and powers: 'Your If is the only peacemaker; much virtue in If' (V.4.102–3). Cominius' 'If', like Touchstone's, is a kind of peacemaker. Set off by the cautious appeal to an opinion in 'it is held', it introduces a slight but significant tremor of doubt into what in Plutarch had been fact, rock-hard and incontrovertible. Cominius goes on to celebrate Coriolanus in battle as a huge, irresistible force – a ship in full sail, bearing down and cleaving the aquatic vegetation of the shallows, a planet, the sea itself – but 'If' continues to mediate between martial prowess as a traditional all-sufficing good and the possible claims of other human ideals. It is as though Shakespeare's Cominius already had an intimation of that later Rome in which Marcus Curtius would be obliged to demonstrate to a forgetful city that valour was indeed her 'chiefest virtue'.

In writing *Coriolanus*, Shakespeare depended primarily upon Plutarch, as he had for *Julius Caesar* and *Antony and Cleopatra*. Once again, North's translation provided him with the dramatic skeleton, and even some of the actual words, of his play. But this time, he also had recourse to Livy, the chronicler of Coriolanus, Marcus Curtius, and the fortunes of republican Rome. It has long been recognized that lines 134 to 139 in Menenius' fable of the belly, those concerned with the distribution of nourishment through the blood, derive from Livy's, not Plutarch's, version of the tale. Those six lines are important in that they provide tangible evidence that Livy's *Ab Urbe Condita* was in Shakespeare's mind when he was meditating *Coriolanus*. But they matter far less than a series of overall attitudes, attitudes peculiar to this play, which I believe Shakespeare owed not to any one, particular passage in Livy, but to his history as a whole – in itself, and also as it had been interpreted by another, celebrated Renaissance reader.

As an author, Livy is likely to have impinged upon Shakespeare's consciousness at a relatively early age. Selections from his work were often read in the upper forms of Elizabethan grammar schools, ranking in popularity only behind Sallust and Caesar.[3] As a young man, Shakespeare drew material from Book 1 in composing his 'graver labour', *The Rape of Lucrece*, published in 1594, six years before Philemon Holland's translation made the whole of Livy available in English. Shakespeare customarily consulted more than one historical source. He had never, before *Coriolanus*, written a play set in republican Rome, in a mixed state of the kind that, for various reasons, was attracting considerable attention in Jacobean England. Livy was the acknowledged, great repository of information about this republic, as well as its fervent champion. It was almost inevitable that Shakespeare should return to *Ab Urbe Condita*, now handsomely 'Englished' by Holland, in order to remind himself of what was happening in Rome at the beginning of the fifth century BC. What he found there was an account of Caius Martius which, although the same in its essentials as that of Plutarch in his 'Life of Coriolanus', was different in emphasis, and radically altered by a context from which it could not be disentangled.

Unlike Plutarch, the biographer of great men, author of *Lives* carefully paired for moral and didactic purposes, Livy was pre-eminently the historian of a city. Throughout the thirty-five extant books of his history, he never breaks faith with the intention expressed in his very first sentence: to record the *res populi Romani*, the achievements of the people of Rome. By *populi*, Livy does not just mean plebeians. He means everyone, all classes, the rulers and the ruled, the leaders and the led. In Livy's eyes, no man, no matter how great, should regard himself as superior to the state, or even coequal. Plutarch consistently plays down the political concerns of Dionysius of Halicarnassus, one of his main sources of information as to the nature of Rome's past. Livy, by contrast, is far less interested in individual destiny than he is in the changing character of Rome's institutions, her expansion through the Mediterranean, and the increasingly complex social and economic equilibrium worked out within the city over a long period of time. So, characteristically, he does not find it especially important to determine whether Coriolanus himself was, in fact, killed by his Volscian allies after he turned back

[3] T. W. Baldwin, *William Shakspere's Small Latine & Lesse Greeke*, 2 vols. (Urbana, 1944), II, pp. 573–4.

from the gates of Rome, or whether he survived, eating the bitter bread of exile, into old age. Either ending is possible. What really matters to Livy in the Coriolanus story is, first, that thanks to the intervention of the women, Rome herself escaped destruction and even acquired a fine new temple dedicated to Fortuna Muliebris. Secondly, that a new stage was reached in the protracted but necessary struggle between patricians and plebeians – a struggle in which there was right on both sides.

Although Collingwood perversely tried to deny it, Livy is essentially a developmental historian. As T. J. Luce writes in his study of the composition of Livy's history, 'the central theme of his narrative is that the growth of Rome and the genesis of her institutions was a gradual, piecemeal process that took many centuries'. Book 2, in which the story of Caius Martius is told, addresses itself specifically to the question of how *libertas* was achieved, actually, and in men's minds. It begins with threats from without: Lars Porsinna of Clusium and the attempt of the exiled Tarquins to regain control of the city. It ends with the overcoming of threats from within, represented by Spurius Cassius, and by Coriolanus.[4] In describing the arrogance of Coriolanus, his stubborn refusal to countenance the tribunate, Livy writes with the Tarquin kings and their tyranny in mind, and also in full awareness of what (historically) was to come: an increase in the number of tribunes to ten, publication of the laws, permission for plebeian/patrician intermarriage, and the opening of the highest civic offices, including the consulship itself, to plebeians. Livy himself went on to chronicle these changes, leaving Coriolanus almost entirely forgotten in the past, except as the focus (intermittently remembered) of a cautionary tale. However useful in time of war, men like Coriolanus are a threat to the balance of the state, to an evolving republic which must try to take them with it but, if it cannot, has no option but to discard them by the way.

Although the populace in *Julius Caesar* includes one witty shoemaker, and there are – temporarily – two sceptics among the followers of Jack Cade, it would be hard to claim that Shakespeare displays much sympathy for urban crowds in the plays he wrote before *Coriolanus*. In depicting the fickle and destructive mob roused so skilfully by Mark

[4] T. J. Luce, *Livy: The Composition of His History* (Princeton, 1977), p. 238 and *passim*.

Antony, the ignorant and brutal rebels of *2 Henry VI*, even those xenophobic Londoners rioting over food prices in the scene he contributed to *Sir Thomas More*, he is savagely funny, but also almost wholly denigratory. That is no reason for assuming, as critics tend to do, that his attitude in *Coriolanus* must be similar. In fact, this play is unique in the canon for the tolerance and respect it accords an urban citizenry. The very first scene of the tragedy presents plebeians who arrest their own armed rebellion in mid-course, not because of outside intervention by a social superior – the persuasive tactics of a Flavius and Marullus, a Lord Clifford or a Sir Thomas More – but freely, of their own volition, because it is important to them to enquire exactly what they are doing, and why. The Roman people here are not distinguished by personal names. They speak, none-theless, as individuals, not as a mob. They care about motivation, their own and that of their oppressors, and they are by no means imperceptive. Even the belligerent First Citizen thinks it important to establish that hunger has forced him into violence, not a 'thirst for revenge' (1.1.2–5). Not one of the citizens attempts to deny that Caius Martius has served Rome nobly, whatever his attitude towards them, nor do they make the mistake of thinking that he stands out against a distribution of surplus corn to the commons because he is personally covetous. The First Citizen contents himself with sug-gesting that this man's valorous deeds have been performed for suspect reasons: out of pride, and a desire to please his mother, rather than from disinterested love of his country. This is not very far from the truth. The Second Citizen has already cautioned the First against speaking 'maliciously' (line 35), and yet the events of the play will, to a large extent, justify the latter's analysis.

The Roman people in this play are politically unsophisticated and, sometimes, confused and naive. Like Williams and Bates confronting the disguised Henry V on the eve of Agincourt, they can be blinded by rhetoric, even though theirs is in fact the stronger case. The English common soldiers allowed themselves to be diverted from the crucial issue of whether or not Henry's cause in France was 'good'. The citizens of Rome are so impressed by the fable of the belly that they fail to detect the logical flaw in its application: the fact that in the present famine the senators are indeed selfishly 'cupboarding the viand' (1.1.100) of last year's harvest in their storehouses, that the belly, by withholding nourishment from the rest of the body politic, has ceased to perform its proper social function. They also allow themselves to be manipulated by their tribunes. And yet it matters that, unlike the crowd in *Julius Caesar*, a crowd which has no opinions of its own, merely those which are suggested to it, first by Brutus and then by Mark Antony, the citizens of the republic can think for themselves. They draw their own conclusions, quite unaided, about the behaviour of Coriolanus when he stands in the market-place and insultingly demands their voices. If, as the First Citizen says in that scene, the price of the consulship is 'to ask it kindly' (II.3.75), Coriolanus at the end of it has been given something for nothing. The people sense this, although even here a dissenting voice is raised: 'No, 'tis his kind of speech, he did not mock us' (II.3.161–2). 'Almost all' the citizens, we are told – not all, because there are other, independent opinions – 'repent in their election' (lines 254–5). The tribunes deliberately inflame the commons against Coriolanus, finally transforming them from angry but rational individuals into 'a rabble of Plebeians' (III.1.179 SD). They are right, however, when they claim that they have a mandate from the people, that the sudden reaction against Coriolanus is 'partly... their own' (II.3.262).

The worst thing the plebeians ever do is something for which Coriolanus himself never berates them. He is not present in Rome to witness their panic-stricken reaction to the news of his league with Aufidius, or the irrational fury they unleash upon Junius Brutus, their own tribune. This is almost the only occasion on which their behaviour can be said to approximate to that of Shakespeare's earlier crowds. In this play, it is exceptional rather than characteristic. It is true that, when cunningly prompted to do so by the tribunes in Act III, the plebeians claim that they alone embody Rome: 'the people', they shout, 'are the city' (III.1.199). This is patently false, as they themselves know in their calmer moods. Rome cannot be identified solely with her commons. But then, the assumption with which Menenius begins the play is equally false, when he tells the citizens that, however great their sufferings in the present dearth, they cannot strike against

> the Roman state, whose course will on
> The way it takes, cracking ten thousand curbs
> Of more strong link asunder than can ever
> Appear in your impediment. (I.1.69–72)

The Roman state, according to this formulation, is not only exclusively patrician, excluding the proletariat, it resembles Corio-

lanus himself on the field of battle: a titanic machine, its motion
timed with dying cries, mowing down every human obstacle in its
path. Of course the city is not the exclusive property of the people,
but neither does it belong solely to the upper class.

In the course of the play, Menenius, Cominius, their colleagues in
the Senate, even Volumnia, will be forced to recognize that this is so.
Although a few young hot-heads among the patricians may flatter
Coriolanus that he does the 'nobler' to tell the mutable, rank-scented
meinie just what he thinks of them, how unworthy they are to possess
any voice in the government of Rome, although a few may toy with
the idea, after his banishment, of abolishing the newly established
institution of tribunes, these are not serious or consequential
responses. Brutus and Sicinius are scarcely lovable men. There is a
world of unsavoury implication in Brutus' reaction to the news of
Coriolanus' alliance with the Volscians in Act IV: 'Would half my
wealth / Would buy this for a lie' (IV.6.158–9). But they are clearly
right in their belief that, once established as consul, Coriolanus would
wish to strip from the people the hard-won concessions they have just
gained. Such a course of action could only be disastrous. The
tribunate, however selfish or inadequate their own performance in
the office, is now a political fact. Once granted, however reluctantly,
the right of the Roman people not just to rubber-stamp a consular
election by exercising their ancient and vulgar prerogative of
examining patrician scars in the market-place, but to make their own
needs and wishes felt through their representatives, cannot be
withdrawn.

Significantly, in the crisis of Act III, Menenius stops talking about
a patrician juggernaut flattening dissenting plebeians like so many
weeds. He asks rather that there be 'On both sides more respect'
(III.1.180), begins to refer to 'the whole state' (III.2.34), appeals to
'good Sicinius' (III.1.191), 'worthy tribunes' (III.1.264), and admits
that the division which has cleft the city 'must be patch'd / With
cloth of any color' (lines 251–2). The tribunes, he admits, are the
'people's magistrates', and likely to remain so (III.1.201–2). When
Sicinius says to him, 'Noble Menenius, / Be you then as the people's
officer' (III.1.327–8), he accepts the designation without demur, and
goes off to plead with Coriolanus to submit himself to judgement. Of
course Menenius, like the other patricians, is trying to be tactful and
conciliatory in what has suddenly become a desperate situation.
Although it amuses him to observe the ebb and flow of popular life in

the market, Menenius' basic contempt for the 'beastly plebeians', Rome's 'rats', her 'multiplying spawn', is deep-rooted. Attitudes like these are not changed overnight. Yet he recognizes, like all the patricians except Caius Martius, that a change in the structure of government has become inevitable. Not one of them welcomes the innovation, but they also see that if civil strife is not to 'unbuild the city, and to lay all flat' (line 197), to 'sack great Rome with Romans' (line 314), they have no alternative but to move with the times.

Only Coriolanus refuses to accept that a new stage has been reached in the evolution of Rome.[5] In Act I, he affirmed bluntly that he would rather 'the rabble... unroof'd the city' (1.1.218) than that any concessions to them should be made. He never relinquishes this opinion. For him, the patrician compromise of Act III, the refusal of the nobles to entertain the prospect of such destruction, take his advice, and try to trample the new power of the tribunes in the dust, constitutes a betrayal both of himself, personally, and of an older Rome to which, in his eyes, only he now remains true. This is why, despite the manifest loyalty and grief of Cominius, Menenius, and the young nobility of Rome, those 'friends of noble touch' (IV.1.49) – Cominius even tries to accompany him into exile – he can tell Aufidius later that 'our dastard nobles' have 'all forsook me' (IV.5.75–6). Menenius, in Act I, made the mistake of reducing the Roman state to her patrician members. The plebeians, briefly, were persuaded to identify the city with themselves. But only Coriolanus ever deludes himself that he, a single individual, constitutes Rome's best and only self. It is a delusion which manifests itself in the magnificent absurdity of his response to the tribunes' sentence of banishment in Act III – 'I banish you!' (III.3.123) – where he effectively tries to exile most of Rome's population, that plebeian majority he detests. Because he thinks in this way, it is possible for him to betray his country without ever admitting to himself that he is, like the petty spy Nicanor, introduced (significantly) just before Coriolanus' arrival at the house of Aufidius in Act IV, a Roman traitor.

[5] In the discussion which followed this paper as originally presented at the 1984 Shakespeare Conference in Stratford-upon-Avon, Professor John W. Velz drew my attention to contemporary knowledge of Lucius Annaeus Florus' *Epitome Bellorum Omnium Annorum*, with its account of Rome's passage through infancy, youth and manhood, to old age. Velz's own article, 'Cracking strong curbs asunder: Roman destiny and the Roman hero in *Coriolanus*' (*English Literary Renaissance*, 13 (1983), 58–69), examines Shakespeare's indebtedness to Virgil in *Coriolanus* in ways that are important and persuasive, arriving at a reading of the play similar, in some ways, to my own.

In a sense, the possibility of such a betrayal has been present throughout Coriolanus' adult life. It is bound up with his essential and crippling solitariness, and also with his failure ever to consider how much his heroism has truly been dedicated to Rome as a city, and how much to his own self-realization and personal fame. Never, it seems, has it occurred to him that the two motives, the public and the private, might under certain circumstances conflict, or that the one might require adjustments and concessions from the other. Of course, he did not mean to be taken literally when he declared of Tullus Aufidius in Act I that,

> Were half to half the world by th'ears, and he
> Upon my party, I'd revolt, to make
> Only my wars with him.   (I.1.233-5)

The lines are revealing, nonetheless, in the way they elevate a purely personal competition above the claims of a country or a cause. Rome will always need great soldiers, dedicated generals and strong defenders. Livy makes this quite clear. Nonetheless, it is an urban republic, not the plains of Troy, a society which no longer, whatever may have been the case in the past, is based exclusively, or even primarily, upon an ethos of war.

One of the great themes running through and unifying Livy's history of Rome is that of the gradual adjustment over the centuries of the claims of peace and war. Numa Pompilius, as the tribune Brutus reminds us in Shakespeare's play (II.3.237-40), was one of Coriolanus' ancestors, that legendary king of Rome who decided in the eighth century BC that it was time steps were taken to civilize his people. Accordingly, as Livy writes (in Holland's translation), he began

by good orders, lawes, and customes, to reedifie as it were that cittie, which before time had been new built by force and armes. Whereunto, he seeing that they might not be brought and framed in time of warre, whose hearts were alreadie by continuall warfare growne wild and savage: and supposing that this fierce people might be made more gentle and tractable, through disuse of armes, he therefore built the temple of *Janus* in the nether end of the street Argiletum, in token both of warre and peace.[6]

Shakespeare could have read about Numa, the great lawgiver and architect of a social and religious order, in Plutarch. There, Numa

---

[6] Livy, *Romane Historie*, p. 14.

has a 'Life' of his own, paired with that of the Spartan ruler Lycurgus. He is also mentioned in the 'Life of Coriolanus'. But it is only Livy who patiently teases out the intimate connection, unfolding over a vast stretch of years, between Rome's need to cultivate the arts of peace as well as war, and the internal struggle between her patricians and plebeians. Over and over in the days of the republic, as Livy makes plain, the patricians depended upon war as a way of stifling civic dissension, busying giddy minds with foreign quarrels in order to keep them distracted from injustices and inequalities at home. Sometimes, this strategy worked, uniting Rome temporarily against a foreign foe. But increasingly, over the years, it did not. Rome could not wage war without the help of common soldiers, could not (indeed) even protect her own frontiers. And so, unhappy and mistreated plebeians either declined to enlist or, if impressed, refused once they arrived on the battlefield to fight. It was virtually the only weapon they possessed in their attempt to wrest some rights and privileges from the ruling class.

In Shakespeare's play, Caius Martius appears, significantly, to be the only patrician who still believes that the internal difficulties of the city can be resolved by a Volscian war. The fact that the people are starving need not oblige the patricians to diminish their own stores: 'The Volsces have much corn; take these rats thither / To gnaw their garners' (1.1.249–50). Plutarch, in his 'Life of Coriolanus', describes how at this time the patricians as a group hoped to rid the city of its difficult and seditious elements by way of a military campaign. But, in Shakespeare, it is only Caius Martius who welcomes war with the Volscians, for its own sake, but also because enforced national service may annihilate 'Our musty superfluity' (1.1.226), by which he means the commons, not the stored-up corn. Moreover, Shakespeare altered the order of events as they occur in both Plutarch and Livy. It is plain in *Coriolanus* that only after tribunes have been granted them do the citizens stop stirring up strife in the city and agree to provide soldiers for the Volscian campaign.

In that campaign, although Coriolanus – not to mention many of the play's critics – later chooses to forget this fact, the plebeians acquit themselves with credit. Cominius is forced initially into an honourable retreat, but he judges that the field has been 'well fought' (1.6.1). When, beyond all hope or probability, Coriolanus reappears through those gates of Corioli which he entered by himself, the soldiers are galvanized into action: they not only rescue him but take the city. Coriolanus could not have done this alone – even though later, just before his death, he seems to think that he did. A thing of blood, looking, as Cominius says, 'as he were flea'd' (1.6.22), Caius Martius then becomes a deadly weapon in the hands of common soldiers who, because they possess him, like a living icon of War, become for a crucial moment heroes too. And so the Roman victory is assured.

This is the one instance of real communion and understanding between Coriolanus and the Roman plebeians in the tragedy, but it is ephemeral and special. Upon it, nothing can be built. Later, back in Rome, he will remember only that 'being press'd to th' war, / Even when the navel of the state was touch'd, / They would not thread the gates' (II.1.122–4). He neglects to remember – even as he neglects to remember the name of the poor citizen of Corioli who once used him 'kindly' (1.9.83) – that the common soldiers did in fact enter the gates of Corioli, at the second opportunity, if not, in response to his threats and insults, at the first. Or how men who seemed to him at the time each worth 'four Volsces' (1.6.78) caught him up in their arms and cast up their caps in their eagerness for action. The only memory that sticks with Coriolanus is the initial prudence (for him, cowardice) of these soldiers, and the contemptible concern of poor men, after the battle is over, for plunder, in the pitiable form of cushions and leaden spoons. A biased, an unfairly selective representation of the campaign, it does nonetheless point to something that is true about the Roman plebeians.

From an early age, as Volumnia tells us, Caius Martius has been dedicated to war, and to achieving excellence in it. It is his metier, his life's work. But the attitude of the Roman people – even, to a large extent, of his fellow patricians – is different. Although the commons can, under exceptional circumstances, be fired with martial enthusiasm, they would really prefer, in Sicinius' words, to be 'singing in their shops, and going / About their functions friendly' (IV.6.8–9). For these small shopkeepers and traders, orange sellers, makers of taps for broaching wine-barrels, military service is something they are obliged to undertake from time to time, when the necessities of the state require it. But they had far rather pursue their normal, peacetime occupations than be out slitting Volscian throats. For Coriolanus, such a preference is contemptible. His view, however, is not endorsed by the play as a whole. The fact is that in an increasingly complex and finely balanced society, one in which even

Cominius can hint that valour may not any longer be the chiefest virtue, Volumnia's son is something of an anachronism, out of line even with the other members of his class. Like that dragon to which he likens himself in Act IV, and to which Menenius and Aufidius also compare him, he is an archaic, semi-mythical creature, armour-plated, gigantic, corporeally invincible, a bulwark for the city in war, but something of an embarrassment in peace, because given then to blundering about the market in a bellicose fashion, breathing fire not on Rome's enemies but on the members of her own lower class.

In the second scene of Act III, after Coriolanus has been forced to take refuge from the crowd in his home, Volumnia (who is in large part responsible for her son's scorn of the people, 'woollen vassals', as she has taught him to call them, 'things created / To buy and sell with groats' (lines 9–10), and who also recognizes that, as consul, he would quickly show them how he is really 'dispos'd' (line 22), nonetheless begs him now to speak to them not 'by th'matter which your heart prompts you', but falsely, in 'syllables / Of no allowance, to your bosom's truth' (lines 54–7). The only hypocrisy that Coriolanus manages to utter, before anger and his bosom's truth overtake him, is this:

> Th'honored gods
> Keep Rome in safety, and the chairs of justice
> Supplied with worthy men! plant love among's!
> Throng our large temples with the shows of peace,
> And not our streets with war!   (III.3.33–7)

His sarcasm is barely concealed, but the First Senator responds enthusiastically, 'Amen, Amen', and Menenius, 'A noble wish' (lines 37–8). Both of them, unlike Coriolanus, mean what they say. The Rome they want is the one set on its course by Numa: vigilant, strong in its own defence, but also a citadel of justice and religion, and paying equal honour, as befits worshippers in the temple of Janus, to the claims of war and peace. What Coriolanus disdainfully fabricates has become for the rest of the city, including the patricians, a genuine political and social ideal, even if tribunes are now required to help achieve it.

I have been trying to argue that, although Shakespeare is unlikely, while actually writing *Coriolanus*, to have kept a copy of Livy open beside him, as he apparently did with Plutarch, nonetheless the attitudes and interests of *Ab Urbe Condita*, as we understand that work now, live to a striking extent in this last of his Roman plays. But, it might be asked, is it reasonable to assume that Shakespeare in 1607–8 would have read Livy in at all the manner we read him today? As a man of his time, would Shakespeare not have been more likely to value the book for the individual stories embedded in it, for what it had to say about the lives of great men, than for an overall historical view of the kind I have been concerned to stress? Not, I think, necessarily. Here, it seems important to point out that Shakespeare's understanding, in *Coriolanus*, of the development and strengths of the Roman republic, as outlined by Livy, is markedly similar in many ways to that of his great Italian contemporary, Niccolò Machiavelli.

Machiavelli's *Discorsi*, his commentary on the first ten books of Livy, was not published in English until 1636. It circulated widely, however, in Elizabethan and Jacobean England in Italian (a language which, on the evidence of his use of Cinthio for *Othello*, Shakespeare could read) and also in various manuscript translations, three of which survive.[7] The notion that Machiavelli reached sixteenth-century England only as a stock stage villain, a caricature agent of hell, has long since been exploded. Among Shakespeare's contemporaries, Sidney, Spenser, Gabriel Harvey, Nashe, Kyd, Marston, Bacon, Fulke Greville, Ralegh, and Ben Jonson, to name only a few, were clearly familiar not only with the devilish practices and opinions popularly attributed to Machiavelli, but with what he had actually written. Neither then nor, indeed, at any time is a first-hand knowledge of Machiavelli tantamount to approval of what he has to say. The commentary on Livy is morally less outrageous than *Il Principe*, yet even Edward Dacres, its seventeenth-century translator, felt constrained to announce on his title-page that he was presenting this work, designed to instruct its dedicatee James, Duke of Lennox in how best to cope with the perils of the political world, fenced round 'with some marginall animadversions noting and taxing [the author's] errours'.[8] It seems to have been relatively common in Elizabethan and Jacobean England for writers to allude to Machiavelli as a caricature bogeyman or as a serious thinker, according to the needs of any specific occasion. The case of Spenser is especially interesting. In one work, *Mother Hubberds Tale*, it suited him to present the stereotype Machiavel – irreligious, perjured, self-

---

[7] Felix Raab, *The English Face of Machiavelli* (London, 1964), pp. 52–3.
[8] *Machiavels Discourses upon the first Decade of T. Livius*, trans. Edward Dacres (1636).

seeking, hypocritical and cruel. But later, in his *View of the Present State of Ireland*, Spenser could, without a flicker of irony, offer Elizabeth's government detailed counsel as to the best way of pacifying that unhappy colony which he took straight out of *The Prince* and, to a lesser extent, the *Discorsi*.[9]

I think myself that it would be more surprising if it could be proved that Shakespeare had managed to avoid reading Machiavelli than if concrete evidence were to turn up that he had. Certainly, the example of Spenser ought to caution one against believing that York's reference in *1 Henry VI* to Alanson as 'that notorious Machevile' (v.4.74), or the intention of the future Richard III to 'set the murtherous Machevil to school' (*3 Henry VI*, III.3.193), in any way precludes the demonstration of genuine understanding elsewhere in the Shakespeare canon. (Significantly, when the Host in *The Merry Wives of Windsor* asks the rhetorical question, 'Am I politic? Am I subtle? Am I a Machivel?' (III.1.101), he has just rendered a signal service to the community, using deceit – the end justifying the means – in order to prevent Windsor's parson and her physician from trying to kill each other in a foolish cause.) There is, however, no real need to make an issue of Shakespeare's actual acquaintance with the *Discorsi*. What matters is the way Machiavelli's interpretation of Livy bears upon *Coriolanus*, however the parallels between the two works arose.

Even critics fundamentally unsympathetic to Coriolanus as a character have a way of applauding the supposed political wisdom of his tirade in the first scene of Act III:

> when two authorities are up,
> Neither supreme, how soon confusion
> May enter 'twixt the gap of both, and take
> The one by th'other,   (lines 109–12)

his attack upon what he scorns as 'this double worship... where gentry, title, wisdom, / Cannot conclude but by the yea and no / Of general ignorance' (lines 142, 144–6). But what Coriolanus is repudiating here is in fact precisely the equilibrium in which, for Machiavelli, Livy had located the strength of the Roman republic. It is one of the central themes of the *Discorsi* that the struggle between patricians and plebeians was positive, not negative, that indeed, as the heading of Chapter 4 in the First Book announces, 'the

[9] Edwin A. Greenlaw, 'The Influence of Machiavelli on Spenser', in *Modern Philology* 7 (1909–10), 187–202.

disagreement of the People and the Senate of Rome made the Commonwealth both free and mighty'.

Machiavelli is careful to distinguish dissension from faction. Faction finally destroyed the republic, in the time of the Gracchi, when the attempt to enforce the old agrarian laws split the city into two warring camps between whom communication and compromise became impossible. The result was a blood-bath, of just the kind that senators and tribunes alike, in *Coriolanus*, fear and make concessions to avoid, 'Unless by not so doing, our good city / Cleave in the midst and perish' (III.2.27–8). But between the expulsion of the Tarquins in the sixth century BC and the end of the second century BC – over three hundred years – dissension between patricians and plebeians was not only relatively bloodless, compromises made on both sides ensured a balance of aristocratic and popular interests in which each individual, however humble, while subordinating his private interests to those of the state, was nonetheless able to cultivate his own *virtu*. It was a balance brought to perfection when, at just the right moment, tribunes of the people were added to the pre-existing political institutions of consuls and senate. Then, for a while, Rome had almost within her grasp that ideal condition of which Machiavelli dreamed, even if he was sadly aware that it was never likely to be realized in his own Italy: that of a free and stable state, the potential insolence and disorder of its people restrained by the power of the nobles, aristocratic ambition and arrogance checked by the people, a state so strong that it could afford to live at peace, with no need to expand, and no neighbours so foolhardy as to molest it.[10]

Although he recognizes that Livy grumbles from time to time about the inconstancy of the multitude, their inadequacies and failings, for Machiavelli the merits of the Roman people are vindicated in the great sweep of Livy's history as a whole. They were, to an extent which perhaps Livy himself never consciously recognized, essential to what the republic achieved. As Machiavelli writes at the end of Book 1: 'the Cittie that imployes not their people in any glorious action, may treate them after their owne manner, as otherwhere it was argued. But that, which will take the same course Rome tooke, must make this distinction'.[11] Even the humblest citizen

---

[10] In his essay, 'Machiavelli's use of Livy' (chapter 4, in *Livy*, ed. T. A. Dorey, London, 1971), J. H. Whitfield stresses the importance of the passage in chapter 6, book 1 of the *Discorsi* in which Machiavelli formulates this ideal. Cf. pp. 83–4.

[11] Machiavelli, *Discourses*, book 1, chapter 60, p. 243.

of the Roman republic was given his chance to achieve 'glory', whether military or civic. As for the desire of the commons to conclude military campaigns as speedily as possible and return to their peacetime occupations, Machiavelli regards it as entirely proper. In his eyes, a man who is a professional fighter, a soldier and nothing else, is valueless to the state and may even endanger it. In the Roman republic, although every able-bodied man was expected to help fight her wars, war was nobody's occupation. And there were so many brave and victorious commanders all serving at one time (as do Cominius, Titus Lartius and Coriolanus), that the people did not need to worry about one of them making himself pre-eminent and so possibly tyrannical.

Machiavelli believed that no human being was either wholly good or wholly bad. An individual's natural qualities, his bent, shape themselves early and cannot thereafter be changed. People also, as they mature, learn certain ways of proceeding, accustom themselves to particular patterns of behaviour. States do this too. But around both, times and circumstances change. It is extremely difficult for individuals, and also for political institutions, to vary at need, to accommodate themselves to the demands of new situations. And yet their failure or success depends, ultimately, upon their ability to do so. A republic, Machiavelli suggests in the *Discorsi*, is likely to fare better in this respect than a monarchy,

because shee can better fit her selfe for severall accidents, by reason of the variety of her Subjects, that are in her, then can a Prince: for a man that is accustomed to proceed in one manner, never alters, as it is sayd, and must of necessitie, when the times disagree with his way, goe to wracke.[12]

In effect, once again, the pluralism, the contentious but firmly shared responsibility of the mixed state, work to its advantage.

As might be expected, Machiavelli's view of Coriolanus himself is harsher than Livy's, and much more dismissive than that of Shakespeare. Machiavelli deals with Caius Martius in Book 1 of the *Discorsi*, in Chapter 7, entitled: 'How useful accusations are in a Republike for the maintenance of liberty'. For him, the story of Caius Martius was interesting simply because it displayed the triumph of

---

[12] Machiavelli, book 3, chapter 9, p. 498. In *Machiavelli* (Oxford, 1981), Quentin Skinner describes Machiavelli's conviction, established early in his life, that 'the clue to successful statecraft lies in recognising the force of circumstances, accepting what necessity dictates, and harmonising one's behaviour with the times' as his 'central political belief' (p. 38).

democratic law. Coriolanus aroused the indignation of a famished populace by declaring in the Senate that corn ought not to be distributed gratis until the people agreed to subject themselves to the nobles and relinquish the tribunate. But the very tribunes Coriolanus wanted to abolish saved his life. If they had not intervened, accused him formally, and summoned him to appear before them and defend himself, he would have been slain in what Machiavelli's seventeenth-century translator calls 'a tumult', as he left the Senate. This episode, Machiavelli declares, shows 'how fit and usefull it is, that the Commonwealths with the lawes give meanes to vent the choler, which the universalitie hath conceiv'd against any one citizen. For when they have not these ordinary meanes, they have recourse to extraordinarie; and out of question these are of worse effect then those.'[13] In exiling Coriolanus, and never permitting him to return, the Roman state was guilty of no error or ingratitude, 'because he alwayes continued his malicious mind against the people'.[14]

It is true in general that 'contempt and contumely begets a hatred against those that use it, without any returne of advantage to them'.[15] But in a republic, above all, the man who is proud and uses insulting language, who openly displays his contempt for the commons, is intolerable: for 'nothing is more odious to the people, especially those that injoy their liberty'.[16] There is only one further reference to Coriolanus in the *Discorsi*, a passing mention of how his mother persuaded him to turn back from the gates of Rome, used to introduce a debate on the relative merits of a good army or an able commander. Machiavelli does not bother to comment directly on Coriolanus' league with the Volscians. What he thought about it, however, can fairly be deduced from the heading to chapter 47 near the end of Book 3: 'That a good Citizen for the love of his country ought to forget all private wrongs'.

Although Machiavelli took no interest in the nature of Coriolanus' life in exile, Shakespeare did. Caius Martius cannot possibly 'banish' the people who have driven him out of the city, restoring Rome to the condition of an ancient, warrior state. On the other hand, I believe, contrary to most critics, that he does find 'a world elsewhere'

---

[13] Machiavelli, book 1, chapter 7, pp. 38–9.
[14] Machiavelli, book 1, chapter 29, p. 125.
[15] Machiavelli, book 2, chapter 26, p. 398.
[16] Machiavelli, book 3, chapter 23, p. 559.

(III.3.135). Historically, the Volscians were a semi-nomadic, cattle-raiding people, hill-dwellers to the south, who envied the rich lands of the Latin campagna. From Livy, Shakespeare would have learned that Rome was at odds with them, off and on, for some two hundred years. She crushed them in the end, but the struggle was long and hard. What seems to have mattered most to Shakespeare, working on hints provided by both Livy and Plutarch, was that in the time of Caius Martius, Volscian society was clearly different and far simpler than that of Rome. According to Plutarch, 'Corioles' was the 'principall cittie and of most fame'[17] – modern archaeologists, by the way, still cannot discover where it was – but it clearly had nothing like the centrality and importance for this nation that the seven-hilled city on the Tiber had for the Romans. Antium, indeed, where Tullus Aufidius presides as a kind of feudal lord, seems equally prominent. This is why Shakespeare can so blithely confuse the two places in the final scene. According to Plutarch, Coriolanus was killed in Antium. That is where Shakespeare's scene begins. But by line 90, Antium has turned into Corioli: 'Dost thou think', Aufidius exclaims, 'I'll grace thee with that robbery, thy stol'n name / Coriolanus, in Corioles?' (v.6.87–9). Shakespeare is being careless, but it is a carelessness made possible by the fact that whereas Rome is unique, one Volscian town looks much like another.

Neither in Antium nor Corioli are there tribunes or aediles. There most certainly is an upper class, designated almost invariably in speech prefixes and in the text as 'lords'. (Only once, from Aufidius, do we hear the term 'senators', IV.5.132.) There are also 'people'. If there is the slightest friction between the two, we are never told about it. Moreover, in this society, everyone seems to regard war as a natural and even desirable condition of existence. In Shakespeare's play, the Volscians are always the aggressors, never the Romans. According to Plutarch, the Volscian lords were in fact reluctant after the sack of Corioli to break the truce agreed so recently with Rome. They had to be tricked, by Aufidius and Coriolanus, into renewing hostilities. In Livy, it is the Volscian commons, broken and dispirited by plague and by the loss of so many young men in the last war, who need to be deceived into resuming arms. Shakespeare ignored both accounts. When Coriolanus arrives, in Act IV, at the house of Aufidius, the Volscian lords have already assembled there to plan a

---

[17] *Plutarch's Lives*, in Bullough (vol. 5), p. 511.

new campaign. While the plebeians, represented here by the servingmen, are overjoyed to hear that there is like to be 'a stirring world again' (IV.5.218–19). War, they declare, 'exceeds peace as far as day does night ... Peace is a very apoplexy, lethargy, mulled, deaf, sleepy, insensible, a getter of more bastard children than war's a destroyer of men' (lines 221–6). Moreover, as the First Servingman maintains, 'it makes men hate one another'. The Third Servingman knows the answer to this apparent paradox: 'Reason: because they then less need one another. The wars for my money' (lines 230–2). In effect, the Volscian plebeians freely accept what in Rome has become a desperate and doubtfully successful patrician strategy: that you can hold a society together, create a bond more important than any social, political or economic inequalities by involving the whole nation in war.

As representatives of the Volscian commons, the three servingmen at Antium do not emerge well from a comparison with their equivalents in Rome. Their behaviour, in fact, on a smaller scale, resembles that of Shakespeare's earlier crowds. Some of the Roman citizens in this play (the Second Citizen in the third scene of Act II, for instance) are slower-witted than others, and likely to be teased about it by their companions. But they are consistently shown as capable of holding an intelligent discussion, and they do not all think alike. The Volscian servingmen, by contrast, constitute a miniature herd. All three of them treat the meanly dressed stranger who has invaded the house with the same high-handed contempt – giving Coriolanus his first taste of what it is like to be thought poor and unimportant. When they discover who he is and how highly their master and the other lords regard him, they swing immediately, and in unison, to the opposite extreme:

SECOND SERVANT: Nay, I knew by his face that there was something in him. He had, sir, a kind of face, methought – I cannot tell how to term it.
FIRST SERVANT: He had so, looking as it were – Would I were hang'd but I thought there was more in him than I could think.   (IV.5.154–9)

The general drift is plain enough, but these men are not very successful at putting their considered opinion of Coriolanus into words. Not, at least, by comparison with the Roman citizens of the first scene, or the two anonymous officers laying cushions in the Capitol in Act II who can discern both that Caius Martius 'hath deserv'd worthily of his country' and that 'to affect the malice and displeasure of the people is as bad as that which he dislikes, to flatter them for their love' (ii.2.21–4). When the third Volscian servant tries to impress his companions with a big word, he immediately gets it wrong: 'Directitude?', the First Servant asks, 'What's that?' (line 209). 'Discreditude' seems to have been what his friend was trying to say. Mistaking of words is a common enough lower-class phenomenon in Shakespeare. It does not, however, seem to afflict the citizens of Rome.

Among the Volscians, Coriolanus is universally admired. The common soldiers 'use him as the grace 'fore meat, / Their talk at table, and their thanks at end' (iv.7.3–4). They flock to him, 'He is their god', following him

> with no less confidence
> Than boys pursuing summer butterflies,
> Or butchers killing flies. (iv.6.90, 93–5)

This is not the kind of special, momentary blaze of admiration that Coriolanus was able to strike out of Roman soldiers in an extremity, in the heat of battle. In this less complicated, archaic warrior state, it surrounds him every day and it is bestowed by nobles and commons alike. Only Tullus Aufidius resists. A man significantly out of touch with the simplicities of his society, even as Caius Martius was with the comparative sophistication of his, this Volscian lord is reflective and intelligent as his rival is not. Ironically, Aufidius would have found it perfectly easy to be politic in Rome, to 'mounte bank' the loves of her people, and do all those compromising, diplomatic things at which Coriolanus rebelled. What he cannot do is overcome the Roman hero in a fair fight, and he has apparently tried no fewer than twelve times. His own retainers know this: 'here's he that was wont to thwack our general, Caius Martius' (iv.5.178–9). Among the Volscians, such physical supremacy counts for much more than it does in Rome. It means that Coriolanus, for the first time in his life, becomes genuinely 'popular'. It also means that Aufidius, who stumbles on a real truth when he says, 'I would I were a Roman, for I cannot, / Being a Volsce, be that I am' (i.10.4–5), who decided after his defeat in Act i that he could maintain the heroic reputation so important in his society only through guile ('I'll potch at him some way, / Or wrath or craft may get him', lines 15–16), becomes desperate to destroy his new colleague: a man now worshipped by a nation savagely widowed and unchilded at his hands as he never was in his own country.

'Bring me word thither / How the world goes, that to the pace of it / I may spur on my journey' (1.10.31–3). Those seemingly casual words which Aufidius addresses to a soldier at the end of Act 1 are telling. Aufidius is adaptable. Like Machiavelli, he understands the importance of accommodating one's behaviour to the times. He has also divined (as, for that matter, did the Second Citizen in the opening scene) that his rival is fatally inflexible, that he cannot move 'from th'casque to th'cushion', cannot 'be other than one thing' (IV.7.43, 42). In this judgement, Aufidius is almost, if not entirely, right. Coriolanus in exile is a man haunted by what seems to him the enormity of mutability and change. This is the burden of his soliloquy outside Aufidius' house: 'O world, thy slippery turns' (IV.4.12–26). The commonplaces upon which he broods – dear friends can become foes, former foes, dear friends; it is actually possible to hate what one once loved, love what one hated – have just struck him, as the result of his recent experiences in Rome, with the force of revelation. But fundamentally, nothing has altered in his own nature. Menenius may be puzzled when Coriolanus does not keep his parting promise to write to his family and friends – 'Nay, I hear nothing; his mother and his wife / Hear nothing from him' (IV.6.18–19) – and initially incredulous that he could have joined with Aufidius. But the Coriolanus who has found a home and adulation among the Volscians remains, in this other country, the man he always was.

Only the embassy of the women can shatter his convictions, force him into a new way of seeing. The scene with the women, outside Rome, when Coriolanus holds his mother by the hand 'silent', when he recognizes that he is not, after all, 'of stronger earth than others' (v.3.29), has been written about often and well. It is, of course, the moment when Coriolanus finally recognizes his common humanity, the strength of love and family ties. But the victory won here is not, I think, as so often is assumed, that of a private over a public world. Shakespeare is at pains to assert that, in republican Rome, the two are really inseparable. Hence the mute, but important presence of the lady Coriolanus greets as

> The noble sister of Publicola,
> The moon of Rome, chaste as the icicle
> That's curdied by the frost from purest snow
> And hangs on Dian's temple.   (v.3.64–7)

Valeria is a character many critics have felt Shakespeare would have done well to jettison, most especially here. (I have even seen it suggested that the only excuse for her existence in the play is to show us the sort of strong-willed woman Coriolanus ought to have married, if only jealous Volumnia had let him.) But, surely, Valeria accompanies Coriolanus' wife and mother on their mission – even though she is not allowed, as in Plutarch, to initiate it – because Shakespeare meant it to be clear that this is by no means a strictly family affair. Valeria, 'greatly honoured and reverenced amonge all the Romaines', as Plutarch puts it,[18] is there to represent all the other women of Rome, those 'neighbours' among whom Volumnia, when she believes her plea has been rejected, is prepared (along with Virgilia and the little Caius Martius) to die.

In the triumphal honours accorded the women on their return to Rome, Valeria has her place, reminding us that although the family of Coriolanus have figured as the crucial agents of persuasion, succeeding where Cominius and Menenius failed, ultimately the victory belongs to the city they have placed above family ties, the Rome for which they spoke. Patricians and plebeians, senators and tribunes have already joined together to pray for the success of this embassy. Now, in celebrating that success, Rome is united as never before in the play. Not even Sicinius thinks of anything but of meeting Volumnia, Valeria and Virgilia to 'help the joy' (v.4.62). That scene of welcome, with its flower-strewn streets, its sackbuts, psalteries, tabors and fifes, contrasts sharply with its equivalent in Antium/Corioli: the parallel entry of Coriolanus bearing the terms of peace.

We are surprised, surely, to learn from Aufidius that Coriolanus means 't'appear before the people, hoping / To purge himself with words' (v.6.7–8), that there is (as the Third Conspirator fears) some danger that he may 'move the people / With what he would say' (lines 54–5). The Folio stage direction following line 69 of this final scene indicates that Coriolanus enters 'with drum and colours, the Commoners being with him'. Coriolanus has found it easier to get on with the Volscian commons than with their more pacific but demanding equivalents in Rome. It is striking, nonetheless, that he is prepared now to explain himself and his actions to lords and people alike, that he presents himself initially not as an heroic individual, but

---

[18] *Plutarch's Lives*, in Bullough (vol. 5), p. 537.

as the servant of a common cause: 'I am return'd your soldier'
(v.6.70). Although he has not been able to make 'true wars', he has
at least framed a 'convenient peace' (v.3.190–1). The attempt fails.
Coriolanus tries here to do something which is new to him, but (as
Machiavelli knew) the habits of a lifetime cannot be transformed
overnight. Aufidius has only to produce that old, inflammatory word
'traitor', so effective before on the lips of the tribunes, and Coriolanus
is lost. He reacts just as he had done in Rome. And, at last, all the
Volscian people remember what, in their adoration of this man, they
had been able for a time to forget: the sons and daughters, the fathers
and friends he once slaughtered. Here, as Machiavelli would have
noted, there are no tribunes to put a brake on their violence as they
demand that Coriolanus be torn to pieces, no intervention of law or
legal process to thwart the conspirators and enforce a compromise
verdict. Coriolanus is simply slain, in 'a tumult', while the Volscian
lords look helplessly on.

There is a sense in which the characteristically shrewd perception
of Aufidius – 'So our virtues / Lie in th'interpretation of the time'
(iv.7.49–50) – might stand as the epigraph for this play as a whole.
Whatever the case in the past, or among the Volscians of the present,
valour in this Rome is no longer 'the chiefest virtue', over-riding all
the rest. It must, as Coriolanus himself finally discovers, learn to
coexist with the values of peace and, even in war, modify its antique,
epic character. There is something both touching and full of promise
in the prayer Coriolanus offers up in Act v at his last meeting with his
son. He asks that little Martius, the soldier of the next generation,
should

> prove
> To shame unvulnerable, and stick i'th'wars
> Like a great sea-mark, standing every flaw,
> And saving those that eye thee! (v.3.72–5)

Shame here is more than a strictly military consideration. Coriolanus
is thinking of his own, complicated misfortunes, of what may befall a
man in peace as well as war. But while the great sea-mark, the
lighthouse beacon standing firm in the storm, remains extra-human,
its prime function is not to destroy but heroically preserve. It is an
image closer to the one old Nestor finds for Hector on the battlefield
in *Troilus and Cressida* – a god 'dealing life' (iv.5.191) – or to Marcus
Curtius dedicating himself to death in the chasm that all of Rome
might live, than it is to that of the juggernaut, the mechanical

harvester, the Caius Martius who was a savage and undiscriminating agent of death.

Coriolanus is a tragedy in that its protagonist does finally learn certain necessary truths about the world in which he exists, but dies before he has any chance to rebuild his life in accordance with them. Paradoxically, it is only in his belated recognition and acceptance of historical change, of that right of the commons to be taken seriously which the other members of his class in Rome have already conceded, that he achieves genuinely tragic individuality. The play is predominantly a history – indeed, Shakespeare's most political play, the only one specifically about the *polis*.[19] I believe that Livy's account of an evolving republic and also, in all probability, Machiavelli's commentary on *Ab Urbe Condita*, helped to shape it, that although it is certainly a better play than Jonson's *Catiline*, or even his *Sejanus*, it is perhaps more like them in its focus upon Rome herself at a moment of historical transition than is usually thought.

To the question of why Shakespeare should have felt impelled to write such a play at this particular moment, there can be no confident answer. The corn riots in the Midlands and, more especially, the anti-enclosure riots of 1607 which affected his native Warwickshire may well have had something to do with it. It is clear too that there was considerable interest in Jacobean England at this time in classical republicanism, in theories of the mixed state. In his book *Coriolanus in Context*, C. C. Huffman assembles an impressive amount of evidence to show that as James's absolutism declared itself more and more plainly, an educated minority came to believe that the King was trying to tamper with the fundamental nature of English government. England, they argued, was a tripartite state, composed of king, nobles and commons. In it, each element had its rights, with Parliament standing as the safeguard against tyranny. James was entirely aware of this line of thought, and of its roots in republican Rome. In 1606, he was fulminating against what he called 'tribunes of the people whose mouths could not be stopped' – by which he meant his antagonists in parliament. His concern, and the terms he chose to express it, were prophetic. In the great clash that was to come between king and parliament ('the in-justest judgement-

---

[19] In her essay 'To starve with feeding: the city in *Coriolanus*' (*Shakespeare Studies* 11 (1978), 123–44), Gail Kern Paster points out that the Spevack Concordance lists 88 uses of the word 'Rome' in *Coriolanus* as against 38 in *Julius Caesar* and 30 in *Antony and Cleopatra*. The word 'Capitol' occurs 15 times, against 2 instances in *Julius Caesar* and only one in *Antony and Cleopatra*.

seate that may be', as James protested) the theory of mixed government was to become a deadly weapon in the hands of the opposition.[20]

Unfortunately, Huffman uses all this historical material to introduce a reading of *Coriolanus* as Shakespeare's apology for Jacobean absolutism, even going so far as to suggest that the dramatist believed Rome would have been better off in ashes, with Volumnia, Virgilia and little Martius dead, than left at the mercy of an institution so wicked as the tribunate. As so often, the settled conviction that Shakespeare's view of history was orthodox, conservative, rooted in the political theories expounded in the Homilies, has blinded the critic to what is actually there on the page. But why should we assume that, in the words of a well-known essay on *Coriolanus* and the Midlands insurrection, 'Whether or not Shakespeare had been shocked or alarmed by the 1607 rising is anyone's guess; but it is fairly certain that he must have been hardened and confirmed in what had always been his consistent attitude to the mob'?[21] Assertions like these encouraged Edward Bond to interpret the extremely ambiguous documents relating to the Welcombe enclosures of 1614 entirely to Shakespeare's discredit. One may dislike Bond's *Bingo*, with its portrait of a 'corrupt seer',[22] a brutal and reactionary property-owner victimizing the rural poor, but there is a sense in which it simply spells out and exaggerates the received notion about Shakespeare's political attitudes. There is no reason why such a view should persist. Although he remained as fascinated by history as a process in 1607 as he had been in the early 1590s, when he was writing the *Henry VI* plays, the man who conceived *Coriolanus* gives every indication of being more tolerant of the commons than before. He looked attentively at the young Roman republic delineated by Plutarch and by Livy, and chose to emphasize what was hopeful, communal and progressive in it, when writing his interpretation of the time.

[20] C. C. Huffman, *Coriolanus in Context* (Lewisburg, 1971), *passim* but especially pp. 148, 189.
[21] E. C. Pettet, '*Coriolanus* and the Midlands Insurrection of 1607', in *Shakespeare Survey 3* (Cambridge, 1950), 34–42.
[22] Edward Bond, in his Preface to *Bingo* (1974), p. xiii.

CHAPTER 8

Leontes and the spider: language and speaker in Shakespeare's last plays (1980)

HERMIONE: Come, sir, now
  I am for you again. Pray you sit by us,
  And tell's a tale.
MAMILLIUS: Merry, or sad shall't be?
HERMIONE: As merry as you will.
MAMILLIUS: A sad tale's best for winter. I have one
  Of sprites and goblins.
HERMIONE: Let's have that, good sir.
  Come on, sit down, come on, and do your best
  To fright me with your sprites; you're powr'ful at it.
MAMILLIUS: There was a man –
HERMIONE: Nay, come sit down; then on.
MAMILLIUS: Dwelt by a churchyard. I will tell it softly,
  Yond crickets shall not hear it.
HERMIONE: Come on then,
  And give't me in mine ear.
  [*Enter*] LEONTES, ANTIGONUS, LORDS [*and others*].
LEONTES: Was he met there? his train? Camillo with him?
I LORD: Behind the tuft of pines I met them; never
  Saw I men scour so on their way. I ey'd them
  Even to their ships.
LEONTES: How blest am I
  In my just censure! in my true opinion!
  Alack, for lesser knowledge! How accurs'd
  In being so blest! There may be in the cup
  A spider steep'd, and one may drink; depart,
  And yet partake no venom (for his knowledge
  Is not infected), but if one present
  Th'abhorr'd ingredient to his eye, make known
  How he hath drunk, he cracks his gorge, his sides,
  With violent hefts. I have drunk, and seen the spider.
  Camillo was his help in this, his pandar.
  There is a plot against my life, my crown;
  All's true that is mistrusted. That false villain

> Whom I employ'd was pre-employ'd by him:
> He has discover'd my design, and I
> Remain a pinch'd thing; yea, a very trick
> For them to play at will.   (*The Winter's Tale*, II.1.21–52)

The Winter's Tale begins where many of Shakespeare's earlier comedies had ended. Friendship, no longer love's rival, has found a spacious if subordinate place for itself within the domain of marriage. Leontes enters the play with his wife Hermione and his friend Polixenes: three people apparently in possession of that harmonious, adult relationship which the youthful protagonists of *The Two Gentlemen of Verona*, *Love's Labour's Lost*, *The Merchant of Venice*, *Much Ado About Nothing* and *All's Well That Ends Well* had struggled painfully, over five acts, to achieve. Mamillius and Florizel, the children whose birth is predicated at the end of so many Shakespearean comedies, actually exist. The story is, or should be, over. So powerful is this sense of being in a place just beyond the normal terminus of Shakespeare's comedies that, even at the beginning of Act II, when Leontes has perversely begun to un-build his paradise, it is possible to hear the echoes of another and less disturbing winter's tale:

> Now it is the time of night
> That the graves, all gaping wide,
> Every one lets forth his sprite,
> In the church-way paths to glide.
> (*A Midsummer Night's Dream*, V.1.3.379–82)

Mamillius' whispered story 'of sprites and goblins' will be as harmless as Puck's fifth-act account of the terrors of the night: a ghost story carefully qualified, in *A Midsummer Night's Dream*, by the final benediction of the fairies. Safe in her warm, domestic interior, Hermione listens indulgently to a child's tale of grave-yard horrors. Neither of them notices that, as in Peele's *The Old Wives Tale*, someone has appeared on stage to tell Mamillius' tale for him. It is Leontes' story of the night, not Mamillius', that the theatre audience actually hears, and this adult fantasy is neither harmless nor amusing.

Leontes, like Othello before him, asserts passionately that ignorance is bliss:

> I had been happy, if the general camp,
> Pioners and all, had tasted her sweet body,
> So I had nothing known.   (*Othello*, III.3.345–7)

Othello's sophistical insistence that a man is robbed only if he knows he is had concentrated attention upon Othello himself: a man constitutionally incapable of existing – whether for good or ill – except in a state of certainty and total commitment. His false logic, engendered by the psychological pain of the moment, had been an unavailing attempt at self-delusion discredited by the speaker in the very moment of constructing it. Othello, in agony, deliberately plays with the idea of a blessed ignorance from which, through Iago's insinuations, he has effectively been debarred. He invents the gross 'pioners' as a form of self-torture, while trying simultaneously to persuade himself that paradise would not be lost even if he were the only man who still believed in it. But he knows that he cannot any longer believe.

Leontes' speech in *The Winter's Tale*, for all its superficial similarity, is very different from Othello's. The little inset story of the spider is palpably an old wives' tale: a piece of unnatural natural history which Leontes trots out as part of his self-defeating effort to make something out of nothing, to give substance to a bad dream. As such, it functions in ways of which the speaker is himself unaware, tells a truth he consciously rejects. If Leontes sees himself as being in Othello's situation, we do not. Othello, with some excuse, could not distinguish between Desdemona's truth and Iago's cunning falsehood. He was not the only person in the play to make this mistake. Leontes, on the other hand, inhabits a world of clear-cut black and white, one in which there is no Iago, and even the herd of anonymous gentlemen at the court always know that Hermione is innocent. Leontes' mind, as his words involuntarily but quite explicitly inform us, has poisoned itself, breeding madness from an illusory evil, even as the minds of people doomed by voodoo or black magic are supposed to do. Whether visible or not, the spider in the cup is itself innocuous: it is the human imagination that is destructive and deadly. This is the most important thing Leontes has to tell us. It is characteristic, however, of the last plays, that the speaker should be quite unconscious of what, for the theatre audience, is the primary meaning of his own words.

In his earlier plays, Shakespeare had very occasionally anticipated this technique. Usually, he did so for straightforward comic effect – one thinks of the word 'ass' as Dogberry indignantly applies it to himself, or as Bottom uses it, innocently, after his translation. Fools who luxuriate in words without understanding their proper meanings, as Dogberry does throughout *Much Ado About Nothing*, Touch-stone's Audrey with the epithet 'foul', or Cleopatra's clown (more profoundly) with the term 'immortal', are given to making sense of a kind they would consciously repudiate. It is part of the character of the Hostess in the *Henry IV* plays that she should remain blithely unaware of the bawdy double entendres which other people detect in her speech, unintentional indecencies which tend to overbear her own meaning. Only in *Troilus and Cressida*, however, did Shakespeare exploit the device in ways that were, fundamentally, not comic. The play is conditioned throughout by the audience's foreknowledge of the fate of Troy, and of the destiny of each individual character. A unique and all-encompassing irony ensures that characters seldom speak out of their own, present moment of fictional time without an audience interpreting their words in the light of the myth as a whole. So, when Helen suggests languidly that 'this love will undo us all' (III.1.110–11), what for her is mere badinage converts instantly into a sinister and alien truth. Pandarus regards it as a jocular impossibility that Cressida should ever be false to Troilus. Should his niece falter, 'let all pitiful goers-between be called to the world's end after my name; call them all Panders. Let all constant men be Troiluses, all false women Cressids, and all brokers-between Pandars! Say, amen (III.2.200–4). It is only for the audience, painfully aware that this is precisely the significance which these names now have, that 'amen' sticks in the throat.

 Troilus and Cressida is a special case. (Indeed, it is interesting that Shakespeare should have wished to stress the ineluctable end of the Troy story in this fashion, as he did not with what might have been regarded as the equally predetermined patterns of English history.) In general, the compulsion to drive a wedge between dramatic speech and the nature and intentions of the speaker becomes important only in his late plays. One must be careful, I think, not to confuse this late stylistic development with ordinary ambiguity – the shadowy penumbra of meanings, not necessarily in the control of the speaker, which may surround a given word. Nor is it the same as that kind of implicit, underlying irony which becomes visible only when a passage is analysed in the study, or remembered from the special vantage point of the fifth act. When Henry V, before Harfleur, exhorts his soldiers to imitate tigers, greyhounds, cannons, or pitiless granite escarpments, his words are a successful incitement to action. Only in the context of the whole play, and *after the dramatic moment is*

past, leaving us to confront an immobile Bardolph and Pistol, is it
possible to reflect that he is asking men to be both more and
considerably less than human. Obviously, Henry himself does not see
the terms he employs as equivocal, an impoverishment as well as an
epic magnification. The point is that, in the theatre, neither do we.
Or, at least, the speech as heard projects this sense in a way that is
almost subliminal.

Similarly, when Othello, in Cyprus, exclaims of Desdemona,

> Perdition catch my soul
> But I do love thee! and when I love thee not,
> Chaos is come again,   (III.3.90-2)

or Macbeth asserts, 'Had I but died an hour before this chance, / I
had liv'd a blessed time' (II.3.91-2), the literal but at this instant
merely potential truth lurking behind the hyperbole is secondary to
the meaning of the lines as the speaker intends them, but also as we
hear them in the moment of utterance. Othello and Macbeth, like
Pandarus and Leontes, speak more truly than they know, but the
bitter prophecy inherent in their words – like the unwitting predic-
tions of Buckingham, Lady Anne, or Richard himself ('Myself myself
confound') in *Richard III* – will always be submerged in the theatre
by other and more immediately arresting considerations. Even if
one's mind does flicker forward to 'the tragic loading of this bed',
here, in the particular stage-present of Act III, Othello's lines make
themselves felt essentially as Othello himself feels them: as a
spontaneous declaration of love and faith. Macbeth's cry, while it
certainly prefigures his fifth-act recognition of a life fallen irremedi-
ably into the 'sear, the yellow leaf', concentrates attention as it is
uttered upon the audacity of his dissembled horror. That is the
primary register.

This is not, however, the way we react to Leontes' spider, or to his
assertion that 'I / Play too, but so disgrac'd a part, whose issue /
Will hiss me to my grave' (I.2.187-9). Here, as in his angry words to
Hermione,

> Your actions are my dreams.
> You had a bastard by Polixenes,
> And I but dream'd it,   (III.2.82-4)

it is what we take to be the *primary* meaning of the speech which is
concealed from the speaker. In the last example, Leontes' heavy

irony functions, for us, as a simple statement of truth. This is also true of the convoluted reasoning through which he persuaded himself, in Act I, that because 'affection' may communicate with dreams, be coactive with the unreal, and because it 'fellow'st nothing' (1.2.138–46), it may conjoin with 'something' – and has. It is interesting to compare the false logic here with Brutus' soliloquy in the orchard in *Julius Caesar*: 'Then lest he may, prevent' (II.1.28). All of the passages from *The Winter's Tale* are entirely and almost impersonally apt as descriptions of the dramatic situation as we, but not Leontes, apprehend it. Mirrors of action almost more than of character, they do not focus attention upon Leontes' central self in the way that Othello's and Brutus' assertions had illuminated the needs and complexities of their natures.

A number of critics have felt that Shakespeare, in his last plays, destroyed that close relationship between language and dramatic character which had seemed the permanent achievement of his maturity. Charles Olson observed in 1950 that the later Shakespeare 'very much doesn't any longer bother to keep his music and thought inside the skin of the person and situation, able as he had been to make each person of his play make his or her individual self register its experience of reality'.[1] James Sutherland, confronting the opening lines of *Cymbeline*, suspected that 'the person who is thinking rapidly, breaking off, making fresh starts, and so on, is not the character, but Shakespeare himself'.[2] For Sutherland, this dislocation between verse and character reflected a Shakespeare who, if not exactly 'bored' (Strachey's epithet), was at least a little jaded: a man to whom poetry no longer came as naturally as leaves to a tree, who had to force himself now to create at all, and had taken to writing in a strained and entirely cerebral way. S. L. Bethell also claimed that the twisted rhythms and tortured syntax of the last plays represented 'Shakespeare's mind, not the character's; indeed, it draws our attention *away from* the speaker to what is spoken about.'[3] Unlike Sutherland, Bethell approved of what seemed to him a new technique designed to give prominence to those metaphysical truths which

---

[1] Charles Olson, 'Quantity in verse, and Shakespeare's late plays', in *Selected Writings of Charles Olson*, ed. R. Creeley (New York, 1966), p. 37.

[2] James Sutherland, 'The language of the last plays', in *More Talking of Shakespeare*, ed. John Garrett (London, 1959), p. 146.

[3] S. L. Bethell, Introduction to *The Winter's Tale*, New Clarendon Shakespeare (Oxford, 1956), pp. 22–3.

alone could justify Shakespeare's use of plot material so naive and silly. More recently, Hallett Smith has shifted the emphasis away from Shakespeare himself to the nature of the stage action. 'It is noteworthy', he says of certain passages in *Cymbeline* and *The Winter's Tale*, 'that the speeches do not so much characterize the speaker as dramatize the occasion.'[4]

Smith appears to me to have come closest to the truth. It is not easy to see why a dramatist who had so triumphantly solved what Daniel Seltzer describes as 'the problem of causing verbal expression to spring naturally from the inner life of the stage personality', who had developed 'a technique uniquely Shakespearian: that of expression, moment by moment, of an inner state and an immediate present time',[5] should suddenly decide to sacrifice the accomplishment. But then it is not easy, either, to understand the logic which impelled Michelangelo to forget everything he had painfully learned about the realistic articulation of the human body and return, in the Rondanini *Pietà*, to the stiff, non-naturalistic forms of Romanesque art. For whatever reason, Shakespeare at the end of his writing life chose to subordinate character to action in ways that seem to give Aristotle's conviction of the necessary primacy of the μῦθος a new twist.[6]

Editors of *The Tempest* have often wished to transfer Miranda's verbal assault upon Caliban in Act I ('Abhorred slave, / Which any print of goodness wilt not take') to Prospero. It seems almost inconceivable that her innocence and gentleness should be capable of such rugged and uncompromising vituperation. Examination of the last plays as a group, however, tends to suggest that the Folio is correct. Over and over again, Shakespeare jettisons consistency of characterization because he is more interested in the impersonal quality of a moment of dramatic time. This is what happens near the beginning of Act III of *The Tempest*, when Miranda somewhat

---

[4] Hallett Smith, *Shakespeare's Romances: A Study of Some Ways of the Imagination* (San Marino, California, 1972), p. 177.

[5] Daniel Seltzer, 'Prince Hal and tragic style', in *Shakespeare Survey 30* (Cambridge, 1977), pp. 13, 23.

[6] In *Die dramatische Technik des Sophokles* (Berlin, 1917), T. Wilamowitz argues against the idea of psychologically consistent characterization in Sophocles, and for the centrality of action, in ways that have some bearing on Shakespeare's late style. According to Wilamowitz, Sophocles was always essentially interested in the situation of the moment, and its effect on the theatre audience. This, as opposed to any internal logic, governs the behaviour of his characters and the way we see them. (See the discussion of Wilamowitz's argument by Hugh Lloyd-Jones, 'T. Wilamowitz on the dramatic technique of Sophocles', in *The Classical Quarterly* 22 (n.s.), 1972, 214–28.)

startlingly produces the image of a concealed pregnancy as the means
of declaring her love to Ferdinand: 'And all the more it seeks to hide
itself, / The bigger bulk it shows' (III.1.80–1). That Ophelia, in her
madness, should reveal that she has secretly committed to memory all
the verses of a rude song about St Valentine's Day, certainly says
something about Ophelia, and about the pathos of her attempts to
look in directions sternly prohibited by Polonius and Laertes. It
would obviously be inappropriate and futile to apply the same
reasoning to Miranda's lines. They are there, not to tell us anything
about sexual repression on the island, but because – as the betrothal
masque will later make even more plain – Shakespeare is concerned,
above all, to delineate this marriage in terms of natural fertility and
increase. Even so, Miranda says to Caliban earlier what the situation,
as opposed to maidenly decorum and the pliability of her own nature,
would seem to demand.

Miranda is not the only heroine to be treated in this fashion in the
late plays. As early as *Pericles*, Marina had anticipated Miranda's
confrontation with Caliban in the uncharacteristic venom and
masculinity of her reproof of Boult:

> Thou art the damned door-keeper to every
> Custrel that comes inquiring for his Tib.
> To the choleric fisting of every rogue
> Thy ear is liable; thy food is such
> As hath been belch'd on by infected lungs.   (IV.6.165–9)

The lines, however well suited to the Duke in *Measure For Measure*, are
not easy for an actress to encompass, considering that she will have
spent most of her previous scenes epitomizing a kind of gentle and
melancholy lyricism, coupled with an innocence incapable of even
understanding the Bawd's professional instructions (IV.2.116–23).
One previous abrupt departure from Marina's normal manner,
during her account to Leonine of the sea-storm of her birth
(IV.1.58–64), has at least warned the performer what to expect. In
both passages, Shakespeare appears to be using Marina less as a
character than as a kind of medium, through which the voice of the
situation can be made to speak.

Further instances of this attitude towards dramatic speech may be
found most readily by turning to those passages in the late plays
which, for one reason or another, have aroused critical censure or
disagreement. Dr Johnson found the third-act soliloquy of Belarius in

Cymbeline ('These boys know little they are sons to th'King') positively exasperating in its irrationality and unabashed expository purpose. Belarius is not, elsewhere, so crudely confiding, like a character in an old play. The improbability, however, of the story he has to tell has already been admitted by Shakespeare, indeed brought to our attention, in the opening dialogue between the first and second gentlemen (I.I.57–67). Belarius' speech in Act III reflects, not his own personality or feelings at the moment (elsewhere clearly enough defined), but simply the character of the events he describes: remote, fantastic, and overtly artificial. The same will be true of the highly wrought and convoluted prose in which the courtiers recount the finding of Perdita in *The Winter's Tale*, as it is of Iachimo's insistence, at the end of *Cymbeline*, upon transforming what ought to be an agonized confession of guilt into an intricate and palpable work of fiction. Iachimo's flowery and long-winded account of how Posthumus was led to wager on Imogen's chastity bears little resemblance to the episode we actually saw, back in the fourth scene of Act I. The gentlemen were not, as Iachimo claims they were, sitting at a feast praising their loves of Italy, until their hyperbole stung the melancholy Posthumus into a celebration of his mistress, and then into accepting Iachimo's trial. The reality was different, and more complex than this. Iachimo has tidied it all up, brought it closer – both stylistically and in terms of fact – to a romance world. He does this for reasons which (again) have less to do with his character than with the way *Cymbeline*, in its final scene, deliberately treats its plot material as unreal.

A similar concern to express situation before character allows the wicked Queen in *Cymbeline* to speak of Britain in words that would not misbecome John of Gaunt, when she proudly refuses to pay the Roman tribute. Even Cloten, when he announces that 'Britain's a world / By itself' (III.I.12–13), can expect applause. Arviragus appears to wander off the point in ways of which true grief, even in a verse play, ought to be incapable when he assures the 'dead' Fidele of the kindly attentions of the ruddock's 'charitable bill (O bill, sore shaming / Those rich-left heirs that let their fathers lie / Without a monument!) (IV.2.225–7). His brother Guiderius reproves him for playing 'in wench-like words with that / Which is so serious'. It is Arviragus, however, who is unconsciously faithful to the quality of the situation: Fidele is not dead, but merely asleep, as the result of the Queen's potion. It is interesting to compare Arviragus' lament here with the comic frenzy of the Nurse when she discovers Juliet 'dead' on her wedding day. Like Fidele, Juliet is only drugged into a semblance of death and, in this sense, the Nurse's ludicrous attempts at tragic style ('O day, O day, O day, O hateful day!'; IV.5.52) are entirely appropriate to a situation which is not what it seems to be. With the Nurse, however, one is aware first and foremost of how perfectly *in character* her lamentations are. Presumably, she sounded much the same when poor Susan went to God. This is not true of Arviragus' elegy in *Cymbeline*, a speech which, if anything, seems oddly hard to square with what we know about this princely rustic.

At least two notorious problems in the last plays may result from Shakespeare's use of this dramatic technique. It is always hard to know what to make of Lysimachus' asseveration to Marina, at the end of their interview in the brothel, that he came 'with no ill intent, for to me / The very doors and windows savor vilely' (IV.6.109–10). He has certainly created the impression, in the scene as a whole, that he is a man perfectly at home in a house of prostitution, and intimately acquainted with its ways. 'How now? how a dozen of virginities?' As the Bawd remarks, 'Your honor knows what 'tis to say well enough' (IV.6.20, 31). There is not the slightest hint that the Governor of Mytilene may be dissembling. Is his explanation to Marina a desperate attempt to save face before he too, with the other converts, goes off to 'hear the vestals sing'? Or is the answer simply that Shakespeare is not interested in Lysimachus' motivation: during the dialogue with the professionals, and with Marina, he is a young man of rank in search of a sound whore, because that is what the situation demands. Afterwards, he is not – because he is going to marry Marina. Something similar seems to be happening with Paulina's outburst to Leontes after the 'death' of Hermione.

> I say she's dead; I'll swear't. If word nor oath
> Prevail not, go and see. If you can bring
> Tincture or lustre in her lip, her eye,
> Heat outwardly or breath within, I'll serve you
> As I would do the gods. But, O thou tyrant!
> Do not repent these things, for they are heavier
> Than all thy woes can stir; therefore betake thee
> To nothing but despair. A thousand knees,
> Ten thousand years together, naked, fasting,
> Upon a barren mountain, and still winter
> In storm perpetual, could not move the gods
> To look that way thou wert.   (*The Winter's Tale*, III.2.203–14)

Paulina, of course, is lying – or, at least, she seems to be from the vantage point of the fifth act. In the scene itself, one must assume that she is a woman half crazed with shock and grief, expressing the truth of the situation. For the theatre audience at this point in the play, Hermione, unlike Fidele, is indeed dead. Paulina's voice is faithful to the action. And it is characteristic of the last plays that Shakespeare should not bother, amid the partial revelations of the final scene, to provide any explanation of her previous behaviour.

Never a man who paid much attention to the requirements of neo-classical decorum when constructing character, the Shakespeare of the late plays seems to have abandoned even the basic convention by which, earlier, his servants and lower-class characters generally expressed themselves in homely, colloquial, if vivid, prose. The gardeners of *Richard II*, in their one, brief appearance, had been striking exceptions to this rule: emblematic, verse-speaking custo-dians of a garden more symbolic than literal and, as such, very different from Launce or Speed, Costard, the citizenry of the Roman plays, Cade's rabble, the Dromios, Grumio, Peter, Pompey, or the carriers at Rochester. Posthumus, on the other hand, is a humble, private gentleman but he has mysteriously acquired, in Pisanio, a servant of quite extraordinary verbal sophistication, who can tell Imogen to

> Forget that rarest treasure of your cheek,
> Exposing it (but O, the harder heart!
> Alack, no remedy!) to the greedy touch
> Of common-kissing Titan, and forget
> Your laborsome and dainty trims, wherein
> You made great Juno angry.   (III.4.160–5)

Even the gaoler in *Cymbeline*, although he speaks prose, seems (like Perdita herself, though without the justification of her lineage) to smack of something greater than himself, 'too noble for this place'. To place his meditation on death ('O, the charity of a penny cord'; v.4.157–206) beside that of the grave-digger in *Hamlet* is to see how little Shakespeare is concerned, now, with any attempt at social realism. Even the Old Shepherd of *The Winter's Tale*, and the fishermen Patchbreech and Pilch in *Pericles*, seem to dodge in and out of their status-defined, comic roles in ways for which there are no real parallels in earlier plays. Stephano and Trinculo, in *The Tempest*, do not do this: they are consistently (and relatively realistically) conceived throughout. Shakespeare's orthodox handling of them, however, only serves to throw into relief the inexplicably civilized verse (if not the sentiments) of Caliban.

It is a commonplace of criticism to separate Imogen from the other young heroines of the last plays, to see her as a sister of Rosalind, Viola, Portia, or the Julia of *The Two Gentlemen of Verona*, a character existing somewhat uncomfortably in a romance world not really designed to accommodate her. There is obviously some truth in this judgement, at least when Imogen is measured against Marina, Perdita, and Miranda. She does indeed seem to be more vigorous, complex, and three-dimensional than they, to summon up memories of the earlier heroines. And yet, when Cymbeline, at the very end, recognizes 'the tune of Imogen' (v.5.238), it is not easy to define just what he means. Unlike Rosalind or Viola, Imogen has seemed to manifest herself in several, divergent modes: passionate and chilly, timorous and aggressive, sometimes intensely feminine, sometimes not. This is partly the result of the way she submerges her own personality within that of the fictional Fidele, losing herself in her role, as Rosalind had not when she impersonated Ganymede, or Viola when she acted Cesario. Rosalind's mercurial, feminine self always shines through Ganymede, making Orlando's acceptance of the wooing game credible. Viola constantly reminds us, as she talks to Orsino, Feste, and Olivia, or struggles to overcome her physical cowardice when confronting Aguecheek, of the lonely, isolated girl she really is. The image is curiously double. In the theatre, an audience remains aware that Fidele is really Imogen. Yet her identity is overlaid by another: that of the 'boy' whom Guiderius, Arviragus, Belarius and (later) Lucius see. We share their viewpoint, as we never share Olivia's, Orlando's, or Orsino's. This is not because Imogen is particularly skilled at dissembling – indeed, the bluntness and impatient candour of her behaviour at court during the early scenes suggest precisely the opposite – but because Shakespeare has transformed her so completely, in her dialogue with other characters, into the person she is pretending to be, that we intermittently lose sight of the reality. It is possible that the page Fidele's lament for his dead master,

> Alas,
> There is no more such masters. I may wander
> From east to occident, cry out for service,
> Try many, all good; serve truly; never
> Find such another master   (IV.2.370–4)

made an imaginary situation seem so convincing that Shakespeare was impelled to introduce the subsequent aside (lines 377–9) in order to remind us of the truth.

Shakespeare's handling of Imogen's disguise would seem to be a further example of the subordination, in the last plays, of character to the demands of stage action. It is also part of a new, and sometimes perplexing, attitude towards disguise and deceit generally. Pastoral Bohemia is a land in which ballad stories so improbable that they are virtual synonyms for fiction can eagerly be swallowed as true. There, no one sees through the various disguises of Autolycus, Florizel, Polixenes and Camillo. Elsewhere, however, dissembling and deceit tend to be transparent as they were not in earlier plays. 'Here comes the Lord Lysimachus disguis'd', the Bawd remarks calmly in the fourth act of *Pericles* (IV.6.16–17). One almost wonders why he troubled. When one considers how complex and vital an issue it had been in earlier plays – both the comedies and tragedies – to distinguish truth from falsehood, seeming from reality, how difficult to arrive in particular cases at Hamlet's understanding that 'one may smile, and smile, and be a villain', the sudden diminution or disappearance of this problem from the last plays is startling. It would seem, however, to be to a considerable extent responsible for their special character and flavour.

Where Bassanio had agonized long over the riddle of the caskets at Belmont, Pericles solves Antiochus' conundrum without effort and at once. Later, at Pentapolis, his rusty armour and dejected manner fail to conceal his innate nobility and worth from King Simonides and his daughter. Both are eager, before they know his identity, to press this seemingly unequal marriage. Lysimachus stands more upon his dignity, but even he requires only the assurance of a birth certificate to offer his hand to the girl he met first in the stews. At Cymbeline's court, everyone but the king himself can see clearly that the queen is evil and not to be trusted, and also that Cloten is a boor, and the lowly Posthumus the only man worthy of such a jewel as Imogen. Courts are not usually so perceptive. Cornelius will not give the queen the poisons for which she asks. Pisanio will neither betray Posthumus by entering the service of Cloten, nor believe Posthumus when he brands Imogen as unchaste. Imogen herself sees through Iachimo's slander of Posthumus. Guiderius and Arviragus know, although they cannot explain why, that Fidele is akin to them as Belarius is not.

In *The Winter's Tale*, although Antigonus misinterprets a dream (and pays heavily for it), Leontes is really the only person who believes in Hermione's guilt. Everyone else, including the nameless gentlemen of the court, sees clearly that he is deluded. Camillo tells Leontes to dissemble with Polixenes: 'with a countenance as clear / As friendship wears at feasts, keep with Bohemia' (1.2.343–4), and the king accepts his advice. 'I will seem friendly, as thou hast advis'd me.' Just how successful this attempt is emerges at the end of the act, when Polixenes assures Camillo that 'I do believe thee: / I saw his heart in's face' (1.2.446–7). Duncan had lamented that 'there's no art / To find the mind's construction in the face' (*Macbeth*, 1.4.11–12), but in the last plays it seems to be true more often that no art is required: faces tell all, even when, as in the case of Leontes, their owners are making strenuous attempts at hypocrisy. Prospero, through his magic art, understands the true nature of everyone on the island. The knowledge adds doubtfully to his happiness. It contributes, however, to the general sense in this, as in the other Romances, that the real problem, now, is not one of distinguishing good from evil but of deciding what to do with a knowledge which often seems to be acquired involuntarily rather than through any conscious effort at discrimination.

The involuntary plays a significantly new part in the last plays. Although, in general, good and evil are oddly transparent and recognizable for what they are, a few individual characters are arbitrarily deprived of this knowledge. Sealed off from everyone around them, they inhabit a strange, isolated state of consciousness in which they not only make false judgements, but cannot be reached or reasoned with by anyone else. These extreme states of mind are not arrived at, as it seems, by any logical, or psychologically comprehensible, process: they are simply 'caught', like the 'flu. This happens to Pericles towards the end of the play. He appears in Act v as a living dead man, one who has not spoken to anyone for three months. Only Marina can break through the barrier, and even she comes close to being defeated by the task. In the case of King Cymbeline, his delusion has come upon him before the beginning of the play, an inexplicable blindness which prevents him from seeing what is apparent to everyone else. Only the death of the wicked queen releases him from the spell. *The Tempest* stands slightly apart from the other Romances, in that the trance which enwraps Alonso, Antonio, and Sebastian after the enchanted banquet is directly attributable to Prospero's art. Again, however, it has the effect of creating a distinction between a special, almost somnambulist state and a waking world of preternatural clarity and moral definition. Posthumus, in *Cymbeline*, shuts himself off from the light in Act II. Philario is a minor character, and he has never met Imogen, but even he can see that Iachimo's tale 'is not strong enough to be believ'd / Of one persuaded well of' (II.4.131–2). Posthumus, however, has suddenly entered the troll kingdom of *Peer Gynt*, and no longer sees the world with the eyes of other men.

The madness of Leontes would seem to be generically like that of Pericles, Cymbeline, Posthumus and (with reservations) the three men of sin in *The Tempest*. But Shakespeare allows us to watch its inception and development at much greater length, a privilege which only serves to make the affliction itself more mysterious. Leontes comes to believe that he is the only person in Sicily capable of distinguishing truth from falsehood. In fact, he is the only person who cannot. What he describes, in the speech about the spider and the cup, as 'my true opinion' is a chimera, a self-deception of the grossest kind. And indeed, only a few lines later, he is repeating this talismanic word *true* in a sentence which means one thing to him and, as so often, something quite different to the audience: 'All's true that is mistrusted.' Editors of *The Winter's Tale* tend to feel that the phrase is sufficiently obscure to require a gloss. They explain carefully that Leontes is justifying the truth of his own suspicions about Hermione and Polixenes – and so he is. The word order, on the other hand, is oddly convoluted. (Compare Ford's superficially similar statement in a similar situation in *The Merry Wives of Windsor*: 'my intelligence is true, my jealousy is reasonable'; IV.2.148–9). *The Winter's Tale* inversion draws attention to a rival, and even more important, interpretation. What Leontes is telling us, without being aware that he does so, is that everything he thinks false is, in fact, true.

Throughout his writing life, Shakespeare displayed a marked predilection for analysing situations by way of contraries or antitheses. Dualities and polar opposites are a striking feature of his style, superimposed upon the individual verbal habits of particular characters: darkness and light, frost and fire, summer and winter, love and hate. Elizabethans, trained as they were in the discipline of formal rhetoric, often thought in such patterns. With Shakespeare, however, certain words seem to summon up their opposites almost automatically, as the result of an ingrained habit of mind almost

more than from the requirements of a particular situation or
rhetorical pattern. This is the case especially with the true–false
antithesis, as even a quick glance at the two words in the Shakespeare
concordance will reveal. They are surprisingly constant companions.
In the last plays, however, something odd seems to happen to
antithesis generally, and to the true–false figure in particular.

'Metaphysical' is a term frequently invoked to describe the stylistic
peculiarities of the Romances. And indeed, there is much to be said
for using it, in Dr Johnson's sense of heterogeneous ideas yoked
together by violence, analogies so ingenious it seems a wonder they
were ever found at all. Characteristic of all four plays, but of *The
Winter's Tale* in particular, is a form of similitude, usually employing
the conjunction *as*, in which antithesis is employed to define resemblance in a fashion both unexpected and only superficially logical.
When Antonio wants to assure Sebastian that Ferdinand is surely
dead, he complicates a fundamentally simple assertion by explaining
that ''Tis as impossible that he's undrown'd, / As he that sleeps here
swims' (II.1.236–7). Time, in *The Winter's Tale*, warns the theatre
audience that he will 'make stale / The glistering of this present, as
my tale / Now seems to it' (IV.1.13–15). Hermione is sure that her
past life 'hath been as continent, as chaste, as true, / As I am now
unhappy' (III.2.34–5), and Paulina informs Leontes that she is 'no
less honest / Than you are mad' (II.2.71–2). Iachimo, purloining the
sleeping Imogen's bracelet, finds it 'as slippery as the Gordian knot
was hard' (II.2.34). There are many other instances. In all of them,
a negative and a positive statement are oddly conjoined. Moreover,
although the syntax often appears to be setting up a clear-cut polarity
(honest–dishonest, chaste–falsely accused), in fact the figure slides off
into the oblique. The terms compared are not really antithetical:
they are merely *different* in a way that makes one wonder why these
particular instances have been made to confront each other at all.

The words *false* and *true* continue, in the last plays, to evoke one
another, but Shakespeare tends to treat them, now, in an almost
vertiginous way. Earlier true–false antitheses (e.g. 'As false, by
heaven, as heaven itself is true'; *Richard II*, IV.1.64) had been clear
cut. Although the complications attendant upon broken vows
produced, in *Love's Labour's Lost* and *King John*, three isolated
examples prophetic of the future,[7] it is only in the Romances that

---

[7] *Love's Labour's Lost*, V.2.772–4. *King John*, III.1.27–8 and V.4.28–9.

truth and falsehood come to engage habitually in a balancing act in which, at one and the same time, they remain polarities and seem to exchange identities. In the light of similar passages in *Cymbeline* and *The Winter's Tale*, Pericles' meditation on Antiochus at the beginning of the play sounds like an authentic and uncorrupted piece of Shakespearean text:

> If it be true that I interpret false,
> Then were it certain you were not so bad
> As with foul incest to abuse your soul.   (I.1.124-6)

Even so, Cornelius, when deceiving Cymbeline's queen about the nature of the drug he gives her, describes himself as 'the truer, / So to be false with her' (1.5.43-4). Pisanio performs the same gyration in Act III, when he informs the absent Cloten that 'true to thee / Were to prove false, which I will never be / To him that is most true' (III.5.157-9), and reiterates the paradox in Act IV: 'Wherein I am false, I am honest; not true, to be true' (IV.3.42). Leontes argues that even if women were as false as 'o'er-dy'd blacks', as water, wind or dice, 'yet were it true / To say this boy were like me' (1.2.134-5).

Imogen's anguished investigation of what it means 'to be false' extends the exercise:

> True honest men being heard, like false Aeneas,
> Were in his time, thought false; and Sinon's weeping
> Did scandal many a holy tear, took pity
> From most true wretchedness. So thou, Posthumus,
> Wilt lay the leaven on all proper men;
> Goodly and gallant shall be false and perjur'd
> From thy great fail.   (III.4.58-64)

Hermione on trial sees the same problem from the opposite side, but she delineates it in similar terms:

> Since what I am to say must be but that
> Which contradicts my accusation, and
> The testimony on my part no other
> But what comes from myself, it shall scarce boot me
> To say 'Not guilty'. Mine integrity
> Being counted falsehood, shall (as I express it)
> Be so receiv'd.   (III.2.22-8)

The pessimism of both women is unwarranted. Except for characters like Leontes and Posthumus, who have suddenly and arbitrarily gone blind, distinguishing between falsehood and truth as *moral* entities is no longer difficult. All of these riddling passages remind us of this fact. At the same time, they suggest, in their deliberate confounding of opposites, the presence of another kind of true–false confusion: one which is central to these plays.

On the whole, efforts to distinguish the fictional from the 'real', art from life, tales from truth, come in the Romances to replace the older, moral concern with identifying hypocrisy and deceit. It is not easy for characters to make these distinctions – nor, in some cases, for the theatre audience. Leontes, when he applies the story of the spider in the cup, mistakes a fiction of his own devising for fact, with disastrous results. He forces the imaginary to become true, even as Antonio does before *The Tempest* begins, when

> having into truth, by telling of it,
> Made such a sinner of his memory
> To credit his own lie – he did believe
> He was indeed the Duke.   (1.2.100–3)

Both of these are false and destructive fictions, credited only by their creators. And in both plays they can be countered only by another, and benevolent, kind of illusion: Prospero's restorative art, or the pastoral make-believe of Bohemia.

In Bohemia, almost all the special techniques of the last plays with which this essay has been concerned are on view simultaneously. People are constantly expressing the truth of the situation without grasping what, for us, is the primary meaning of their own words – as in the reiterated description of the lowly Perdita as a 'queen'. It has often been remarked that Polixenes and Perdita, in their debate on Art and Nature, perversely argue against their own position and intentions as they understand them at this point. Polixenes, after all, has come to the sheep-shearing precisely in order to prevent his gentle scion from grafting himself onto wild stock. Perdita, for her part, intends to make just such an 'unnatural' marriage. Their words, inconsistent with the purpose of the two speakers, focus attention not upon them but upon the real nature of the situation.

Perdita dislikes acting as much as she dislikes nature's bastards in her rustic garden. It worries her that her own identity should be submerged so completely in that of the festival queen she plays, that her robes should change her disposition. In fact, she does lose herself in her part, even as Imogen had in that of Fidele, although in this case the scene in which she distributes the flowers seems to operate as a healing counterbalance to the earlier 'play' in which her father, another unwilling actor, had fancied himself hissed off the stage in the role of cuckold. It is with great reluctance that Perdita agrees to continue in her royal part after Polixenes has revealed himself. Camillo's counsel to her to 'disliken / The truth of your own seeming' (IV.4.652–3) not only brings truth and falsehood into a linguistically dizzying relationship, in the manner characteristic of these plays; it expresses a truth beyond Camillo's ken. Like Imogen, Perdita must consent to 'disguise / That which, t'appear itself, must not yet be / But by self-danger' (*Cymbeline*, III.4.144–6).

Autolycus, a man of various and willing disguises, may seem at first sight to be a hypocrite and dissembler in the manner of earlier plays. His real association, however, is with fictions rather than with genuine evil. Certainly his decision not to take the obviously profitable step of acquainting Polixenes with Florizel's intended flight – because to do so would be an honest action, and Autolycus prefers to remain true to his own falsehood – is scarcely that of a man whose villainy we can take seriously. At the end of the play, the Clown, his chief victim, is cheerfully defending his oath that Autolycus is 'as honest a true fellow as any is in Bohemia' on the grounds that 'if it be ne'er so false, a true gentleman may swear it in the behalf of his friend' (v.2.157, 162–3). Justice Shallow's man Davy, pleading for the notorious Visor because 'the knave is mine honest friend' (*2 Henry IV*, v.1.50), never confounded the moral connotations of 'knave' and 'honest', despite his concern to mitigate the pejorative side. The Clown, on the other hand, calls precisely this polarity into doubt in ways that make it impossible for us to regard Autolycus as anything but what he is: a creator of fictions who, by not betraying Florizel to Polixenes, and by inventing a tale which frightens the Old Shepherd and the Clown into Sicily with the all-important fardel, is in fact the agent of the happy ending.

In Bohemia, people constantly confuse fact with fiction. Mopsa and Dorcas are almost obsessive in their desire to be assured that the pedlar's fantastic ballads are true. Their naiveté is comic and yet, later in the play, we find ourselves humbly sharing their impulse. The second gentleman announces that 'such a deal of wonder is broken out within this hour that ballad-makers cannot be able to express it' (v.2.23–5). The preservation of Perdita and her reunion with her father are, as Shakespeare continually reminds us, 'like an old tale', more improbable even than Autolycus' ballads. It is, however, a story that we too, in reading or watching the play, want to believe. This is even more true with the awakening of Hermione from marble to flesh, a resurrection which is as much a miracle for the theatre audience as for the characters involved. 'It is requir'd', Paulina says, 'you do awake your faith' (v.3.94–5). What kind of faith?

Several kinds of fiction, as it seems, have operated in *The Winter's Tale*. The comedy ending which was the original point of departure dissolved almost at once into a dark tale of sprites and goblins. Then, it metamorphosed into a traditional comedy plot. Florizel and Perdita stand together in the last moments of the play as lovers who have won through, despite parental opposition and mistakes about identity, in the immemorial way of comedy. It is true that there is something they lack. Mamillius ought to be standing beside them: Florizel's friend, as Polixenes was Leontes'. But Mamillius, like Antigonus, is dead. Hermione, too, is wrinkled and older after the passing of sixteen years. Leontes does not get back exactly what he threw away. Still, he gets back far more than men can realistically expect. *The Winter's Tale* admits something that Shakespeare's Elizabethan comedies had tried to deny: happy endings are a fiction. A fiction, but not quite a fairy-tale.

Paulina declares of Hermione in the last scene:

> That she is living,
> *Were it but told you*, should be hooted at
> Like an old tale; but it *appears* she lives.
>
> (v.3.115–17; *my italics*)

The words are true, once again, in a way not comprehended by the speaker. It is, after all, because of the dramatic form in which this implausible fiction has been embodied, because of our complex, theatrical experience of this μῦθος, that we can give *The Winter's Tale* a kind of assent we deny to Greene's *Pandosto*. In the world as we know it, the dead do not return. Lost children generally stay lost, and shepherds' daughters do not attract the sons of kings. Ageing widows are not married off quite so neatly as Paulina. Shakespeare not only does not try to conceal, he positively emphasizes the fact that his material is the archetypal stuff of legend and fairy-tale. That we respond to it as something far more powerful and engaging than 'Cinderella' or 'Beauty and the Beast' testifies to the subtlety with which Shakespeare has adjusted his language and dramatic art to the demands of a new mode: one in which plot, on the whole, has become more vivid and emotionally charged than character. And also, to a desperate artistic honesty which could admit, now, to creating fictions, while making us understand why and how much we should like those fictions to be real.

CHAPTER 9

'Enter Mariners wet': realism in Shakespeare's last plays (1986)

On the twenty-ninth of June 1613, realism – that most elusive and shifting of aesthetic concepts – contrived to burn the Globe theatre to the ground. The play involved was almost certainly Shakespeare's *Henry VIII*, presented under its alternative title, *All Is True*. According to Sir Henry Wotton, who described the catastrophe a few days later in a letter to his nephew, unusual efforts had been made by the King's Men to reproduce the ceremonial, dress, orders and insignia of Henry's court, 'even to the matting of the stage'.[1] Wotton had his doubts about such fidelity to fact. The effect, he grumbled, was 'within a while to make greatness very familiar, if not ridiculous'. Indeed, there is a distinctly judgemental note in Wotton's account of how the theatre cannon, shot off here not as the usual Elizabethan and Jacobean shorthand for a battle (something always difficult to stage) but simply to dignify Henry's arrival as a masquer at York House, accidentally set fire to the playhouse thatch, a calamity which went unnoticed until too late by 'eyes more attentive to the show'.

Thirteen years earlier, the Chorus of *Henry V*, Shakespeare's penultimate English history, had admitted humbly that only an impossible set of conditions – 'a kingdom for a stage, princes to act, / And monarchs to behold the swelling scene' – could possibly bring forth 'the warlike Harry, like himself' (Chorus. 1.3–5). In effect, the only satisfactory way of telling this story would be for it actually to happen again, on 'the vasty fields of France' (12). The *Henry VIII* Prologue, by contrast, makes not the slightest apology for the inadequacies of the theatre this play was destined to destroy. The spectators, it predicts calmly, will 'think ye see / The very persons of our noble story / As they were living' (25–7). Nor do they have to make any special imaginative efforts to 'piece out our imperfections

[1] Sir Henry Wotton, quoted in Geoffrey Bullough, ed., *Narrative and Dramatic Sources of Shakespeare*, IV (London, 1962), p. 436.

with your thoughts' (*Henry V* Chorus. 1.23), 'play with your fancies', or 'eche out our performance with your mind' (Chorus. III.7, 35). They need only admire the stage pictures, weep for the characters and, above all, recognize that what they are about to see is 'true' (21).

But in what sense 'true'? Ignoring Philip Sidney's dictum in the *Apology for Poetry* – that the poet 'never maketh any circles about your imagination, to conjure you to believe for true what he writes', that he gives names to men 'but to make their picture the more lively, and not to build any history'[2] – dramatists in the period frequently laid claim in their titles to factual truth. This is the case, above all, with history plays, a relatively new form lacking classical sanction and driven, as a result, to seek it elsewhere, and also (for similar reasons) with domestic tragedy. Hence *The True Tragedy of Richard III* (1591), *The True Chronicle History of the Whole Life and Death of Thomas Lord Cromwell* (1600), *The True and Honorable History of Sir John Oldcastle* (1599) – the last a riposte to what the four joint authors dismissed as the 'forg'de invention' of Shakespeare's *Henry IV* plays[3] – or *A Yorkshire Tragedy: Not So New, as Lamentable and True* (1606). Even Heywood's *The Four Prentices of London With the Conquest of Jerusalem* (1600), an egregiously wild invention, billed itself as *True and Strange*.

The majority of such claims are scarcely more serious than those of Autolycus in *The Winter's Tale*, when he assures the shepherdesses Mopsa and Dorcas that the ballads he has for sale – about usurers' wives who give birth to money-bags, or hard-hearted maids turned into fish, who repent tunefully 'forty thousand fadom above water' (IV.4.277) – are all 'very true' (267). Heywood, indeed, made a joke out of his alternative title in the Prologue to *The Four Prentices of London*:

1 Touching the name why is it called, True and Strange, or The foure Prentises of London? A Gentleman that heard the subject discourst, sayd it was not possible to be true; and none here are bound to beleeve it.

2 'Tis true, that Alexander at thirty-two years of age conquered the whole world; but strange he should do so. If we should not beleeve things recorded in former ages, wee were not worthy that succeeding times should believe things done in these our ages.

[2] Sir Philip Sidney, *An Apology for Poetry*, ed. Geoffrey Shepherd (Manchester, 1973), p. 124.
[3] See the Prologue to *Sir John Oldcastle*, in *The Shakespeare Apocrypha*, ed. C. F. Tucker Brooke (Oxford, 1908), p. 129.

1 But what authority have you for your History? I am one of those that wil believe nothing that is not in the Chronicle.

2 Our Authority is a Manuscript, a Booke writ in parchment; which not being publicke, nor generall in the World, we rather thought fit to exemplifie unto the publicke censure, things concealed and obscur'd, such as are not common with every one, than such Historicall Tales as every one can tell by the fire in Winter...

1 You have satisfied me; and, I hope, all that heare it.[4]

That supposed manuscript authority, the 'Booke writ in parchment', is oddly premonitory of those fake documents upon which the early English novel, from Defoe and Richardson to Scott, so often pretended to rely. Long before the word itself came into common usage, new and heterodox types of fiction were already seeking support from what we should now find it natural to designate as the 'real'.

Henry VIII takes a number of liberties with the historical facts of Elizabeth's father's reign. Yet, on the whole, it honours the contract its Prologue makes with 'such as give / Their money out of hope they may believe' (7–8). Certainly, by comparison with Samuel Rowley's earlier dramatization of Henry's life, *When You See Me, You Know Me* (1604) – a cheerfully preposterous piece in which bluff King Hal, disguised, had exchanged fisticuffs with a rogue called 'Black Will', endured a night in one of his own prisons on a disorderly conduct charge, and jettisoned Anne of Cleves for Katherine Parr in the space of four lines – the relatively sober and accurate account which the King's Men were offering might well claim to represent 'truth' (9, 18). The trouble with this truth is that it is so naked and unmediated, so cunningly full but contradictory and unshaped, as to create serious problems of interpretation. As is so often the case in Shakespeare's late plays, characters and their motivations, viewed from outside rather than from within, remain riddling and opaque. No soliloquies resolve the question of Buckingham's innocence or guilt, divulge Henry's genuine reason for divorcing Katherine, the extent of Wolsey's fidelity to the crown, or make it plain in what spirit Anne makes her way to Henry's bed. Judgement, as a result, or even understanding of these events which (in one sense) are being so accurately presented, becomes almost impossible. As one critic has

---

[4] Thomas Heywood, *The Four Prentices of London*, in *The Complete Dramatic Works of Thomas Heywood*, 4 vols. (London, 1874), II, pp. 165–6.

observed, 'It is not the presence of fact or chronicle-matter in *Henry VIII* but the restraint of the imagination's transforming power that is distinctive.[5]

Consistently, where analysis or personal revelation might be expected, the play offers spectacle instead: Buckingham formally escorted to his execution, the masque and banquet at York House, Queen Katherine's state trial, the great procession at the coronation of Anne, and then at Elizabeth's christening, the vision which appears to the sleeping Katherine shortly before her death. With the significant – and deliberately puzzling – exception of the last, all of these ceremonies and pageants are versions of things which the members of Shakespeare's audience might reasonably be expected to encounter outside the theatre. They were also events which a company with the resources of the King's Men could represent plausibly on the stage. (Although there is much talk, for instance, about the Field of the Cloth of Gold, with its horses and knightly combats, no attempt is made to include it in the action.) The tableaux of *Henry VIII*, moreover, appear to be there purely for their own sake: they serve no essential plot or thematic purpose. When Heywood, in *If You Know Not Me, You Know Nobody* (1604), had shown Elizabeth on the way to her coronation receiving a Bible and a purse from the Lord Mayor of London, and scrupulously named the lords she confirmed in their offices, while receiving from them the insignia of rule, he was making a powerful statement about support for a Protestant queen among the nobility and in the City. Shakespeare, by contrast, in stage directions so elaborate that they might almost belong to a film script, specifies that Anne returned from Westminster Abbey preceded by trumpets, two judges, the Lord Chancellor 'with purse and mace before him', choristers, the Lord Mayor of London, Garter, then 'Marquess Dorset, bearing a sceptre of gold, on his head a demi-coronal of gold. With him, the Earl of Surrey, bearing the rod of silver with the dove, crowned with an earl's coronet. Collars of Esses', and so on, down to the 'old Duchess of Norfolk' who carried the queen's train, merely (as it seems) because this, with surprisingly few alterations and omissions, was how this procession had looked, according to Holinshed, in 1533.

In objecting to what might be described as the documentary aspect of *Henry VIII*, to its concern to reproduce certain public events of the

[5] Judith H. Anderson, *Biographical Truth: The Representation of Historical Persons in Tudor-Stuart Writing* (New Haven, Conn., 1984), p. 132.

last century as they might have appeared to people living then, Wotton displayed an uneasy sense that the theatre was over-reaching itself. To claim that, thanks to the indulgence and imaginative efforts of the spectators, a cockpit, a wooden O, might for a little while pretend to 'hold the vasty fields of France' was one thing. The English theatre had played this game, in one form or another, for centuries. What seems to have disturbed him about *Henry VIII* were its trespasses upon the real, a confident annexing of the actual which appeared to threaten the integrity and status of the things imitated. The term itself was not available to him, but in effect Wotton was made uneasy by the *realism* of *Henry VIII* as performed at the Globe.

'The terminology of "the real"', J. P. Stern has written, 'is no more than the dispensable cultural option of an era.'[6] As he remarks, the word 'reality' does not appear in the whole of Shakespeare. But then, apart from a very few, special instances, it cannot be traced anywhere until the late seventeenth century. 'Real' makes its entrance much earlier, but for long remained an uncommon word, the precise sense of which, as the OED notes, tends in context to be difficult to define. Towards the end of Elizabeth's reign, it could apparently be regarded as affected. In *The Scourge of Villanie* (1598), Marston has a fling at three 'new-minted Epithets' of 'Torquatus', one of which turns out to be 'Reall'.[7] It has been claimed that Torquatus was meant to represent Ben Jonson, in whose work the word does appear seven times: five times in the plays, twice in non-dramatic poems. But, apart from the fact that none of these Jonson texts was available to Marston at the time he was writing his satire, it seems odd that the word as Jonson uses it – invariably in the traditional scholastic sense of idea or essence as opposed to accidental particularity or mere name[8] – should attract derisory attention.

Shakespeare's three uses of 'real' (in *All's Well That Ends Well*, 'A Lover's Complaint' and *Coriolanus*) are more complex and innovative. Moreover, he found its converse 'unreal', a word he may

---

[6] J. P. Stern, '"Reality" in early twentieth-century German literature' in *Philosophy and Literature*, ed. A. Phillips Griffiths, Royal Institute of Philosophy Lecture Series: 16. Supplement to *Philosophy* 1983 (Cambridge, 1984), p. 47.

[7] John Marston, 'To those that seeme judiciall perusers', *The Scourge of Villanie*, in *The Poems of John Marston*, ed. Arnold Davenport (Liverpool, 1961), p. 100.

[8] Jonson's use of this word is discussed, usefully, in vol. 9 of the Oxford edition of Jonson's *Works*, ed. C. H. Herford and Percy and Evelyn Simpson, 11 vols. (Oxford, 1925–53), p. 436. Jonson's Oxford editors, while admitting the possibility, in some instances, of other connotations, stress the primacy of the scholastic meaning.

well have invented, necessary to him twice, in *Macbeth* and *The Winter's Tale*. The incidence of 'real' in Shakespeare is, of course, slender when compared with his lifelong reliance upon the word 'true' and its cognate forms. That vocabulary cluster fills nine and a half columns in the Spevack Concordance. 'Real' and its partner 'unreal', however, are very special words as Shakespeare employs them. If, as has recently been suggested, both *All's Well That Ends Well* and 'A Lover's Complaint' are Jacobean works,[9] then these are terms which come into play only during the second half of Shakespeare's writing life. Three out of the five passages are cited in the OED as being the earliest recorded use of the word in this particular sense. All constitute a deliberately chosen alternative to the word 'true', or to its usual Shakespearean antonym.

The prefix 'un-' was a particular favourite of Shakespeare's, a way of negating something within a specific context while continuing to affirm its general existence. A number of these compounds seem to have been original with him: 'unknowing', 'unfellowed', 'unpolluted', 'unaneled', and many more.[10] Others – 'unhappy', for instance, or 'unworthy' – were already in common use. So was the word 'untrue'. Yet whereas two hundred and fifteen instances of 'happy' in the Concordance are matched by forty-one uses of 'unhappy', and two hundred and thirty-eight of 'worthy' by thirty-nine of 'unworthy', the massive entry for 'true' – eight hundred and forty-nine – is countered by only seven examples of 'untrue'. Normally, Shakespeare locates the obverse of 'true' in the monosyllable 'false', a word he employs three hundred and thirteen times. Lexically independent of 'true', 'false' is autonomous as compounds beginning with an 'un-' prefix are not. Yet the two contrasting words were so closely associated in Shakespeare's mind that the one tended to summon up the other automatically, sometimes within the same line, more often at a little distance. Usually, this partnership serves to activate the moral connotations implicit in both, even in contexts where such a meaning is far from primary.

'Real' and 'unreal', on the other hand, never keep company in Shakespeare. Neither harbours any sense of moral judgement. In 'A

---

[9] In his edition of *The Sonnets and A Lover's Complaint* (Harmondsworth, 1986), John Kerrigan argues persuasively for a Jacobean date for the latter poem. I am indebted to Gary Taylor, co-editor of The New Oxford Shakespeare, for outlining to me his reasons for believing that *All's Well That Ends Well* must now be placed later than *Measure For Measure*.

[10] S. S. Hussey, *The Literary Language of Shakespeare* (London, 1982), p. 55.

Lover's Complaint', the forsaken maid is bitterly accusatory when she describes her beautiful seducer as being able, in his personal conduct, to 'livery falseness in a pride of truth' (105). The young man is a 'false jewel' (154), a deceiver whose smooth tongue makes specious use of words like 'truth' and 'troth'. Only his horsemanship, so uncanny that beholders were led to question its basis, was no illusion. In defending the integrity of this one quality, its foundation in fact, Shakespeare's maid shies away from the slippery and contaminated word 'true'. His 'real habitude', she declares, 'gave life and grace / To appertainings and to ornament' (114–15). Appertainings and ornament, false appearances, guileful shows, lies that look like truth: these are common currency in the courtly world of 'A Lover's Complaint'. That is why the unusual word 'real' has to be invoked in order to characterize the single, wholly amoral activity of the young man which tangibly is what it seems to be.

Again, in *Coriolanus*, the protagonist reaches out for the word 'real' when trying to convince his fellow patricians that to allow the plebeians any sway in the government of the state must be to sacrifice 'real necessities' to 'unstable slightness' (III.1.147–8). 'Real necessities' are not the same as 'true needs'. Nor do they have anything to do with the idealist/nominalist debate. They are part of that world of solid, firm, visible entities, of scars and swords, oak garlands and brazen instruments of war, in which Coriolanus feels at home. Diplomacy and compromise, patrician willingness to adapt to the times, can only (in his eyes) violate 'the fundamental part of state' (151). The 'real', for Coriolanus, is what can be touched and felt and seen. It does not inhabit words or 'voices' – the 'yea and no / Of general ignorance' (145–6) – but, taking the word back to its primal Latin root in *res*, seen actions and changeless, massy things.

The 'real' in Shakespeare is neither good nor bad, and only in a morally neutral sense 'true'. 'Unreal', its converse, is similarly amoral. All the associations of this word are with ambiguous, riddling, intangible things: ghosts and shadows, dreams, nothingness, or names without substance. Macbeth tries to rid himself of Banquo's all too palpable ghost by addressing it as 'horrible shadow! / Unreal mock'ry' (III.4.105–6). Leontes, commenting more acutely than he knows upon his predicament, observes that 'affection' communicates with 'dreams': 'With what's unreal thou co-active art, / And fellow'st nothing' (*The Winter's Tale* 1.2.138–42). In the most complicated of the three instances, the supposedly dead Helena, in

All's Well That Ends Well, forces from the King of France the startled enquiry: 'Is't real that I see?' (v.3.306). Her immediate disclaimer – 'No, my good lord, / 'Tis but the shadow of a wife you see, / The name, and not the thing' (306–8) – reinterprets the King's question. France wondered if some 'exorcist / Beguiles the truer office of mine eyes' (304–5), whether he was looking at a living woman or a ghost. Helena understands this. She also plays with the familiar nominalist/ idealist distinction. Yet her reply is addressed fundamentally to Bertram, not the King. She wants her husband to concede that she is fully and physically his wife, not merely the possessor of an empty title. Only Bertram's acknowledgement that this is so: 'Both, both. O pardon' (308), can now make Helena 'real'.

For most of Shakespeare's characters, seeing is believing. 'If there be truth in sight', Duke Senior announces confidently, in the moment that 'Ganymede' metamorphoses into the lost Rosalind, 'you are my daughter' (*As You Like It* v.4.118), and he is echoed by Orlando and Phebe. Horatio would not have credited the ghost in *Hamlet*, for all that Bernardo and Marcellus have to say about it, 'without the sensible and true avouch / Of mine own eyes' (1.1.57–8), and Thersites finds it particularly exasperating that Troilus should refuse to accept what he has not only overheard but – more importantly – seen outside Calchas' tent: 'Will 'a swagger himself out on's own eyes?' (*Troilus and Cressida* v.2.136). Although eyes may, on occasion, play tricks on their owners (Macbeth, confronted with the airy dagger, is unsure whether they 'are made the fools o'th'other senses', or are 'worth all the rest' (11.1.44–5)) normally, they are the highest and most reliable of the five senses. Yet they cannot guarantee, or even significantly control, a correct understanding of what they communicate. Othello did actually see the handkerchief in Cassio's hand, Gloucester the blood flowing from Edmund's self-inflicted wound, and Claudio and Don Pedro a 'ruffian' being outrageous without rebuke outside Hero's bedroom window. Eyes were not to blame for what followed, only the misinterpreting mind ensnared in a carefully constructed deceit which has known how to make false use of the visually true.

In the romances, characters continue to misconstrue or be baffled by the evidence presented to their eyes. Yet it is rare, now, for such uncertainties to result in *moral* confusion. Apart from a few isolated blunderers – Leontes, Posthumus, or King Cymbeline – upon whom moral obtuseness descends suddenly, like a disease, characters in

these plays usually find it simple to separate honesty from dissembling, white from black. So, everyone in *Cymbeline*, except the
King, recognizes effortlessly that Imogen and Posthumus are good,
and worthy of each other, the Queen wicked, and her son Cloten a
brute. No one but Leontes, in *The Winter's Tale*, makes the mistake of
believing Hermione unchaste. The incestuous solution to the riddle
game at Antioch is so obvious that King Pericles can scarcely miss it
– something which certainly could not have been said of the caskets
facing Bassanio in Portia's Belmont. In *The Tempest*, only Caliban,
and the equally inexperienced Miranda who naively includes
Antonio in her 'brave new world', misjudge the people around them.
The very words 'true' and 'false', in these plays, although they
continue to summon up one another, are no longer highly charged
opposites. Indeed, they often seem to change places, as they do in
Pisanio's paradox: 'Wherein I am false I am honest; not true, to be
true' (*Cymbeline* IV.3.42). The overall result is to shift attention away
from 'what our seemers be' (*Measure for Measure* I.3.54) towards more
specialized, aesthetic concerns: issues which we would find it natural
to speak of now in terms of the unreal and the real.[11]

In *Pericles*, 'absolute Marina' (Chorus. IV.31) is said to be so skilful
with her needle, composing

> Nature's own shape of bud, bird, branch, or berry,
> That even her art sisters the natural roses;
> Her inkle, silk, twin with the rubied cherry.   (Chorus. V.6–8)

Like the painted cherries of Zeuxis, at which real birds pecked,
Marina's embroidery obliterates a boundary, inviting misinterpretation as substance rather than shadow. Such conceits, of a visual
art rivalling life, or even more lifelike than life itself, were of course
common in the Renaissance. Usually, however, they concede some
degree of failure, as in the poem appended to the Droeshout
engraving of Shakespeare in the First Folio, where the artist's 'strife'
to delineate his subject's 'wit' as well as his features, and 'out-doo the
life', ends in defeat. Because it makes (apparently) no attempt to
imitate the human form, let alone mind or personality, Marina's
needlework satisfies realistic criteria more easily than the work of

---

[11] See my earlier essay, 'Leontes and the spider: language and speaker in Shakespeare's last
plays', in *Shakespeare's Styles: Essays in Honour of Kenneth Muir*, ed. Edwards, Ewbank and
Hunter (Cambridge, 1980). The present essay is in many ways a complement to this piece,
reprinted above.

artists whose subject matter is more animate and ambitious. Buds and branches, berries, roses or cherries, after all, do not require her to apologize for needlework's inability to incorporate motion and sound. Only the bird might be thought to suffer any diminution in consequence of being, perforce, both voiceless and immobile.

When, on the other hand, Iachimo praises the unknown sculptor responsible for the carved chimney piece in Imogen's bed-chamber ('chaste Dian bathing') as 'another Nature, dumb', a man who 'outwent her, / Motion and breath left out' (*Cymbeline* II.4.84–5), the qualifications make significant inroads on the praise. Movement and sound are components too important in this mythological scene not to make their absence felt, for all the artist's skill, even as they are in the 'conceit deceitful' of that 'skillful painting made for Priam's Troy' before which Shakespeare's Lucrece momentarily forgets herself, tearing at the image of Sinon, Tarquin's surrogate, with her nails, only to rebuke herself at once: '"Fool, Fool,", quoth she, "his wounds will not be sore"' (*The Rape of Lucrece* 1423, 1367, 1568). Lucrece is particularly distressed by Hecuba's speechlessness: the painter 'did her wrong, / To give her so much grief, and not a tongue' (1462–3). For all his cunning with foreshortening and perspective, with things which 'seem' real, the Troy artist was no 'god'. All he created, in the end, was the 'liveless life', 'in scorn of nature', of things which can neither speak nor move (1374).

'Seems' and 'seem'd' recur frequently in the account of the Troy painting. Although morally neutral, they carry with them an underlying sense of inadequacy which can slide easily into disparagement. It is rare, in Shakespeare, for the visual arts to escape some kind of contact with the dubious vocabulary of scorn and mockery, counterfeiting and deceit. Only for an instant do the painted eyes of 'fair Portia's counterfeit', which Bassanio discovers in the leaden casket, seem to move. In the next moment, he is recognizing how painfully 'this shadow / Doth limp behind the substance' (*The Merchant of Venice* III.2.115, 128–9). Even the vainglorious Painter in *Timon of Athens*, flattered by the Poet that his work is so lifelike that 'to th'dumbness of the gesture / One might interpret', feels it necessary to brush the hyperbole away: 'It is a pretty mocking of the life' (I.1.33–5). He may, as Timon later accuses him, with a deliberate play on words, draw 'a counterfeit / Best in all Athens', and 'most lively': he cannot escape the limitations of his medium, a medium which perpetually invites description not in the morally neutral terms of the unreal and the real, but in the more pejorative ones associated with falsehood and truth (v.1.80–3).

When Paulina, in the fifth act of *The Winter's Tale*, unveils the statue of Hermione, she avails herself of just this suspect vocabulary: 'prepare / To see the life as lively mock'd as ever / Still sleep mock'd death' (v.3.18–20). In speaking about the statue earlier, the anonymous third gentleman had described its supposed creator, Julio Romano, in familiar terms: Nature's 'ape', a man who might indeed put her out of business if only he possessed personal immortality and 'could put breath into his work'. One of the marvels reported about Hermione's statue (the gentleman does not say that he credits it) is that it is so lifelike the beholder might be tempted to address it, 'and stand in hope of an answer' (v.2.94–102)). Perdita, in fact, will do just this, while her father stands torn between his rational knowledge that no 'fine chisel / Could ever yet cut breath', that if the eyes of the image seem to move, that is because 'we are mock'd with art' (v.3.78–9, 68), and a delirious persuasion that he may be right in supposing that 'it breath'd...and that those veins / Did verily bear blood?' (64–5).

'Verily' is an interesting choice. In the first act of *The Winter's Tale*, Polixenes' recourse to just this word had let him in for a good deal of affectionate teasing from Hermione. Shakespeare often treats that group of relatively new and still uncommon English words derived from the Latin *veritas* – 'verily', 'verity', 'verify', 'veritable' – as mildly comic and affected. Hamlet makes 'verity' an ingredient in his parody of Osric's inflated rhetoric (v.2.116); Kent in *King Lear* uses it to satirize courtly language (II.2.105). 'Verified' is one of the grandiose words Dogberry flaunts without understanding (*Much Ado About Nothing* v.1.218), while both 'verify' and 'verily' suffer as a result of the attentions, however well meaning, of Fluellen in *Henry V* (III.2.71, v.1.61). In *The Winter's Tale*, Archidamus has already inflicted some damage on 'verily' in the opening scene by relying on it (in vain) to help him finish a particularly stilted and ineffective sentence of compliment (I.1.11). Hermione's subsequent mockery of what she calls Polixenes' 'dread "verily"' (I.2.55) threatens to finish the word off. Yet at the end of the play, Leontes will need 'verily', not as a pretentious term, but for reasons akin to his earlier need for 'unreal': because, in a scene which carefully avoids 'true' and 'false', the uncommon and arresting adverb 'verily' is better able to suggest what is special and extraordinary about a stone image which, by laying claim to motion and speech, is about to break through the barrier dividing even the most realistic sculpture from life.

Shakespeare never provides an answer to Polixenes' baffled enquiry in the last moments as to just how Hermione has 'stol'n from the dead' (115). Was Paulina, like everyone else, including the theatre audience, deceived in Act III by a semblance of death from which the queen later revived? Or did she lie to Leontes when assuring him that 'she's dead; I'll swear't. If word nor oath / Prevail not, go and see' (III.2.203–4). According to his own admission in Act v, Leontes did 'go and see', and what he found was a corpse (v.3.139–40). How this particular 'dead' queen re-lives is indeed 'to be question'd' (139). All that can be said with any confidence, however, is that the life she regains is specifically that of the theatre, the one art whose prerogative it was to present images which can both move and speak, as those of the painter and sculptor cannot.

For both audiences, the one on and the one off stage, Paulina carefully defines the nature of the miracle:

> that she is living,
> Were it *but* told you, should be hooted at
> Like an old tale; but it *appears* she lives,
> Though yet she *speak* not. (v.3.115–18, *my italics*)

Report, addressed solely to the ear, without visual confirmation, would be as suspect as those ballads peddled by Autolycus, fictions to be credited only by hearers as naive as Mopsa and Dorcas. But Hermione's resurrection is not dependent upon narrative, a tale told at secondhand. She 'appears' to live. In the late sixteenth and early seventeenth centuries, the meaning of the verb 'appears' was almost always straightforward: 'to come forth into sight' (sometimes from a place of concealment), 'to become visible'. When the music wakes her, and she steps forward to embrace her husband, Hermione satisfies that criterion of reality. Leontes' cry, 'O, she's warm!' adds further tangible confirmation and yet, significantly, it is still not enough. 'She hangs about his neck', Camillo exclaims wonderingly, but he goes on to demand: 'If she pertain to life, let her speak too' (112–13). Prompted gently by Paulina, Hermione formally blesses her daughter and, in the moment that she utters these words, her metamorphosis from stone to flesh becomes complete.

Shakespeare set up this *coup de théâtre* with enormous care. Critics, while recognizing that the dramatist would naturally have been reluctant to risk either anti-climax or a repetition of the earlier reunion of Pericles and Marina, have often felt dissatisfied nonetheless with the scene which immediately precedes the final one: that conversation between Autolycus and the three Sicilian gentlemen which is as close as Shakespeare allows us to get to the highly charged moment, off-stage, when the farthel was opened and Leontes recovered his lost child. The scene itself is cast entirely in prose, of an ornate and consciously distanced kind, a narrative mode reminiscent, both in sentence structure and in many of its conceits, of that employed by Sidney in *The Countess of Pembroke's Arcadia*. It has not infrequently been attacked as long-winded, undramatic, and excessively contrived. Yet Shakespeare is doing something here of crucial importance to our understanding of the statue scene. Of the three gentlemen, the Second (Rogero) knows about the finding of Perdita only from report. He and, as he suggests, others in the same position are by no means able to believe what they have heard: 'This news, which is call'd true, is so like an old tale, that the verity of it is in strong suspicion' (v.2.27–9). The word 'verity', whatever it may have been for Kent and Hamlet, is in this context no more risible than Leontes' 'verily' will be a few moments later. It too is being asked to extend and complicate the meaning of 'true'. The First Gentleman has been somewhat more fortunate than the Second. He was actually present when the farthel was produced, and 'methought, I heard the shepherd say, he found the child' (6–7). At this point, however, he and all the other courtiers were ordered to leave the room. The last thing he took away with him was the sight of Leontes and Camillo standing staring at one another like a pair of carved or painted images. Like the Poet in *Timon of Athens*, he was struck by the eloquence of these silent figures: 'There was speech in their dumbness, language in their very gesture.' The passion expressed was clearly that of 'wonder', but whether 'they had heard of a world ransom'd, or one destroy'd', the First Gentleman could not say. As he points out, even 'the wisest beholder, that knew no more but seeing, could not say if th'importance were joy or sorrow' (13–19).

Only the Third Gentleman, Paulina's steward, permitted as it seems to stay behind when the others left, can banish the doubts of that courtier who has heard about the finding of the king's daughter without seeing it, and also content the First Gentleman by discovering the meaning of what he has merely seen. His interlocutors accept the combined evidence he offers of eye and ear. Yet the Third Gentleman finds explication extraordinarily difficult. 'That which you hear', he begins confidently, 'you'll swear you see, there is such unity in the proofs' (31–2). But as he proceeds with his account of what happened in the palace, narrative, although pushed to its figural and descriptive limits, reveals itself increasingly as inadequate to its task. The meeting between Polixenes and Leontes, the Third Gentleman is obliged to confess, was 'a sight which was to be seen, cannot be spoken of' (42–3). As for what ensued, it 'lames report to follow it, and undoes description to do it'. These events become, in fact, when related, once more 'like an old tale, which will have matter to rehearse, though credit be asleep' (57–8, 61–2), as even their narrator is aware.

Such a story, the Third Gentleman muses prophetically near the end of the steward's account, deserves to be staged before an 'audience of kings and princes, for by such was it acted' (80–1). This is the old, seemingly impossible set of conditions of which the Chorus in *Henry V* had dreamed: 'a kingdom for a stage, princes to act, / And monarchs to behold the swelling scene'. But, as the three gentlemen depart for Paulina's house in order to admire, along with the members of the royal party, a rare work of art whose existence has never before been mentioned in the play, those conditions are about to be realized. Before an on-stage audience of kings and princes, there will be enacted the resurrection of a real, not a player queen. And, when Paulina's show is over, although no one in either the stage or theatre audience can be entirely clear as to the nature of what they have both heard and witnessed, it cannot be easily dismissed, 'hooted at like an old tale'. 'The art itself is Nature' (IV.4.97), not because, as Polixenes claimed earlier in the sheepshearing scene, human meddling with the integrity of the original creation is itself part of that creation, but because of the special relationship which the theatre enjoys with the real.

In a scene from *The Two Noble Kinsmen* which was almost certainly the work of Shakespeare, not of his collaborator Fletcher, Theseus tries to persuade his sister Emilia to be present at the combat between her suitors Palamon and Arcite:

> She shall see deeds of honor in their kind
> Which sometimes show well, pencill'd. Nature now
> Shall make and act the story, the belief
> Both seal'd with eye and ear.   (V.3.12–15)

These lines carry Sidney's (and Aristotle's) paradox, that 'Oft cruell fights well pictured forth do please',[12] one crucial step further. Recognizing that Emilia shrinks from what she calls the 'dread sights' (v.3.10) of a tournament which must end with the death of one of her lovers, Theseus complicates Sidney's position by establishing Nature itself as an actor/dramatist whose creations, surpassing those of the painter's pencil because incorporating movement and sound, may nonetheless be viewed with that aesthetic detachment which makes tragedy possible as a form. His argument is unsuccessful. Like Perdita with Polixenes, Emilia refuses either to debate the issue or to abandon her previous resolution. Shakespeare makes her do so, at least in part, because – as with the Field of the Cloth of Gold in *Henry VIII* – the tournament in question could not have been enacted in any but the most perfunctory and unrealistic way. Here, close to the end of his career as a dramatist, the Shakespeare who once (however apologetically) allowed 'four or five most vile and ragged foils / (Right ill-dispos'd in brawl ridiculous)' to represent the glories of Agincourt (*Henry V* Chorus. iv.50–1) seems to have felt disinclined to stage anything the King's Men could not invest with some significant degree of visual realism. So Emilia, and the theatre audience, remain behind when Theseus and his train depart for the lists, to learn the fortunes of the day only by report.

That the King's Men, working at the Globe and at their new indoor theatre in Blackfriars, were now capable of much that would have seemed almost miraculous to the audiences of the 1580s and even 1590s is obvious from the texts of *Pericles*, *Cymbeline*, *The Winter's Tale*, *The Tempest*, *Henry VIII* and *The Two Noble Kinsmen*. Dream visions, elaborate pageantry, or the sudden descent on a golden eagle of a god wielding thunder have all become theatrical opportunities, not moments which provoke lamentation for the inadequacies of the stage. The oft-cited influence of the Jacobean court masque upon such things as Queen Katherine's dream in *Henry VIII*, the disappearing banquet in *The Tempest*, Jupiter's appearance in *Cymbeline* and Diana's in *Pericles*, the dance of satyrs in *The Winter's Tale*, or the initial tableau and later temple scenes of *The Two Noble Kinsmen* certainly cannot be discounted. Yet it is also true that, in a theatre with technical resources comparatively recently developed, the plot material to which Shakespeare now seems to have been

---

[12] Sidney, 'Astrophil and Stella', 34, in *The Poems of Sir Philip Sidney*, ed. W. A. Ringler (Oxford, 1962), p. 181.

drawn encouraged him to re-think the function of the eye in determining 'belief'.

About 1596, when he wrote the 'Pyramus and Thisbe' scenes for *A Midsummer Night's Dream*, Shakespeare had mocked the antiquated plays of the early Elizabethan period,[13] and also the literal-mindedness they encouraged in Bottom and his associates, men unacquainted with the theatre and its ways. The mechanicals are parody realists. Faced with the fact that Thisbe and her lover met by moonlight, their initial reaction was to enquire of the almanac whether there would be a moon on the night of their performance at court. There is one, they discover, and yet Peter Quince remains doubtful that, merely by leaving a casement open in the window of the chamber where they are to play, its beams can be introduced effectively into the action. Hence the second-best but (to their minds) necessary expedient of equipping one of their number with lantern, dog and bush and allowing him to introduce himself as 'Moonshine'. The wall which divided the lovers has to be similarly tangible, and so Snout plasters himself over with loam and rough-cast and comes in carrying a stone. What worries them about their lion – Snug the joiner in a beast's skin – is that it is likely to terrify the ladies in the audience unless it explains its true nature: 'Nay; you must name his name, and half his face must be seen through the lion's neck, and he himself must speak through, saying thus, or to the same defect: "Ladies", or "Fair ladies"' (III.1.36–9).

Although Time in *The Winter's Tale* speaks verse far better than any at Moonshine's disposal, he is a personification of the same general kind. As Presenter, effortlessly preparing the audience for what it is about to see as well as hear, old Gower in *Pericles* seems more akin to Peter Quince as Prologue – rambling, unstrenuous, confident that only a slight effort is required to participate imaginatively in the stage events towards which he points – than he does to that anxious Chorus which cajoles and nags its way through *Henry V*. The audience of *Pericles* can 'sail seas in cockles, have and wish but for't' (IV.4.2). For the three dumb-shows he introduces, themselves obvious relics of the Elizabethan past, Gower makes no apology: 'Like motes and shadows see them move a while, / Your ears unto your eyes I'll reconcile' (IV.4.21–2). Like the pageantry at the courts of Antiochus and the good king Simonides, these silent tableaux contribute to the

---

[13] In his book, *Something of Great Constancy: The Art of A Midsummer Night's Dream* (London, 1966), David Young provides a full account of the older dramatic material parodied.

new emphasis upon visual realization evident throughout *Pericles* and the last plays generally: a readjustment of the claims of eye and ear in which the literalism of the mechanicals, no longer just a case of comic misunderstanding, takes unexpectedly sophisticated and ambiguous forms. Even 'Lion' reappears in the form of that notorious bear which chases Antigonus off stage in Act III of *The Winter's Tale*.

Like 'Lion', this bear may have been played by an actor costumed as an animal. But it is also possible that, for at least the first few performances of the play, it was real. There seems to have been a vogue (as yet unexplained) for stage bears in 1610–11, when *The Winter's Tale* appeared. Two were called for in Jonson's masque *Oberon*. More important is the revival, by the King's Men, of the anonymous play *Mucedorus* (*c.* 1590), 'Amplified with new additions... before the king's Maiestie at White-hall on Shrove-Sunday night'. Prominent among those additions is a scene in which the clown, Mouse, falls over a bear. In the earliest text of *Mucedorus* (1598), the stage directions had called for the heroine Amadine and her cowardly lover Segasto to enter 'runing... being persued with a beare'.[14] The Jacobean bear has a significantly larger part, and it is tempting to believe that this is so because the King's Men, arrestingly, had found it possible to replace the fake bear of the original *Mucedorus* with a live animal, presumably better trained and more biddable than most, which had become temporarily available. This hypothesis at least goes some way towards explaining why such a creaking, old romance should suddenly receive a court performance before James, and also why it became, after that performance, astonishingly popular, running through four quarto editions over the next five years.

Mucedorus was one of the plays attributed to Shakespeare during the Restoration. No one now accepts that attribution. It may be, however, that his hand in the 1610 additions has been too readily dismissed. As resident dramatist for the King's Men, Shakespeare would have been expected to alter and refurbish old plays for revival by the company.[15] C. F. Tucker Brooke, the most recent editor of *Mucedorus*, concedes that the additions 'are of greater poetic merit than the rest of the comedy, and somewhat more in Shakespeare's

---

[14] *Mucedorus*, in *The Shakespeare Apocrypha*, ed. Brooke, pp. 107–8. See Brooke's discussion of the difference between the two texts in his introduction to the volume, pp. xxiii–xxvi.

[15] Gerald Eades Bentley, *The Profession of Dramatist in Shakespeare's Time, 1590–1642* (Princeton, N.J., 1971), pp. 235–63.

manner',[16] without arguing for his authorship. All that can be said, perhaps, is that there does seem to be some kind of link between the bear in *The Winter's Tale* and the one featured in *Mucedorus* as performed in the same year by the same company, and that a live animal – far more than an actor in a bearskin – would have upset ordinary audience assumptions about stage illusion in a way that seems consonant with the practice of Shakespeare's late plays. After all, even in the twentieth century, animals tend to elicit a confused response in the theatre. In Peter Hall's RSC production of *Richard II* in 1964, a horse, caparisoned for the lists, trotted across the stage just before the combat between Mowbray and Hereford. 'Is that horse *real?*' one member of the Stratford audience was heard to enquire anxiously on the opening night. Real it was, and it had no business appearing in *Richard II* at all, but the uncertainty it provoked is revealing. For a Jacobean audience, conditioned to expect that wild beasts in plays would all be superior versions of the impersonation contrived by Snug the joiner, the entrance of a live bear must, for a moment at least, have been bewildering. Certainly the clown's joke in the bear scene added to *Mucedorus* in 1610 becomes far more piquant if the animal described here, and just about to make its first appearance on stage, was going to turn out to be real: 'A Beare? nay, sure it cannot be a Beare, but some Divell in a Beares Doublet: for a Beare could never have had that agilitie to have frighted me.'[17]

Although it called for a lion, the story of Pyramus and Thisbe at least did not require the mechanicals to cope with the problem of staging a shipwreck. If, like many plays of the period, it had, Bottom and Peter Quince would surely, in line with their approach generally, have insisted upon drenching the actors involved with water, so that they entered after the event demonstrably wet. And here, for once, according to the canons of the professional theatre in the time, their realism would not have been misplaced. On the Elizabethan and Jacobean stage, wet actors seem to have been almost as mandatory a shorthand for disaster at sea as alarms and excursions were for a battle. It did not matter in the least that most plots of this kind were egregiously far-fetched and fantastic. The condition of the newly shipwrecked was 'real'. So, the anonymous *Thracian Wonder* (1599) contains the direction: '*Enter old Antimon bringing in Ariadne ship-wrecked, the Clown turning the Child up and down, and wringing the clouts*:

[16] Brooke, *The Shakespeare Apocrypha*, p. xxvi.   [17] *Ibid.*, 1.2.3–6 (p. 107).

they pass over the stage: exeunt. Enter Radagon, all wet, looking about for shelter as shipwrecked.[18] In *The Four Prentices of London*, Heywood made not the slightest effort to render the catastrophe itself plausible – all four brothers are cast away simultaneously on Goodwin Sands, yet one is washed ashore near Boulogne, the second several hundred miles down the French coast, the third off Ireland, and the fourth in the region of Venice – but they arrive in these different locales in the approved manner: 'all wet', or 'all wet with his sword'.[19] When Jonson composed his parody shipwreck for the collaborative play *Eastward Ho!* (1606), he mocked this theatrical convention. The usurer Security emerges from the Thames 'wett', according to the stage direction, and it is plain from the dialogue ('I see y'ave bene washt in the *Thames* here') that the other survivors of the wreck were also depicted as soaked to the skin.[20]

In *Twelfth Night*, interestingly enough, Shakespeare had declined to follow this practice. Although the Folio text was almost certainly set from a theatre prompt-copy, there is not the slightest indication in either stage directions or dialogue that Viola – or her twin brother Sebastian – was meant to be shipwrecked into Illyria 'wet'. Malone, on the other hand, was responding sensitively and almost certainly accurately to the text when he added the stage direction 'Enter Pericles wet' to that scene at the beginning of Act II in which the shipwrecked king stumbles ashore numbed with cold to be rescued by the fishers. Certainly Shakespeare himself was responsible for its equivalent, 'Enter Mariners wet', in the first scene of *The Tempest*. And here, what is ordinarily a somewhat naive piece of realism suddenly becomes complex. That frightened crowd of sea-soaked mariners which stumbles in just before Alonso's ship drives on to the rocks was clearly designed to make the calamity as convincing and tangible as possible, for characters and theatre audience alike. Modern directors rarely retain Shakespeare's wet mariners, preferring to bypass what presumably seems to them the crude literalism of the Jacobean stage in favour of sound and lighting effects not available to the King's Men. But an audience which has not actually seen those drenched garments in the opening scene loses some of the carefully planned contrast with the one that follows. For Shakespeare's contemporaries especially, accustomed as they were to

---

[18] *The Thracian Wonder*, in *The Dramatic Works of John Webster*, ed. William Hazlitt, 4 vols. (London, 1857), IV, p. 135 (1.3).   [19] *The Four Prentices of London*, p. 177.
[20] Ben Jonson, *Eastward Ho!*, in *Works*, ed. Herford and Simpson, IV.1.32.

regarding 'wet' actors as straightforward indications of disaster at sea, Prospero's calm revelation that the storm was a triumph of art, and that no one has suffered the slightest harm, must have been completely unexpected. It matters too that although the realistic presentation of the seamen seems to foreshadow the condition in which Ferdinand, Alonso and the other members of the court party must arrive on the island, in fact it does not. Prospero describes Ferdinand as 'something stain'd' to Miranda, but it is with grief for his father's loss, not sea-water (1.2.415). Not only are the courtiers' clothes not wet, it seems to Gonzalo that although 'drench'd in the sea, [they] hold notwithstanding, their freshness and glosses, being rather new dy'd than stain'd with salt water' (II.1.63–5). This, he admits, 'is indeed almost beyond credit' (59–60), and indeed neither Antonio nor Sebastian will credit it. Here, as with the related argument as to whether the island is really the green and balmy place Gonzalo apprehends, or Antonio and Sebastian's barren fen, the theatre audience, already disorientated by Shakespeare's cunningly inconsistent use of the dramatic code of 'playing wet', could not have been quite sure what it was meant to believe.

Characters in the last plays are continually having to revise their standards of the 'real'. Even those two pragmatists, Antonio and Sebastian, confronted with the magical banquet in Act III, find their grasp on the actual badly shaken: 'Now I will believe / That there are unicorns; that in Arabia / There is one tree, the phoenix' throne, one phoenix / At this hour reigning there' (III.3.21–4). Old tales, attested to by the eye as well as the ear, become true. 'If I should tell my history', Marina confesses to King Pericles, 'it would seem / Like lies disdain'd in the reporting' (v.1.118–19). Her admission, anticipating Paulina's statement in *The Winter's Tale* that 'were it but told you', Hermione's return to life 'should be hooted at like an old tale', governs much in the last plays. Here, Pericles, who has not seen what we have seen of Marina's life at Tharsus and in the brothel at Mytilene, nonetheless consents to listen to her story because of what his eyes, confusedly but urgently, convey: 'falseness cannot come from thee, for thou lookest / Modest as Justice... I will believe thee, / And make my senses credit thy relation / To points that seem impossible, for thou lookest / Like one I lov'd indeed' (v.1.120–3).

In the romances, an odd kind of credit attaches itself to things which, in narration, would seem blatantly fictional. Shakespeare, in his a-typical handling of the frame in *Pericles*, comes close to spelling this out. A Presenter, speaking to the audience directly, Gower and his tale ought to seem closer and more real than the stage action he conjures up. As a story-teller, his attitude is intimate and confiding, and yet the rhyming octosyllabics employed by this ghostly medieval poet, full of archaisms, self-consciously literary, are clearly much further removed from ordinary speech than the iambic pentameters of the inset play. Those portions of Pericles' story which Gower tells seem, as a result, far more remote, less immediate and believable than what we see enacted. By turning the frame inside-out in this way, planes of reality are made to shift and blur in a fashion characteristic of the late plays.

Not only Old Gower, but the statue scene in *The Winter's Tale*, the bear, the wet mariners and deceptive spectacles of *The Tempest*, the unexpected appearances of gods, all seem designed to perplex a theatre audience, at least momentarily, as to the existential status of what it sees. Even *Henry VIII*, generally so much more straight forward in its realism than the romances, has its moment of mystification. The celestial vision which appears to the sleeping Queen Katherine is unequivocal only for her. Her attendants, Patience and Griffiths, although they sit wide awake in the chamber, are aware of nothing, even as Lysimachus, Helicanus, Marina and the others on board the Tyrian galley cannot hear Pericles' music of the spheres. The theatre audience is more privileged. But how is it to interpret what it has been given? Up to this point in Act IV, all the pageantry with which *Henry VIII* is filled – trial scenes and coronation processions, feasts and masquings – has been entirely earthly and rational. The 'six personages, clad in white robes, wearing on their heads garlands of bays, and golden vizards on their faces' look, as they dance ceremoniously about the queen, very like masque figures. But that cannot, in context, explain what they are. When Shakespeare abruptly introduced the god Hymen at the end of *As You Like It* in 1599, he made it possible to recognize in this figure Corin or Amiens in disguise, an option which the theatre has usually taken up. The garlanded dancers of *Henry VIII*, by contrast, like Jupiter in *Cymbeline*, or Diana at the end of *Pericles*, suddenly disrupt the audience's previous understanding of the 'real', leaving it in its own version of Gonzalo's uncertainty; 'Whether this be, / Or be not, I'll not swear' (*The Tempest* v.1.122–3).

Ultimately, of course, the spectators unlike the characters know that what they are watching is a dramatic spectacle, only a play.

Outside the theatre lies a reality superior to anything the stage can contrive. Yet, in the last plays above all, Dr Johnson's eminently sensible view of an audience as always rationally conscious of stage artifice, aware that what it sees is a performance, pure and simple, seems to break down. This is partly because of the special dramatic techniques which they employ, the obfuscations and the sleights of hand. It is also, surely, because they appeal so poignantly to our sense of how we should like the world to be, and know that it is not: ultimately gracious and restorative, a place where losses are not final, and even the most terrible mistakes can be redeemed. Like those 'subtleties o'th' isle' of which Prospero speaks in *The Tempest*, the plays themselves will not quite 'let you / Believe things certain' (v.1.124–5). That paradox is responsible in large part for their special quality, a quality which can be fully experienced only in the theatre – the place where the statue visibly moves and, in doing so, forgives our illusions.

PART II

CHAPTER 10

The king disguised: Shakespeare's *Henry V* and the comical history (1975)

In the worst moment of the French campaign, when the night before Agincourt finds the English army reduced, dispirited, and ailing, 'even as men wrack'd upon a sand, that look to be wash'd off the next tide' (IV.1.97–8), Henry V pays two quite different visits to his despondent troops. Although the first of them, made in his own person as king, is not enacted, the Chorus testifies eloquently to its success:

> every wretch, pining and pale before,
> Beholding him, plucks comfort from his looks.
> A largess universal, like the sun,
> His liberal eye doth give to every one,
> Thawing cold fear, that mean and gentle all
> Behold, as may unworthiness define,
> A little touch of Harry in the night.   (IV.41–7)

Later, in the first scene of Act IV, Henry borrows a cloak from Sir Thomas Erpingham, conceals his royal identity, and ventures alone among soldiers no longer able to recognize him as their king. His fortunes in this second sally are altogether less prosperous. Thorny and disquieting from the start, his conversation with Williams, Court, and Bates ends in an open quarrel. Moreover, it provokes Henry's only soliloquy in the play: a bitter examination of kingship itself and of the irremovable barriers isolating the monarch from a world of private men.

Shakespeare may well have remembered from Holinshed, or from *The First English Life of Henry V*, that the historical Henry 'daylie and nightlie in his owne person visited the watches, orders and stacions of everie part of his hoast'.[1] Nowhere, however, is it suggested that he

---

[1] Quoted in Geoffrey Bullough, ed. *Narrative and Dramatic Sources of Shakespeare*, vol. IV (London, 1962), p. 362.

ever did so incognito. Geoffrey Bullough has argued that when Shakespeare made Henry muffle himself in Erpingham's cloak he was thinking of a passage from Tacitus' *Annals* in which Germanicus disguises himself on the eve of a battle in order to assess the morale of the Roman legions.[2] Germanicus, however, lurks outside his soldiers' tents as a mere eavesdropper; he never attempts a personal encounter. Although the passage cannot be discounted entirely as a source for Henry's disguise, its importance has surely been over-estimated. For those Elizabethans who watched *Henry V* in the new Globe theatre in 1599, the king's behaviour before Agincourt would have had analogues far more striking and immediate. There is a surprising number of disguised kings to be found in those English history plays which have survived from the period 1587–1600. A few of these princes are driven to dissemble their identity for a time out of political necessity, as Marlowe's Edward II does after the triumph of Young Mortimer and Queen Isabella, or Shakespeare's Henry VI in the last part of the trilogy, when he rashly steals across the border into England 'disguised, with a prayer-book', only to be recognized despite this precaution by the two Keepers and haled away to the Tower. A larger and more interesting group is composed of kings who, like Shakespeare's Henry V, adopt disguise as a caprice, for reasons that are fundamentally exploratory and quixotic.

Toward the end of *George a Greene, the Pinner of Wakefield* (?Robert Greene, *c.* 1590), an unspecified King Edward of England decides to 'make a merrie journey for a moneth'[3] along with his friend King James of Scotland, for the purpose of meeting the folk hero George a Greene, a loyal pinner in the north country who has been instrumental in putting down a rebellion against the Crown. The two monarchs travel on foot and in disguise. At the town of Bradford they yield meekly to the insolent demands of the locals, trailing their staves in order to pass without argument through the town. George a Greene, disgusted by such pusillanimity, berates the two kings soundly for cowardice and forces them to hold up their staves. King Edward gains a vivid and somewhat disconcerting idea of the character and temper of his subject before the revelation of his royal identity puts an end to the game. All is forgiven. George is offered a knighthood, which he politely refuses, preferring to remain an

[2] *Ibid.*

[3] *George a Greene*, in *The Life and Complete Works in Prose and Verse of Robert Greene*, ed. Alexander B. Grosart, 15 vols. (London, 1881–3), XIV, p. 940.

English yeoman. Edward unites him with Bettris, his love, over-riding the snobbish objections of her father, and the play ends harmoniously with a feast at which King Edward, King James, George a Greene, Robin Hood and Maid Marian, and all the shoemakers of Bradford sit side by side as friends and good companions.

Peele's *Edward I* (*c.* 1591) also associates the king in disguise with the Robin Hood stories. Lluellen, the rebellious Prince of Wales, his mistress Elinor, and his friend Rice ap Meredith have taken to the greenwood in the company of a friar, 'to live and die together like Chamber Britaines, Robin Hood, little John, Frier Tucke, and Maide marrian'.[4] King Edward, intrigued to learn of this little society, decides to pay it a secret visit, disguised, and accompanied only by Lluellen's brother, Sir David of Brecknock:

> as I am a Gentleman,
> Ile have one merrie flirt with little John,
> And Robin Hood, and his Maide marrian.
> Be thou my counsell and my companie,
> And thou maist Englands resolution see.   (10.1548–52)

In the forest, Edward adjudicates in a dispute between two rogues who have tried to cozen one another, agrees with Lluellen that his purse will belong to whichever man can overcome the other in a fair fight, and (exactly as his prototype Richard Coeur de Lion had done in the ballads) sends 'Robin Hood' sprawling. The exigencies of Peele's plot made it impossible for this forest scene to end with reconciliation and pardon in the ballad tradition. Lluellen, rebellious to the end, is killed in battle later in the play. It is remarkable, however, how close this personal encounter between the outlaw and the king he cannot recognize – in both senses of that word – has come to healing the breach between them. When 'Longshanks' has gone, his identity disclosed, Lluellen admits ruefully that 'his courage is like to the Lion, and were it not that rule and soveraigntie set us at jarre, I could love and honor the man for his valour' (12.1917–19).

The two anonymous plays *Fair Em* (*c.* 1590) and *The True Chronicle History of King Leir* (*c.* 1590) both present kings who disguise themselves in the cause of love. William the Conqueror, in *Fair Em*,

---

[4] Frank Hook, ed., *Edward I*, in *The Life and Works of George Peele*, gen. ed. Charles T. Prouty, 3 vols. (New Haven, 1952–70), II, lines 1199–1201.

falls in love with a picture of Blanch, Princess of Denmark, and travels to see her in her father's court under the name of Sir Robert of Windsor. Finding the lady less glamorous in reality than she seemed in her portrait, he tries to elope with Mariana, a lady promised to his friend and travelling companion, the Marquis of Lubeck. Mariana, however, not only surmounts the temptation to abandon Lubeck for a crown but contrives to substitute a masked and love-sick Blanch for herself at the rendezvous appointed. William, who discovers the fraud on arrival in England, is understandably put out but decides that although Blanch is not Mariana she is nonetheless tolerable, and certainly preferable to war with Denmark. At the end of the play, William marries Blanch and, at the same time, restores Godard the supposed miller to his rightful place in society and bestows his daughter Em upon Valingford, the suitor who best deserves her.

In *King Leir*, the Gallian king comes to England disguised as a pilgrim, in order to determine which is the best and most marriageable of Leir's three daughters. He meets Cordella after her disgrace, finds her fair and good, and pretends that he has been sent as an ambassador by his royal master to make her the Gallian queen. Cordella, who has most perspicaciously fallen in love with the humble palmer himself, spurns this splendid offer and bids him 'cease for thy King, seeke for thy selfe to woo'.[5] After this gratifying proof that Cordella loves the man and not the monarch, the palmer reveals his identity and the two are married immediately and return to France. Disguise, however, remains a feature of their court. In scene 24, the Gallian king and queen mingle with their subjects in the guise of country folk and, thus obscured, discover and are reconciled with the wretched Leir and his counsellor Perillus on the seacoast of Brittany.

Finally, *The First Part of King Edward IV*, a play written by Thomas Heywood before 1599, presents two quite separate royal disguises. Edward conceals his identity when he goes into Lombard Street for the first time to lay amorous siege to Mistress Shore. More relevant to *Henry V*, however, is his encounter with John Hobs the tanner. The king, hunting incognito at Drayton Basset, becomes separated from his queen and courtiers. Hobs, meeting him in the forest, suspects him at first for a thief ('How these roysters swarme in the country, now

---

[5] *The History of King Leir*, 1605, ed. W. W. Greg, Malone Society (London, 1908), line 691.

the King is so neare'[6]), but is persuaded at length that Edward is a minor hanger-on at court: in fact, the king's butler. Under this delusion, he prattles on merrily about the two kings of England, Edward at court and the deposed Henry VI in the Tower. Edward, slyly anxious to know how he is regarded by this outspoken subject, receives some disconcertingly frank answers to the questions he puts. The commons of England, according to Hobs, love King Edward

as poor folks love holidays, glad to have them now and then; but to have them come too often will undoe them. So, to see the King now and then 'tis comfort; but every day would begger us; and I may say to thee, we feare we shall be troubled to lend him money; for we doubt hees but needy. (p. 45)

Even more improbable in its light-hearted political inconsequence is Edward's amused acceptance of the tanner's shifting loyalties. 'Shall I say my conscience?' he enquires cunningly. 'I think *Harry* is the true king.'

HOBS: Art advised of that? *Harrys* of the old house of *Lancaster*; and that progenity do I love.
KING: And thou doest not hate the house of *York*?
HOBS: Why, no; for I am just akin to *Sutton* Windmill; I can grind which way soe'er the winde blow. If it be *Harry*, I can say, 'Well fare *Lancaster*.' If it be *Edward*, I can sing, '*Yorke, Yorke*, for my mony.' (p. 45)

Basically, as it turns out, Hobs approves of King Edward for reasons that have nothing to do with his government of the realm: 'He's a frank franion, a merry companion, and loves a wench well (p. 47).' To his way of thinking, the king ought not to encourage patents and monopolies, but Hobs is willing to believe that Edward does so out of ignorance, because he has been misled by greedy counsellors and because he cannot see for himself how the system operates. As subject and king converse, Edward's respect for this 'honest true tanner' and for his powers of observation grows. Hobs, for his part, comes to like the supposed butler so well that he invites him home to his cottage for dinner and the night. The tanner has a pretty daughter and there is even some talk of a match, although Hobs would like his prospective son-in-law to have a steadier

---

[6] *The First and Second Parts of King Edward IV*, ed. Barron Field, *The Dramatic Works of Thomas Heywood Now First Collected*, 4 vols. (London, 1874), I, p. 41.

profession, not one of these fly-by-night court posts. Not until
daybreak does Edward tear himself away from the tanner's hospitality to return to London and the troubles of a kingdom in revolt.
Again, the meeting between subject and king in disguise has
generated harmony, good fellowship, and mutual understanding.

In all these English histories – and there must have been many more
plays like them, now lost – the king's disguise demands to be seen as
a romantic gesture. Edward IV, William the Conqueror, Edward I,
the Gallian king, or the brace of monarchs in *George a Greene*, all
conceal their identities in much the spirit of Haroun al Raschid, the
caliph of *The Arabian Nights* who liked to walk the streets of Baghdad
incognito, in search of the marvellous and the strange. Moreover, the
people they meet come from the world of balladry and legend. Robin
Hood and Maid Marian, the folk-hero George a Greene, the miller
and his daughter, thieves and outlaws, the beggar-maid destined to
become a queen, or the tanner of Tamworth: all were characters
nurtured in the popular imagination. Maurice Keen, in *The Outlaws
of Medieval Legend*, describes the informal meeting of commoner and
king as the wish-dream of a peasantry harried and perplexed by a
new class of officials, an impersonal bureaucracy against which the
ordinary man seemed to have no redress:

They only knew that the King was the ultimate repository of a law whose
justice they acknowledged, and they saw treason against him as a betrayal
of their allegiance to God himself. If they could only get past his corrupt
officers, whose abuse of the trust reposed in them amounted to treason in
itself, and bring their case before the King, they believed that right would be
done. Their unshakeable faith in the King's own justice was the most tragic
of the misconceptions of the medieval peasantry, and the ballad makers and
their audiences shared it to the full.[7]

In the ballads, king and unsuspecting subject meet time after time
and discover unanimity of opinion and mutual respect. Richard
Coeur de Lion banquets in Sherwood Forest on stolen venison,
forgives Robin Hood and his men, and confounds the sheriff of
Nottingham. Henry II so enjoys the rough but generous hospitality
of the miller of Mansfield that he makes him a knight and gives him
a royal licence to keep the forest of Sherwood. Other ballads describe
the meeting of Edward I and the reeve, King Alfred and the

[7] Maurice Keen, *The Outlaws of Medieval Legend* (London, 1961), p. 156.

shepherd, Edward IV and the tanner, Henry VIII and the cobbler, James I and the tinker, William III and the forester, and many similar encounters.

That conversations of this sort represent a fantasy, the 'misconception', as Keen terms it, of a victimized agrarian class, is obvious. They derive from attitudes far removed from anything which the hard-headed citizens of Elizabeth's London actually believed. Yet the old roots ran deep. This type of ballad not only survived through Jacobean and Caroline times: the idea behind it remained oddly resonant and haunting. Real Tudor monarchs sometimes played at enacting it. Henry VIII, as Hall tells us, graciously allowed himself to be 'waylaid' and dragged off to a reconstruction of Coeur de Lion's feast with Robin Hood, Maid Marian, and their fellows.[8] Queen Elizabeth, walking in Wanstead gardens, suddenly found herself confronting a group of supposed country folk: 'Though they knew not her estate, yet something there was which made them startle aside and gaze upon her.'[9] Cunningly, Philip Sidney proceeded to involve the queen in a dispute between a shepherd and a forester for possession of the Lady of May, requesting her, after she had heard the rustic arguments of both sides, to award the lady to the suitor she considered most deserving. Traces of this kind of situation can be seen as well in some of the masques at court, but it was in the drama proper that the idea of the king's personal engagement with his subjects and their problems flowered and was most fully exploited.

There are a few Elizabethan plays in which the king manages to mingle with his subjects freely and dispense justice without resorting to disguise. At the end of Dekker's *The Shoemaker's Holiday*, Henry V in his own person sweeps away the snobbery of his officers and nobles:

> Dost thou not know, that love respects no bloud?
> Cares not for difference of birth, or state,
> The maide is yong, well borne, faire, vertuous,
> A worthy bride for any gentleman.[10]

As benevolent *deus ex machina*, he joins the hands of Rose, the citizen's daughter, and Lacy, nephew to the Earl of Lincoln. Annihilating

[8] *Hall's Chronicle, containing The History of England*, ed. Sir Henry Ellis (London, 1809), pp. 513, 582.

[9] 'The Lady of May', *The Complete Works of Philip Sydney*, ed. Albert Feuillerat, 4 vols. (Cambridge, 1912–26), II, p. 330.

[10] *The Shoemaker's Holiday*, *The Dramatic Works of Thomas Dekker*, ed. Fredson Bowers, 4 vols. (Cambridge, 1953–61), I, v.5.104–7.

objections based upon wealth or class, he acts from principles of perfect equity as soon as he examines the case himself, just as the medieval minstrels had always believed he would. Yet even Dekker's Henry, in a play which could scarcely be described as realistic, worries about the constraints and inhibitions which his declared royal presence may impose on London's madcap mayor, Simon Eyre, at the Shrove Tuesday banquet where these events take place. Most Elizabethan dramatists seem to have accepted the idea that disguise was an essential prerequisite for the ease and success of the meeting between private man and king. Only if the king's identity was concealed could there be natural conversation, frankness, and a sense of rapport. It is the fundamental premise of all these plays that the king, rightly considered, is but a man, and a remarkably understanding man at that. If only, they seem to suggest, king and commoner could talk together in this way, without formality or embarrassment, how many problems would be solved, how many popular grievances redressed. Humanity and humour, an easy cameraderie: these qualities, usually obscured by ceremony, distance, and that hierarchy of officials standing between the monarch and his people, emerge clearly as soon as he steps down from his throne to speak, for a little while, as a private man.

When Shakespeare sent Henry V to converse incognito with Williams, Court, and Bates on the night before Agincourt, he was surely influenced by plays like these far more than by any distant memory of how Germanicus had behaved in the war against Arminius. Generically, Shakespeare's disguised king belongs with Peele's Edward I, Heywood's Edward IV, or the accommodating monarchs of *George a Greene*. Yet the *Henry V* episode is unique. By 1599, the king who freely chooses disguise had become the hallmark of a particular kind of play. Polonius almost certainly would have defined the mode (quite shrewdly) as the 'comical-historical'. *Henry V*, however, is not a comical history. Far more ironic and complicated than the plays which belong properly to that genre, it introduces the time-worn and popular dramatic motif of the king disguised into its fourth act in order to question, not to celebrate, a folk convention. In itself, the gesture could be relied upon to generate certain clearly defined emotional expectations in an Elizabethan audience powerfully conditioned by both a ballad and a stage tradition. Shakespeare built upon this fact. He used Henry's disguise to summon up the memory of a wistful, naive attitude toward history and the relationship of subject and king which this play rejects as attractive but untrue: a nostalgic but false romanticism.

As the royal captain of a ruined band, a sun-god radiating his beams indiscriminately upon the soldiers among whom he walks, Henry is effective, as the Chorus makes plain. Throughout this play, the relation between the Chorus's unequivocal celebration of Henry and his war in France and the complicated, ambiguous, and sometimes flatly contradictory scenes which these speeches are made to introduce is productive of irony and double focus. This duality of attitude is particularly striking in Act IV, where the Chorus's epic account of the king dispensing comfort to his troops in his own person leads directly into that altogether more dubious scene in which Henry visits the army a second time, disguised, in the manner of a ballad king. Once he has obliterated his identity, Henry falls into a series of non-encounters, meetings in which the difficulty of establishing understanding between subject and king is stressed, not the encouraging effect of 'a little touch of Harry in the night' (IV.47).

It is true that Ancient Pistol, the first man Henry faces, is scarcely capable of rational discourse. Pistol lives in a wholly private world, a heightened and extravagant realm where everything appears twice life size. His overcharged style of speech, filled with contempt for Fortune, exotic geography, and resounding proper names, derives from Marlowe and from those lesser dramatists who imitated Marlowe. Pistol's language is a tissue of play scraps. In his own mind, as Leslie Hotson has pointed out, he is Tamburlaine.[11] 'As good a gentleman as the Emperor' (IV.1.42), he appears blatantly literary, a mere stage king, as soon as he confronts Henry. Linguistically, Shakespeare's early histories had been intermittently Marlovian. Here, at the end of his Elizabethan cycle, he effectively laid the ghost of Tamburlaine as a hero, making it impossible for him to be taken seriously again until the Restoration. By deliberately weighing Pistol's egotism, his histrionics, against the workaday prose of the true king, he indicated the distance between one kind of theatrical fantasy and fact.

Perhaps because he fears recognition by his captains, Henry makes no attempt to speak to Fluellen and Gower. He waits in silence until the entry of Williams, Court, and Bates: three ordinary soldiers for

---

[11] Leslie Hotson, 'Ancient pistol', *Shakespeare's Sonnets Dated, and Other Essays* (London, 1949), pp. 57–75.

whom the king has always been an unapproachable and distant figure. This encounter is, of course, the mirror image of all those scenes in plays like *George a Greene* or *Edward IV* in which the king and his humble subject reach a frank and mutual accord. Here, nothing of the kind occurs. Instead, Henry finds himself embroiled in a tough and increasingly embarrassing argument. He is rhetorically dexterous, and he succeeds in convincing the soldiers that the king cannot be held responsible for the particular state of soul of those individuals who die in his wars. The other question raised by Williams, that of the goodness of the king's cause in itself, his heavy reckoning at that latter day when he must confront the subjects who have been mutilated and have died for him in a war that perhaps was unjust, Henry simply evades. Here, as in the play as a whole, it is left standing, unresolved.

Even worse, Henry discovers with a sense of shock that his soothing account of the king as 'but a man, as I am' (IV.I.IOI–2), sensitive to the disapprobation or approval of his humblest subject, is treated as flatly absurd. For Williams, the gulf between commoner and king is unbridgeable. A man 'may as well go about to turn the sun to ice with fanning in his face with a peacock's feather' as expect his 'poor and private displeasure' to influence the behaviour of a monarch (IV.I.198–201). This shaft strikes home, exposing the speciousness of Henry's pretence that he can really be the friend and brother of these soldiers, as well as their king. The conversation ends in a quarrel, a failure to arrive at understanding which contradicts the romantic, ballad tradition. Left alone, Henry meditates acrimoniously on the pains of sovereignty, the doubtful worth of the 'ceremony' that divides the king from a world of private men without providing him with any adequate compensation for his isolation and his crippling weight of responsibility.

Subsequently, after Agincourt has been won, Williams learns that it was the king himself whom he offended and with whom he has promised to fight. Like the outlaws of medieval legend, Williams meets not only with pardon but with royal largesse. He receives his glove again filled with golden crowns by Henry's bounty. Yet this gift, unlike its archetypes in the ballads and in Elizabethan comical histories, seems strangely irrelevant. Consciously anachronistic, it provides not the ghost of an answer to the questions raised during this particular encounter between common man and king disguised. Is the king's cause just? If not, what measure of guilt does he incur for requiring men to die for anything but the strict necessity of their country? Can the opinions and judgements of private men influence the sovereign on his throne? Henry is generous to Williams, but it is a dismissive generosity which places the subject firmly in an inferior position and silences his voice. The two men do not sit down at table together to any common feast, in the manner of Dekker's Henry V or Heywood's Edward IV. Indeed, Williams himself seems to be aware that the answer represented by the glove full of crowns is inadequate. He never thanks Henry for the present, accepting it without a word and turning, in the next instant, to repudiate the shilling offered him by Fluellen: 'I will none of your money' (IV.8.67). That gift he can dare to refuse. Even his plea for pardon is filled with suppressed anger and resentment:

Your Majesty came not like yourself. You appear'd to me but as a common man; witness the night, your garments, your lowliness; and what your Highness suffer'd under that shape, I beseech you take it for your own fault, and not mine.   (IV.8.50–4)

   Henry V is a play concerned to force upon its audience a creative participation far more active than usual. The Chorus urges an unceasing visualization, bright pictures in the mind, of horses, ships under sail, silken banners, or the engines of siege warfare. Within the play itself, Shakespeare suggests without indicating priority a multiplicity of possible responses to every character and event. Celebration and denigration, heroism and irony exist uneasily side by side. The Chorus may regard England's despoliation of France as a species of sacred obligation. Elsewhere, the attitude is far less clear-cut. Always in the background there hovers a disconcerting memory of Canterbury and Ely in the opening scene, busily fomenting the war in France to divert attention from the temporal wealth of the Church. Behind that lurks Henry IV's deathbed advice to his son to 'busy giddy minds / With foreign quarrels' (*2 Henry IV* IV.5.213–14) in the hope that the shaky legitimacy of Lancastrian rule might thus escape scrutiny. Among Shakespeare's other histories, only *Henry VIII* is so deliberately ambiguous, so overtly a puzzle in which the audience is left to forge its own interpretation of action and characters with only minimal guidance from a dramatist apparently determined to stress the equivalence of mutually exclusive views of a particular complex of historical events.
   In both *Henry V* and *Henry VIII*, the fact that the mind and heart

of the king are essentially opaque, that his true thoughts and feelings remain veiled behind a series of royal poses – as those of Richard II, Richard III, King John, Henry VI, or even Henry IV do not – contributes to the difficulty of assessment. Even Henry's soliloquy before Agincourt is strangely externalized and formal, in no sense a revelation of the private workings of a mind. Neither here nor anywhere else in the play is the whole truth about the king's personal decision to invade France disclosed. This reticence is not accidental. Henry is, by secular standards, an extraordinarily successful example of the God–man incarnate. The conception of kingship in this play derives not from the relaxed and essentially personal tradition of the ballads but from a complicated, inherently tragic Tudor doctrine of the king's two bodies.[12] Shakespeare had previously dealt with the violence of divorce or incompatibility between the twin natures of the king. Henry V, by contrast, has achieved a union of body natural and body politic difficult to flaw. Yet the price he pays for his subordination of the individual to the office is heavy, in personal terms. There is loss as well as gain in the gulf that now divides Henry from his old associates Bardolph and Pistol, from a world of private men in which he alone speaks out of a double nature. Hal's sudden unavailability as a person, his retreat into an oddly declamatory series of stances, reflects neither his own nor Shakespeare's weakness. It is simply a measure of the signal effectiveness of this man's incarnation as king.

In many respects *Henry V* is a success story. Agincourt, at least from one angle, is a splendour. Within its own limited sphere the rhetoric of the Chorus rings true. Henry himself can be described as an 'ideal' sovereign, God's gift to an England weary of rebellion, usurpation, and civil war. At the same time, it is not easy for any mere mortal to support the psychological and moral burden of a double self. At a number of points in the play, particularly in situations which seem to demand an essentially personal response, the strain involved in maintaining such a constant ventriloquism becomes obvious. Even when Henry tries temporarily to obliterate one half of his identity, as he does in the scene with Williams, Court, and Bates, he finds it impossible to produce a natural and unforced imitation of a private man. Richard II, ironically enough, had experienced similar difficulties after his deposition. In Henry's case, the suppression of

---

[12] Ernst Kantorowicz, *The King's Two Bodies* (Princeton, 1957).

one side of his nature is only momentary, the product of whim rather than political defeat. Nevertheless, his awkwardness with the soldiers points to the irrevocability of that mystic marriage of king and man accomplished in the ceremony of coronation. Only death can dissolve this union.

Meanwhile, the king must contrive to deal with a world of single-natured individuals from which he himself stands conspicuously apart. Henry cannot have personal friends as other men do. There is a sense in which the rejection of Falstaff at the end of 2 Henry IV leads directly on to the rejection of the traitor Scroop in the second act of Henry V. Precisely because Scroop is someone Henry has imagined was bound to him as a man by private ties of affection and liking, his treason is far more painful than the more neutral betrayal of Cambridge and Grey. With the latter he deals in an efficient, almost perfunctory fashion. Only Scroop evokes a long and suddenly emotional remonstrance in which Henry effectively bids farewell to the possibility of personal relationship. Significantly, this scene at Southampton is placed between the two episodes in London dealing with the death of Falstaff. The epic voyage to France is thus preceded by three scenes dealing not merely with the death of former friends but with the final severance of the new king's remaining personal ties. Thereafter in the play, he will use the term 'friend' in a special sense.

Not by accident, Henry abruptly abandons the royal 'we' when he turns to accuse Scroop. In Act I he had spoken almost entirely from this corporate position, allowing himself only infrequently to be jolted into an adventurer's 'I'. The Southampton scene is also one which insists throughout upon the double nature of the king and makes that nature grammatically clear through his habitual use of a plural first person. Cambridge and Grey, it seems, have conspired to kill 'us' (II.2.85–91): 'But O, / What shall I say to thee, Lord Scroop?' (II.2.93–4). In his long, passionate speech to this false friend 'that knew'st the very bottom of my soul' (II.2.97), Henry grieves more as man than as king. Not until the moment comes for sentencing all three conspirators does he regain his balance, discriminating calmly between the offence intended to his body natural and his body politic:

> Touching our person seek we no revenge,
> But we our kingdom's safety must so tender,
> Whose ruin you have sought, that to her laws
> We do deliver you. Get you therefore hence,
> Poor miserable wretches, to your death. (II.2.174–8)

The voice here is impersonal, speaking from behind the mask of kingship, deliberately avoiding the first person singular of individual response.

Once arrived in France, Henry refers to himself far more often as 'I' or 'me' than he does as 'we' or 'us', at least up to the council of Troyes in the fifth act. As leader of an English host stranded in a foreign country and in a position of increasing danger, Henry finds it not only possible but necessary to simplify his royalty to some extent. After much painful marching in the rain-drenched field, he can describe himself as a soldier, 'a name that in my thoughts becomes me best' (III.3.5–6). In this role he achieves a measure of escape from the royal impersonality demanded under more ordinary and formal circumstances. When he warns the governor of Harfleur of the horrors that lie in store for his city if it fails to capitulate, when he exchanges badinage with Fluellen, or celebrates honour in the Crispin Day speech in terms that Hotspur would have understood, he is playing a part – much as Prince Hal had done in the tavern scenes of the *Henry IV* plays or among the alien but imitable chivalries of Shrewsbury. In this context, the infrequent appearances of the royal 'we' in Acts III and IV become purposeful and striking reminders of the ineluctable reality of the king's twin nature – a nature temporarily obscured by the adventurer's pose appropriate to the French campaign.

Gravely, Henry reminds Williams that 'it was ourself thou didst abuse', before he dismisses him with pardon and reward (IV.8.49). When his old associate Bardolph is summarily executed for robbing a church, Fluellen informs the king and, describing the dead man's face in terms so vivid that there can be no possible mistake, enquires somewhat tactlessly: 'if your Majesty know the man' (III.6.101–2). Henry's stiff reply to this appeal to his memory of a time before his coronation is more than a politic evasion: 'We would have all such offenders so cut off.' His sudden use here of the first person plural of majesty, occurring as it does in a scene where even the French herald Montjoy is addressed by Henry as 'I', constitutes the real answer to Fluellen's question. As a twin-natured being, the king is stripped not only of personal friends but also of a private past. To recognize Bardolph, let alone to regret him, is impossible.

The war in France provides Henry with 'friends' of a rhetorical and special kind. It also allows him an ambiguous use of the pronoun 'we' which momentarily clothes the abstract doctrine of the king's

two bodies with flesh. Before Harfleur, Henry rallies 'dear friends' to
the breach, or urges them to 'close the wall up with our English dead'
(III.1.1–2). The good yeomen whose limbs were made in England are
asked to 'show us here / The mettle of your pasture' (III.1.26–7).
Later, before Agincourt, he will tell his cousin Westmoreland that 'if
we are mark'd to die, we are enow / To do our country loss' and
speak of 'we few, we happy few, we band of brothers' (IV.3.20–1, 60).
His encounter with Williams, Court, and Bates in Act IV is prefaced
by a speech addressed to Bedford and Gloucester in which the
pronouns 'we' and 'our' are by implication both royal and collective:

> Gloucester, 'tis true that we are in great danger,
> The greater therefore should our courage be.
> Good morrow, brother Bedford. God Almighty!
> There is some soul of goodness in things evil,
> Would men observingly distill it out;
> For our bad neighbor makes us early stirrers,
> Which is both healthful and good husbandry.
> Besides, they are our outward consciences
> And preachers to us all, admonishing
> That we should dress us fairly for our end.
> Thus may we gather honey from the weed,
> And make a moral of the devil himself.   (IV.1.1–12)

In passages like these, where Henry's 'we' and 'our' seem to refer
both to himself as king and to the nobles and soldiers around him as
a group, a community in which he participates, the idea of the king's
two bodies acquires a meaning that is concrete and emotionally
resonant. Rightly considered, Henry's soldiers are part of his body
politic and thus extensions of his own identity. But it is only in
moments of stress and mutual dependence that the doctrine
articulates itself naturally, allowing the king an easy jocularity which
is familiar without being intimate, essentially distant at the same time
that it creates an illusion of warmth and spontaneity. As the peril of
the situation in France grows, so does Henry's sense of fellowship. It
is almost as though he extracts from danger a kind of substitute for the
genuinely personal relationships abandoned with Falstaff and
Scroop.

Ironically, Henry's dazzling victory at Agincourt necessarily spells
the end of this special accord. The king who speaks in the council
chamber at Troyes in Act V is once again firmly entrenched behind a
royal 'we' that is a diagram rather than a three-dimensional fact.

Somewhat disconcertingly, he insists upon using the first person plural even in his request that the girl he intends to marry should remain in the room with him when the peers of France and England depart to discuss terms of peace:

> Yet leave our cousin Katherine here with us:
> She is our capital demand, compris'd
> Within the fore-rank of our articles.   (v.2.95–7)

For all its political realism, this seems a desperately awkward beginning to a declaration of love. In the wooing scene that follows, Henry falls back upon his soldier's persona. He resurrects this 'I' to deal with a situation of peculiar difficulty. How should a king, encumbered by twin natures, embark upon what is necessarily the most personal of all relationships, that of love? Henry's particular compromise is witty, and yet the problems of communication in this scene do not spring entirely from the fact that the king's French is even more rudimentary than the lady's English. Most of Henry's blunders, his various solecisms, derive from his uncertainty as to whether at a given instant he is speaking as Harry or as England, and whether the girl he addresses is the delectable Kate or the kingdom of France. Certainly the princess, when informed that her suitor loves France so well that 'I will not part with a village of it; I will have it all mine. And, Kate, when France is mine and I am yours, then yours is France and you are mine,' might well be excused for complaining that 'I cannot tell wat is dat,' even if her linguistic skills were considerably greater than they are (v.2.174–7). The loving monarchs of *Fair Em* and *King Leir* recognized no such problems of expression. Whatever this wooing scene was like in the lost, original text of *The Famous Victories of Henry V*, it has been made in Shakespeare's play to serve the theme of the king's two bodies: the dilemma of the man placed at a disadvantage in the sphere of personal relations by the fact of a corporate self.

The first part of *Sir John Oldcastle*, a play belonging to the Lord Chamberlain's rivals, the Admiral's Men, was staged by 1600. Its four authors, Michael Drayton, Anthony Munday, Richard Hathway, and Robert Wilson, were certainly painfully conscious of Shakespeare's Henry IV plays and probably of *Henry V* as well. In the absence of any Elizabethan equivalent to Vasari, a writer who would have relished and also recorded the whole imbroglio, there seems no way of knowing precisely what steps the Brooke family took to try and dissociate their ancestor Sir John Oldcastle, the Lollard martyr, from Shakespeare's Falstaff. That Shakespeare had originally christened his fat knight Oldcastle is clear from surviving allusions within *1 Henry IV*, from the public apology in the epilogue to the second part – 'for Oldcastle died a martyr, and this is not the man' – and from the malicious references of contemporaries as anxious to press the connection as Sir Henry Brooke was to repudiate it.[13] Whether Shakespeare was forced to remove Falstaff from *Henry V* because of the protests of the Brookes and then permitted to display him at full length in *The Merry Wives of Windsor* at the direct request of Queen Elizabeth remains conjectural. It seems likely, however, that the Brooke family eventually realized that their repressive tactics were only serving to make them ridiculous and, in desperation, decided to fight fire with fire: to appeal to the stage itself to counteract the slanders of the stage.

There is no positive evidence that the mysterious sum of money received by Philip Henslowe 'as A gefte'[14] to the four authors of *Sir John Oldcastle* came from Sir Henry Brooke. On the other hand, everything about the first and only surviving part of their history suggests a work especially commissioned as an answer to the Falstaff plays:

> The doubtfull Title (Gentlemen) prefixt
> Upon the Argument we have in hand,
> May breede suspence, and wrongfully disturbe
> The peacefull quiet of your setled thoughts.
> To stop which scruple, let this briefe suffise:
> It is no pamperd glutton we present,
> Nor aged Councellor to youthfull sinne,
> But one, whose vertue shone above the rest,
> A valiant Martyr and a vertuous peere;
> In whose true faith and loyaltie exprest
> Unto his soveraigne, and his countries weale,
> We strive to pay that tribute of our Love,
> Your favours merite. Let faire Truthe be grac'te,
> Since forg'de invention former time defac'te.[15]

13 Leslie Hotson, 'Two Shakespearean firsts – the Earl of Essex and Falstaff', *Shakespeare's Sonnets Dated*, pp. 147–60.
14 *Henslowe's Diary*, ed. R. A. Foakes and R. T. Rickert (Cambridge, 1961), p. 126.
15 *Sir John Oldcastle*, *The Shakespeare Apocrypha*, ed. C. F. Tucker Brooke (Oxford, 1908), Prologue.

That the 'pamperd glutton', the 'aged Councellor to youthfull sinne' referred to in this prologue is Shakespeare's Falstaff admits of no doubt. Drayton, Munday, Wilson, and Hathway were out to soothe the Brooke family by presenting their ancestor as a hero, claiming in the process that they spoke truth where Shakespeare had lied. Furthermore, they had to construct an effective dramatic entertainment: a play which could support inevitable comparison with the popular Henry IV and V plays offered by the rival Lord Chamberlain's Men at The Globe. The result is curious. The first part of *Sir John Oldcastle* is, in effect, a detailed demonstration of how to turn a tragical into a comical history.

The four *Sir John Oldcastle* authors faced from the beginning a problem even more difficult than that of rivalling Shakespeare's invention. The historical Sir John Oldcastle, a follower of Wicliffe, had eventually given his life for the Protestant faith. As such, he was entirely eligible for the status of Elizabethan hero. Unfortunately, he happened to live in the reign of Henry V, a king who not only was not a Protestant himself, but one who firmly put down any outbreaks of this heresy that came to his attention. In writing his own Henry V play, Shakespeare had been able to ignore the inconvenient fact of the Henrician persecutions. The Oldcastle authors, on the other hand, could scarcely evade the religious issue, given a hero who was remembered solely because of it. Neither could they ask an Elizabethan audience to accept Henry V, the hero-king of the Agincourt ballad, the conqueror of France, as a villain. Because the second part of *Sir John Oldcastle* has been lost, it is impossible to know how they treated the awkward fact of the martyrdom itself. Part 1, however, is remarkable for the consistency with which it romanticizes and obscures political and religious issues that were potentially dangerous. Carefully, and unhistorically, the four dramatists dissociated Oldcastle from a Lollard uprising aimed against the king as well as the pope. The rabble in the play is confused about its religious motives and activated chiefly by the hope of plunder. With this irresponsible and seditious mob the character Oldcastle is shown to have no connection. It is only the bishops, and certain nobles jealous of his popularity, who pretend that he leads the rebels. Henry himself is in no way distressed by Oldcastle's Protestantism, so long as it remains unconnected with the elements of political disorder in the state. It is almost suggested that Henry yearns to become a Protestant himself, except that the time is somehow not right. (There were, after all, limits to the liberties Elizabethan dramatists could take with history.)

That the Oldcastle authors were perfectly familiar with Shakespeare's histories is obvious. Indeed, they seem to have spent a good deal of their time wondering how to convert the fine things in the possession of the Lord Chamberlain's Men to their own uses. Like *Henry V*, *Sir John Oldcastle* opens just before the expedition to France. Here too, the clergy are scheming to divert attention from the wealth and rich livings of the church through the judicious dispensation of a portion of their gold: some is destined to help finance the war; some is offered to the Earl of Suffolk as a bribe to persuade him to speak against the troublesome Oldcastle – the most articulate opponent of ecclesiastical wealth and ceremonies – to the king. At the beginning of Act II, a summoner engaged by the wicked Bishop of Rochester arrives before Oldcastle's house in Kent to serve a summons upon its master. Unluckily for him, he meets Harpoole, Oldcastle's brusque but loyal steward, first. Harpoole examines the legal document carefully:

HARPOOLE: Is this processe parchment?
SUMMONER: Yes, mary.
HARPOOLE: And this seale waxe?
SUMMONER: It is so.
HARPOOLE: If this be parchment, & this wax, eate you this parchment and this waxe, or I will make parchment of your skinne, and beate your brains into waxe: Sirra Sumner, dispatch; devoure, sirra, devoure.

(II.1.56–65)

After a comic struggle, in the course of which the wretched summoner is threatened with a beating and administered a cup of sack with which to wash down the last scraps, he duly eats the summons including the seal. 'Waxe,' as Harpoole opines, is wholesome: 'the purest of the hony' (84).

This episode has its obvious parallel in *Henry V*. In Act V, Fluellen invokes the aid of a cudgel to force a reluctant and histrionic Ancient Pistol to eat the leek he had previously mocked. The New Arden editor regards the similarity here as part of the evidence that the Oldcastle authors were familiar with *Henry V* as well as the two parts of *Henry IV* when they wrote their own play.[16] He is probably right. Yet it is surely important to note that there is a third scene of this kind,

[16] *Henry V*, ed. John H. Walter, The New Arden Shakespeare (London, 1954), p. xi.

earlier than either *Henry V* or *Sir John Oldcastle*, which should be taken into account. In *George a Greene*, Sir Nicholas Mannering arrives at the town of Wakefield bearing a commission from the rebellious Earl of Kendall for the requisition of victuals for his soldiers. George a Greene himself, outraged both by the request and by Mannering's insolence in urging it, first tears the parchment and then compels this traitor to King Edward's throne to eat the seals that were attached to it:

> MANNERING: Well, and there be no remedie, so, George:
>   [*swallows one of the seals.*]
>   One is gone: I pray thee, no more nowe.
> GEORGE: O, sir,
>   If one be good, the others cannot hurt.
>   So, sir;
>   [*Mannering swallows the other two seals.*]
>   Nowe you may goe tell the Earle of Kendall,
>   Although I haue rent his large Commission,
>   Yet of curtesie I haue sent all his seales
>   Back againe by you.   (144–53)

The episode involving Harpoole and the Summoner in *Sir John Oldcastle* may well have been inspired by Pistol's encounter with Fluellen; it is nevertheless with this older scene from *George a Greene* that its real affinities lie. Like the pinner of Wakefield, Harpoole is a man of the people, someone who clings to a vanishing world of immediate feudal loyalties. His aggression stems not, like Fluellen's, from the need to avenge a personal affront but from the desire to defend his master from traitors who obscure simple right and wrong with the aid of a new and suspect legalism. The spice of the incident lies in the audacity of the under dog: the simple, honest man converting rotten parchment bonds into matter-of-fact fodder. It reflects one of the wish-dreams of a lower class victimized by legislation forced upon it from above, by a sea of paper which it could not understand. In both *George a Greene* and *Sir John Oldcastle*, the plain old loyalties of master and servant, subject and king, achieve a triumph in the moment that the parchment (or the seals) slides down the officer's unwilling throat. When Shakespeare converted the original legal document into a vegetable, the dapper courtier worsted by the pinner into an entirely personal matter involving Fluellen's Welsh pride and Pistol's unconsidered boasting, he was moving away from traditional forms in response both to the spirit of the time and to the shape of his own history play. By 1599, the comical history was a consciously reactionary, an outdated dramatic mode. That cycle of Shakespearean plays which begins with *Richard II* and ends with *Henry V* had helped to make it so. Yet Elizabethans could still be made to respond emotionally to the ballad and folk material upon which the genre depended, while withholding actual belief in such distant and half-legendary types of social protest.

Harpoole himself has nothing but praise for the constable who enters immediately after the discomfited summoner has crept away. This functionary has been sent to make hue and cry after a thief who has robbed two clothiers. He means to search the ale-house for the culprit, but because that building stands in Oldcastle's 'libertie' he refuses to exercise his function 'except I had some of his servants, which are for my warrant' (II.1.140–1). In effect, the constable of his own free will recognizes and honours an older order of jurisdiction and responsibility based on the autonomy of the great house and its demesne. That the inviolability of Oldcastle's 'libertie' from outside interference is no longer something taken for granted is apparent in Harpoole's cry of relief: 'An honest Constable! an honest Constable!' The steward is old-fashioned, a believer in relationships and prerogatives which, in his time, were beginning to be questioned and superceded. Later in the play, he will engineer his master's escape from the Tower and loyally, without hope of reward, accompany Oldcastle and his Lady in their flight. His taste in literature reflects his attitudes toward society and the proper relationship of vassal and overlord. When the Bishop of Rochester orders the 'heretical' books in Cobham's house to be burned, Harpoole makes a heated defence of his own personal library: 'for I have there English bookes, my lord, that ile not part with for your Bishoppricke: Bevis of Hampton, Owleglasse, the Frier and the Boy, Ellenor Rumming, Robin hood, and other such godly stories' (IV.3.166–70).

Harpoole and his library are by no means the play's only links with the ballad and romance tradition. The cast of characters includes another Sir John besides the hero: Sir John the parson of Wrotham. This cleric is a hanger-on of precisely those covetous bishops who cause Oldcastle so much trouble. He follows them, however, purely to serve his own ends:

> Me thinkes the purse of gold the Bishop gave
> Made a good shew; it had a tempting looke.
> Beshrew me, but my fingers ends do itch

To be upon those rudduks. Well, 'tis thus:
I am not as the worlde does take me for;
If ever woolfe were cloathed in sheepes coate,
Then I am he, – olde huddle and twang, yfaith,
A priest in shew, but in plain termes a theefe.
Yet, let me tell you too, an honest theefe,
One that will take it where it may be sparde,
And spend it freely in good fellowship.
I have as many shapes as *Proteus* had,
That still, when any villany is done,
There may be none suspect it was sir John.
Besides, to comfort me, – for whats this life,
Except the crabbed bitternes thereof
Be sweetened now and then with lechery? –
I have my Doll, my concubine, as t'were,
To frollicke with, a lusty bounsing gerle.   (1.155–73)

As an example of Shakespearean influence, this speech would be hard to surpass. It is perfectly evident that Sir John of Wrotham represents an attempt on the part of the *Oldcastle* authors to make use of precisely the character their play was designed to discredit and obliterate from the memory of Elizabethan audiences: Sir John Falstaff. Somehow, Drayton, Munday, Hathway, and Wilson were going to contrive to introduce the Gad's Hill robbery into their work too. Doll, the parson's paramour, is sister to Falstaff's Doll Tearsheet and, in the course of the play, will display the same mixture of tenderness and fury as her prototype. The line about Proteus has been stolen from one of the speeches of the future Richard III, in *3 Henry VI* (III.2.192). Otherwise, the speech appears on the surface to be all fake Falstaff. Yet something about the tone is alien. Falstaff, after all, was scarcely 'an honest theefe', concerned to 'take it where it may be sparde'. A purse was a purse for him, whether it belonged to a wealthy traveller or was to be extracted from poor Mistress Quickly at the cost of all her plate. It is in the outlaw ballads of the late Middle Ages, particularly those centred upon Robin Hood, that the source of this Sir John's attitude may be found. What the *Oldcastle* authors have done is to reach back through Falstaff to resurrect the far older figure of Friar Tuck.

When Shakespeare's Henry V adopted disguise, the night before Agincourt, he found himself confronting men who enquired into the nature of the king's responsibility with uncomfortable particularity. The *Oldcastle* Henry V also resorts to disguise, perhaps in imitation of

Shakespeare's play. At the end of Act III, the king sets off to
Westminster alone and incognito to gather news about the rebellion.
On Blackheath he encounters Sir John disguised in green, the colour
traditionally worn by the followers of Robin Hood. Courteously and
wittily the chief relieves his unknown sovereign of a purse containing
one hundred pounds in gold. This Henry V, unlike his Shakespearean
counterpart, evinces no hesitation in speaking about his disreputable
past and old associates:

Wel, if thou wilt needs have it, there 'tis: just the proverb, one thiefe robs
another. Where the divel are all my old theeves, that were wont to keepe this
walke? Falstaffe, the villaine, is so fat, he cannot get on's horse, but me
thinkes Poines and Peto should be stirring here abouts.   (III.4.59–65)

Sir John, informed that his victim is a gentleman of the King's
chamber, professes himself doubly pleased: this traveller can spare his
money without hardship and may also be useful in future to 'get a
poor thiefe his pardon' (III.4.82). With this latter contingency in
mind, the concealed parson breaks a golden angel between them so
that they may know each other again. Sir John swears that this token,
when produced, will forestall any second robbery. Henry, in return,
is to remember his promise of a pardon. In high good spirits, and
without the least animosity on either side, the two men shake hands
and separate.

   Henry, now quite penniless, but delighted by this irregular
encounter, proceeds on his way and joins his army in a field near
London after dark. His lords greet their king ceremoniously, but find
him strangely reluctant to abandon his disguise. 'Peace, no more of
that', he tells Suffolk, who has addressed him formally as 'your
Highnesse':

> The King's asleepe; wake not his majestie
> With termes nor titles; hee's at rest in bed.
> Kings do not use to watch themselves; they sleepe,
> And let rebellion and conspiracie
> Revel and havocke in the common wealth...
>   ... this long cold winters night
> How can we spend? King Harry is a sleepe
> And al his Lords, these garments tel us so;
> Al friends at footebal, fellowes al in field,
> Harry, and Dicke, and George. Bring us a drumme;
> Give us square dice, weele keepe this court of guard
> For al good fellowes companies that come.   (IV.1.6–10, 29–35)

Predictably, Sir John is the first good fellow to wander in. In the gaming that ensues, the disguised king wins back his hundred pounds. When the parson produces his half of the broken coin as a final stake, Henry matches it, and challenges the thief to a combat. The two take up their positions and are about to engage when a horrified noble intervenes and reveals the identity of the king. Without this interruption, the episode would fairly clearly have terminated in the manner sanctioned by the Robin Hood ballads and actually demonstrated in Peele's *Edward I*: with a victory for the king that vindicated his strength and manly prowess.

In *Sir John Oldcastle*, Henry amuses himself for a few moments by adopting a pose of mock severity toward this Friar Tuck. Reminded, however, by the culprit that 'the best may goe astray, and if the world say true, your selfe (my liege) have bin a thiefe' (IV.1.182–4), the king freely admits the fact and contents himself with urging upon the parson a repentance and reclamation like his own. He makes him a free present of the stolen gold, a gift which Sir John receives with an unfeigned gratitude and delight that is worlds away from Williams' taciturn acceptance of the glove filled with crowns in Shakespeare's play: '*Vivat Rex* & *currat lex*! My liege, if ye have cause of battell, ye shal see sir John of Wrootham bestirre himself in your quarrel' (IV.1.197–9). One may well suspect the parson's ability to forswear cards and wine and become an honest man – indeed, on his next appearance, in Act V, he is confessing to Doll that drink, dice, and the devil have consumed the hundred pounds and preparing to recoup his fortunes by way of another robbery – but not the sincerity of his admiration for King Henry as a man.

Consistently, in borrowing from Shakespeare, the *Oldcastle* authors turned their material back in the direction of balladry and romance. That doctrine of the king's two bodies which underlies all of Shakespeare's histories from *Richard II* to *Henry V* is nowhere visible in their play, any more than it is in *George a Greene*, *James IV*, or the old *Famous Victories of Henry V*. The *Oldcastle* Henry shifts from the first person singular to the plural form much as he might put on a furred cloak for a state occasion: to mark the momentary appropriateness of formality. This king is first and foremost a man, an understanding good companion, happy to try conclusions with a thief, prevented only by lack of time and the necessary affairs of state from engaging more often in the kind of light-hearted, picaresque adventure he so clearly loves. Not even his confrontation with the traitors Cambridge,

Scroop, and Grey in Act v can shake his confidence in the possibility of personal relations. The whole idea of kingship in this play is uncomplicated, stripped of sacramental overtones, and essentially gay. It is also deliberately unreal, a fiction deriving from a distant and half-legendary past. *Henry V* may seem, by comparison with Shakespeare's other histories, to be optimistic and celebratory, a simplified and epic account of certain events in the Hundred Years' War. To set it for an instant beside *Sir John Oldcastle* is to realize, not only that Shakespeare was an incomparably finer dramatist than his four rivals put together, but that his conception of history, even when he was chronicling one of England's moments of glory, was fundamentally tragic.

In the absence of any formal dramatic theory which could be said to connect with the productions of the public stage, Elizabethan drama seems to have developed to a large extent through a curious kind of dialogue among specific plays. The world of the London playhouses was small and intimate: everyone, as it seemed, knew everyone else. Kyd once shared a room with Marlowe, and lived to regret it; Ben Jonson loved Shakespeare but prided himself on being able to beat Marston and take his pistol from him; Shakespeare suffered from the animosity of Greene and was defended by Chettle; the so-called War of the Theatres sent a number of poets into battle with each other for reasons that must have been aesthetic and personal in about equal measure. The true history of the hostilities and allegiances, the jealousies and discipleships among the dramatists writing between 1587 and 1600 can never be recovered now. Yet the plays that have survived from this period are in a sense projections and records of these long vanished relationships and artistic controversies. Because the history play was a relatively new genre, without the classical sanction possessed by comedy and tragedy, and also because its brief flowering was effectively bounded by the reign of Elizabeth, it can provide a particularly rewarding study of the way writers tended to articulate their own dramatic ideas by reference to pre-existing plays. No Puttenham or Abraham Fraunce, no Sidney or Ben Jonson ever troubled to distinguish between the comical and the tragical history as dramatic forms. It is only from the plays themselves that these categories emerge as something more real and consequential than the private lunacy of a Polonius, or the rodomontade of Elizabethan printers concerned to imp out a title-page with words.

The roots of the tragical history lie, fairly obviously, in those Tudor entertainments which A. P. Rossiter called the 'interlude[s] of church and state'.[17] The consequential dialogue between plays begins, however, in 1587 when Marlowe used the memory of Preston's *Cambises* (1561) and plays like it to launch his own counterstatement in the form of *Tamburlaine the Great*. Plays like the anonymous *Locrine* (1591) or *Selimus* (1592) reveal much about the impact of Marlowe upon his contemporaries: the need to assimilate and learn from *Tamburlaine* but also to domesticate and render it harmless. In *Edward II* (1592), on the other hand, Marlowe himself seems to have felt impelled to imitate Shakespeare's new style of history play, much in the way that Raphael, painting in the Vatican Stanze della Segnatura, suddenly was led to create figures patently Michelangelesque after he had been shown the unfinished Sistine ceiling. Because Vasari thought such things important, the details of how and when Raphael managed to see the tormented grandeurs of the Sistine Chapel are known, even as the long hours Michelangelo himself had spent absorbing the figure style of Masaccio in the Brancacci Chapel are known. Without the testimony of Vasari, there would only be certain stylistic features from which to construct a hypothesis that Raphael's experience of the Sistine ceiling was so unexpectedly intense that for a time it altered the character of his own work, or that Michelangelo learned from Masaccio. The problem of identifying reaction and specific indebtedness would, in fact, strongly resemble the one which confronts the Elizabethan scholar trying to make sense of the development of dramatic forms during the crucial years 1587–1600.

As it was defined by Shakespeare, the tragical history became a serious, and politically a somewhat incendiary, examination into the nature of kingship. At the heart of the form lay the Tudor doctrine of the king's two bodies, which, in the fullness of time, was to provide justification for the execution of Charles I. Shakespeare himself, absorbed by the difficulties of royal incarnation, never wrote a comical history, unlike Peele, Greene, Heywood, Dekker, and a host of other contemporary dramatists. Yet he must have been aware of it as an alternative form, stemming originally from ballads and romances, made dramatic at least as early as 1560, and still wistfully alive in his own time. Certainly he introduced its most characteristic

[17] A. P. Rossiter, *English Drama From Early Times to the Elizabethans* (London, 1950), p. 113.

motif, that of the king disguised, into *Henry V* because he expected to gain, by his atypical handling of it, a calculated and powerful emotional effect. For Shakespeare, *Henry V* seems to have marked the end of his personal interest in the tragical history. He had virtually exhausted the form, at least in its English version, and not only (as it turned out) for himself. When the four *Oldcastle* authors accepted the doubtful task of competing with Shakespeare's Henry IV and V plays, it cannot have been only the religious difficulties posed by their subject matter which led them to turn tragical history so completely into comical. *Sir John Oldcastle* is a tribute to Shakespeare not only because it is haunted everywhere by characters, episodes, and turns of phrase taken from his own cycle, but also because its entire style and anachronistic ethos as a play stand as silent witness to the fact that in the English tragical history, the more consequential form Shakespeare had made peculiarly his own, little, as it seemed, was left for anyone else to do.

'He that plays the king': Ford's *Perkin Warbeck* and the Stuart history play (1977)

In the Prologue to *The Chronicle History of Perkin Warbeck : A Strange Truth* (1633), John Ford claimed that he was reviving a mode now conspicuously 'unfollowed' and 'out of fashion'.[1] Historians of the theatre have agreed. Apart from a few belated survivals, among which *Perkin Warbeck* itself and Shakespeare's *Henry VIII* stand out, the chronicle history seems to have died with Elizabeth. Various explanations have been advanced for the disappearance of plays focussed upon the reigns of more or less historical English kings: a decline in 'national spirit', the accession of a Scottish king, the rarefied tastes of the private theatre audience, a tendency to transform history into romance, or merely the exhaustion of what was perhaps a limited dramatic form. The massive achievement of Shakespeare's nine Elizabethan histories, plays dealing with the reigns of seven English kings from John to Richard III, may well have contributed to a contemporary feeling that the chronicle history had fulfilled its potentialities and should now be put aside. Certainly Shakespeare's decision, at the beginning of the seventeenth century, to turn from English to Roman history seems (quite apart from its own internal artistic logic) to herald the general abandonment of the genre. Plays concerned with the lives of English kings had been written during the last decades of the sixteenth century not only by Shakespeare, but by Marlowe, Peele, Greene, Heywood, Munday, Wilson and by all those anonymous authors responsible for such works as *The Troublesome Raigne of King John* (1588), *Edward III* (1590), *Jack Straw* (1591), *The True Tragedy of Richard III* (1591), and *Woodstock* (1592). Many other plays of this type have been lost. The decline, after only one year of James's reign, in the popularity of a dramatic genre which flourished so richly under Elizabeth raises

[1] John Ford, *The Chronicle History of Perkin Warbeck*, ed. Peter Ure, The Revels Plays (London, 1968), p. 11. All subsequent quotations from the play refer to this edition.

questions about the genre itself. It may also lead one to ask whether theatrical interest in the nature and development of the English monarchy really did fail abruptly in the early seventeenth century, or whether it simply went underground, manifesting itself in new and characteristically Stuart forms.

Any list of the English histories written between 1603 and the closing of the theatres in 1642 must always be subjective, conjectural and incomplete. Some plays have vanished. Others survive only as disembodied titles suggestive of a type. Even the extant histories reliably assigned to the period can be difficult to disentangle from lost, Elizabethan plays on the same subject. Most perplexing of all is the problem of classification. The English history play had been, from the beginning, an amorphous and ill-defined genre, always inclined to blur or submerge its identity in that of the neighbouring, and more established, forms of comedy and tragedy. Elizabethans were notoriously careless about nomenclature, blithely describing the same play as a 'comedy', a 'tragedy', or a 'history' as the humour took them. Such contradictory baptisms are understandable. Modern critics, confronted with plays like Shakespeare's *Richard III* (1593) and *Richard II* (1595), with Greene's *James IV* (1590), the anonymous *Look About You* (1599) or the second part of Heywood's *Edward IV* (1599), tend to shift their terms in a not dissimilar way. Any decision as to whether *Richard II*, for instance, is properly to be classed as a history or a tragedy is likely to depend less upon objective criteria than upon a particular, critical interpretation of the play. In the Stuart period, as the history play adopts new and subtle disguises, the difficulties increase. *Macbeth* (1606) is surely as much a history play as *Richard II*. The fact that it is almost invariably discussed as a tragedy would seem to reflect not so much its First Folio grouping (*Cymbeline*, after all, appears among the tragedies too), as it does critical preconceptions about the protagonist, plus an underlying and guiding conviction that tragedy is the dominant Jacobean form.

Ironically, in view of its subsequent eclipse, the traditional history play received an invigorating gift of new subject matter as the immediate effect of the accession of James I. During the reign of Elizabeth no one, for obvious reasons, had dared to represent either the great queen herself, or her father Henry VIII, on the public stage. Even Henry VII, the founder of the Tudor dynasty, was sparingly handled. Shakespeare distanced him as a kind of icon of majesty at the end of *Richard III*, an emblem of righteousness and peace more

than a fallible human being. He never wrote a play about Henry
VII, attractive though much of the historical material must have
seemed to him. Robert Wilson did. Henslowe records a payment to
him for the second part of *Henry Richmond* on 8 November 1599. Both
this play and its presumed first part are lost, as is an *Owen Tudor* of
1600 on which Wilson collaborated with Drayton, Hathway and
Anthony Munday. Judging from the extant *I Sir John Oldcastle* (1599)
produced by the same dramatists, and from the titles of several other
lost histories in which Wilson had a hand, his two plays about the
Tudors probably tempered fact with a strong and, under the
circumstances, prudent admixture of fantasy. The very fact that he
called his play *Henry Richmond*, not *Henry VII*, suggests a shying away
from the actual reign of Elizabeth's grandfather in favour of passages
from his early life: a strategy altogether understandable in 1599. As
for Henry VIII, it is significant that the king does not appear as a
character in either *Sir Thomas More* (1595) or *The True Chronicle
History of Thomas Lord Cromwell* (1600), despite his overwhelming
importance to the lives (and deaths) of these two servants of the
Crown. Almost certainly, the same was true of the two lost plays
concerned with the life of Cardinal Wolsey recorded in 1601.

The beginning of James I's reign, by contrast, is marked by no
fewer than five extant histories in which Tudor monarchs are
assigned prominent speaking parts: *Sir Thomas Wyatt* (1604), *When
You See Me You Know Me* (1604), *1* and *2 If You Know Not Me, You
Know Nobody* (1604-5), and *The Whore of Babylon* (1606). It is just
possible that the Dekker and Webster collaboration *Sir Thomas Wyatt*
is based upon the lost *1* and *2 Lady Jane* of 1602, but even if it was, that
stage coronation of Queen Mary to which the 1607 title-page so
proudly draws attention, together with the portrayal of Elizabeth's
half-sister herself, must be Jacobean additions. Rowley's *When You See
Me You Know Me*, clearly a play with which Shakespeare was familiar,
follows Henry VIII affectionately through three marriages and the
disgrace of Wolsey, while recording the struggles of emergent English
Protestantism, a faith championed most effectively by Will Sommers,
the king's canny fool. In Heywood's two-part *If You Know Not Me,
You Know Nobody*, Elizabeth strives gallantly to retain her life and
liberty despite the persecutions of Queen Mary, to be rewarded at
last for her acumen and courage by the great Protestant victory of
1588. *The Whore of Babylon*, an hysterical anti-Catholic blast by
Dekker, presents Elizabeth thinly disguised as Titania the Fairie

Queene (by courtesy of Spenser, who would not, one feels, have been much gratified) and again moves to its climax with the defeat of the Armada.

In his address to the readers of *The Whore of Babylon*, Dekker claimed that his intention was 'to set forth (in Tropicall and shadowed collours) the Greatnes, Magnanimity, Constancy, Clemency, and other the incomparable Heroical vertues of our late Queene'. These he compares to a pyramid lost in the clouds, beyond the achievement of any pen, or to a stream so profound as to be unfathomable. Time, the presenter of the play, will fetch back 'all those golden years / He stole', and 'lay the Dragon at a Doves soft feete'.[2] This is not the language of court flattery – Elizabeth, after all, was dead, and no son of hers succeeded – but of myth. The same kind of glorification of Elizabeth's early reign informs Heywood's diptych *If You Know Not Me, You Know Nobody*, where the very title isolates Elizabeth as the wonder of the western world. Rowley's portrait of Henry VIII is more intimate and personal, never attempting to slur over the king's well known inequalities of temper. Henry emerges, however, with all his idiosyncrasies, as a mythological figure of another, and more traditional, kind. The death of Elizabeth and the consequent replacement of the Tudor by a Stuart monarchy has allowed Rowley to celebrate Henry, most implausibly, as a ballad king-in-disguise: walking incognito among his subjects, talking with them familiarly, proving his physical supremacy by defeating Black Will in a hand to hand fight, uncovering and redressing hidden wrongs. The play continues the old, romantic line of *George A Greene* (1590), *Fair Em* (1590), *King Leir* (1590), *Edward I* (1591), *I Edward IV* (1599), and *I Sir John Oldcastle* (1599), all of them histories in which a great king pretends for a time to be a private man and, in this disguise, vindicates his inherited right to rule others by demonstrating his personal strength, intelligence, imagination, judgement and compassion.[3] *When You See Me You Know Me* is distinctively Jacobean only in that, before 1603, it would not have been possible to add Henry VIII to this theatrical line of historical kings who acquire the status of folk hero.

---

[2] Thomas Dekker, *The Whore of Babylon*, in *The Dramatic Works of Thomas Dekker*, ed. Fredson Bowers, 4 vols. (Cambridge, 1953–61), II, pp. 497, 499.

[3] See my essay 'The king disguised: Shakespeare's *Henry V* and the comical history', originally published in *The Triple Bond*, ed. Joseph G. Price (Pennsylvania and London, 1975), pp. 92–117 and reprinted above.

The little flurry of plays mythologizing the reigns of Henry VIII and his daughter Elizabeth was soon over, Shakespeare's *Henry VIII*, with its ecstatic prophecy of the glories of Eliza's time, standing as a curiously belated example of the phenomenon. After 1604, only a few plays were written which seem to extend the old-style Elizabethan history. Rowley's *The Birth of Merlin* (1608 or possibly 1620) is a conjuror play tenuously linked to the life of a British king, in the manner of *Friar Bacon and Friar Bungay* (1589), *John a Kent and John a Cumber* (1589), or *Look About You*. The anonymous *Welsh Ambassador* (1623) is reminiscent of *Locrine* (1591) or *Edward III* in its delineation of a monarch tempted to be unkingly because of lust. Celebration of the safely distant heroics of ancient Britons, adumbrated in the titles of such lost Elizabethan plays as *1* and *2 The Conquest of Brute* (1598), *Uther Pendragon* (1597), *King Lud* (1599), or *Arthur King of England* (1598), finds its Stuart echo in *Cymbeline* (1609), Fletcher's *Bonduca* (1613), the unintentionally hilarious *The True Trojans* of 1625, and *The Valiant Welshman* (1612). More interesting, however, in terms of the distinctively seventeenth-century development of the English history, are those plays in which a vanished, and usually heroic, ideal of royalty, related to the ideal glorified in the nostalgic Tudor histories written around 1604, is explored without direct reference to the Tudors, and in forms which depart consciously from those of the Elizabethan period.

Nostalgia can assume many shapes. Massinger, in *The Emperor of the East* (1631), surely invokes the memory of Elizabeth in the character of Pulcheria, the wise and good regent of Constantinople, who has in time to surrender her throne to a younger brother who is foolish, uxorious, swayed by his favourites, and weak.[4]

> she indeed is
> A perfect Phoenix, and disdaynes a rivall.
> Her infant yeeres, as you know, promis'd much,
> But growne to ripenesse shee transcendes, and makes
> Credulitie her debtor ...
> Her soule is so immense,
> And her strong faculties so apprehensive,
> To search into the depth of deepe designes,
> And of all natures, that the burthen which
> To many men were insupportable,
> To her is but a gentle exercise.   (1.1.18–22, 52–7)

---

[4] Philip Massinger, *The Emperor of the East*, in *The Plays and Poems of Philip Massinger*, ed. Philip Edwards and Colin Gibson, 5 vols. (Oxford, 1976), III (1.1.18–22, 52–7, 64–78).

This royal paragon, sought after in marriage by many foreign kings, 'scornes to weare / On her free necke the servile yoke of marriage'.

> And for one loose desire, envie it selfe
> Dares not presume to taint her. *Venus* sonne
> Is blinde indeed, when he but gazes on her;
> Her chastity being a rocke of Diamonds,
> With which encountred his shafts flie in splinters,
> His flaming torches in the living spring
> Of her perfections, quench'd: and to crowne all,
> Shee's so impartiall when she sits upon
> The high tribunall, neither swayd with pittye,
> Nor awd by feare beyond her equall scale,
> That 'tis not superstition to beleeve
> *Astrea* once more lives upon the earth,
> *Pulcheriaes* brest her temple.   (1.1.64–78)

The young emperor Theodosius shows signs of repenting of his wicked ways at the end of the tragi-comedy, but clearly, he will never attain the kind of magical and epic royalty associated with this elder sister who fades away so mysteriously at the end of Act v. Massinger's hyperbole, far exceeding Shakespeare's description of the 'fair vestal throned by the west', makes one understand how the author (probably Ford) of *The Queen: or The Excellency of her Sex* (1628) could rely upon his audience to react instantly against Alphonso, a character who seeks 'to free wrack'd *Arragon* from ruin, / Which a fond womans government must bring'. The Queen, as it turns out, is no Elizabeth. Still, she is not a bad ruler, and Alphonso's blind prejudice against a 'female Mistriss of the Crown'[5] tells against him because of the memories of the great queen that are inevitably aroused.

Nostalgia of a different, and less specific, kind seems to inform Shakespeare's treatment of Duncan and of Edward the Confessor in *Macbeth*. There are no real analogues to these remote and saintly kings in his Elizabethan work. Edward's success in touching his subjects for the evil may indeed represent a compliment to James I; the fact remains that Edward himself, as he is described by Malcolm and the English doctor, is a living legend of a kind that even the most assiduous and obsequious of the Jacobean masque writers could not create around the person of James. It has sometimes been suggested that there are scenes missing from the fourth act of *Macbeth*, that it is

---

[5] John Ford (?), *The Queen*, ed. W. Bang, *Materialen zur kunde des älteren englischen Dramas* xiii (Louvain, 1906), lines 247–50, 257–8.

strange that so much emphasis should be placed upon the healing and prophetic gifts of a monarch we are never allowed to see. Edward the Confessor as an absent presence, on the other hand, obviously contributes to the pattern of a play concerned throughout to contrast an older, sacramental kind of kingship with something more brisk and modern. Duncan too is 'a most sainted king' (IV.3.109) who becomes, in death, a sort of royal icon: 'his silver skin lac'd with his golden blood' (II.3.112). Both he and Edward represent images of monarchy associated with the past and, as such, contrasted not only with Macbeth the savage usurper but also with the young king who inherits the throne of Scotland at the end. That strange scene in which Malcolm investigates Macduff's willingness to accept a rightful king who is, by his own confession, a lecher, a miser, and a promise-breaker, devoid of all 'the king-becoming graces' (IV.3.91), has always seemed disturbing. One is surely intended to take Malcolm at his word, to believe that he blackens his character falsely as a way of testing Macduff. And yet, whatever one thinks of Macduff for countenancing as much as he does of this impressive catalogue of royal vice, Malcolm himself emerges from the scene obscurely tainted. Even if he is none of the dreadful things he has artfully pretended to be, it seems clear that he will prove a politic and ordinary king, neither saint nor hero. It is hard to imagine Duncan or Edward the Confessor, however uncertain the times, playing Malcolm's trick upon Macduff. Had Duncan practised such wiles, he might have lived longer, but he would have been a different kind of king.

Interestingly enough, in at least two Stuart histories, men who share some of the mythic quality of Shakespeare's Duncan and Edward are presented as reluctant kings, elevated unwillingly to thrones they have no wish to possess. Shakespeare's Richard II and Henry VI had each had moments of wishing for the status of a private man. These, however, were momentary aberrations, products of despair, or a particularly sinister political situation. Elidure in *Nobody and Somebody* (1605) and Constantius in Middleton's *The Mayor of Queenborough* (1618), by contrast, both regard monarchy as an unwelcome assault upon the integrity of their private lives. Bookish and religious men, they find, as Constantius says, that their 'true kingdom' is within, and wonder that 'men so much should covet care'.[6]

---

[6] Thomas Middleton, *The Mayor of Queenborough*, in *Thomas Middleton*, ed. Havelock Ellis, The Mermaid Series (London, 1890), II (1.2). *Nobody and Somebody*, ed. J. S. Farmer (Tudor Facsimile Texts) (London, 1911) G1.

Like Duncan, the saintly Constantius is murdered, but not before he
has persuaded the future queen of England, Vortiger's consort-to-be,
that worldly power is despicable and corrupting. Elidure, after
suffering the agony of being crowned three times, as a result of
factional strife, is left at the end of his play as an established king who
has no choice but to reign. One can only speculate as to the nature of
that intriguingly titled lost play, *Two Kings in a Cottage* (1623), but
Dekker and Webster's Lady Jane Grey certainly makes it clear that
the only kingdom she desires is that of her husband's love, enjoying
which, 'What care I though a Sheep-cote be my Pallace?' Were the
pains of sovereignty 'rightly scand', she asserts, 'wee scarce should
finde a King in any Land'.[7]

Despite some suggestions in *1* and *2 Henry IV* and *Henry V*, this idea
of kingship as something which violates and destroys a private life
which rivals it in value, would seem to be a peculiarly Stuart
phenomenon. It was strengthened by the consciousness of a new kind
of rift which had opened, in the seventeenth century, between the
private and the public man. Elizabethan histories had often traced
the calamities of a reign to a war between man and office, a conflict
between the needs of the king's body natural and his body politic.
Almost invariably, however, they assumed that the 'king-becoming
graces' listed by Malcolm,

> As justice, verity, temp'rance, stableness,
> Bounty, perseverance, mercy, lowliness,
> Devotion, patience, courage, fortitude,   (IV.3.92–4)

were also those to which a private man and good Christian ought to
aspire. A great king was by definition a good and complete man, an
idea which helps to explain the persistence on the stage of that ballad
tradition in which royalty in disguise continues to command the
respect and admiration of the unsuspecting subject. Kings like
Richard II, or Locrine, or Edward II and III, imperil their thrones
when they are tempted to behave in ways that would also be wrong
– if less cataclysmic in their consequences – in a private individual.

On the plains of Scythia, or before Damascus, the brilliant ferocities
of Tamburlaine might be acceptable. They were not to be admired,
even covertly, in an English king. This fact surely helped to shape
Marlowe's sudden change of style and attitude when he turned to
English history in *Edward II* (1592). The subtle trains and amoral

---

[7] Dekker, *Sir Thomas Wyatt*, in Bowers, I (1.2.13–18, 31–2).

behaviour of Machiavelli's Prince were expected as a matter of course from usurpers like Shakespeare's John, or from characters like Marlowe's Mortimer who were in chase of a crown. Elizabethan dramatists exercised the greatest caution in attributing such qualities, patently at odds with the traditional virtues, to legitimate English rulers. It is extremely interesting to watch Shakespeare, arguably the greatest political realist among the Elizabethan writers of history plays, carefully white-washing the surface of *2 Henry IV*, *Henry V* and (later) *Henry VIII*, while leaving the reality behind the official facade delicately open to question. To what extent did Henry IV (and Prince Hal) approve Prince John's distasteful stratagem at Gaultree? Is the expedition to France really the holy war Henry V and the Chorus claim, or something more Machiavellian? What is the real motive governing Henry VIII's divorce? It is impossible to be sure. Only Shakespeare, perhaps, could have raised such issues, even obliquely, before 1603 in connection with a 'good' English king.

After the death of Elizabeth, it seems to have become increasingly difficult, not only to mythologize the English monarchy, but even to believe that an effective king was necessarily a good man. The changed temper of James's reign was surely responsible, in large part, for this shift of attitude. A great many of Elizabeth's subjects had been perfectly aware of just how hard-headed and devious she was as a ruler. Nevertheless, particularly in her last years, this knowledge co-existed quite happily with an acceptance of her as a Phoenix, a secular Virgin Mary, a bejewelled and magical icon of state. She had a way of turning even her miscalculations into triumphs. The so-called 'Golden Speech' of November, 1601 in which she used her defeat in the matter of monopolies as an occasion to express her love for her people, not only strengthened the ties of loyalty to the Crown at the time but, as C. V. Wedgwood has demonstrated, lived on into the Commonwealth period as an emotional weapon to be employed against the Stuart Kings.[8] James I's honeymoon with the English people was quickly over. After an initial period of relief that the succession had been resolved so smoothly, dissatisfaction gradually mounted with a king whose foreign policy seemed positively pusillanimous and a betrayal of the Protestant cause at home and abroad, whose ambiguous sexual tastes gave increasing power to his favourites, who could think of nothing better to do with a man like

---

[8] C. V. Wedgwood, *Oliver Cromwell and the Elizabethan Inheritance* (London, 1970).

Ralegh than to lock him up, who was personally anything but charismatic, let alone heroic, and whose financial dodges, though cunning, seemed unworthy of a great king. Even Ben Jonson must often have found it trying to be obliged to celebrate a monarch who could fall asleep during the serious portion of a court masque and, upon awaking, demand crossly that somebody should dance. The doctrine of the divine right of kings so dear to James's heart was all very well in the abstract: there was little about James personally or his court to encourage dramatists to embody it in a new wave of history plays. The reign of Charles I, although different in quality, proved no more propitious in this respect.

Stuart dramatists who wished to treat English history seriously, without retreating into the mists of pagan Britain, found that they had very little room for manoeuvre. A real king, as the Stuart monarchy reminded them constantly, now appeared to be a practical, cautious, unheroic individual, greatly occupied with questions of cold cash. Elizabeth must have looked fairly grotesque in her last years, but she was a magnificent monster, a mythic beast, which is more than could be said of 'the wisest foole in Christendome', in Sir Anthony Weldon's famous description, with his thin beard and circular walk, his tongue too large for his mouth, weak hams, and shapeless clothes artificially padded out as a protection against possible assassins.[9] As the hero of a play, even if the image was reflected at a distance, such a figure was not artistically attractive. It was always more rewarding to write about Macbeth, or even Duncan, than about Malcolm. The English history play was created during the reign of Elizabeth: a problematic figure, but nobody's Malcolm. The form withered away after 1603, partly because dramatists seem to have found it difficult to invest historical English kings with majesty and significance once James I confronted them as the visible representative of monarchy. There seem to have been only two lines of genuinely fresh development, neither of them responsible for many plays. Both lines meet in Ford's *Perkin Warbeck*, an achievement magnificent in itself which also represents the brilliant, if temporary, solution of an artistic dilemma.

In the Elizabethan history, love had almost always been something a

---

[9] Sir Anthony Weldon, quoted in *Portraits in Prose*, ed. Hugh Macdonald (London, 1946), pp. 20–4.

prince had to overcome, a temptation to him to stray from the path of kingly duty. This is its role in *Locrine*, *James IV*, *Fair Em*, *Friar Bacon and Friar Bungay*, *1* and *3 Henry VI*, *Edward III* and (with a difference) *Edward II*. Davenport's *King John and Matilda* (1631) is the first English history to give the king's name in the title equal weight with that of the lady he loves. The play itself suggests that John's failure to subjugate the beautiful Matilda is quite as important as his defeat by the barons on the field of Runnymede. An impulse largely diffused before 1642 in tragi-comedies (especially those of Fletcher), with only the most tangential relationship to the English history play, the conflict between love and the claims of monarchy became during the Restoration a guiding principle of the English histories written by Crowne, Orrery and Banks. It formed a special sub-section of the general love and honour debate. In his adaptation of Shakespeare's Henry VI plays (1680, 1681), Crowne reinforced virtually every political motive with one derived purely from the heart, even going so far as to make Warwick defect from Edward IV not so much because of the dishonoured French marriage treaty as because Warwick was in love with Lady Grey himself. Orrery managed to suggest, in 1664, that the battle of Agincourt was almost trivial compared with the struggle between Henry V and Owen Tudor for the favour of Katherine of France, while John Banks, in *The Unhappy Favourite* (1681), reduced Elizabeth, that Amazonian queen, to a love-sick maiden who is literally 'no more but e'en a woman' when the machinations of a jealous rival deprive her of Essex, her true love.

Although its Restoration and eighteenth-century progeny were more numerous, the Stuart love history is ultimately less interesting than a little group of plays in which an amoral and unglamorous monarch, a warrior for the working day, is used to set off a king figure of another and more nostalgic kind. In this latter character, traditional 'king-becoming graces' like those enumerated by Malcolm and celebrated in Elizabethan history plays and ballads are resurrected. Shakespeare, earlier, had created a contrast of this kind in *Richard II* and in *King John*. It was plain, however, that the charismatic figures there, Richard and the young Arthur, were the true kings of England, even if they were forced to yield both their thrones and their lives to a politic usurper. The Stuart plays are different. In them, the individual who looks and speaks like a monarch is, in some sense, a pretender: a claimant whose actual title to the throne, whatever the emotions aroused by his personality, is fictional, or impossible to prove. They seem to turn the ancient story of 'the waking man's dream' upside down, with results that are characteristically Stuart.

The sleeping beggar who awakes in splendour, to be assured by everyone that he is a prince whose memories of rags and poverty are all an unfortunate delusion, then finds himself back in his old life when the 'dream' breaks, was traditionally a comic figure. The ineptitude of his attempts to behave like a nobleman amused Haroun al Raschid in *The Arabian Nights*, Shakespeare's nameless Lord in the induction to *The Taming of the Shrew* and, presumably, the historical Philip the Good of Burgundy and the Emperor Charles V, both of whom are said to have practised the trick. The ineptitude was, indeed, the point of the joke. Christopher Sly, elevated to the aristocracy, remains unable to suppress his plebeian appetite for beef and small ale, or to address his 'wife' and servants as a great man should. Bottom encounters similar difficulties as the consort of the fairy queen. The dream of monarchy in which Ancient Pistol is more or less permanently lost appears to be entirely self-induced, but again the effect is comic for everyone but Pistol himself. In *2 Henry VI*, even the followers of Jack Cade finds his lunges at kingly rhetoric ('We John Cade, so term'd of our suppos'd father' IV.2.31) and his claim to be the son of Mortimer and a Plantagenet mother, hilarious. Falstaff fares no better when he tries to impersonate Henry IV in the Boar's Head, only to be met by Prince Hal's amused contempt: 'Dost thou speak like a king?' (*1 Henry IV* II.4.433) These Shakespearean examples, various though they are in terms of the characters and situations involved, are typical in their view of the pretender figure as funny. Not until the seventeenth century does the man who plays the king begin to appear more genuinely royal than the legitimate monarch.

Almost certainly, there was a Stuart play about Perkin Warbeck before Ford's. Gainsford mentions one in 1619, and implies that it took a strongly denigratory view of Perkin. Given Gainsford's own hostile attitude towards the pretender in his *True and Wonderfull History of Perkin Warbeck* (1618), one of the prose sources for Ford's play, this is scarcely surprising, and may not be an accurate reflection of the lost work. The dedicatory verses to the quarto edition of 1634 suggest that even in the case of Ford, contemporary opinion was oddly divided with respect to the right way of responding to Perkin. Of the five poems printed, two, after making it prudently clear that they do not support the pretender's claim to be Richard, Duke of York, nonetheless celebrate him as 'Glorious Perkin', whose 'lofty spirit soars yet', another reduces him to a trickster who 'ran his wily ways', while the remaining two decide to ignore the issue entirely. Subsequent criticism has perpetuated this uncertainty of attitude. Within recent years, however, the number of Perkin's admirers has tended to increase, while Henry VII, a character scrupulously passed over in all five of the 1634 poems, now seems a more dubious figure than nineteenth- and early twentieth-century critics were prepared to admit.

In an important article published in 1970, 'Perkin Warbeck as anti-history', Jonas Barish first queried the conventional reading of Ford's play as a lesson in kingship in which Henry emerges as an admirable or even, in some interpretations, an ideal monarch while Perkin himself, for all his personal grace, becomes an interesting study in aberrant psychology. Barish stressed Ford's strange and persistent refusal to commit himself as to the truth of Perkin's claim. The historical Perkin confessed, before he died, that he was an impostor. The dramatic character does not. 'As in *Richard II*', Barish concludes, 'we find a contrast between the storybook monarch, the one who plays the king beautifully, and the manipulator who rules adroitly without commanding love... Perkin Warbeck reminds us of how, in our dreams, we would like kings to appear, and how in reality, it is nearly impossible that they should'.[10]

Philip Edwards has linked *Perkin Warbeck* as a pretender play with Massinger's *Believe As You List* (1631). It is known that Massinger originally wrote his play about Don Sebastian of Portugal. He transferred it to the safe distance of the classical world only because his version of a recent European *cause célèbre* ran foul of the censors. Both dramatists then, as Edwards points out, have taken a pretender who, historically, was discredited and invested him with dignity. Both resurrect the myth of the hero who returns from the dead to save his oppressed people, and they do so in ways which suggest, delicately, that their real subject is England under the rule of Charles I. These nostalgic and conservative plays use Henry VII and Flaminius, Massinger's representative of Rome, to personify what seemed at the time to be the dangerous innovation and autocracy of Charles's rule. Standing against these politicians, and doomed to lose, is a king

---

[10] Jonas Barish, '*Perkin Warbeck* as anti-history', in *Essays in Criticism* 20 (1970), 151–68.

figure of another and more traditional kind: a man who not only 'has a kind of beauty of being', but who 'is the guardian of the idealized, authentic, undivided life, when truth and government were not separated'. Massinger's Antiochus really is a king. Perkin's position is far more ambiguous, but Ford hints, in Daubeney's first speech and in the exchange between Huntly and Dalyell on the subject of Katherine's royal blood, at the uncertainty of all these titles to a throne: 'At best, Henry the usurper faces Richard the son of the usurper.'[11]

Edwards' essay on *Perkin Warbeck* and *Believe As You List* is illuminating, not only in itself, but for what it suggests about the changed form and function of the Stuart history under Charles. Certainly the two plays make a revealing pair, whatever their precise relationship to each other in terms of date of composition and intentionally parallel subjects. Massinger may let his audience know the truth about the pretender, as Ford does not: his title *Believe As You List* stresses the dilemma confronting all the stage characters who meet Antiochus, a dilemma which Ford has simply extended so that it affects the theatre audience as well. We too believe as we like and as we are emotionally and politically predisposed. The total inability of Antiochus, the true king of the Asians, to prove his identity politically, as opposed to personally, suggests that the ironic words of Ford's James IV lie at the heart of both plays:

> Kings are counterfeits
> In your repute, grave oracle, not presently
> Set on their thrones with sceptres in their fists.   (II.3.37–9)

By implication, the converse is also true: any man actually sitting on a throne, grasping the appropriate regalia, is now by definition a king, whoever he is, and however he got there in the first place. It does not do much for the theory of divine right.

Ford was always a dramatist who liked to invoke and build upon his audience's memory of earlier plays, in particular those of Shakespeare. Often, he seems to use Shakespeare in something of the way Euripides used Aeschylus: to set off and define his own, strikingly different treatment of subject matter superficially similar. *Perkin Warbeck* is filled with deliberate echoes of this kind. Perkin himself, as

[11] Philip Edwards, 'The royal pretenders in Massinger and Ford', in *Essays and Studies* 27 (1974), 18–36.

has often been pointed out, greets the soil of England when he steps
ashore at Cornwall in Act IV in words that recall Richard II's
salutation of his kingdom's earth when he returns from Ireland.
Again like King Richard, Perkin in chains parts forever from his wife
in a London street, surrounded by ungentle men who make a
mockery of the marriage oath. Most brilliantly of all, perhaps,
Richard's defiance of Henry IV in the deposition scene – 'You may
my glories and my state depose, / But not my griefs; still am I king of
those' (IV.1.192–3) – becomes Perkin's affirmation at the end that he
is king at least over death, and also of one woman's heart.

> Spite of tyranny,
> We reign in our affections, blessed woman!
> Read in my destiny the wrack of honour;
> Point out, in my contempt of death, to memory
> Some miserable happiness: since herein,
> Even when I fell, I stood enthroned a monarch
> Of one chaste wife's troth pure and uncorrupted   (v.3.121–7)

In Shakespeare's play, Richard's rhetoric is almost always ambiguous, arousing in his auditors both on and off stage a mixture of
admiration and impatience. Ford calculatedly rendered the already
complicated situation in Shakespeare's play still more mysterious,
when he gave this noble, but oddly anachronistic, language not to an
anointed king but to a pretender.

Perkin, however, is not the only rhetorician in the play, nor is
Richard II the only play by Shakespeare that Ford invokes. The first
two acts of *Perkin Warbeck* imitate the structure of *Antony and Cleopatra*
in the way they alternate, scene by scene, between England
and Scotland. There was, as it seemed, only one woman in the Rome
of Octavius, and she was a political pawn. There are none at all in the
court of Henry VII, or at least none who are granted a stage life.
Daubeney reminds us in the first scene that 'Edward's daughter is
king Henry's queen' (1.1.38) but this queen, the possession of whom
constitutes a large part of Henry's title to the throne, never appears
in the play. Ford was probably remembering what Bacon said about
Henry VII's resentment of a queen whose title was considered by
many to be far stronger than his, and his insistence upon keeping her
in eclipse. He was also, as Shakespeare was in *Antony and Cleopatra*,
drawing a contrast between a limited world and one which, for all its
faults, is complete. Of the three other women with whom Henry VII

is concerned, two are, like the queen, important but invisible
marriage tokens. His own daughter, Margaret, is used to buy off
James IV. King Ferdinand's daughter Catherine is, in the course of
the play, contracted to Henry's son Arthur, at the price of the life of
the imprisoned Earl of Warwick – a Yorkist pretender even more
alarming than Perkin in that his identity is beyond question. The
third woman, Perkin's Scots wife Katherine Gordon, discovers when
she is brought before Henry in Act v that he will not admit the fact
of her marriage. It is politically inconvenient, and therefore does not
exist. As she tries desperately to speak of her husband, Henry
pointedly offers her the compliments appropriate to a young,
unmarried beauty, and presses her to accept an annuity of a thousand
pounds.

It has often been remarked that the opening scene of *Perkin Warbeck*
recalls the beginning of Shakespeare's *1 Henry IV*. Here once again is
a king formally 'supported to his throne' by his nobles. Even his
opening speech seems, at first sight, to echo that of the earlier Henry:

> Still to be haunted, still to be pursued,
> Still to be frighted with false apparitions
> Of pageant majesty and new-coined greatness,
> As if we were a mockery-king in state,
> Only ordained to lavish sweat and blood
> In scorn and laughter to the ghosts of York,
> Is all below our merits; yet, my lords,
> My friends and counsellors, yet we sit fast
> In our own royal birthright.   (1.1.1–9)

There is a querulous tone here absent from Henry IV's declaration,
'So shaken as we are, so wan with care...' It seems odd that Ford's
king should begin by advertising his own 'merits', and even stranger
that he should talk about a 'royal birthright' which, in his case,
palpably does not exist. The whole speech, with its nervously repeated
'yet', sounds like a cunning appeal for reassurance, for an affirmation
of allegiance. The Bishop of Durham, for the first of many times in the
play, provides it, marshalling the other lords behind him in a chorus
which seems, in its unqualified abuse of Perkin and celebration of
Henry, too unanimous and strident.

In the intricate structure of Ford's play, Durham is a character
parallel to Perkin's chief follower Frion. Durham has material of
better quality than Frion's with which to work – the peers of
England, as opposed to a motley collection of tailors, scriveners,

merchants and small town mayors – but he moulds and directs these inferior intelligences in the same way. Consistently, in the early part of the play, Durham is the man who speaks first on all important issues and trains the rest obediently after him. He and Henry operate as a team almost in the manner of Richard III and Buckingham. Consummate actors, they make sure between them, not only that Stanley should die, but that it will be the nobles and not the 'merciful' king who insist upon his execution. There is no evidence that Stanley's guilt in the play extends any further than it did in Bacon's *Life*: a mere unguarded assertion, made to Clifford, who later turns informer, that he would not take up arms against a true Yorkist claimant to the throne. As with the execution of Warwick, announced later in the play, Ford obviously had to be careful how he handled the question of Stanley's 'treason'. There can be no doubt, however, as to the dignity with which Stanley faces death, or to where our sympathies lie in that strange scene in which he marks the informer's cheek with the sign of the Cross. Stanley dies praying for the king (II.2.67–9, 97–8), but it is not clear which king he has in mind. His last message to his brother, 'that I shall stand no blemish to his house / In chronicles writ in another age' (II.2.101–2), reinforces the ambiguity inherent in his final couplet:

> I take my leave, to travel to my dust:
> Subjects deserve their deaths whose kings are just.   (II.2.108–9)

With Stanley out of the way, Durham hastens up north. There, characteristically, he will brush aside the 'gay flourishes' (IV.1.60) of the single combat proposed between King James and Surrey, in favour of a hard-headed and successful appeal to James's self-interest. By now, Durham has the English nobles sufficiently well-trained that they can bark in chorus without a conductor:

> HENRY: Lords, we may reign your king yet; Daubeney, Oxford,
>   Urswick, must Perkin wear the crown?
> DAUBENEY: A slave!
> OXFORD: A vagabond!
> URSWICK: A glow-worm!   (IV.4.32–4)

For services such as these, Henry determines that, should the present archbishop of Canterbury obligingly 'move / To a translation higher yet', his good Fox of Durham 'deserves that see. / He's nimble in his industry, and mounting' (IV.4.71–4).

Quite apart from the dubious joke about 'translation', one may wonder if nimbleness and a mounting mind ought really to be the chief prerequisites for an archbishop of Canterbury. Henry's piety, although frequently on public view, is like so much of his behaviour a façade. He may assure his followers that, 'When counsels fail, and there's in man no trust, / Even then an arm from heaven fights for the just' (1.3.137–9), or claim that

> A guard of angels and the holy prayers
> Of loyal subjects are a sure defence
> Against all force and counsel of intrusion.   (1.1.73–5)

The aphorism by which he actually lives would seem to be: 'Money gives soul to action' (III.1.29). It is like Henry that after the defeat of the Cornish rebels in Act III – men who have rebelled because of his financial exactions, not because of the Yorkist claim – the king should direct that cash should be distributed among his troops, 'which shall hearten / And cherish up their loyalties (III.1.112–13). 'O, happy kings,' he muses after giving this order, 'whose thrones are raiséd in their subjects' hearts!' (117–18). Hearts, in this instance, would appear to be a euphemism for pockets.

Ford's Henry VII is not a villain, like Shakespeare's Richard III or King John. He is simply a king with the soul of an unscrupulous merchant banker. His cash, as he says proudly, 'flows through all Europe', and he likes to think of himself as 'steward' of 'such voluntary favours as our people / In duty aid us with' (IV.4.46–54). The 'voluntary' nature of these contributions is certainly open to question, but not the skill with which Henry bribes and rewards informers, churchmen, soldiers, foreign ambassadors and other kings. He is a monarch in a new and wholly unromantic style: an administrator rather than 'God's substitute, his deputy anointed in His sight'. Such a concept of kingship is modern, and not very appealing, which is why Henry spends so much of the play pretending to emotions and scruples he does not feel. Whatever Perkin may be doing, Henry VII certainly plays the part of king, in the sense that he tries to conceal the thing he is behind a mask of traditional 'king-becoming graces'. He even essays the personal. Henry's staged grief in the scene in which Clifford publicly impeaches Stanley suggests that he has taken hints from a combination of the deposition scene from Shakespeare's *Richard II* (the mirror) and Henry V's reaction, at Southampton, to the treachery of Scroop. As an actor, Henry VII is

not very accomplished. Later, in the speech in which he agrees to
Stanley's execution, the truth constantly slips out from behind the
pose:

> What a coil is here
> To keep my gratitude sincere and perfect!
> Stanley was once my friend and came in time
> To save my life; *yet to say truth, my lords,*
> *The man stayed long enough t' endanger it.*
> But I could see no more into his heart
> Than what his outward actions did present;
> And for 'em have rewarded him so fully,
> As that there wanted nothing in our gift
> To gratify his merit, as I thought,
> Unless I should divide my crown with him
> And give him half; *though now I well perceive*
> *'Twould scarce have served his turn without the whole.*
> But I am charitable, lords; let justice
> Proceed in execution, whiles I mourn
> The loss of one whom I esteemed a friend.   (II.2.26–41, *my italics*)

Even without the peevish, and altogether characteristic, emphasis
upon reward unprofitably bestowed, it is clear that genuine sorrow
would be incapable of Henry's jests. Oxford and Surrey may conclude
that the king is 'composed of gentleness'. Durham's comment –
'every man is nearest to himself, / And that the king observes; 'tis fit
'a should' – seems, as usual, more perceptive (II.2.50–2).

By preference, Henry avoids personal encounters, even as he
avoids participation in a battle (II.2.143–5). He makes his tender
heart the excuse for refusing to see Stanley, although it does not
prevent him from eavesdropping on the whole scene. In Act III, he
again declines to see the rebel leaders he has just condemned to death.
Significantly, Perkin when captured is thrust into Henry's presence
before he has time to prevent it, and with embarrassing results. Peter
Ure once pointed out that Perkin accomplishes the seemingly
impossible when he manages to take Henry's condescending first
speech away from him, turn it in the opposite direction, ennoble it,
and set it free.[12] Not even Shakespeare's Richard II had done
anything quite like this to Bolingbroke. Language and personal
appearance may be all that Perkin has to rely upon; with them he

---

[12] See Ure, p. lxxvii. There is also a perceptive account of Ford's complex handling of audience
expectations in the chapter on *Perkin Warbeck*, in Tucker Orbison's *The Tragic Vision of John
Ford*, Salzburg Studies in English Literature (Salzburg, 1974).

dominates the scene. Even the owlish Mayor of Cork, apparently the silliest of Perkin's tattered followers, begins to sound like a disconcertingly wise fool:

For I confess, respectively, in taking great parts, the one side prevailing, the other side must go down... For my own part, I believe it is true, if I be not deceived, that kings must be kings and subjects subjects. But which is which – you shall pardon me for that. (v.2.105–6, 113–16)

One sees why Henry terminates the interview with speed and refuses, thereafter, to see Perkin again.

Ford never asserts either that Perkin is the rightful king of England or that, if he possessed a throne, he would be a better ruler than King Henry. If anything, the suggestion is that this is a man born out of his time, an anachronism in a world where power now resides in the royal exchequer and the 'king-becoming graces' are an irrelevance. The same is true of Massinger's Antiochus, another man whose royalty must be measured in terms of his language and his personal relationships, and who also goes down in defeat, betrayed (like Perkin) by his own followers. Both pretenders grow in stature in the course of their play. Antiochus learns to put in practice the stoic philosophy he studied in his Athenian exile. He may lose the world, but he gains quiet possession of his own soul. Consigned to the galleys, he knows that 'every place shall bee / A temple in my paenitence to me'.[13] Although, like Perkin, he refuses under torture to deny that he is a king, he carefully prevents the old friends who recognize him at the end from proclaiming his identity and so bringing on themselves the anger of Rome. Perkin's new self-possession declares itself when James IV casts him off. He is entirely aware of the sordid traffic between the English, Scottish and Spanish courts. In a desperate situation he chooses, however, to remember only James's past kindness, not his present treachery nor the breaking of his kingly oath. He asks simply that the wife James gave should remain his: 'Such another treasure / The earth is bankrupt of' (iv.3.103–4). The speech is characteristic of Perkin in the way it translates wealth into personal value, inverting Henry's normal metaphoric practice. It is like Perkin too that when Dalyell asks to accompany the woman he still loves, in her exile, he grants the suit freely, without jealousy or suspicion.

Through Katherine Gordon, Ford manipulates our feelings about

---

[13] Massinger, *Believe As You List*, ed. Edwards and Gibson (iv.4.74–5).

Perkin with particular subtlety. Henry VII, as the play points out more than once, acquired a kingdom through his politic union with Edward IV's daughter. Perkin asks courteously for a kingdom of another kind when Katherine becomes his wife:

> An union this way
> Settles possession in a monarchy
> Established rightly as is my inheritance.
> Acknowledge me but sovereign of this kingdom,
> Your heart, fair princess, and the hand of providence
> Shall crown you queen of me and my best fortunes. (II.3.78–83)

Half in love with Dalyell at the beginning of the play, Katherine was moved to tears by the pretender's initial speech at the court of King James without placing firm trust in his story, and certainly without desiring him as a husband. Neither a sentimentalist nor a fool, she listens doubtfully to his early promises to crown her 'empress of the West', conceding only that her bridegroom has 'a noble language' (III.2.162–3). Yet what began inauspiciously as a marriage high-handedly arranged, against the will of Huntly, and half against that of Katherine herself, ends as Perkin's one, incontrovertible triumph. The English lords are scandalized when Katherine insists upon joining the pretender, a man dishonoured, dirty, racked and tortured, in the stocks. They are sure her father will disown her. Instead, Huntly not only approves her action but, for the first time, accepts Perkin as her husband and a gentleman. In the moments before he goes to his death, Perkin is supported by people who, like himself, cannot be bought for cash. And in Katherine, whose language has come now to express something far more passionate than mere duty ('O my loved lord ... my life's dearest'), he finds, as Lear did briefly with Cordelia, a personal kingdom that can mock at the pretensions of those packs and sects of great ones, that ebb and flow by th' moon.

Although *Perkin Warbeck* and *Believe As You List* were the most impressive pretender plays written in England during the reign of Charles I, they do not stand alone in their period. Two other dramas survive to indicate that Ford and Massinger were not the only playwrights for whom the old story of 'the waking man's dream' had acquired a new significance. A third play pushes the debate between the new style king and the ghost from the past back into the reign of Edward I. Aston Cokain's *Trappolin Supposed A Prince* (1633) is based upon a favourite theme of the *commedia dell' arte*, one for which a number of scenarii survive. Probably, Cokain saw a performance by the Affezionati troupe in Venice in 1632, from which he remembered enough to write a play of his own in which virtually every incident can be traced back to an Italian source.[14] *Trappolin Supposed A Prince* is the closest of the Stuart plays to the traditional, comic treatment of the pretender. Trappolin himself is a simple, sensuous, pacific soul, fond of food and drink and not above a bit of pimping, whose theatrical ancestry stretches back to the comic heroes of Aristophanes. His principal ambition is to get his girl Flametta out of the clutches of the lecherous courtier Barbarino, and marry her himself. Unjustly banished from Florence by Barbarino in the absence of the Duke, Trappolin encounters a kindly magician in a forest who not only transforms him into the exact likeness of the Duke, but gives him the power to change the real Duke, when he returns, into Trappolin. The complications which result are, in large measure, farcical. And yet the mock-Duke is not just a figure of fun in the manner of Christopher Sly. That the Florentine courtiers should believe their prince has gone mad is a comment upon their society and upon the degeneration of a royal ideal quite as much as it is upon Trappolin's inability to assume the airs and graces of the genuine Duke.

'Whatever I do, though never so bad', Duke Trappolin muses at one point, 'passeth with approbation. Poor Trappolin turned Duke! 'tis very strange, but very true'.[15] Ford gave *Perkin Warbeck* the sub-title *A Strange Truth*. It seems impossible to determine in what order the two plays were written, but they are not so dissimilar in their concerns as might appear. Like the traditional king of ballads and folk stories, Trappolin is just, shrewd and personal as the real Duke of Florence is not. 'Though I am the Duke' he says, 'yet I love to do no hurt, as other men in authority would' (p. 172), and the action of the play bears him out. Like Dekker's Henry V in *The Shoemaker's Holiday* (1599), Trappolin recognizes that social snobbery should not keep true lovers apart. The real Duke of Florence has forbidden his sister Prudentia to marry Brunetto because he is only the younger son of the Duke of Savoy. Trappolin, who knows an honest man when he sees one, perplexes Brunetto by treating him as a friend and equal, and unites him with Prudentia. He also presides over a mad court of

[14] K. M. Lea, 'Sir Aston Cokayne and the "Commedia dell' Arte"', *Modern Language Review* 23 (1928), 47–51.
[15] Sir Aston Cokain, *Trappolin Supposed a Prince*, in *The Dramatic Works of Sir Aston Cokain*, ed. J. Maidment and W. H. Logan (Edinburgh, 1874), p. 151.

justice which, examined more closely, is not so lunatic after all. Trappolin's decisions are unorthodox and little beholding to legal conventions, but they are emotionally and personally just – as when he rules that there is something grotesque about a plaintiff who demands money in compensation for a child's death. As a law giver, Trappolin is very like Sancho Panza, who also ends up governing his island more wisely than the real Duke and Duchess had anticipated. It was not just in England that the motif of 'the waking man's dream' underwent important changes in the seventeenth century. Calderón's *La vida es sueño*, in which the dreamer behaves atrociously during his brief reign, is returned to bondage, and then miraculously is allowed to play the king's part a second time and get it right, was written in 1635.

Cokain's Trappolin returns happily to the status of private man at the end of the comedy. The suggestions of social and political heresy dissolve, tactfully, in laughter. Stuart dramatists, after all, were obliged to tread with caution. This was especially true when they found themselves facing a monarch who was both sensitive on the subject of kingship, and an inveterate reader of plays. Charles I objected personally to the title of Massinger's lost *The King and the Subject* (1638) and to a passage describing royal methods of raising money, even though the play seems to have been set in Spain. That unknown J.W. (Gent.) responsible in the previous year for *The Valiant Scot* clearly had to exercise great care in writing a chronicle history about the Scottish rebellion of 1297, given the fact that the king of England was emphatically not his hero. Something very strange has happened to Edward I in this play. Peele's warrior king, and the hero of other, lost Elizabethan history plays as well as of ballads, has shrunk into a reticent, calculating man who exists chiefly, as it would seem, as a foil for Wallace and (ultimately) for Bruce. As it is in *Perkin Warbeck*, Scotland is here portrayed as a romantic, turbulent country where old ideals of chivalry and personal valour linger on as they do not in England. Wallace himself is not, as he was in the ballad by Blind Harry which underlies the play, an uncriticized folk hero. His revenges against the English are excessive, and destroy the innocent as well as the guilty. He can also be as stubbornly individualistic and vain as Dryden's Almanzor. The dramatist never suggests that this man should rule Scotland. On the other hand, Edward I, for very different reasons, is equally incompetent to do so.

Among the English, Clifford behaves in a fashion for which there was no authority in J. W.'s ballad source. He sets himself passionately to oppose all the schemes proposed by his party to 'snare' or 'intrap' Wallace, as opposed to killing him nobly in the field. The hunting imagery here is exactly that favoured by Ford's Henry VII in describing the campaign against Perkin. Not only does Clifford repudiate the view held by Edward and his other nobles, that 'All strategems are lawfull 'gainst a fo'[16]: he goes so far as to persuade the Scottish Bruce to forswear his allegiance to Edward and join with Wallace. In this play, a shadow king of Scotland travels a road exactly opposite to that of Ford's King James. Bruce discovers that he cannot exist with honour in the politic world of Edward I, and exchanges it for something rougher but more heroic. Bruce's change of sides comes too late to prevent Wallace from being trapped at last and sent to execution by Edward, but his first act after being crowned – Edward having abruptly decided to be magnanimous to the Scots he finds he cannot rule, and give them their own king – is to slay with his own hand the Scots informer responsible for Wallace's death. What Wallace chiefly lacked, as Clifford remarks, was the tempering quality of noble blood. Edward's deficiencies go unspecified, but they are clearly those of a man content to rule at a distance, through officers of doubtful probity, and undistinguished in himself for human sympathy or understanding. At the end, having assimilated the complementary lessons of both Wallace and Edward, Bruce is left standing on the brink of a mythic career as saviour of Scotland which the dramatist, understandably, was content to leave implicit.

Cartwright's *The Royal Slave* (1636), in many ways the most interesting play of the three, was admired so greatly by Charles I and Henrietta Maria when they saw it at Christ-church on 30 August that they requested a repeat performance at Hampton Court by professional actors. Music by Henry Lawes and unusually elaborate and costly sets and costumes by Inigo Jones have usually been given credit for the quite remarkable success of this play. The answer is unlikely to be so simple. *The Royal Slave* is set in Sardis, in the aftermath of a great battle in which the Persians have defeated an army of Ephesians and taken many of them captive. Persian custom dictates that, after such a conquest, one prisoner should be crowned king and, after taking an oath of fealty to Persia, allowed to reign

---

[16] J.W. (Gent.) *The Valiant Scot* (London, 1637) E4v.

unchecked for three days, after which he is to be sacrificed to the gods. Arsamnes, the Persian king, examining the possible victims in his prison, finds them all disappointing until the gaoler produces Cratander, a man initially passed over because 'wondrous heavy and bookish, and therefore I thought him unfit for any honour'.[17] Cratander, who appears to have been educated in the same Stoic school as Massinger's Antiochus, unwittingly convinces Arsamnes that he is indeed a worthy candidate for the starring role in *The Golden Bough*. What happens thereafter is surprising. Informed of the dubious honour which has fallen upon him, Cratander fails to emulate all his predecessors and call for the wine and the dancing girls. He contents himself with questioning whether the gods can really feel honoured by a custom so barbaric, after which he gets down to the serious business of ruling Persia: 'Our Reigne is short, and businesse much, be speedy. / Our Counsels and our deeds must have one birth' (B4R).

After one day of Cratander's reign, the Persian court is in chaos. Half of Arsamnes' councillors find the pretender so impressive that their desire to extend the duration of his monarchy verges on treason. The other half, although it finds him equally formidable, is passionate to get rid of him. Atossa, Arsamnes' queen, has fallen in love with him, and Arsamnes himself is suffering agonies of jealousy and trepidation. Astonishingly, everything works out happily. Cratander not only spurns (like Antiochus) all the sensual baits laid in his path to trap him, but refuses to betray Persia to Ephesus. The queen manages to convince her husband that what draws her to Cratander is 'a faire likenesse / Of something that I love in you' (G3v). He is, in fact, a neo-Platonic essence of kingship, from which Arsamnes can learn to correct what is unkingly in himself: his jealousy, his levity, his endurance of false courtiers and, finally, his deplorable sanction of human sacrifice. Cratander faces death calmly at the end of his three days, when the priests insist. The gods, however, intervene. At the end of the play, Cratander returns to Greece to be a king in earnest, not in jest.

That he should do so is all the more remarkable because of Cartwright's hint that this man was a slave not simply because of his misfortune in war, but also in his native land. The Ephesians who creep into Sardis in disguise from the shattered remnants of the army

---

[17] William Cartwright, *The Royal Slave* (Oxford, 1639) B2v, B4, G3v, D3v.

outside the walls tempt Cratander to 'Come then a King home, that went'st out a Slave'. The implication here is one that Cratander seems to accept in his reply:

> I am so still; no sooner did I come
> Within the Persian Walles, but I was theirs.
> And since, good *Hippias*, this pow'r hath only
> Added one linke more to the Chayne. I am
> Become *Arsamnes* Instrument: I've sworn
> Faith to his Scepter. (D3v)

At least one of Cratander's actions in the play, his scornful treatment of a hard-drinking courtier and of the achievement of remaining upright 'after the hundreth Flagon', seems to refer directly to an episode in the life of Charles I as recounted, later, by Clarendon.[18] The implied association of Cratander, as paragon of kingship, with Charles himself becomes all the more remarkable in view of Cartwright's refusal ever to make the orthodox discovery that, really, this man possesses noble blood. Shakespeare's Perdita seems to everyone who sees her like a queen, but then she truly is the daughter of a king. The same is true of the nobility of the hero in Massinger's *The Bondman* (1623). Only Jonson, perhaps, dared to go as far as Cartwright when he allowed 'Sovereign Pru', Lady Frampull's chambermaid in *The New Inn* (1629), to display an innate aristocracy so convincing during her one day as pretender queen that a real lord, Latimer, recognizes it for what it is and takes her to wife. Cartwright was, of course, a university man. Like Massinger's Baldock in *Edward II*, but in very different terms, Cratander's gentry is really something he fetches 'from Oxford, not from heraldry'. Cartwright may also have been thinking of Epictetus when he fashioned his philosopher king out of a common slave. The play seems to suggest, for all its fanciful and remote setting, and its ornate musical and visual trappings, the logical end of the Stuart history: as visible kings are reduced to petty and undistinguished private men, private men of a certain kind may come to seem like kings as kings once were.

History, however, had the last word. There is something very poignant about all those royalist pamphlets which describe the last days of Charles I as a stage play, laboriously analysing the machinations of Parliament, the Army, and Cromwell as a drama

---

[18] Compare the incident at E2v with Clarendon's account of the character of Charles I in *The History of the Rebellion* (World's Classics selected edition, ed. G. Huehns, Oxford, 1955, p. 318).

replacing the suppressed activities of the public stage. One remembers, too, the haunting little vignette of those stage players who were surprised in a clandestine performance at Salisbury Court on the first of January 1649, how 'with many Linkes and lighted Torches they were carried to White-Hall with their Players cloathes upon their backs. In the way they [the soldiers] oftentimes tooke the Crown from his head who acted the King, and in sport would oftentimes put it on again'.[19] It would be interesting to know the name of the interrupted play. When Marvell immortalized Charles I in his death, in the 'Horatian Ode', as a 'royall Actor', a man snared and hunted by his adversary, he was using ideas from the Stuart histories which had attached themselves now to the real king. Charles, moreover, found his own dramatists. In Germany, Gryphius hammered out *Carolus Stuardus* (1649), a play drawing (like *Perkin Warbeck*) upon memories of *Richard II*, in which Charles compares his death to that of Christ in a Passion Play. The English author of the anonymous, and unperformed, *Famous Tragedy of Charles I* (1649), a man closer to the pain of the event, could not bring himself to represent the king himself – any more than those dramatists writing before the death of Elizabeth could put the Tudors on the stage. He contented himself with a spectacular revelation of the king's mutilated body in the last scene, a discovery in the tradition of Hieronymo's revelation of his murdered son in *The Spanish Tragedy* (1587). Charles I had liked plays, even if he expected them to keep their place. He would perhaps have smiled wryly at this last coming together of Stuart history and its mirror image on the stage.

[19] Quoted in Leslie Hotson, *The Commonwealth and Restoration Stage* (Cambridge, Mass., 1928), p. 40.

CHAPTER 12

Oxymoron and the structure of Ford's *The Broken Heart* (1980)

At the end of *The Broken Heart* (1629) two unexpected deaths raise Nearchus, prince of Argos, to the throne of Sparta. The man who came to Sparta in Act III as a suitor for the hand of the Crown Princess Calantha remains there as Lacedaemonian king in his own right: chief mourner for a native, and now extinguished, royal house. Almost nothing that has happened in the last two acts was predictable. Nearchus admits as much in a concluding couplet:

> The counsels of the gods are never known
> Till men can call th'effects of them their own.[1]   (v.3.105–6)

Ford may well have been remembering Euripides. The Choruses of *Alcestis*, *Helen* and (with slight variations) *Medea*, *Andromache* and *Bacchae* all make the same statement at the end. Although human beings often pride themselves, mistakenly, on being able to anticipate their development, the plots devised by heaven are impenetrable until the final scene:

> Many are the forms of what is unknown.
> Much that the gods achieve is surprise.
> What we look for does not come to pass;
> God finds a way for what none forsaw.
> Such was the end of this story.[2]

In making this discovery, the Euripidean Chorus – like Nearchus later – speaks for the members of a disconcerted theatre audience.

The Broken Heart is the only one of Ford's plays set in a scrupulously maintained pagan world. The Sparta of Ithocles, Orgilus, Penthea and Calantha may exhibit a number of anachronistic Renaissance

---

[1] John Ford, *The Broken Heart*, ed. T. J. B. Spencer, Revels Series (Manchester, 1980). All subsequent quotations from the play refer to this edition.

[2] Euripides, *Alcestis* and *Helen*, both trans. Richmond Lattimore, in *The Complete Greek Tragedies*, eds. David Grene and Richmond Lattimore, 4 vols. (Chicago, 1953–9), lines 1159–63, 1688–92.

features: this icily passionate study in aristocratic stoicism (a tragedy without a villain, as it has been called)[3] rigorously excludes Christian reference. Its gods are frightening and opaque, speaking only in sinister riddles. Although the goodwill of Apollo and other deities is constantly being invoked, it rarely seems to manifest itself. Characters can be certain only of heaven's tireless surveillance and understanding of their most jealously guarded secrets. Armostes' melancholy realization that 'our eyes can never pierce into the thoughts, / For they are lodged too inward' (IV.1.17–18) is an experience common to all the men and women of the play. But heaven, as Euphrania says, 'does look into the secrets of all hearts' (I.1.113–14). Not even Tecnicus, the philosopher and servant of Apollo, can hope to rival the 'quick-piercing eyes' (I.3.5) of these divine spies:

> Our mortal eyes
> Pierce not the secrets of your hearts. The gods
> Are only privy to them.   (III.1.10–12)

In a society where virtually everyone but Bassanes conceals motivations and deep feelings fiercely and with great skill, such supernatural clairvoyance must be particularly disturbing. Remote and incomprehensible on their heights, the gods not only shape the action towards unforeseen conclusions, they see through the reticences, prevarications and disguised emotions of everyone else. It is precisely the position to which all the major characters of the tragedy aspire, and which not even Calantha can attain.

In another play, the omniscience of the gods might have been shared by the theatre audience. Ford, however, chose to turn the very sophistication, the theatrical expertise of a group of habitual Caroline playgoers against them. To be well acquainted with Shakespeare, with the conventions of Elizabethan and Jacobean revenge tragedy, with standard character types and the normal configurations of plot within a five-act structure is to be hindered, not helped, in understanding this play as it unfolds. Ford begins with a skilful recreation of the third scene of *Hamlet*. Here again is a young man embarking on a journey, taking leave of a testy and overly protective father while, at the same time, forbidding his sister to form an attachment of which he disapproves. But the parallel between Crotolon, Orgilus and Euphrania, and Polonius, Laertes and Ophelia is deliberately deceptive. Unlike Laertes, Orgilus has no

---

[3] Roger T. Burbridge, 'The moral vision of Ford's *The Broken Heart*, *SEL* 10 (1970), 397–407.

intention of leaving home. He surprises the audience two scenes later by turning up, disguised, in the palace gardens. There, he puts on something remarkably like Hamlet's antic disposition, and is employed by the unsuspecting Prophilus, Euphrania's lover, to carry letters between the two, in secret, 'at nine i' th' morning, and at four at night' (1.3.155). Any audience watching Prophilus and Euphrania fall into this trap, and hearing the ominous soliloquy with which Orgilus concludes the scene, might be forgiven for feeling confident about the direction that the action is going to take:

> Put out thy torches, Hymen, or their light
> Shall meet a darkness of eternal night.
> Inspire me, Mercury, with swift deceits.
> Ingenious fate has leapt into my arms,
> Beyond the compass of my brain.   (1.3.175–9)

It comes as a shock to discover, not only that no love-letters ever materialize upon which Orgilus can exercise his 'swift deceits', but that two acts later he will freely bestow his sister upon Prophilus, his enemy's best friend, and wish the bridal pair nothing more sinister than 'comforts lasting, loves increasing' (III.4.70).

Kenneth Muir has complained about two 'structural flaw[s]' in *The Broken Heart*: first, the 'clumsy' way in which Penthea is left in the palace garden to await her brother but, when Ithocles is suddenly taken ill, finds herself confronting Orgilus, her former affianced lover, instead; and, secondly, the abrupt shift of focus on to Calantha at the end.[4] But, arguably, such *non sequiturs* are deliberate, the dramatic principle upon which the entire tragedy is based. Ford is calculatedly evasive as to just where, among Penthea, Calantha, Orgilus, Ithocles, Amyclas, Nearchus and even Bassanes, his tragic centre lies. Interest is diffused among the different members of a society: an aristocratic social order whose well-being is ultimately more important than that of any of its components. This kind of structure possesses obvious affinities with that of comedy. And indeed, despite the brooding presence of Orgilus, it is by no means clear at first that the material of *The Broken Heart* must necessarily be tragic.

If the opening scene summons up memories of *Hamlet*, its successor immediately subverts the prognostication by suggesting the jubilant early stages of *Much Ado About Nothing*. A war has been triumphantly concluded, and its returning heroes are clearly ripe for falling in love

---

[4] Kenneth Muir, 'The case of John Ford', in *The Sewanee Review* 84 (1976), 614–29.

and re-populating the world they have just diminished. The old king of Sparta feels himself transformed and 'ent'ring / Into his youth again' (1.2.4–5). Lord Ithocles, described in the first scene as 'insulting' (50), a man 'proud of youth, / And prouder in his power' (39–40), turns out to be a victorious general of great modesty and tact. Groneas and Lemophil, the two courtiers-turned-soldier, initiate a subsidiary comic intrigue when they resolve to ignore Chrystalla and Philema in future, instead of pursuing them, and hope that then 'they'll follow us' (147). Even Bassanes, the jealous monster introduced at the beginning of Act II, arouses comic expectations through his unabashed derivation from Jonson's Kitely and Corvino, and (to a lesser extent) Shakespeare's Ford.

All of these comedy expectations prove false. Despite Amyclas' own confidence that his life is renewing itself – 'It will, it must' (1.2.10) – and in the midst of rumours that the rejuvenated king has grown a new beard of 'a pure carnation colour' (II.1.47), the old man suddenly sickens and dies. Ithocles, although not to be contained within the hostile and simplistic description offered by Orgilus in the opening scene, still has more than a trick of the old self-centred arrogance about him. When he displays it in Act IV, the consequences are fatal. The putative intrigue involving Groneas, Lemophil and Calantha's two maids of honour breaks off, perplexingly, in scene 2, exactly where it began. It is never heard of again. In her final testament, Calantha arbitrarily disposes of Chrystalla as wife to Nearchus' friend Amelus, and sends Philema into perpetual seclusion as a vestal virgin. Considering that their names, as Ford points out in the list of *Dramatis personae*, mean 'Crystal' and 'A Kiss' respectively, one might think that these destinies ought more appropriately to have been reversed. Calantha, however, appears to be a dramatist as perverse as Ford himself. As for Bassanes, he contradicts his apparent comic type by becoming, first, a genuinely tragic figure as he contemplates the wreck of Penthea's sanity, and then ending the play as the newly created Marshal of Sparta, an infinitely sadder but also transformed man at whom nobody is any longer tempted to laugh.

Five deaths dispersed through Acts IV and V make the final movement of *The Broken Heart* unequivocally tragic. The pattern, however, is one that both summons up and obstinately refuses to conform to the requirements and expectations of the traditional revenge play. Even as the paradigm of *Romeo and Juliet* lurks behind *'Tis Pity She's A Whore* (1632), making the star-crossed love of

Giovanni and Annabella something that it is impossible either to endorse or condemn, so *The Broken Heart* uses *The Spanish Tragedy*, *Hamlet*, and their Jacobean successors to deceive the theatre audience about Orgilus and his function in the action. Misleading clues and cunningly laid false trails gesture towards a kind of shadow revenge tragedy always promising to emerge through the fabric of the unconventional one Ford actually wrote. In this ghost play Orgilus, disguised as the poor scholar Aplotes, not only uses his role as go-between to trouble the love of Prophilus and Euphrania, he inflames Nearchus' jealousy of Ithocles until the prince takes steps to ensure that 'low mushrooms never rival cedars' (IV.1.98). Penthea's self-control does not survive her encounter with Orgilus in the garden. The woman who can so fervently invoke 'wild fires' (III.2.47) to scorch, before they finally consume, her brother's heart, in retribution for what he has made of her life, is surely not going to plead his love-suit to Calantha.

Most striking of all, perhaps, is the indication that Orgilus, like so many Elizabethan and Jacobean revengers, will bring his purposes to fruition in a deceiving show:

> If these gallants
> Will please to grace a poor invention,
> By joining with me in some slight device,
> I'll venture on a strain my younger days
> Have studied for delight. (III.4.84–8)

It might be Kyd's Hieronymo assembling his unsuspecting actors for the slaughter. When Groneas, Lemophil and Ithocles all volunteer to take part in Orgilus' device to honour the nuptials of Prophilus and Euphrania, the knowledgeable theatre audience primes itself for the holocaust. The 'Soliman and Perseda' play at the end of *The Spanish Tragedy*, the fencing match in *Hamlet*, and the barriers at court in *The White Devil*, the murderous masques of *The Revenger's Tragedy*, Middleton's *Women Beware Women*, and Marston's *Antonio's Revenge* (not to mention Hippolyta's lethal contribution to the wedding feast in Ford's own '*Tis Pity*) all lend their weight to the supposition that, as so often in the past, the 'entertainment' will explode into violence. Alert members of the audience, remembering Prophilus' early claim that Ithocles was a friend 'in which the period of my fate consists' (1.2.42) might even expect the bridegroom to join Ithocles and the other amateur actors in the list of victims.

Every one of these clues is false. The course of Prophilus' and Euphrania's love runs smoothly to its happy conclusion. Nearchus, once he is convinced that Calantha returns Ithocles' passion, magnanimously withdraws his own suit:

> ...affections injured
> By tyranny, or rigour of compulsion,
> Like tempest-threatened trees unfirmly rooted,
> Ne'er spring to timely growth.   (IV.2.205–8)

He will only pretend to be jealous 'of what privately I'll further' (IV.2.211). Penthea, forgetting her own wrongs, bravely speaks for her brother to Calantha, and earns a royal rebuke. Orgilus presents no show at his sister's wedding. Before the revels begin, he has caught Ithocles in the imprisoning chair and killed him. It is a 'device' of a kind, but scarcely to be identified with the 'strain my younger days have studied' which Orgilus offered back in Act III, and it has no audience apart from the dead Penthea. The 'shows' of Act V turn out to be the formal court dance which Calantha refuses to interrupt for tidings of calamity, Orgilus' ritual suicide – described by Bassanes as though it were halfway to being a work of art (V.2.131–4) – and its complement and corrective: the supreme effort of will through which Calantha transforms her coronation into a wedding which is also a funeral.

In the epilogue to *The Broken Heart*, Ford briefly borrowed the voice of Ben Jonson:

> Where noble judgements and clear eyes are fixed
> To grace endeavour, there sits truth not mixed
> With ignorance. Those censures may command
> Belief which talk not till they understand.   (1–4)

Ford's insistence that his aim was 'well to deserve of all, but please the best' (12), like his plea that no one should presume to criticize before they 'understand', recalls the arrogant Jonson of *Cynthia's Revels*, *Poetaster*, and the two addresses to the reader prefixed to *Catiline*. On the other hand, his prediction of a contradictory and confused response to *The Broken Heart* reflects the problems posed specifically by his own play. This tragedy, Ford seems to be saying, will not be easy to decode. Indeed, different members of the audience may well end up by criticizing it for what seem to be mutually exclusive faults:

> Let some say, 'This was flat'; some, 'Here the scene
> Fell from its height'; another, that 'the mean
> Was ill observed in such a growing passion
> As it transcended either state or fashion'.   (5–8)

Apparently, *The Broken Heart* is vulnerable to the charges of being flat and dull, but also sensational, feverish, and over-wrought.

Ford was shrewd. The warring responses which he anticipated in his epilogue have been perpetuated in the critical history of this play. *The Broken Heart* has regularly been accused of flatness, of being, as Robert Ornstein put it, 'pale', while other critics have seen a puzzling monotony of plot and character.[5] Conversely, it has been felt to be exaggerated and shrill: a decadent study in extreme and implausible emotional states, which employs excessive and elliptical forms of speech. The possibility that both reactions might point towards intrinsic qualities of the play, antinomies explored and ultimately reconciled within it, has proved more difficult to entertain. Yet this is surely the solution to the riddle posed by Ford's epilogue: the 'strain' which those who 'understand' are asked to countenance and allow, so that 'THE BROKEN HEART may be pieced up again' (14). The tragedy is like that poem which Yeats hoped one day to offer his Connemara fisherman: 'cold and passionate as the dawn'.[6]

The rhetorical term *oxymoron*, although not noted by the *OED* before 1640, was probably known in England before that date. It occurs in fourth-century Latin commentaries on Virgil, in its present sense: a figure by which 'contradictory or incongruous terms are conjoined so as to give point to the statement or expression' (*OED*). Although rhetoricians also employed *conciliatio* in a similar fashion, the latter term tended to be reserved for verbal structures larger than a mere noun and its modifier. *Oxymoron* is an interesting word because it enacts its own meaning. Two antithetical words, ὀξύς (*sharp*) and μωρός (*dull*) are rammed together in a way that forces reappraisal of each. It is tempting to speculate that Ford may have had the term *oxymoron* specifically in mind when he prophesied disagreement among his audience, in the epilogue, as to whether *The Broken Heart* ought to be castigated for being too high-pitched, or for being dull. Certainly the play makes repeated and striking use of the figure. Most

---

[5] Robert Ornstein, *The Moral Vision of Jacobean Tragedy* (Madison, Wisconsin, 1960), p. 213.

[6] Charles O. McDonald has used this line from Yeats's poem 'The Fisherman', to describe *The Broken Heart*, in 'The design of John Ford's *The Broken Heart*: A study in the development of Caroline sensibility', *Studies in Philology* 59 (1962), 141–61.

of these oxymorons are generated by the predicament of Penthea, the irresolvable dilemma at the heart of the tragedy, and by the consequent behaviour of Orgilus. But the figure is central to *The Broken Heart* as a whole: the most intense and undiluted way of expressing the contradictoriness of life in this society, and something of its sense of claustrophobia and impasse.

The Broken Heart is the only one of Ford's plays which does not relax into a single line of prose. Even Phulas and Grausis, Bassanes' retainers and the only non-aristocratic characters in the tragedy, speak verse. In general, the language of the play gravitates towards paradox. Ithocles is 'a friend/Firm and unalterable. But a brother/ More cruel than the grave' (1.3.62–4). Penthea, 'old in griefs' and yet 'in years…a child' (III.5.50–1), is one 'buried in a bride-bed' (II.2.38). Her husband Bassanes, whose uxorious passion is 'nurse unto a fear so strong and servile' (1.1.62), discovers by possessing Penthea that 'the way to poverty is to be rich' (II.1.70). Orgilus defines himself as 'no brave, yet no unworthy enemy' (v.2.139), and the newly created Marshall of Sparta, contemplating Calantha at the end, finds that he 'must weep to see / Her smile in death' (v.3.97–8). That Apollo's oracle at Delphi should speak in riddles – 'The lifeless trunk shall wed the broken heart', and 'Revenge proves its own executioner' (IV.1.134–9) – is only to be expected; less predictable is the compulsion felt by virtually all the characters towards verbal compression, towards the unmediated and painful confrontation of warring terms.

Compound and hyphenated words are a feature of *The Broken Heart*. The 'lover-blest heart' (III.2.45) of 'life-spent Penthea' has been ground into dust by 'death-braving Ithocles' (1.2.11). The 'monster-love' of Bassanes leads him to accuse his wife of living in 'swine-security of bestial incest' (III.2.150) with her own brother. Ithocles dies into a 'long-looked-for peace' (IV.4.70). It may be that the unusual frequency of such compounds in this play is another indication of Ford's scrupulosity about his Spartan setting: he must have known that the tendency 'to peece many words together to make of them one entire, much more significative than the single word', had been stressed by Puttenham and other rhetoricians of the period as characteristic of the ancient Greeks.[7] A few of the compound

---

[7] George Puttenham, *The Arte of English Poesie*, ed. G. D. Willcock and A. Walker (Cambridge, 1936), pp. 156–7.

words in *The Broken Heart* (e.g. 'monster-love') gesture towards the condition of oxymoron. Essentially, however, they imply unity and equivalence, of a perilous and uneasy kind. In this sense they are unlike those stifling noun/adjective relationships through which the genuine incompatibilities of the play are expressed: 'noble shame' (IV.2.150), 'excellent misery' (V.2.66), 'dreadful safety' (V.2.117), 'married bachelors' (IV.2.131), 'honourable infamy' (V.2.123), or Penthea's own description of herself as 'a ravished wife/Widowed by lawless marriage' (IV.2.146–7).

The work of Glenn Blayney and Peter Ure on the status of formal betrothals in the sixteenth and seventeenth centuries has at least rescued Penthea from the old critical charge of being some kind of hysterical Platonic: a girl who conceals her fundamental abhorrence of sex behind an exaggerated notion of the importance of her previous contact with Orgilus.[8] In fact, her position resembles that of Clare in Wilkins's *Miseries of Enforced Marriage* (1606), after her affianced lover has obeyed a guardian and married someone else:

> A wretched maid, not fit for any man,
> For being united his with plighted faiths,
> Whoever sues to me commits a sinne,
> Besiedgeth me, and who shal marry me:
> Is like my selfe, lives in Adultery, (O God)
> That such hard Fortune, should betide my youth.
> I am Young, Fayre, Rich, Honest, Virtuous,
> Yet for all this, who ere shall marry mee
> I am but his whore, live in Adultery...
> I must be made a strumpet gainst my will.[9]

Wilkins's heroine stabs herself to avoid such a fate; Penthea, in *The Broken Heart*, actually experiences it. Both of her contracts, the one with Orgilus solemnized in the presence of her father, and the 'noble shame' of her enforced marriage to the wealthy Lord Bassanes, are legally and emotionally binding. Each one contaminates and nullifies the other. She behaves to both men with extraordinary probity and restraint, but the situation itself is intolerable, and would be so even if Bassanes were not a jealous lunatic. The cruelty of Ithocles has created a 'divorce betwixt my body and my heart' (II.3.57),

[8] Glenn Blayney, 'Enforcement of marriage in English drama (1600–1650)', in *Philological Quarterly* 38 (1959), 459–72. Peter Ure, 'Marriage and the domestic drama in Heywood and Ford', *English Studies* 32 (1951), 200–16.
[9] George Wilkins, *The Miseries of Enforced Marriage*, Tudor Facsimile Texts, ed. John S. Farmer (London, 1913), C4v.

condemning Penthea to live out a kind of perpetual and agonizing Marvellian 'Dialogue Between the Soul and Body', in which the two partners perpetually accuse and torment one another.

When a penitent Ithocles foresees that his sister will become a martyr to whom 'married wives' (III.2.85) direct their orisons, the apparent redundancy of his formulation is purposeful and telling. It reflects his belated awareness that, thanks to him, this is not in fact Penthea's condition. Addressing Calantha later, Penthea plays pathetically with the epithets 'virgin wives' and 'married maids' (III.5.52, 56), beneficent oxymorons which express a Spenserian ideal of purity and chastity within a betrothed or married state. Her own position, as she knows, is that of chaste whore and 'ravished wife'. It cannot be maintained. Calantha's disingenuous, if understandable, snub when Penthea tries to win her for Ithocles snaps a sanity and will already stretched to breaking point. Penthea gives way to the anorexic's terrified passion for purity, to that 'dilemma of the self whose boundaries feel infinitely vulnerable to invasion from surrounding territory, either because of some constitutional fragility, or insensitive impingement from the environment, or both'.[10] She puts an end to the warfare between body and heart by choosing to punish the former for its involuntary corruption:

> Penthea's, poor Penthea's name is strumpeted.
> But since her blood was seasoned by the forfeit
> Of noble shame, with mixtures of pollution,
> Her blood——'tis just——be henceforth never heightened
> With taste of sustenance. Starve. Let that fullness
> Whose plurisy hath severed faith and modesty –
> Forgive me. O I faint!   (IV.2.148–54)

Psychologically, the reaction is entirely comprehensible. Its consequences, however, are tragic in a way Penthea herself did not foresee.

When Orgilus tells Bassanes, in Act IV, that Penthea 'is left a prey to words' (IV.2.44), he surely does not mean (as one of the play's recent editors would have it) that the insanity which afflicts her in her last hours exposes her to 'scandal'.[11] The line is both more literal and more far-reaching. Once 'the empress of her soul, her reason' (IV.2.48) has been deposed, Penthea becomes the victim of all those

---

[10] Rosemary Dinnage, reviewing three clinical books on anorexia in *The New York Review of Books*, 22 February 1979, p. 8.

[11] *The Broken Heart*, ed. Donald K. Anderson Jr, Regents Renaissance Drama Series (London, 1968), p. 75.

turbulent feelings of love and hate, of that desire for vengeance, which she has suppressed so gallantly up to this point. The woman whose conscious will forbade her to repay the insufferable Bassanes in kind, to encourage Orgilus' passion in the garden, or to revenge herself on her brother when the opportunity offered itself, is now left 'a prey to words' which her rational and waking mind would never have permitted her to utter.

Once again, and at a crucial moment in the play, Ford was remembering *Hamlet*. Ophelia too not only exposed a carefully concealed private self in her madness ('To-morrow is Saint Valentine's day'), she whetted Laertes' desire to be revenged on Prince Hamlet — something from which her conscious mind would have recoiled. Ophelia directs no blame towards the man she loves. But Laertes, as he watches her distribute her pathetic flowers, puts words into her mouth: 'Hadst thou thy wits and didst persuade revenge, / It could not move thus' (IV.5.169-70). Penthea, whose roses were all gathered in Act II, does make an accusation. Pointing to her brother Ithocles, she summons up the ghost of her ruined happiness and reminds Orgilus of who destroyed it: 'that is he... that's he, and still 'tis he' (IV.2.116, 122). And Orgilus, a potential revenger who has recently seemed to waver in his purpose, finds that

> She has tutored me.
> Some powerful inspiration checks my laziness...
> If this be madness, madness is an oracle.   (IV.2.124-5, 133)

From this moment on, the tragedy is inevitable in human as well as divine terms. It is a tragedy made more poignant because the magnanimous and loving Penthea, when sane, would have done anything to prevent it. Her madness has produced a different kind of divorce between body and heart, unleashing all the weaknesses and passionate, vindictive impulses which her conscious emotional self had overcome at such crippling cost.

For Orgilus too, Ithocles' arrogant violation of the pre-contract has resulted in a divorce between body and heart:

> All pleasures are but mere imagination,
> Feeding the hungry appetite with steam
> And sight of banquet, whilst the body pines,
> Not relishing the real taste of food.
> Such is the leanness of a heart divided
> From intercourse of troth-contracted loves.   (II.3.34-9)

Like Penthea, Orgilus can find no way out of the impasse, except through the creation of a body/heart division of another kind. When Orgilus betrays Ithocles at last, kills him, and so avenges his own and Penthea's wrongs, he is a man divided in his feelings about the act as no previous revenger had been in sixteenth- and seventeenth-century drama. His hesitations are not Hamlet's, nor are they the compunctions of the hero in Marston's *Antonio's Revenge*, before he murders the inoffensive little son of his enemy Piero. Tecnicus' rejection of the revenge code as an example of false honour has touched his pupil not at all. Orgilus not only nurses an acute sense of personal injury, he believes that the martyred Penthea has given him a mandate to kill. Unfortunately, he also finds when the moment of decision comes that he admires and respects his victim.

It is true that the selfishness of Ithocles, after Calantha has accepted him as her husband on a pre-contract, makes it easier for Orgilus to proceed:

> ORGILUS: I was myself a piece of suitor once,
> And forward in preferment too; so forward,
> That, speaking truth, I may without offence, sir,
> Presume to whisper that my hopes and, hark'ee,
> My certainty of marriage stood assured
> With as firm footing, by your leave, as any's
> Now at this very instant – but –
> ITHOCLES: 'Tis granted.
> And for a league of privacy between us,
> Read o'er my bosom and partake a secret.
> The princess is contracted mine.   (IV.3.114–23)

Ithocles' interruption is grossly insensitive in itself. Even worse is the way he brushes aside the parallel between Orgilus' blighted expectation of happiness and his own, present anticipation of joy. Orgilus will remind Ithocles later of this lapse, of how his rapture at the prospect of enjoying Calantha and a crown not only made him neglect Penthea's sufferings, but rendered 'my injuries... beneath your royal pity' (IV.4.36–7). Even before he stabs Ithocles, however, Orgilus has begun to prove the truth of his prisoner's cool injunction: 'On to the execution, and inherit / A conflict with thy horrors' (IV.4.50–1).

Revengers in seventeenth-century drama do not usually take their victims' hands in token of heart-felt regard before delivering the fatal blow, encourage them during their death-throes, and praise them dead. Orgilus bids Ithocles farewell as 'fair spring of manhood' (IV.4.71), and couples him with Penthea: 'Sweet twins, shine stars forever' (IV.4.74). He is a revenger emptied of rancour, his action almost as mechanical as the chair he uses to guarantee success, and he is quietly resolved on his own death. Not for an instant does he consider what he later calls the 'dreadful safety' of flight, so magnanimously recommended by his dying enemy. Instead, he seeks out Calantha at once and confesses that 'brave Ithocles is murdered, murdered cruelly' (V.2.16). Orgilus never admits that his reasons for killing Ithocles were anything but 'just and known' (V.2.46). He does not regret what he has done. He simply divorces the almost impersonal necessity for the action, as he sees it, from what he acknowledges to be the butchery (V.2.41) of its accomplishment, and the worth of his victim: 'Never lived gentleman of greater merit, / Hope, or abiliment to steer a kingdom' (V.2.47-8). Once again, the only resolution of this conflict, of the 'honourable infamy' (V.2.123) of Orgilus' condition, lies in death.

In an essay called 'The task of cultural history', Johan Huizinga once tried to distinguish between what he called aristocratic and popular cultures:

An aristocratic culture does not advertise its emotions. In its forms of expression it is sober and reserved. Its general attitude is stoic. In order to be strong it wants to be and needs to be hard and unemotional, or at any rate to allow the expression of feelings and inclinations only in elegant forms... The populace is always anti-stoic. Great waves of emotion, floods of tears, and excesses of feeling have always been breaks in the dikes of the popular soul, which then usually swept along the spirit of the upper classes.[12]

Racine comes most immediately to mind as the dramatist of a tragic aristocracy struggling against overwhelming odds to subdue or at least shape its passionate emotions. But he was anticipated by Ford in *The Broken Heart*. The play has in common with *Phèdre* or *Bérénice* a sense of almost unendurable repression, of torrents of feeling made to flow in channels too narrow and constricted to contain them. Explosion is always imminent, a violation of decorum which will shake this world apart. The code which governs Spartan society demands that people should maintain a rigid self-control. Because these characters are all passionate by nature, and because their

---

[12] Johan Huizinga, *Men and Ideas: History, the Middle Ages, the Renaissance*, trans. James S. Holmes and Hans van Marle (New York, 1970), pp. 47-8.

situations either are or become extreme, such control is possibly only through various forms of self-imposed psychological violence. The outward stillness towards which everyone but Bassanes strives is excruciatingly difficult to maintain. The lava crust is thin on the top of the volcano and, when the explosion comes, it tends to be all the more devastating because it has for so long been held artificially in check.

Book in hand, the conscious replica of Hamlet mad in craft, Orgilus disguised as the scholar Aplotes had bestowed upon his sister and Prophilus in Act I a 'distracted' meditation with method in it:

> Say it. Is it possible
> With a smooth tongue, a leering countenance,
> Flattery, or force of reason – I come t''ee, sir –
> To turn or to appease the raging sea?
> Answer to that. Your art? What art to catch
> And hold fast in a net the sun's small atoms?
> No, no. They'll out, they'll out. Ye may as easily
> Outrun a cloud, driven by a northern blast,
> As fiddle faddle so. Peace, or speak sense.   (1.3.102–10)

The speech recognizes the potency of powerful, uncivilized forces. Like the sun, the sea and the wind, human emotions naturally evade regulation and capture – whether in the form of Tecnicus' rational counsels, or (more painfully) the attempts of individuals to conform to a demanding aristocratic code. In itself, this code is neither arid nor ridiculous. It governs Tecnicus' rigorous but compassionate surveillance of them all, and his rejection of revenge as untidy and irrational, the dignity with which King Amyclas accepts the fact that he is not about to regain his youth after all, but to die, Nearchus' generous renunciation of Calantha, and the 'undaunted spirit' (v.2.42) of Ithocles when facing the death of a trapped animal. It also dictates Penthea's irreproachable behaviour to Orgilus, to her brother Ithocles, and to the husband who makes her life a hell. At the end of the play, Calantha will bring it to the point of apotheosis: a vindication made even more impressive because she alone forges a wholeness and rapport between Sparta's social ideal and the heart's truth. That is why she, and not Penthea, is ultimately the heroine of *The Broken Heart*.

Although Orgilus has threatened from the beginning to tear through and destroy the ideals of his class, it is the nobleman Bassanes who provides the fullest and most depressing exposition of what Ford sees in this play as the alternative. When he appears for the first time in Act II, talking of ear-wigs, warts, pimples, city housewives, hounds' heads, wag-tails and jays, bitch-foxes, bed-posts and collops, he introduces a language alien to that spoken by anyone else in the play. This is partly because of its unremitting lowness and physicality, partly because of a specificity which throws into relief the other characters' predilection for the abstract. Bassanes' speech, like his imagination, is populated with monsters of his own invention: horned beasts, nightmares, rotten maggots, human beings with the features of dogs, cats, foxes and swine, and 'the deformed bear-whelp/Adultery' (II.1.5–6). For those around him, he is himself a freak of nature. Orgilus, attempting to describe Bassanes' schizoid attitude toward his wife, calls it 'monster-love' (I.1.61). Ithocles, when accused of incest with Penthea, flings the epithet 'monster' at Bassanes (III.2.153) and, even for his servant Grausis, he is an 'animal' (III.2.178).

Not until he has been forcibly separated from the wife he both adores and reviles can Bassanes see that he is himself a beast more hideous than anything his diseased mind has been able to conjure up: 'of those beasts/The worst am I' (IV.2.28–9). Purified by this recognition, his language now takes on an abstract quality and dignity like that of the other characters. From being the one inhabitant of the court wholly incapable of controlling his passions, a man accustomed to vent all his private emotions and fears, he moves to an extreme of stoicism in the face of disaster:

> Make me the pattern of digesting evils,
> Who can outlive my mighty ones, not shrinking
> At such a pressure as would sink a soul
> Into what's most of death, the worst of horrors.
> But I have sealed a covenant with sadness,
> And entered into bonds without condition
> To stand these tempests calmly. Mark me, nobles,
> I do not shed a tear, not for Penthea.
> Excellent misery! (V.2.58–66)

The culminating oxymoron makes it plain that Bassanes' new attitude is agonizing and, in a sense, unnatural. But this excruciating self-restraint, a forcible subordination of passion to the dictates of reason and the will, is preferable to the hysteria and self-indulgence of his earlier self. Restored to his rightful place in Sparta's aristocratic society, Bassanes ceases to be an aberrant, comic character.

Amid the pure, consciously restricted diction of *The Broken Heart*, 'monsters' acquire something of the prominence and special significance that the word *monstre* possesses in *Phèdre*. Ithocles humbly admits to the sister he has wronged that 'ingratitude of nature / Hath made my actions monstrous' (III.2.81–2). Armostes fears that his nephew's ambition for Calantha's hand will result in some prodigious birth, like the centaur Ixion fathered on a cloud (IV.1.69–73). The mad Penthea's imagination runs on sirens, half woman, half bird. Her desperate resolution to starve herself will tempt Nature to 'call her daughter, monster' (IV.2.156). Orgilus is rumoured to have fled to Athens on a fiery dragon (II.1.54), and to have returned to Sparta through the agency of hobgoblins (III.3.36). Meeting him after the secret murder of Ithocles, Bassanes is uniquely and tellingly impelled to revert to the disordered language he employed before his reformation:

> I will not aught to do with thee of all men.
> The doubles of a hare or, in a morning,
> Salutes from a splay-footed witch...
> Are not so boding mischief as thy crossing
> My private meditations. Shun me, prithee.
>
> (v.1.11–13, 16–17)

Here, for once, the monstrosity Bassanes senses is actual, and not merely a product of his own diseased imagination.

However it manifests itself, the monstrous is at odds with Sparta's rational, demanding aristocratic ideal. Revenge, whether it takes the form of Orgilus' futile murder, or Ithocles' earlier revival of an obsolete family feud, is monstrous: a false honour, 'proceeding from the vices of our passion, / Which makes our reason drunk' (III.1.36–7). Penthea's collapse into inanition and lunacy, however pathetic and understandable under the circumstances, is nonetheless grotesque, a surrender to the irrational which proves horribly destructive to the people she most loves. As *The Broken Heart* nears its ending, Ford poises against these failures a number of triumphs: the self-control of Nearchus, the way Ithocles and Amyclas face death, the redemption of Bassanes and, most memorable of all, Calantha's demonstration of the fundamental strength and cohesion of this social order, when she refuses to shatter the formal patterns of the courtly dance for the individual deaths of her father, her friend Penthea, and her affianced lord.

Like *Antony and Cleopatra* and *The Duchess of Malfi*, *The Broken Heart* possesses a divided catastrophe. Where Shakespeare and Webster had drawn the line of demarcation between Acts IV and V, Ford chose to contain it within Act V. The effect, however, is the same. An apparent climax, an expected ending, is set up and then denied. The tragedy surprises its audience by continuing, and by doing so in a way that forces a radical re-adjustment of attitudes, and a perspective on the action, that had seemed settled. Calantha has consistently been the most opaque and unknowable of the major characters in the play. Only two small hints – her choice of Ithocles rather than Nearchus to lead her off-stage at III.4.75–6, and the ambiguous business with the ring at IV.1.25–34 – have betrayed the inner workings of her heart. Penthea goes to her death believing that her love embassy has failed. When, in Act IV, Calantha ceremoniously asks her father to give her Ithocles for her own, the old king obviously believes that she is assuring him of favour in what will shortly be the new reign. He does not realize that he has just given parental sanction to a pre-contract which cuts out the Prince of Argos. For the theatre audience, however, which overhears Calantha's aside to Ithocles, 'Th'art mine. Have I now kept my word?' (IV.3.88), the shock is considerable. It becomes plain that in a scene Ford has high-handedly refused to show us, these two have made a mutual declaration of love. They stand before us as a betrothed couple, although just how they have arrived at this understanding remains unclear. Ithocles' passion for Calantha, strong enough to make him sicken physically, as well as possessing his mind, has been amply displayed. The nature and depth of her feelings for him are altogether less certain. In the absence of the betrothal scene itself, the answer seems to be provided by her behaviour in the dance.

Meditating on ambition in the specific context of what then seemed to be his hopeless passion for Calantha, Ithocles in Act II had reflected that

> Morality applied
> To timely practice keeps the soul in tune;
> At whose sweet music all our actions dance.
> But this is form of books and school-tradition.
> It physics not the sickness of a mind
> Broken with griefs. (II.2.8–13)

Like Orgilus in the habit of Aplotes, Ithocles impatiently rejects the rational ideal honoured in Sparta as something inadequate in practice, however persuasive in the abstract. Calantha, by contrast, turns the abstraction of Ithocles' fancied 'dance' into a concrete reality, and demonstrates that it not only should but can over-ride personal anguish. In doing so, she summons up ideas that are more than narrowly aristocratic:

> *Dauncing* (bright Lady) then began to be,
> When the first seedes whereof the world did spring,
> The Fire, Ayre, Earth and Water did agree,
> By Loves perswasion, Natures mighty King,
> To leave their first disordred combating;
>   And in a daunce such measure to observe,
>   As all the world their motion should preserve...
>
> Loe this is Dauncings true nobilitie.
> Dauncing the child of Musick and of Love,
> Dauncing it selfe both love and harmony,
> Where all agree, and all in order move;
> Dauncing the Art that all Arts doe approve:
>   The faire Caracter of the worlds consent,
>   The heav'ns true figure, and th'earths ornament.[13]

Sir John Davies's long poem 'Orchestra Or a Poeme of Dauncing', printed in 1596, provides a gloss on the dance in Act v of *The Broken Heart*, linking it with a great Renaissance and classical tradition. Through the exercise of will, Calantha holds the court together in an order and harmony sanctioned and repeated by the seasons, the constellations, the tides, and the fruitful marriage of the elements. She defends a society threatened by chaos and monstrosity. Precisely because she does not break up her lines to weep, she vindicates Sparta's exacting code of reason, measure and self-control as something which can be exemplified by human beings, not merely by the books they write.

Structurally, the unviolated symmetry and closure of the dance in Ford's play answers all of those masques, shows, plays within the play and other entertainments which had disintegrated into confusion at the end of so many Elizabethan and Jacobean revenge tragedies. It gains its effect largely because of the way it contradicts an established theatrical tradition, becoming an affirmation rather than an agent of destruction.[14] The last change concluded, Calantha begins her reign 'with a first act of justice' (v.2.67). She sentences Orgilus to death,

---

[13] Sir John Davies, 'Orchestra or a poeme of dauncing', in *The Poems of Sir John Davies*, ed. Robert Krueger (Oxford, 1975), pp. 94, 115.

[14] It is possible that Ford remembered Marston's use of a court dance in *The Malcontent*, some years earlier, to conduct the play towards a final social harmony.

reminds the company that the departed must have paid their debt to mortality one time or another, and announces that 'we'll suddenly prepare our coronation' (v.2.93). This line seems to bring the tragedy to its end, on a note at once admirable and chilling. The 'masculine spirit' (v.2.95) of Calantha has elicited from the awed members of the court a reaction which speaks for the theatre audience as well: a compound of wonder, humility, relief, and a certain discomfort. This woman who has just lost her father, her lover, and her friend seems, in her iron self-control, both more and less than human. The suspicion arises that, paradoxically, the high, rational ideals of Sparta can only be embodied by someone who is emotionally a monster.

Ford allows such an ending to flicker as a possibility, and then unexpectedly moves beyond it. It seems that Orgilus' execution is to take place not only within the time span of the play, but on stage. The blood-letting itself, detailed, protracted, and made more disturbing by the controlled hysteria of Bassanes' commentary, presents an image of violence *and* repose. This is an oxymoron which operates primarily on a visual level, but it is no less powerful for that. The whole play has worked to create a powerful sense of energies and passions repressed, bottled up within limits too narrow. The release of Orgilus' turbulent, pent-up blood is both ghastly and somehow gratifying: a 'pastime' as Bassanes terms it (v.2.131) in deadly earnest, a game in which the will controls the body, an 'honourable infamy' (v.2.123). As a stoic display, it is raw, crude, but effective. At its conclusion, the tragedy gestures deceptively once again at an ending:

> The coronation must require attendance.
> That past, my few days can be but one mourning. (v.2.158–9)

Bassanes' valedictory lines sound final. And indeed there appears to be no plot material remaining, no expectations unfulfilled. Orgilus, Ithocles, Penthea and Amyclas are dead, Prophilus and Euphrania united, Bassanes reformed, and Calantha rules in Sparta. Whether or not she eventually accepts Nearchus as husband is a matter of no import. The woman who displayed such 'tokens/Of constancy' (v.3.16–17), as Armostes puts it, in the last scene is clearly capable of governing alone.

Nothing prepares either the theatre audience or its surrogates on stage for another scene, one in which the play's title will be reinterpreted, Calantha's true nature revealed, and the ethos of Sparta made human. The queen's prayer before the altar at the beginning of this scene may well be a request for death, a request granted by the gods. Nevertheless, there is about her extinction the sense of a supreme triumph, a mastery of mind over body which alters, in retrospect, the way we regard Penthea's last will and testament, and her death by starvation, as it modifies the effect of Orgilus' suicide. Like Yeats's old man of Tara, who decided in his 101st year that his life had gone on long enough,

> Saw that the grave was deep, the coffin sound,
> Summoned the generations of his house,
> Lay in the coffin, stopped his breath and died,[15]

Calantha dies through a conscious and calculated movement of the mind. She does not need to starve herself out of existence, like Penthea, nor does she become in the slightest degree irrational. Her final disposition of people, her ordering of the succession and of Sparta's high offices are irreproachable. Unlike Orgilus, she does not even require the aid of a knife. She simply wills herself to stop living, and that will – whose strength has already been demonstrated in her continuation of the dance – performs what is required of it.

Like Ithocles, Orgilus and Penthea before her, Calantha arranges for music to express something she cannot easily say. A lyric relief from the rigours of the play's spare, aristocratic norm of dramatic speech, the four songs of *The Broken Heart* release emotion to flow in freer and less restricted channels, without for an instant dissipating its intensity.[16] This is true even of the song Orgilus sings to bless the marriage of Prophilus and Euphrania, although it appears at a moment less ominous than the other three. For the dying Penthea, the desperate Ithocles of Act III, and Calantha at the end, music crystallizes emotion. It objectifies feelings which have become intolerable, an agony which these people have tried to repress as long as possible. But Calantha's song, written we are told by herself, has a quality all its own. Appropriately, for someone who has elected to

---

[15] William Butler Yeats, 'In Tara's Halls', in *Collected Poems of W. B. Yeats* (London, 1961), p. 374.

[16] A number of scholars (S. P. Sherman, G. M. Carsaniga, Katherine Duncan-Jones) have felt that Ford was drawing attention in his prologue to parallels between Penthea's situation and that of Penelope Devereux, Sidney's Stella. The general indebtedness of *The Broken Heart* to Sidney's *Arcadia* has long been recognized. It may be more than coincidental that Ford's songs appear at an analogous point in the whole, and fulfil a very similar purpose, to those in the second half of Sidney's *Astrophil and Stella*.

become queen, bride, and corpse all in the same moment, it focusses upon the paradox of Time:

> Crowns may flourish and decay,
> Beauties shine, but fade away.
> Youth may revel, yet it must
> Lie down in a bed of dust.
> Earthly honours flow and waste.
> Time alone doth change and last.
> Sorrows mingled with contents prepare
>   Rest for care.
> Love only reigns in death; though art
> Can find no comfort for a broken heart.   (v.3.85–94)

In a world of transience and mutability, 'Time alone doth change and last'. But Time, as both Crotolon and Penthea have observed earlier, has a 'daughter': 'Truth is child of Time' (III.5.62, IV.3.38). The riddles of the gods and the dark complexities of human feelings are alike impenetrable until 'events/Expound their truth' (IV.3.37–8). No amount of interpretation or attempted analysis on the part of other characters – or a theatre audience – can plumb them until the moment is ripe. Calantha's unpredictable funeral wedding, mingling sorrows with contents, is the last of the oxymorons in *The Broken Heart*. But it is different from its predecessors. In the tableau she stages at the end, the conflicting demands of an impersonal, public world and a private realm of the emotions, mind and body, stoicism and passion, are at last reconciled. In revealing the strength of her commitment to the murdered Ithocles, she fuses the contradictory terms which have bedevilled her society. Love still leads to death, but at least it is a death freely and intelligently chosen, and its legacy to others is order, not destruction. Unlike Penthea, Orgilus, or even Ithocles, Calantha in dying honours all the demands that life makes on people in Sparta. Unimaginable before it actually happens, the second catastrophe of *The Broken Heart* both exemplifies the aristocratic code at its best, and makes its peace with the heart's necessities. Far from being a structural fault, the last of the surprises Ford prepared for his theatre audience was an inspiration. It sets the seal on a dramatic technique – unorthodox, sometimes puzzling, but brilliant – which has operated throughout this play as a metaphor for the unknowability of fate.

CHAPTER 13

Shakespeare and Jonson (1983)

In 1618, when Ben Jonson made his famous journey to Scotland and talked with (or more properly, at) William Drummond of Hawthornden, Queen Elizabeth had been dead for fifteen years. Prince Henry, briefly cherished as Astraea's true heir, had been in his grave for six years, and William Shakespeare for two. The Jonson who conversed with Drummond had arrived at a seeming impasse as a writer of comedy. Indeed, he may well have made a private decision to abandon the stage. *The Staple of News*, his next new play, did not appear until 1626, eight years after the meeting with Drummond and ten years after *The Devil is an Ass*, the last of his Jacobean comedies. The Jonson of 1618 could afford to turn his back on the theatre, or so it must have seemed. A famous and, of late, a much honoured man, he had already published his Folio *Works*, including nine of his plays. He had powerful friends and patrons, was about to receive an honorary MA from Oxford University and, apart from his established position as chief masque writer to the court of King James, he was busy with various literary projects of a nondramatic kind. When his library was destroyed by fire in 1623, Jonson lamented, in 'An execration upon Vulcan', the disappearance of a whole galaxy of precious, unpublished works: several translations, an English grammar, his history of the life of Henry V, a poetic account of his expedition to Scotland, what sounds like the original (and probably much larger) version of *Discoveries* – 'twice-twelve-yeares stor'd up humanitie' – and, rather less expectedly, a number of theological writings. These were the losses that really hurt. He comes close to

---

The argument of this essay is developed in my book, *Ben Jonson, Dramatist* (Cambridge, 1984). Two paragraphs and several sentences necessary for the argument appeared in an article entitled 'Harking back to Elizabeth: Ben Jonson and Caroline nostalgia', *English Literary History* 48 (1981), 706–31. Quotations from Jonson are taken from *Ben Jonson*, ed. C. H. Herford and Percy and Evelyn Simpson, 11 vols. (Oxford, 1925–52).

forgiving the lame god of fire for sweeping away something less consequential: 'parcels of a Play' (line 43).

In talking to Drummond that winter of 1618, Jonson with characteristic highhandedness dismissed a number of celebrated poets, both living and dead, who like himself had begun writing during the reign of Elizabeth. He expressed unqualified impatience at that time with Thomas Campion, Samuel Daniel, Sir John Davies, John Day, Thomas Dekker, Michael Drayton, Edward Fairfax, Sir John Harington, Gervase Markham, John Marston, and Thomas Middleton. Jonson had been for years a notorious dissenter from the mainstream of Elizabethan literature, and this blacklist was obviously far from complete. Anthony Munday, for instance, satirized as Antonio Balladino in the revised version of Jonson's early comedy *The Case is Altered*, is absent. So is Thomas Kyd, the author of that stubbornly memorable play *The Spanish Tragedy*, a play which haunted Jonson even more persistently and cruelly than it did other dramatists of his generation. If Dekker is to be credited. Jonson had himself acted the part of Hieronymo during his days of lowly service 'among the Mimickes', which would help to explain why he could never thereafter get it out of his head.[1] Also, as I believe myself (although I do not want to argue the case here), Jonson *was* the skilful ventriloquist responsible for the famous 'additions' to the play commissioned by Henslowe in 1601–2 and printed in Pavier's edition of 1602.[2] And yet both the language and the revenge form of *The Spanish Tragedy* were peculiarly offensive to his artistic principles. Marlowe too, at least the Marlowe who wrote *Tamburlaine* and was indirectly responsible for so much of that '*scenicale* strutting, and furious vociferation' (778–9) which Jonson later deplored in *Discoveries*, rather surprisingly seems to have escaped censure before Drummond in 1618.

For his friend George Chapman, for one lyric by Sir Henry Wotton, and for Robert Southwell's poem 'The Burning Babe', Jonson did find words of unalloyed praise. But when he came to what seem to us now to be the four great names of Elizabethan poetry – Philip Sidney, Edmund Spenser, John Donne, and William Shakespeare – his response was significantly divided. Jonson had a shrewd sense of what the judgement of posterity on this quartet was likely to

---

[1] *Satiromastix*, in *The Dramatic Works of Thomas Dekker*, ed. Fredson Bowers, 4 vols. (Cambridge, 1953–61), I, IV.1.132.

[2] See my *Ben Jonson, Dramatist* (Cambridge, 1984), pp. 13–28.

be. They were not poetasters. Whatever their faults, they were writers who mattered, which is why Jonson returns to them again and again. Yet the feelings they aroused in him had, for a long time, been contradictory and a little defensive.

Jonson's mixed attitude towards Shakespeare, the scandalous inventor of servant monsters, seacoasts in Bohemia and moldy tales; a man who wrote too glibly and 'wanted Arte' (Drummond, line 50) but who was also the master of 'well torned, and true-filed lines'; in tragedy the peer of Aeschylus, Sophocles, and Euripides, and in comedy of Aristophanes, Plautus, and Terrence – 'not of an age, but for all time' – is famous. Less attention has been paid to the fact that his response to Sidney, Spenser, and Donne displays a strikingly similar inconsistency. Sidney obviously obsessed Jonson as the realization of a personal ideal: the good poet who was also a conspicuously good man, who brought his life and his art into just that harmonious accord which Jonson prized and found it so difficult in his own case to achieve. In 'To Penshurst', Sidney is the poet at whose 'great birth...all the *Muses* met' (line 14). Elsewhere in *The Forest*, and in the *Epigrams*, he is the great, the 'god-like Sydney', who exhausted the wealth of the Muses' springs'. *The Silent Woman* even turns him into a professional man of letters, admittedly by somewhat sophistical means. When Sir John Daw sneers at men who are obliged to live by their verses, Dauphine punningly slaps him down: 'And yet the noble *SIDNEY* lives by his, and the noble family not asham'd' (II.3.117–18).

But how much of Sidney's work did Jonson genuinely admire? The neoclassicism of *An Apology for Poetry* was predictably appealing. *Arcadia* and *Astrophil and Stella*, the fictions through which Sidney in fact 'lives', were another matter. The Jonson who talked to Drummond disapproved of romance literature. Moreover, as he pointed out sourly, in *Arcadia* Sidney violated the principles of classical decorum, failing to distinguish the speech of princes from that of clowns. It is true that Saviolina and Fungoso in *Every Man Out of His Humour* are constantly reading *Arcadia* and introducing its choicer phrases into their discourse. They also happen to be half-wits, whose admiration in no way honours Sidney's book. As for *Astrophil and Stella*, it was largely responsible for the sonneteering vogue of the 1590s, and Jonson made it clear to Drummond that he deplored the sonnet, that tyrannical bed of Procrustes, as he called it, in which sense is distorted in the interests of form. It is all too tempting to dismiss as casual Jonson's poem in *The Forest* in which he assures the Countess of Rutland, Sidney's daughter, that she is (or might become, with a little more effort) a poet quite as good as her father. Unfortunately, Jonson reiterated this opinion in talking to Drummond, and that is altogether more embarrassing.

As for Spenser, Jonson told Drummond that he did not like either his stanzas or his matter. But he crammed his own, personal copy of '*Spenser's* noble book' (line 24), (as he called it in his epigram to Venetia Digby) with marginal annotations.[3] And he not only advised young men, in *Discoveries*, to read Spenser *for* his matter, but informed a presumably bewildered Drummond that, after all, Arthurian material formed incomparably the best subject for an heroic poem. 'In affecting the Ancients', Jonson grumbled, 'Spenser writ no Language.' Yet Drummond records that his guest liked to recite sections of *The Shepherd's Calendar* from memory. In his masque *The Golden Age Restored* of 1615, Jonson had already placed Spenser beside Chaucer as one of those 'sons' of Apollo who accompany Astraea on her return to earth.

John Donne, like Shakespeare, was Jonson's personal friend. Jonson praised him in his *Epigrams* as 'the delight of *PHOEBUS*, and each *Muse*' (Epigram XXIII, 'To John Donne', line 1), and he told Drummond that Donne was 'the first poet in the world in some things' (117–18). He clearly valued Donne's critical judgement, sent him his own poems with a trepidation that seems unfeigned and (again according to Drummond) introduced him as a speaker in his lost apology for *Bartholomew Fair*, under the name of Criticus. Interestingly enough, it was the Elizabethan and not the Jacobean Donne who appealed to Jonson: all Donne's best poems, he claimed, had been written before the age of twenty-five. He himself had memorized all of 'The Bracelet' and parts of 'The Calme'. But this brilliant contemporary, 'whose every worke', Jonson asserted in his *Epigrams*, 'came forth example, and remaines so, yet', was also (it seems) a wilfully obscure poet who 'for not being understood would perish', and who 'for not keeping of accent deserved hanging' (196, 48–9).

Jonson found it easy to condescend to the lesser stars of Elizabethan

---

[3] Since this essay was written, Jonson's copy of Spenser has turned up, in the collection of Paul Getty, Jr. An account, by James A. Riddle and Stanley Stewart, of Jonson's underlinings and annotations in Spenser's 'The ruines of time', and their implications, was published in *Studies in Philology* 87, no. 4 (Autumn, 1990), 427–55. A book-length study of the volume as a whole is forthcoming.

poetry. The four great planets – Sidney, Spenser, Shakespeare, and Donne – compelled respect. Their achievements, however, which he was too intelligent not to recognize, were disquieting. After all, the great men, as well as the poetasters and the lesser lights, had helped to define his own temperamental separation from the main current of late-sixteenth-century poetry and drama. During the 1590s Jonson developed a distinctive poetic and (more particularly) a distinctive comic mode by reacting against a generalized Elizabethan norm. In this respect, he was the exact opposite of Shakespeare, who forged his own style during the last decade of the sixteenth century by assimilating and then transcending the native tradition.

I do not want to deny the influence of Lyly, or of popular morality drama or the Elizabethan pamphleteers on Jonson's early humour plays. It is important to remember, too, that in 1598 Francis Meres was praising Jonson for tragedies, every one of which is lost. In 1618, after the publication of his Folio, Jonson told Drummond that half of his comedies were not in print. We will never know what Jonson's lost Elizabethan popular plays were really like: *The Isle of Dogs*, *Hot Anger Soon Cooled*, *Page of Plymouth*, *Robert II King of Scots*, *Richard Crookback*, and heaven knows how many more. Clearly Jonson was determined that this hackwork (much of which he was writing concurrently with those early humour plays that he did carefully preserve) should sink without trace. But the fact that he produced plays during the 1590s in collaboration with men like Nashe, Dekker, Porter and Chettle – and we know from *Eastward Ho!* later just how proficient and adaptable a collaborator Jonson could be – makes it plain that he had, however reluctantly, served out a literary as well as an actor's apprenticeship to the popular dramatic tradition.

Jonson knew, then, exactly what he was reacting against as a writer of comedy. Shakespeare, a man some eight years his senior, must have seemed to him to exemplify and focus everything from which he himself was trying so hard to break away. And yet Shakespeare was not only a personal friend, very possibly the man who enabled Jonson to escape from his servitude to Henslowe: he was a comic dramatist who had somehow contrived to do most of the things of which Jonson disapproved, to follow false gods, and yet create plays that Jonson simply could not brush away and dismiss as he could work by Greene and Dekker, Heywood, Porter, Chettle, and Munday, even though they derived, apparently, from the same popular quarry. This is why, as I want to argue, Shakespeare was such a thorn in Jonson's flesh. It also, I believe, accounts (at least in part) for the fact that in later years Jonson, in effect, recanted, that he worked out a kind of intelligent rapprochement with what for so long had been the rival comic form.

Almost invariably, comparisons between Jonsonian and Shakespearean comedy resolve themselves into a series of well-worn antitheses. Classical versus romantic, first of all. A comedy of specialized as against one of wide appeal. Jonson's meticulously created urban worlds, usually contemporary London, more or less thinly disguised, against those of a man who insisted upon ruralizing even his cities (Athens or Messina, Milan and Tyre) and upon blurring our sense of historical time. Jonsonian comedy displaying only the most perfunctory interest in love and marriage, tending (Queen Elizabeth always excluded) to debase or simply ignore women, against one presenting marriage as the most valuable of human relationships, and women, even the youngest and most inexperienced, as the natural embodiments and guardians of the values central to a good society. A rigidly moral if not positively punitive art, poised against something far more tolerant and forgiving. Stereotyped humour characters whose obsessions may be brutally shattered but who are fundamentally incapable of growth or change, measured against Shakespearean characters who learn from their experiences, becoming wiser and better in the course of five acts – or even, like Orlando's brother, overnight. Eddying, disjunctive Jonson plots, against an essentially linear and causal story line. Compression and the unities as natural features of comic form, as opposed to a relaxed and cavalier treatment of time and place. Plays which simply stop – because a situation has been fully explored, because 'Mischiefes feed / Like beasts, till they be fat, and then they bleed' (*Volpone*, v.12.150–1), because the time has come to apply the match to the fuse and blow the whole preposterous entanglement sky-high – against a comedy in which the end, characteristically, crowns all.

Like most literary generalizations, these are certainly open to qualification, from both the Jonsonian and the Shakespearean side. Yet they seem at least roughly accurate. I suspect, moreover, that Jonson would have endorsed them, and with some pride. Which does not mean that he could prevent himself from craning his neck from time to time to regard the alien territory on the other side of the fence, with a measure of personal unease. In *Every Man Out of His Humour* of

1599, perhaps the most extreme and defiantly idiosyncratic of all Jonson's Elizabethan comedies, one of the two chorus characters betrays at one point a hankering after a different kind of play. He wonders whether the argument of the satiric comedy they are watching might not have been 'of some other nature, as of a duke to be in love with a countesse, and that countesse to be in love with the dukes sonne, and the sonne to love the ladies waiting maid: some such crosse wooing, with a clowne to their serving man' (III.6.196–9). From this alarmingly prescient account of *Twelfth Night*, a play Shakespeare had not yet written, he is haled away sternly by Cordatus, a character described as 'the Authors friend', who informs him that comedy should be what Cicero said it was: an imitation of life, a glass of manners and an image of truth – pleasant, ridiculous, and designed, above all, for the correction of social abuses. Anything else, and most certainly a romantic plot of the kind just outlined, is mere window dressing for the vulgar. So much for Shakespeare. And yet at the end of this very play, Jonson cannot forbear looking across the fence again in what seems to be an uncritical, indeed almost an admiring, fashion. He allows one of his characters to describe another as 'a kinsman to justice *Silence*', in full consciousness of the very different comic kingdom that reference will conjure up. While Macilente, that lean, raw-boned anatomy and uncompromising satirist, who to some extent speaks for Jonson himself, begs for applause in the last lines by suggesting that audience approval might have the power to transform him into his comic antitype, rendering him, as he says, as fat as Sir John Falstaff.

Jonson's ten surviving Elizabethan and Jacobean comedies often seem to invoke conventions, themes, or situations associated with specific Shakespearean plays in a deliberately distorted form. So the mock combat between the two cowards Daw and La Foole in *The Silent Woman*, each one falsely convinced of the ferocity of his opponent, replays the reluctant encounter between Viola and Sir Andrew Aguecheek. The collegiate ladies in the same play, living apart from their husbands in a little single-sex society that is rudely shattered by their sudden, collective passion for Dauphine, seem to glance uneasily not only at a contemporary feminist affectation but at Navarre's abortive scheme for an Academe in *Love's Labour's Lost*. It seems doubtful that Puntarvolo in *Every Man Out of His Humour* would have been accompanied by so palpably engaging and omnipresent a dog had Jonson not been remembering Launce and his friend Crab in *The Two Gentlemen of Verona*. (But, Jonson being Jonson, Puntarvolo's dog is poisoned in the end.) The balcony scene from *Romeo and Juliet*, as critics have long recognized, reappears in a most disturbing and dubious form in *Poetaster*, when Julia and her exiled lover Ovid are obliged to part. Indeed, what appears to be the current critical deadlock over exactly how Jonson intends us to take this scene – whether as condemnation of the erring couple or celebration – derives precisely from our uncertainty as to what the dramatist's attitude really is to his Shakespearean model.

None of these echoes can be pinned down or dismissed as simple parody. They are odder and more mixed than that. Moreover, they associate themselves with other episodes, harder to relate to a particular Shakespeare play, which nonetheless seem to point stubbornly but ambiguously in the general direction of Jonson's great competitor. Only three characters in Jonson's twelve surviving Elizabethan and Jacobean plays could be said to transform themselves in a positive, Shakespearean manner, as a result of their experience in the course of the action, as opposed simply to being smashed (like Humpty Dumpty falling off his wall) or remaining, for better or worse, just what they were at the start. They are Kitely in the revised *Every Man In His Humour*, the miser Sordido in *Every Man Out of His Humour*, and the Banbury preacher Zeal of the Land Busy in *Bartholomew Fair*. The handling of all three suggests a Jonsonian desire to experiment with the rival mode, coupled with a weird failure of conviction at the crucial moment.

Kitely tells us, at the end of *Every Man In*, that he is now cured of causeless jealousy of his young wife, and then instantly undercuts this recantation by announcing that he has taken it, word for word, from 'a jealous man's part, in a play' (v.5.82–3). In *Every Man Out*, the heartfelt curses of the rustics when they discover the identity of the would-be suicide they have cut down, impel Sordido abruptly into blank verse and a resolve to spend the rest of his life doing good to his neighbours. The speech itself comes close to sounding plausible. But, again, Jonson cannot maintain a serious attitude towards his conversion. Moments later, the rustics are pointing out that Sordido's tears trill as softly down his cheeks as the vicar's bowls along his green. Absurdly, they plan to ask the town clerk to enter the miser's conversion in the Acts and Monuments. As for Zeal of the Land Busy's perfunctory and anticlimactic collapse before the uplifted garment of Leatherhead's puppet – 'For I am changed, and will

become a beholder with you' (v.5.116–17) – neither in the theatre
nor in the study does it really convince as the effective re-education
of that terrific opponent of Baal, Dagon, and idolatrous groves of
Images detected among the humble wares of a gingerbread stall. It is
as though Jonson wants to flirt with another kind of comedy, but
finds that when it comes to the point he cannot rid himself of the
attitude he expressed in his 'Epistle to Sir Edward Sackville':

> Men have beene great, but never good by chance,
> Or on the sudden. It were strange that he
> Who was this Morning such a one, should be
> *Sydney* e're night!   (lines 124–7)

Jonson found a more characteristic, and also more successful,
compromise solution to the problem in *The Alchemist*, a comedy in
which a bewildering variety of people find their way to Subtle's house
of illusions precisely because they are longing to be transformed, to
discover a more spacious and glamorous way of life, whether as
gallant, roaring boy, captain, great lady, or master of the philosopher's stone. The dreams all fail. These lives are about as likely to
turn into gold as are Sir Epicure's andirons. But that is something
Jonson can understand, and also (more than many of his critics have
been willing to allow) something for which he has a kind of sneaking
sympathy.

   Jonson told Drummond that he had once begun to write a comedy
based on the *Amphitruo* of Plautus, but abandoned it because, as he
said, he could never find two pairs of actors so like each other in
appearance that he could 'persuade the spectators they were one'
(422–3). This is a revealing comment. Plautus had not had to worry
about persuading his audience that Jupiter and Amphitryon,
Mercury and Sosia were indistinguishable, for the simple reason that
Roman actors wore masks. Elizabethan actors did not wear masks.
Moreover, they performed in close proximity to the audience, usually
in full daylight. Jonson's hesitation is entirely understandable. And
yet Shakespeare, when faced with exactly the same difficulty, treated
it with a joyous unconcern. I suppose it is just possible that there was
one set of identical twins in the Lord Chamberlain's Company
around 1593, when *The Comedy of Errors* was first performed –
although T. W. Baldwin's researches certainly did not reveal them.
The mind boggles at the thought of there being *two* sets. In effect,
Shakespeare simply did not care that his two Dromios and his two

Antipholuses were not visibly identical on the stage in the manner demanded by his plot. In a comedy largely concerned with the transformations effected by the mind, he was perfectly willing to let this blatant theatrical incongruity take its place in the argument of the whole. Moreover, in *Twelfth Night* a few years later he did it again. Despite the chorus of wonder that breaks out when Sebastian finally appears to confront Viola his twin – 'An apple, cleft in two, is not more twin', 'How have you made division of yourself?' – most members of any theatre audience will always be more struck by the *dissimilarity* in appearance of these supposedly identical twins than by the likeness everyone is hailing as so miraculous. Far from trying to minimize the inevitable discrepancy between verbal statement and visual fact, Shakespeare calmly called the attention of the whole theatre to it. He did so, I think, in both *Twelfth Night* and *The Comedy of Errors*, for reasons that have to do with his interest in the complex relation between imagination and truth: in the extent to which, in fact, we create the world we say we perceive.

Ben Jonson refused, unlike Shakespeare, to have anything to do with the *Amphitruo* in a theatre which could neither provide him with two sets of identical twins to play the parts nor bypass the problem of verisimilitude by way of the mask. He rejected, in fact, precisely that hinterland of experience, between fantasy and fact, sleep and waking, with which Shakespearean comedy is largely concerned. Jonson's Jacobean comedies deal extensively with deceit, with playacting, and pretence. But always as weapons of imposture. They are never, as so often in Shakespeare – in *The Taming of the Shrew*, for instance, in *As You Like It*, *Twelfth Night*, or *Much Ado About Nothing* – a means of uncovering truth. When Pertinax Surly in *The Alchemist*, or Justice Overdo in *Bartholomew Fair*, are so misguided as to try to use disguise in this sense, they not only make fools of themselves. They do so in ways that call certain fundamental assumptions of Shakespearean comedy into question. It was like Jonson to reverse Shakespeare's favourite device of the heroine who masquerades as a boy, in doublet and hose, as he does with Epicoene's pretence in *The Silent Woman*, or with Wittipol's disguise as an improbably gigantic Spanish lady in *The Devil is an Ass*. When, in his Elizabethan and Jacobean plays, he does turn transvestism the Shakespearean way round, in Lady Would-Be's mistaken conviction that Peregrine is 'the most cunning curtizan, of *Venice*' (III.5.20) merely posing as a man, or in the corrupt courtier Anaides' habit of forcing his punk Gelaia to wait on him in male attire, as his page, in *Cynthia's Revels*, we seem to be looking at Shakespearean comedy through a distorting glass.

By comparison with his own Elizabethan comedies, let alone with Shakespeare's, Jonson's Jacobean plays are strikingly pessimistic. For all their hilarity, their energy and inventiveness, the view of man and of social relations that they put forward is essentially despairing. And there are no longer any moral arbiters, characters like Justice Clement from *Every Man In His Humour*, or Asper, Crites, and Horace in the Elizabethan comical satires, to affirm the possibility of other and better ways of behaving. And yet it is important to remember that, with time, even Shakespeare seems to have found optimistic comedy difficult to sustain. *Measure For Measure* is Shakespeare's most Jonsonian play. This is so not only because of its urban setting – Vienna is a city that we really do believe in as a surrogate for London – but because the play creates a sense of complex, ineradicable human evil beyond the capacity of its own comic conventions to control. The comedy may end with marriages in the usual Shakespearean way. Apart from the contract between Claudio and Juliet, two people who are given nothing whatever to say to each other in the final scene, none of these unions possesses any emotional reality. It is not even certain that Isabella accepts the Duke. Lucio's wedding is a punishment which he regards as equivalent to whipping and hanging. Angelo has no words of love, or even of ordinary thanks, for Mariana – to whom he owes his life. This is a comedy ending which goes through all the usual Shakespearean motions, but it does so in a way that robs them of vitality and conviction.

Measure For Measure seems to have been the last comedy Shakespeare ever wrote. After it comes an unbroken string of tragedies, halted only by *Pericles* in 1609. And *Pericles* is a very different kind of play. Like its three successors, *Cymbeline*, *The Winter's Tale*, and *The Tempest*, it represents a break with Shakespeare's earlier style so radical as to make the very word *comedy* seem inappropriate as a description. *Romances*, if you like, or *final plays*, but not *comedy*, or at least not in the sense in which we apply that word to *As You Like It* or *A Midsummer Night's Dream*. I want to argue that *Bartholomew Fair* turned out, in a sense, to be Jonson's *Measure for Measure*. With this play, he seems to have arrived at a crisis in the development of his own kind of comedy which parallels the one Shakespeare had experienced some years before, even though the reasons for it were very different.

Most recent critics seem to have agreed that *Bartholomew Fair* displays a tolerance and geniality new in Jonson's work. No one is punished. At the suggestion of Quarlous, they all go home to Justice Overdo's to a feast, and to hear out the remainder of Littlewit's play. This conclusion is certainly not punitive, but neither (as it seems to me) is it very sunny. This off-stage feast may be an improvement on the violent and disordered banquets in *Every Man Out of His Humour*, *Poetaster*, and *The Silent Woman*, but it still falls considerably short of being a Shakespearean 'one feast, one house, one mutual happiness'. (*The Two Gentlemen of Verona* v.4.173). Jonson has simply resigned himself to the fact that human beings are fundamentally ineducable, that appetite and a shared impulse towards aggression – symbolized respectively by the feast and by the knockabout and degradation of the puppet play – are the only things upon which a social order can be realistically based.

I should be prepared to maintain that *Bartholomew Fair* is Jonson's greatest play. Certainly it is his richest and most ambitious. But it was also the end of a road. Unlike Shakespeare, Jonson was a basically accumulative artist, who tended to reuse the same character types and situations in play after play. In *Bartholomew Fair*, he finally managed to get his entire comic world, painstakingly assembled over a period of years, on stage at once, to make a grand culminating statement. This is a play which stretches the capacities of Jonson's own achieved comic form to the breaking point. With well over thirty speaking parts, an enormous number for a Renaissance comedy, it maintains the most delicate balance between order and chaos, between structure and a seemingly undisciplined flow which is like the random, haphazard nature of life itself. All the world's a Fair, Jonson seems to be saying, and all the men and women merely angry children, even those like Winwife and Quarlous, Grace and Justice Overdo, who begin by regarding themselves as rational, superior beings in a society of thieves and zanies. Jonson aimed here at an inclusiveness he had never sought before. The result is brilliant, but it precipitated him into artistic bankruptcy.

Jonson's next play, *The Devil is an Ass*, two years later in 1616, reveals just how crippling an overdraft was incurred by *Bartholomew Fair*. An astonishing amount of this comedy reworks earlier Jonsonian material. Indeed, it might almost be subtitled 'The Further Adventures of Face and Subtle'. Except that here they happen to be called Merecraft and Engine, and they have obviously been listening,

at some point, to the ravings of Sir Politic Would-Be. The situation of
Fitzdottrel's wife, jealously mewed up at one moment by her
appalling husband, forced by him in the next into the presence of her
aspiring lover – all in the interests of financial gain – derives from
that of Corvino's Celia. There are two gallants in *The Devil is an Ass*,
just as there were in *Bartholomew Fair* – Wittipol and Manly – and
Wittipol repeats the ruse of Epicoene by getting himself up in female
attire and mingling with another collegiate society of absurd and
corrupt ladies. Guilt-head and his son Plutarchus, the careful citizen
and the young man nourishing aristocratic ambitions, are versions of
Sordido and Fungoso from *Every Man Out*, while Fitzdottrel himself
combines the specific vices of Epicure Mammon, Corvino, and Politic
Would-Be. At the end, he simulates diabolic possession in the manner
of the advocate in *Volpone*. Even the words of this comedy often sound
strikingly familiar. Wittipol, wooing Fitzdottrel's wife by her own
husband's agreement, tells her bluntly that 'you are the wife, / To so
much blasted flesh, as scarce hath soule, / In stead of salt, to keepe it
sweete' (1.6.88–90). In *Bartholomew Fair*, Edgeworth had said just this
of Cokes: 'talke of him to have a soule? 'heart, if hee have any more
then a thing given him in stead of salt, onely to keepe him from
stinking, I'le be hang'd afore my time' (IV.2.54–6). Wittipol merely
gives us a verse restatement of Edgeworth's original joke.

The Devil is an Ass is compulsively repetitive of earlier work, as
Jonson himself must have known. And yet it also strikes out bravely
in some new and unexpected directions. Mistress Fitzdottrel, for
instance, is the first woman in a Jonson comedy who can fairly be
described as a heroine. She is beautiful, intelligent, passionate, and
chaste. Significantly, the name 'Fitzdottrel' does not fit her at all –
in the way that 'Otter' or 'Would-Be', earlier, had accurately
described both husband and wife. It is simply another degradation
imposed upon her by her ghastly spouse. In exploring the hell of her
marriage and the strength of her temptation to accept Wittipol as a
lover, Jonson treats Mistress Fitzdottrel with sympathy and respect.
For the first time, he enters the precincts of romantic love – the area
central to Shakespearean comedy, but left untouched in his previous
plays. His means of entry is unusual. Mistress Fitzdottrel is a married
woman, not a maiden. There can be no question of cancelling her
wedding vows and uniting her with Wittipol, the man of sense and
feeling who values her for what she is. But it matters that Jonson
should take her predicament seriously, that he should lament the

waste of so much feminine intelligence, as well as youth and beauty, on a fool. And that we should care, as we did not care about the future of Celia at the end of *Volpone*.

In exploring the Wittipol/Mistress Fitzdottrel situation, Jonson also took his first steps in the direction of a Shakespearean attitude towards play-acting and illusion. When Wittipol discovers that because of her promise to her husband, the lady cannot utter a word in reply to his lovesuit, he adroitly proceeds to change places with her, to impersonate her, and say in her imagined person what he hopes she is thinking and feeling. The result is startling. For a time, Mistress Fitzdottrel behaves as though the real woman has agreed to feel and be guided by the sentiments her imitation has expressed. The theatre dictates to life, not because it is an agent of deceit, as it was in the hands of performers like Volpone, Face, or, in this play, Merecraft the projector, but because it has uncovered a hidden, emotional truth. It was an idea Jonson was to return to and greatly elaborate, years later, when he wrote *The New Inn*.

For the moment, however, he showed no signs of wanting to build on *The Devil is an Ass*. I said at the beginning of this essay that the Jonson who talked to Drummond in 1618 may well have decided to abandon the public stage. He was busy as a masque writer, of course, but he had never found it difficult before to occupy himself both with royal entertainments and with the theatre. I think myself that he turned away from the stage for a whole decade because he could not see his way artistically after *The Devil is an Ass*, could not resolve the problem he had tackled there for the first time: that of forging a new comic style. Shakespeare, in a similar situation, had turned to tragedy. But Jonson had no real gift in this line. *Sejanus* is a very interesting play, but its real value seems to me to lie in the fact that Jonson was able to work through it to *Volpone*, that it was the means by which he broke out of that first, and far less acute, comedic perplexity which assailed him after *Poetaster*. *Sejanus* mediates between the comical satires and Jonson's greater and more sombre Jacobean plays. *Catiline*, on the other hand, does not stand in this kind of relationship to its immediate successor, *Bartholomew Fair*. Nor is it in itself a work which suggests that even if audiences had liked it, which they conspicuously did not, Jonson had an untapped tragic potential left him to explore.

After his return from Scotland, Jonson engaged himself in a host of literary activities. He, after all, unlike Shakespeare, was not dependent upon 'public means which public manners breeds' (Sonnet III). Or not for a while. Then King James died, and Jonson, a man who could not establish with Charles I the relationship he had enjoyed with his father, found himself once again obliged to write for the theatres. His financial position was habitually insecure and, after a stroke left him partially paralysed in 1628, it steadily became worse. It is tempting to wonder, indeed, how often Shakespeare, that solid citizen of Stratford, may have advised his friend to cut his expenditure on books and wine, invest in a sound country property and a parcel of tithes, and generally defend himself in a good, bourgeois way against the realities of old age. If he did, Jonson did not listen. Having no real choice in the matter, he returned to confront an artistic issue he would probably have preferred to avoid: that of a new style in comedy.

Shakespeare himself, when he stood at this same crossroad some years before, had reached back to those traditional dramatic forms with which his own art had always had a basic affinity. *Pericles* deliberately summons up the rambling, episodic plays of the early Elizabethan period: gallimaufries like *Sir Clyomon and Sir Clamydes*, *The Cobbler's Prophecy*, or the original *Mucedorus*. Jonson, understandably, turned at first to a different but equally obsolete form: morality drama. The young Jonson had ostensibly scorned these plays, even as Shakespeare had once felt free to mock the old romances in the Pyramus and Thisbe interlude of *A Midsummer Night's Dream*, but they lay close, all the same, to Jonson's particular temperament and way of seeing. In trying to make a fresh start in comedy, both men began by resurrecting one specific part of their dramatic inheritance: romance and the morality play, respectively. The impulse was similar, and so were some of the consequences.

Here again, *The Devil is an Ass*, with its subplot concerning the adventures of that much put-upon junior demon Pug during his one day's holiday from Hell, had already pointed the way. But *The Staple of News* in 1626, Jonson's first Caroline comedy, is even more completely and anachronistically a morality play. In telling the familiar story of the prodigal son, Jonson employed an outworn Elizabethan dramatic device in the disguise of Penniboy Canter, the father who feigns his own death and then takes service with his son and heir in order to see 'if power change purpose', and 'what our seemers be' (*Measure for Measure* 1.3.54). Jonson had mocked Justice Overdo when he did something similar in *Bartholomew Fair*. But there is no mockery of Penniboy Canter, even as there is none of the two moral conversions (that of the prodigal himself and of the Canter's miserly elder brother) with which the comedy ends. The scepticism which served to undercut the earlier reformations of Kitely and Sordido has no place in *The Staple of News*. Nor does there seem to be any irony about the fact that the Prologue for the court performance takes the very unexpected form, for Jonson, of a Sidneian sonnet.

When Jonson returned to the stage in 1626, both he and the world around him were much changed. He himself was significantly older. He had arrived at that time of life when men are naturally tempted to review their own past, to re-evaluate and assess the opinions and experiences of their youth. In Jonson's case, this tendency can only have been reinforced by the crippling paralysis which confined him to his lodgings, with time on his hands, and, as he outlived his old friends one by one, an ever-diminishing number of visitors. Secondly, in 1623, Heminge and Condell had produced Shakespeare's plays in Folio. Jonson had edited his own plays in Folio seven years before, an enterprise which must have encouraged them. He may have helped Shakespeare's fellow shareholders in their task in ways that went beyond the two poems he contributed to the volume: 'To the Reader' and 'To the Memory of My Beloved, The Author Mr William Shakespeare and what He Hath Left Us'. The impact of those thirty-six Shakespeare plays, eighteen of them never printed before, standing together to confront him as the completed work of a friend whose art he had criticized, but the importance of which he had always conceded, must have been enormous. The consequences, as I have argued elsewhere (*English Literary Renaissance* 9 (1979) 395–418), first declare themselves in *The New Inn*, Jonson's second Caroline play. Here, in 1629 – an ageing dramatist, 'sick, and sad', as he describes himself in the epilogue – he turned away from morality drama to re-think the premises of Shakespearean comedy: in effect, to come to terms with its attitudes and, up to a point, make them his own. Moreover, this impulse is one that perpetuated itself in Jonson's last three Caroline plays: *The Magnetic Lady* (1632), *A Tale of a Tub* (1633), and *The Sad Shepherd*, the pastoral that Jonson left unfinished at the time of his death in 1637.

But it was not only sickness, the inclination of old men to reminisce, or the Shakespeare First Folio that impelled Jonson into what was really a kind of belated Elizabethanism. It was also a spirit abroad in the air around him, one that had been steadily gathering force since the early years of James's reign. Bishop Goodman, himself an apologist for King James, nevertheless found himself obliged to record the fact that although England at the end of Queen Elizabeth's life was

generally weary of an old woman's government...after a few years, when we had experience of the Scottish government, then in disparagement of the Scots, and in hate and detestation of them, the Queen did seem to revive; then was her memory much magnified, – such ringing of bells, such public joy and sermons in commemoration of her, the picture of her tomb painted in many churches, and in effect more solemnity and joy in memory of her coronation than was for the coming in of King James.[4]

In the latter years of James's reign, and throughout that of his successor, more or less hagiographic accounts of the life of the great queen – often concealing a savage, implied comparison with the failures of the Stuart regime – poured from the press. The legend of Good Queen Bess's golden days, a legend containing a good deal of distortion and exaggeration, as such legends usually do, had been unleashed. In the end, it would bear a certain amount of responsibility for sweeping King Charles from his throne.

The whole question of late Jacobean and Caroline nostalgia for the reign of Elizabeth is immensely complex, and one that modern historians of the period are only now beginning to explore. For a number of reasons I cannot consider it at any length here. But it does seem to me important to remember that this attitude took literary, as well as political, forms. Revivals of old, seemingly outmoded Elizabethan plays – many of them at court – including the plays of William Shakespeare, are a feature of the 1630s. Moreover, two of Jonson's oldest and closest friends, Sir Robert Cotton (d. 1631), and William Camden (d. 1623), Jonson's former master at Westminster School, the man to whom he said he owed 'All that I am in arts, all that I know' (*Epigrammes*, XIIII. 'To William Camden', line 2), both moved, near the end of their lives, towards the conviction that Elizabeth, not James, had in fact been the Augustus Caesar of Britain, and her reign a direct parallel to the Golden Age of Rome. It was an opinion shared by Newcastle, Jonson's last patron.

Jonson had always been fascinated by classical myths of a golden age. They turn up again and again in his masques and plays. Ironically, during the last and (on the whole) fairly sour and disillusioned years of Elizabeth's reign, he had actually written a

[4] Godfrey Goodman, *The Court of King James the First*, 2 vols. (London, 1839), I, p. 9.

comedy about the Rome of Augustus. *Poetaster*, with its final establishment of the good poet Horace and the consummately great poet Virgil as acknowledged legislators of mankind, ruling side by side with a just and enlightened emperor, had fairly obviously been intended in 1600 as a contrast to the sorry state of affairs in the England of Elizabeth. At this time, Dekker identified Horace, the satiric poet newly elevated into favour and importance by Caesar at the end, as a flattering self-portrait of Jonson himself. He was right. *Poetaster* was the wish-dream of a disgruntled Jonson acutely conscious that this was not, in fact, the position he occupied in Elizabeth's court, and disinclined to see any connection between either the political or the literary splendours of the classical Rome he venerated and a degenerate contemporary world. But the whirligig of time brought in, if not exactly his revenges, at least a radical recon- sideration of the recent past. Jonson was by no means the only old man who discovered during the decade of the 1630s, as the Puritans gathered strength, that he had actually lived in the Golden Age, without knowing it at the time.

I do not want to push Jonson's late change of heart too far. He associated himself with Horace in *Poetaster* but he would never, not even in his last years, have been able to recognize that the Virgil of the play was really William Shakespeare. Indeed, a late but persuasive tradition recorded by Gildon and Rowe has the old Jonson still arguing grumpily with Suckling and Davenant about the impurity of Shakespeare's art. That was only to be expected. What one could not have predicted were Jonson's four last plays, and the new understanding not only of Elizabethan literature but, more especially, the spirit of Shakespearean comedy that breathes through them all.

In *Bartholomew Fair*, back in 1614, Jonson had for the first time given English literature the role hitherto fulfilled in his comedies by the Greek and Roman classics. When Quarlous selects the name 'Argalus', the knight of true and self-sacrificing love, from Sidney's *Arcadia*, and Winwife chooses 'Palemon', from Chaucer's 'Knight's Tale', as the words to be inscribed in Mistress Grace's table-book, the two men inadvertently damn themselves. The names are talismanic, summoning up stories in which love and friendship were difficult, demanding ideals but untainted by financial or prudential considera- tions. The contrast implied between the mutually distrustful fortune- hunting of Quarlous and Winwife, the cold, detached attitude of

Grace Wellborn, and the passionate loyalty and commitment of Argalus and his lady Parthenia, Palemon, Arcite, and Emily is devastating. Moreover, when he came to the puppet play at the end of *Bartholomew Fair*, Jonson rubbed the judgement in. Here he used *Damon and Pithias*, an early Elizabethan play by Richard Edwards, and Marlowe's great poem 'Hero and Leander' as the paradigms, works of art commenting not only upon Littlewit's travesty of them, but also upon the corresponding debasement of love and friendship in Quarlous, Winwife, and Grace. It is the memory of Edwards, Sidney, Marlowe, Fletcher, and Shakespeare, far more than the Ciceronian maxims so piously mouthed by Justice Overdo, which effectively mock the triumph of appetite and aggression at the Fair.

Jonson's four final plays, *The New Inn*, *The Magnetic Lady*, *A Tale of a Tub*, and *The Sad Shepherd*, carry this kind of Elizabethan nostalgia to a much further extreme. Significantly, three of the four have country settings. *The Magnetic Lady*, as Jonson is at pains to point out in his introduction, actually goes back and rewrites the humour plays of his youth. In doing so, it transforms a brand of comedy originally dedicated to judgement and destruction into one of reconciliation and accord. As for *A Tale of a Tub*, a play apparently set around 1560, early in the reign of the Virgin Queen, it is so filled with archaic words and constructions and with an outmoded early Elizabethan verse that Jonson's Oxford editors were impelled, despite its late position in the posthumous Folio of 1640, to argue for it as a misplaced piece of juvenilia: a play written even before *Every Man In His Humour* and hastily revised by the elderly Jonson to accommodate a satire on Inigo Jones. This early dating was attacked sharply, and I think entirely rightly, by W. W. Greg. In fact, *A Tale of a Tub*, with its fresh, country world, its entirely affectionate handling of a collection of positively Shakespearean local rustics (most of them nostalgically obsessed with parish records, genealogies, and the history of their community) could only have been written in Jonson's last years. The play's linguistic archaisms can be matched in *The Sad Shepherd* and in the two late entertainments commissioned by Newcastle, and only there. It looks very much as though the man who once girded at Spenser because 'in affecting the Ancients, [he] writ no language', came at the end of his life to do exactly this himself.

Although *The New Inn* uses two lines from John Donne's 'The Calme', a poem written during the Essex expedition of 1597, as the pivot upon which its fifth act turns, the spirit which informs it throughout is Shakespearean. The hostelry of The Light Heart at Barnet, among the fields, is a place to which people journey, leaving the city behind them, and in which they are transformed, a place that is heightened and extraordinary. The agents of transformation are twofold: romantic love and theatre. I claimed earlier that for the younger Jonson play-acting and deceit were almost always the weapons of imposters, not ways of discovering truth. In *The New Inn* this is no longer so. The comedy adopts a positively Shakespearean view of the imagination. Something odd, too, has happened to the usual Jonsonian charactonyms or 'speaking names' – names like Politic Would-Be, Fastidious Brisk, or Volpone – which had tended to fix and define characters, depriving them of the freedom and flexibility that most of Shakespeare's people inherit with their more neutral names. In the high plot, they have either vanished, or they are names like Lovell and Frampull, possessing two possible meanings, into the positive one of which the character moves in the course of the action. These are people capable of change.

If the multiple discoveries of the last act of *The New Inn* are odd – the revelation that the supposed son of the Host, who has been acting the part of a girl called Laetitia in the revels, really *is* a girl and called Laetitia, or that a husband and wife estranged and separated from each other for years have both been living under the same roof all along without recognizing one another – they are no more implausible than the events of the final scene of *Cymbeline* or *The Winter's Tale*. Certainly Jonson handles these ostentatiously fictional consonances in an intensely Shakespearean way. Dryden dismissed *The New Inn* and all the rest of Jonson's late plays as 'dotages'.[5] And the appellation, unfortunately, has stuck. But then it used to be common to denigrate *Pericles*, *Cymbeline*, *The Winter's Tale*, and *The Tempest* as the products of Shakespeare's boredom and creative decline in his last years. The last plays of Jonson, like the last plays of Shakespeare, are extreme and difficult works of art. They do not readily yield up their secrets. They constitute a remarkable achievement all the same, and one sorely in need of sympathetic reassessment. Quite as much as the commendatory verses to the Shakespeare First Folio, they can stand as Jonson's real tribute to the man whose different kind of art had both infuriated and haunted him for so long.

[5] John Dryden, *An Essay of Dramatick Poesie*, in *The Works of John Dryden*, xvii, ed. S. H. Monk and A. E. W. Maurer (Berkeley, 1971), p. 57.

CHAPTER 14

London comedy and the ethos of the city
(1979)

More than any other form of art, drama depends upon the city. Whatever its distant, prehistoric origins in vegetation myths and country festivals, the theatre in its developed forms is essentially an urban phenomenon. Unlike music and painting, the novel, architecture or poetry, drama has always sought out the city as its proper home. And the bigger the city in proportion to its satellite towns, the better. Once established in the metropolis, drama gathers strength from what it recognizes as its native soil. Artistically, it becomes more interesting and important. It also becomes extremely difficult to kill, even with the help of plague and political revolution, as the Puritans and the city magistrates of sixteenth- and seventeenth-century London were to discover.

The affinity between drama and the city is both a classical and a Renaissance fact. It is not hard to explain. Other arts can survive quite nicely with an audience of one person, provided that this patron is sufficiently rich, reasonably intelligent, and doesn't become bored. Drama cannot. Even the rarefied form of the Jacobean and Caroline masque, visually accommodated and explicitly addressed to the monarch, also requires a hall packed with courtiers and other hangers-on if it is to succeed. Although the city doesn't always, at least it can provide a large, permanent audience in a way the country cannot. The components of this urban audience will be both changing and fundamentally continuous. This means that the actors, no longer wearisomely peripatetic, can settle down to the important task of training a body of spectators to interpret the increasingly complex shorthand of performance. An experienced audience can be taught to respond to those evolving conventions and techniques without which drama is condemned to presenting only a static and oversimplified abstract of reality. It matters, too, that in the city, drama can afford to build a house of its own; a permanent theatre designed for this purpose, as an inn-yard, a banqueting hall or a village green are not. A specialized building of this kind can and will incorporate a visual and spatial symbolism which supports and enriches the two hour's traffic of the stage.

Virtually all the great drama of the world was written for what Walter Pater liked to call 'the pale people of towns'. That being the case, it is surprising how consistently tragedy, as opposed to comedy, has avoided the city as a setting. Exceptions have to be made for two or three Greek plays, and for a few Elizabethan and Jacobean works which focus upon ancient Rome as a complete, urban entity: a tragic city which is also a social microcosm. Usually, however, tragedy has adopted the isolated great house as its territory: sometimes a palace, at others only the envelope which contains a family in trouble. The voice of the city is sometimes heard in or just outside of this enclosure. In *Hamlet*, Claudius fears reprisal from 'the distracted multitude'. Oedipus has to deal with the distracted citizens of Thebes, seeking deliverance from Apollo's plague. But the town is really peripheral to tragedy, not its proper milieu, never the place where our eyes are fixed. Even Troy looks less like a city in Euripides and Shakespeare than it does like a court: an enormous palace encircled by walls where Priam, Hecuba and their doomed children maintain a kind of feudal existence.

Tragedy is perfectly happy to abandon the great house for the country. It will visit the blasted heath, the peaks of the Caucasus, a forest, a deserted island, or the grove of the Furies outside Colonnus. What it emphatically does not want to know about is the market-place, the bourse, the shop-front, or the row of houses facing one another across an Athenian or a London street. Shakespeare gets Othello and Desdemona out of Venice, the big mercantile city, just as fast as his source material will permit. It is on Cyprus, the island across the sea which has virtually no civic character whatever, that the tragedy unfolds. For Shakespeare and his contemporaries, the enmity between tragedy and the city was to be explained, in part, by a misunderstanding of Aristotle. Aristotle had asserted that the characters in tragedy are, or should be, better than average men, and those in comedy, worse. The sixteenth century misinterpreted this statement and believed, as a result, that the distinction between tragedy and comedy (apart from the nature of their endings) was largely one of social class. Tragedy deals with our social betters, comedy with the little people to whom we condescend. This was not what Aristotle had meant in the *Poetics*, but the misreading happened to tie in conveniently with the quite independent medieval opinion that comedy presents familiar images of everyday life, inventing fictional plots and characters, while tragedy is distant, historical, and exalted.

Virtually all cities, even if for various reasons they draw the aristocracy to them, are middle-class creations. They bear the stamp of the middle class, and they are characterized by middle-class values. They also give rise to a coherent lower-class community, whether of slaves, as in ancient Athens, or, in Renaissance London, of apprentices, domestic servants and unskilled artisans. Secure in their misinterpretation of Aristotle, and encouraged by the example of Aristophanes, Plautus and Terence, theorists and dramatists in the sixteenth and seventeenth centuries understandably regarded the city as an appropriate setting for comedy, but not for tragedy. It was not that the metropolis did not produce tragic material. Many of the surviving broadside ballads of the period relate horrific London stories of duplicity, murder and financial ruin of just the kind that the nineteenth-century tragic novel was going to seize upon as its proper territory. Interestingly enough, there is a brand of Elizabethan 'domestic' tragedy which deals with material of this kind, the characters of which are predominantly middle class. But these plays – *Arden of Feversham* (1591), Heywood's *A Woman Killed with Kindness* (1603), or *A Yorkshire Tragedy* (1606) – are almost invariably news flashes from rural parishes and country towns. They are not, by preference, set in London. What Dickens later did for London, Dostoevsky for St Petersburg, and Balzac for Paris, neither Shakespeare nor any of his dramatic contemporaries wanted to do in tragic terms for the city in which they lived and worked.

Tragic drama does not like the city. Comedy, by contrast, has usually insisted that the urban world constitutes its proper sphere. It confronts its audience with a more or less heightened, a fantasized picture, of that audience's own, day-to-day life in a city which, although it often shelters prudently under other names, tends to be recognizable as a version of the one just outside the playhouse door. This fact would be more glaringly obvious than it is if Shakespeare had not chosen to ignore it. Shakespearean comedy has no real descendants, and not a great deal in the way of direct forerunners. Of the sixteen comedies he wrote, including the last plays, only *Measure For Measure*, *The Comedy of Errors*, *The Merry Wives of Windsor* and parts of *The Merchant of Venice* can be described as genuinely urban. Moreover, although he seems to have spent most of his working life in the place, Shakespeare is almost unique among Elizabethan and Jacobean comic dramatists in that he never availed himself of London as a setting. His English histories, as was inevitable, are filled with London scenes. In comedy, on the other hand, Windsor was geographically as close to the metropolis as he could bring himself to come. This is not to deny the occasional whiff of London air in Shakespearean comedy. When Antonio counsels Sebastian, in *Twelfth Night*, that 'in the south suburbs at the Elephant / Is best to lodge' (III.3.39–40), Illyria suddenly looks like London. Momentarily, a town inserts itself into the empty space between two, great aristocratic houses: that of Olivia and of the Duke Orsino. But this is really the kind of exception that proves the rule. Hymen may be the 'god of every town', as we are told at the end of *As You Like It* (V.4.146). Shakespeare's comedies deliberately bypass the teeming life, not only of contemporary London, but of cities generally. They are filled with evasions of the urban. In *A Midsummer Night's Dream*, Bottom and his friends are described as 'hard-handed men that work in Athens here' (V.1.72), but as soon as they open their mouths, it becomes plain that they live in rural Warwickshire, just as it is clear that the palace of Duke Theseus is really a great Elizabethan country house, a Kenilworth or a Hardwick Hall.

Shakespeare's contemporaries reacted differently. Well over one hundred English comedies survive from the period 1580–1642 which explicitly use London as a setting. Obviously, many more have been lost. London offered comic dramatists of the period what Athens had once offered Aristophanes and his successors: the opportunity to superimpose extravagant and blatantly fictional plots upon a contemporary, urban world which the theatre audience could recognize, sometimes street by street, as its own. To elect Cornhill Street, as opposed to Sicily or the Forest of Arden, as a comedy setting was to incur certain problems, but also to reap tangible rewards. The realistic London background established a tension between the ordinary experience of the theatre audience, and the comedy plot, that was different and more specific than in Shakespeare. Comedy, for instance, has always been given to resurrecting the dead. But such unlikely returns acquire a special quality when, instead of making exotic re-appearances as a living statue in Hellenistic Sicily, an abbess in Ephesus, or an unknown veiled bride in the Messina of *Much Ado About Nothing*, characters literally climb out of their coffins in Cheapside, in a house at Crutched Friars, or just behind Charing Cross. This both is and is not London, a world simultaneously familiar and strange.

London comedy takes many different forms, and adopts a variety of different attitudes – not least towards the city which was its subject. All of these plays, however, whether designed for the public or the private theatres, whether respectful or satiric in their treatment of citizens, exploit that curious interweaving of realism with fantasy that was inherent in the genre. Even more important, perhaps, is the fact that all were written in full consciousness of the City's official disapproval. Even when the likeness turned out to be flattering, London's rulers sat unwillingly for their dramatic portrait. Had Queen Elizabeth not happened, personally, to like plays and to want them tried out in public before she saw the best ones herself, the London magistrates would probably have succeeded in suppressing almost all professional dramatic activity within the city at large. There would be no Elizabethan theatre, or at least none of the immense artistic importance of the one that did survive.

London's civic officials do not seem to have discriminated between London comedy and other kinds of drama in their campaign for wholesale abolition of the stage. Regardless of whether they presented Cooke's *The City Gallant* (1611) or *Hamlet*, the theatres were regarded as places of riot and disorder, distracting citizens from divine service, and encouraging apprentices to waste time that could be more profitably spent. This was not only because playhouses attracted dissolute and wicked elements in the urban population, but because the City seems to have believed that people learned from plays how to lie, cheat, blaspheme, fornicate and rob. Acting was dangerous in itself, an encouragement to depart from the path of sincerity and plain dealing, to adopt false faces in real life, not merely on the stage. Comedies actually set in London and dealing with the day-to-day life of the metropolis must have seemed especially perilous in this respect. They could provide practical instruction in urban chicanery and vice as romantic comedy (let alone tragedy) could not. Clearly heightened and fictionalized though they were, the shifts and dodges of a Luke Frugal, a Cocledemoy, a Spendall, Allwit or Quomodo were nonetheless lessons with an immediate, possible application.

It was true that some, if by no means all, of these London plays meticulously discredited and punished their offending characters, no matter how engaging and clever. Comedy, however, is always an unreliable moral ally. Even when it intends to be orthodox and conservative, it is likely to remain subversive at heart: to reveal a covert attachment to wit for its own sake, and for licence rather than restraint. Its attitudes towards money and property, closely scanned, are usually suspect. A conflict between civic and comedic values marks even those plays which set out to celebrate London and its middle-class ethos. They cannot conceal the fact that they are confronted by an artistic dilemma: that the very ethos, as well as the legislation, of the City which they magnify is fundamentally opposed to the things for which comedy, in any age, has always stood.

In *The Politics of Stability: A Portrait of the Rulers in Elizabethan London*, Frank Freeman Foster describes the middle-class ethos of the City, the code which, despite differences of religion (especially at the beginning of Elizabeth's reign), of background, status and wealth, united the men who governed London between 1558 and 1642. Many of the magistrates who ruled London's twenty-six wards had not themselves been born in the City. Once absorbed, however, into its complex political hierarchy in a position of responsibility and power, they formed an exceptionally cohesive and dedicated group. As Foster writes, 'so great was their abiding loyalty to the City and to each other, so deep and reverent their commitment to City politics, that their profoundest religious impulses seem understandable only if viewed as a blending of the civic and the spiritual'.[1] These men gloried in the City's wealth, its eminence as the economic capital of Europe, its ancient customs, and the rights and independence it had wrested gradually from the Crown. If no other European city in the Renaissance developed a drama that could rival the Elizabethan, it was also true that there was no equivalent to London's intricate system of self-rule, or its ethos of life and work, an ethos that seems to have been shared by all of London's rulers, regardless of their particular guilds, investment interests, social background, aims and personalities.

These, however, were the men who banished the theatres, as physical structures, from the limits of the City over which they had immediate jurisdiction and who sought continually to close them

---

[1] Frank Freeman Foster, *The Politics of Stability: A Portrait of the Rulers in Elizabethan London* (London, 1977), p. 5.

down in the suburbs as well, although their power there was only indirect. Even John Stow, who sometimes writes about London as though it were some sort of terrestrial, and specifically English, version of Augustine's City of God, had no use for its drama.[2] Yet, paradoxically, the City needed the drama, not only as a source of entertainment, but in order to give shape and dignity to precisely that ethos of life and work which was so bitterly opposed to drama as a form. The increasing cost and theatrical elaboration of the annual Lord Mayor's Show is instructive in this respect. These shows are inveterately moral: a celebration of the man embarking upon his year of power in the City, but also a caution to him to use that power well. Characteristically, they stage some kind of emblematic contest between virtue and vice, from which the Lord Mayor, with the help of the livery companies, plus his own implied patience and sagacity, emerges victorious. A number of texts for these shows survive, by Dekker, Middleton, Heywood, Anthony Munday and others – precisely the men who were also writing for the wicked professional players out in the suburbs. Shakespeare's name is conspicuously missing from the list. Otherwise, a surprising number of the public theatre playwrights, including Ben Jonson, had a hand in one civic show or more. Moreover, many of them tried to translate the values and preoccupations of these shows into terms suitable for the professional stage. The result was a series of plays which not only honoured London, but set out to explain the City and its ethos to itself.

Thomas Heywood wrote civic pageants. He was also the probable author of the two parts of *Edward IV*, a history play of about 1599. In Part I, rebels against the Crown pour into London from the country, and are successfully resisted by the City acting in concert, from the Lord Mayor down through the aldermen and liverymen, to those apprentices who 'doe great service', according to Heywood's stage direction, in repelling the assault on the City gates. The aldermen and guildsmen are perfectly aware that these apprentices have far less to lose, should the City be taken, than their masters. This is why they remind them, shrewdly, that 'you may come to be as we are now'.[3] Looked at properly, the wealth of the City concerns them as much as it does their elders. Heywood lays heavy stress upon the treasure of

---

[2] John Stow, *Survey of London*, edited by Charles Kingsford, 2 vols. (Oxford, 1971), I, pp. xl–xli.
[3] *1 Edward IV*, in *The Dramatic Works of John Heywood*, edited by R. H. Shepherd, 6 vols. (London, 1874), I, p. 17.

London. Ostensibly, the country rebels are Lancastrians, men seeking
the release of Henry VI from the Tower, and his re-establishment on
the throne. This motive, however, is really secondary. What their
leader Falconbridge dangles before their eyes is the dazzling
possibility that, once London is taken, they may 'ride in triumph
thorough *Cheape* to *Pauls* / The *Mint* is ours, *Cheape, Lombard Street,*
our own; / The meanest soldier wealthier than a king'.[4] The lines are
adapted quite deliberately from one of the most celebrated speeches
of Marlowe's Tamburlaine:

> Is it not brave to be a King, *Techelles?*
> *Usumcasane* and *Theridimas,*
> Is it not passing brave to be a King,
> And ride in triumph through *Persepolis?*[5]

Heywood did not expect his audience to smile. Marlowe's Persepolis
has found its equivalent in Cheapside and Paul's, in a London of
velvet, satins and silks, quite as fabulous in its way as any city of the
East, where 'chains of gold and plate shall be as plenty / As wooden
dishes in the wild of *Kent*'.[6]

Like Shakespeare's histories, *Edward IV* plays off London against
the Court. This City, however, is not only a far larger and more
carefully defined entity than Falstaff's Eastcheap, or Cade's Blackheath: it is the true hero of the play. Edward himself, in Part I, is a
tardy and blameworthy king who arrives too late to help the citizens
defend London. They are victorious without him, and he must
apologize for what he admits to be his 'slackness in such urgent
need'.[7] All Edward can do is instantly to knight the Lord Mayor, the
alderman Josselin, and the Recorder of London for their services. He
then attempts to knight a man who is not yet a City dignitary, but
who has distinguished himself during the day by his forethought and
valour in her defence: Matthew Shore, a goldsmith. Politely but
firmly, Shore declines this honour. He does so because he feels it is not
right that he, an ordinary liveryman, should be 'advanc'd with
Aldermen, / With our Lord Mair, and our right grave Recorder'.[8]
There is, in other words, an independent City hierarchy which royal
command cannot cancel out. For Shore to accept a knighthood

---

[4] *Ibid.,* 26.
[5] *1 Tamburlaine,* in *The Complete Works of Christopher Marlowe,* edited by Fredson Bowers, 2nd
edn (Cambridge, 1981), II.5.51–4.   [6] Heywood, *Edward IV,* 10.   [7] *Ibid.,* p. 32.
[8] *Ibid.,* p. 33.

would be to suggest that the king's power could level the distinctions accepted in the City. Reluctantly, Edward admits defeat:

> Well, be it as thou wilt; some other way
> We will devise to quittance they deserts,
> And not to faile therein, upon my word.[9]

The words are heavily ironic. Later, at the feast which the City gives to honour Edward IV and the victory that has been won for him, the king falls in love with Shore's wife. He seeks her out in her husband's shop, the Pelican, in Lombard Street. After a brief struggle, she consents to become his mistress, and to leave the City for the Court.

Shore's place of business is not idly named. Just before that ill-omened feast at which Edward first beheld Jane Shore, the Lord Mayor had recalled his own past history. An orphan, abandoned in infancy, he was found by a shoemaker near Cow Cross in Islington, brought up in one of the civic hospitals of London, and then bound apprentice to a grocer. When he rose to power in London, he not only rewarded the citizen who found him, but became the benefactor both of the charitable institution in which he was reared and of the City which taught him a trade. His whole life has been one of grateful return for debts he is glad to acknowledge. Edward IV is also a man deeply obliged to the City. Instead of honouring these obligations, he betrays them by seducing the wife of one of those citizens whose efforts actually kept him on his throne. The pelican is, of course, a symbol of tragic self-sacrifice, associated with Christ himself. According to the bestiaries, it tears open its own breast to nourish its young with its heart-blood, and patiently endures the pain until it dies. Shore does something like this for a king who is about as grateful as were the original beneficiaries of the Crucifixion. The goldsmith does not rage against the adulterous Edward. He does not even revile his former wife Jane – who, in any case, is crushed by a sense of her own guilt, a guilt she tries vainly to expiate by service to the poor of the City. He simply goes on living, a cuckold at whom it is impossible to laugh, in whom patience declares its affinity with the divine. When, at the end of Part II, Edward's dynasty is swept away as though it had never been, this judgment upon his wife and children seems to stem less from any curse on the house of York than from Edward's own violation of trust and family ties in the City. Both Shore, the patient man, and the wife he symbolically re-marries in

---

[9] *Ibid.*, p. 33.

the new reign of Richard III die at the end of Part II. Heywood, however, leaves one in no doubt that the values of the City, especially as exemplified in Matthew Shore, have triumphed over the Court and its essential selfishness.

Although it has moments of comedy throughout, *Edward IV* is really a history play with tragic overtones. As such, it is not only safely distanced in time, but able to keep potentially disruptive comic elements subordinated to the overall pattern. Patience, after all, however highly prized in the City, is not really a virtue with which comedy has much affinity. Efforts to celebrate it in London comedy as a masculine attribute usually run into difficulties or contradiction. This is ultimately true even of the Dekker and Middleton two-part collaboration *The Honest Whore* (1604–5), although it certainly represents one of the most ingenious attempts. The oxymoron of the title and the final repentance and reintegration into respectable society of the heroine probably outraged conservative members of the audience, despite the fact that Bellafront's trials and sufferings before she can be declared 'honest' make the legendary tribulations of Griselda seem slight. Her patience is underpinned, however, in the sub-plot by that of the linen-draper Candido, in whom it appears as a quintessentially civic virtue.

Candido is so imperturbable and calm that courtiers actually seek him out in the City in order to try and vex him, with wagers laid on the outcome. Commercially, this citizen adheres to an extreme version of the belief that the customer is always right. This allows him, when a provoking gallant insists upon having one pennyworth of lawn cut out of the exact centre of a piece of cloth worth twenty pounds, to remark calmly:

> We are set heere to please all customers,
> Their humours and their fancies: – offend none:
> We get by many, if we leese by one.
> May be his minde stood to no more then that,
> A penworth serves him, and mongst trades tis found,
> Deny a pennorth, it may crosse a pound.
> Oh, he that meanes to thrive, with patient eye
> Must please the divell, if he come to buy.[10]

When the gentlemen push the joke further, and steal his best silver-gilt goblet, Candido has the law on them. He retrieves his property,

---

[10] *1 The Honest Whore*, in *The Dramatic Works of Thomas Dekker*, edited by Fredson Bowers, 4 vols. (Cambridge, 1953–61), I.5.121–8.

and then refuses to prosecute. They did it, as he points out quite accurately, as a joke.

Candido is an alderman, and one who takes his duties seriously. His wife hopes to infuriate him at last by locking up the gown he ought to wear to the meeting at the Guildhall and throwing away the key. Candido sighs, but then carefully cuts a hole for his head in his best velvet table-cloth, and goes off to attend the civic meeting in what is at least an approximation of the required dress. At the end of Part I, this almost inhuman equability gets Candido committed to Bedlam as a lunatic. The Duke who releases him suggests that he must surely have learned by now that the man who cannot be angered by any wrong is a fool. Candido smartly puts the aristocrat right. Patience, he points out, is of all virtues 'neerst kin to heaven'. Christ was not only the archetypal patient man but 'the first true Gentle Man that ever breathd'.[11] Floored by this social comment, the Duke can only beg Candido to come to Court, and to teach that Court how, truly, to shine.

Although he never strays from London, or from the ordinary routine of his shop, his guild, and his civic duties in his ward, Candido is a hero. The trouble is that it is impossible, even while recognizing this fact, not to sympathize with the wife and the courtiers who are maddened by this curiously commercial brand of saintliness. Candido is an absolutist, and comedy does not like absolutists. He has carried a recognized virtue to the point of eccentricity, as the sub-title of *The Honest Whore* ('The Humours of the Patient Man') seems to admit. Moreover, although Dekker and Middleton found that the subject of the converted whore was one that provided them with ample material for a second play, Candido in Part II is a distinct embarrassment. There is almost nothing further to be said about him. As a vital quality, the patience which has defined his character is transferred by the dramatists to the former harlot, now decently but extremely unhappily married. This particular situation is one with which comedy has always found it easy to deal. Bellafront's lurid past may be unusual. Her sufferings in marriage, and eventual triumph, link her with the archetypal Griselda, with Greene's forsaken Dorothea in *James IV* (1590), or Shakespeare's Helena in *All's Well That Ends Well*. Even more important, she becomes the sister of a host of other heroines in London comedy: Mistress Arthur

---

[11] *Ibid.*, v.2.495, 499.

in *How a Man May Choose a Good Wife From a Bad* (1602), Luce in *The London Prodigall* (1604) and her namesake in Heywood's *The Wise Woman of Hogsdon* (1604), or the prodigal's wife in Rowley's *A New Wonder, a Woman Never Vexed* (1625). Patience, in all these women, is hailed as exceptional, but it is also time-honoured and familiar comic material: the agent of the happy ending.

In Nathan Field's London comedy, *A Woman is a Weathercock* (1609), a private theatre play belonging to the Children of the Queen's Revels at Whitefriars, the citizen Strange seals his admission to the ranks of the gentry by losing his patience. Both he and his new wife know that the aspersions cast upon her chastity by a disappointed suitor of her own class are false. Strange is disinclined, this being the case, to fight. But Kate, his bride, has other ideas:

> 'Tis thy best course to fight: if thou be'st still,
> And like an honest tradesman eat'st this wrong,
> O, may thy spirit and thy state so fall,
> Thy first-born child may come to the hospital.[12]

Strange accepts this counsel, overcomes the nefarious Captain Pouts in Lambeth Fields, and forces him to a public confession of his slanders. At the end, Strange announces proudly, 'I consecrate my deed unto the city.'[13] Paradoxically, it is precisely because of this action that the City can no longer contain him. He has adopted the ethos of another class, even as the aspiring citizen Spendall does in Cooke's *The City Gallant* when he refuses to pocket up a wrong but, as 'the highest-spirited citizen / That ever Guildhall took notice of', calls his opponent into the field.[14] Spendall later repents, in prison, of the activities implied by his name, but the very raffish and improvident qualities which have landed him in the Counter prove to be his salvation. They attract the (essentially sexual) attention of a rich and beautiful widow, who marries him.

Like *The Honest Whore*, *The City Gallant* was a public theatre play. It must have nourished the fantasies of many a discontented young apprentice in the audience, but it was certainly not intended as a satire on the City. (Neither, for that matter, was *A Woman is a Weathercock*.) The fact was that in comic terms, the behaviour of a Strange or a Spendall was much easier to handle dramatically than the civic virtue of Candido. In Part II, despite all the associations with

---

[12] *A Woman is a Weathercock*, in *A Select Collection of Old English Plays*, edited by Robert Dodsley, with additions by W. Carew Hazlitt, 15 vols. (London, 1874–6), XI, p. 40.
[13] *Ibid.*, p. 85.   [14] *The City Gallant*, in Dodsley, XI, p. 232.

Christ and with a middle-class, commercial ideal, Candido's self-
effacing male patience becomes increasingly peculiar and strained.
Dekker and Middleton themselves seem to recognize this. They
finally permit Candido to lose his temper, and even to threaten to
strike his second, shrewish wife. Thereafter, his demonstrations of
imperturbability are oddly mechanical, and even harsh. He comes
across in the second play less like a model Christian than as a celebrity
with a role to maintain in the City: a man whose calculated patience
becomes the weapon he turns against arrogant courtiers in order to
win points in the class struggle. There is sarcasm, and a sense of
conscious superiority, in the words he addresses to the wanton
gentlemen who have ripped a piece of his best cambric to shreds:
'Thanke you Gentlemen, / I use you well, pray know my shop
agen'.[15] The Candido of Part II is a poseur more than a saint. This
does not seem to be a logical development of the original character.
It looks more like a confession on the part of Dekker and Middleton
that, whatever the situation in real life, in comedy patience is
properly a woman's virtue.

In *The Knight of the Burning Pestle*, a private theatre play of about
1607, Francis Beaumont created a parody confrontation between
comedy and the ethos of the City. George and Nell, the obstreperous
member of the grocer's guild and his wife, clamber onto the stage at
the beginning to protest against a comedy called 'The London
Merchant'. They are convinced it will gird at citizens and abuse the
City. As it happens, their fears are unfounded. 'The London
Merchant', insofar as they allow it to be performed at all, is a
perfectly neutral 'public theatre' play about a virtuous apprentice,
Jasper, whose only sin lies in the fact that he returns the love of his
master's daughter. As Jasper and his Luce struggle through various
trials and setbacks to an eventual happy outcome, Nell and George
consistently produce the wrong reactions. Not only do they not like
'The London Merchant', they reject all the conventions and
ordinary assumptions of comedy which it embodies. The grocer and
his wife positively like misers and penny-pinchers. A foolish suitor
who woos Luce with grotesque mercantile imagery, and insists upon
telling her not only the brand name but the price of the gloves he

---

[15] *2 The Honest Whore*, III.3.122–3. This comedy cautiously claims to be set in Milan. Its street-
names, landmarks and institutions, however (Bedlam, Bridewell, and so on) are unequivocally those of Elizabethan London.

gives her ('They cost me three and two pence, or no money') is 'e'en the kindest young man that ever trod on shoe leather'.[16] They are deeply disappointed that it should be the generous and romantic Jasper who wins the girl, as opposed to this booby. They also disapprove of comic indulgence in food and drink. Jasper's father Merrythought is, indeed, an extreme version of the insouciant and egotistic sensualist so beloved by comic dramatists from the time of Aristophanes: an elderly *enfant terrible* who constitutes a parody of an immemorial comic type. It is true that, in Merrythought, Beaumont has pushed Philocleon, Udall's Merrygreke, and Shakespeare's Falstaff to an extreme, as though consciously experimenting with the comic tolerance of a theatre audience larger and considerably more sophisticated than George and Nell. That, however, scarcely explains the positive ardour with which the two turn from him to embrace the cause of Mistress Merrythought, the old reprobate's dour, skinflint wife, and her pusillanimous younger son.

As George and Nell continue to produce responses to the plot of 'The London Merchant' that are consistently perverse, a kind of shadow play – an inverted comedy – seems to take form behind the one actually being staged. In this play, money is far more important than true love, thrift than generosity. Laughter is suspect, and so are most forms of pleasure except that to be derived from inspecting the contents of the till. Powerful individualism is a doubtful commodity, certainly inferior to self-effacing and sober common sense. Interestingly enough, possessed by a spirit of fun, George Chapman, Ben Jonson and John Marston had actually written the anti-comedy George and Nell want to see a few years before. *Eastward Ho!* (1605), for the Children of the Queen's Revels, is a meticulous, if tongue-in-cheek, exposition of the ethos of the City which ends up by demonstrating how awful civic virtue is. Quicksilver, the mercurial bad apprentice, with his whore, his extravagance, his social ambitions and hoard of exotic quotations from plays, is actually rather attractive. He ends up, however, in prison and in a state of miserable and distinctly overdone repentance. His fellow apprentice Golding, on the other hand, a man whose very marriage is a prudent business transaction, and who even shies away prudishly from the indulgence of a wedding supper, bids fair at the end of the play to become 'one o' the Monuments of our Citty'. Taken into the livery of his company

---

[16] *The Knight of the Burning Pestle*, ed. Sheldon P. Zitner, Revels Series (Manchester, 1984), I, pp. 152, 202–3.

on the first day of this freedom, subsequently chosen commoner and
alderman's deputy with unprecedented speed, Golding evokes
rapturous prognostications as to 'the reward of a thrifty course'. His
father-in-law Touchstone can envisage a day when

> thou and thy Actes become the Posies for Hospitals, when thy name shall be
> written upon Conduits, and thy deeds playid i' thy life time, by the best
> companies of Actors, and be call'd their *Get-peny*. This I divine. This I
> Prophecie.[17]

Golding himself repudiates such fame: 'I had rather my bearing, in
this, or any other office, should adde worth to it; then the Place give
the least opinion to me'.[18] It is an immaculate City response, but also
one at which comedy is bound to laugh.

To do them justice, George and Nell don't want to go to the theatre
merely to misinterpret *Eastward Ho!* They are romantics as well as
being materialists, and something in them craves a magnification of
the City that goes beyond hospitals, conduits, and a meteoric rise in
the civic hierarchy. This is why they dictate to the unwilling actors a
second and rival play, interwoven with the events of 'The London
Merchant', and almost wholly unrelated to it. 'The Knight of the
Burning Pestle' is not only dedicated 'to the eternal honour and glory
of all grocers', it has the advantage of starring their own apprentice
Ralph. Bearing the arms of his livery company throughout, Ralph
involves himself in terrific adventures in Moldavia and points East:
in a wild farrago of dragons and giants, castles and kings. He returns,
however, to London, loyal to his company and to his girl Susan,
despite the temptations of the Princess of Cracovia and a crown. It is
in London that the summit of his career is reached. As the City's
May-Lord, he presides over London's most comedic festival. Subsequently, he drills a band of city militia (at the request of George and
Nell) in the following inspiring terms: 'Gentlemen, countrymen,
friends, and my fellow-soldiers, I have brought you this day from the
shops of security and the counters of content, to measure out in these
furious fields honour by the ell, and prowess by the pound.'[19] This is
the climax of Ralph's career. As he walks taking the air in Moorfields,
like any ordinary citizen, Ralph is overcome by grim Death and
expires, piously consigning his soul not to Heaven but to Grocer's
Hall, its secular equivalent.

---

[17] *Eastward Ho!*, Herford and Simpson, IV.2.70, 54, 74–7.   [18] *Ibid.*, IV.2.64–6.
[19] *The Knight of the Burning Pestle*, V.138–42.

Plate 4   A drawing of Simon Eyre, Lord Mayor in 1445, in his aldermanic robes.

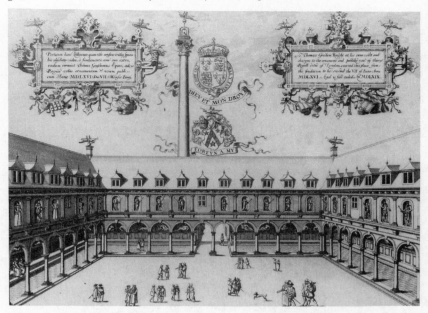

Plate 5   The first Royal Exchange as built in the centre of the City of London by Sir
Thomas Gresham in 1565–9.

Ralph's address to the City militia is interesting because its commercial terminology is both so like and so unlike that of Luce's foolish suitor. Nell and George admire both in a way that makes one understand how they can accommodate 'The Knight of the Burning Pestle' to the shadow play they discern behind 'The London Merchant'. In any case, the grocer and his wife never lose sight of fundamentals as they impel Ralph from one exotic adventure to another. It is not simply a question of their touching faith that the King of Cracovia's daughter must ultimately yield to London's Susan, or that the gorgeous East represents a sphere of influence less important than Mile End or the Strand. George and Nell are really less worried about the monsters and giants Ralph has to encounter than about the possibility that, in an inn or a prince's palace, he may find himself unable to *pay*. They are forever defraying the charges of their own fictional character, leaping up to discharge a reckoning, or ensuring (for the honour of the Grocer's Company) that the servants receive a proper tip. Mad and improbable though Ralph's adventures are, there is a sense in which they never leave the comfortable

Plate 6 Sir Thomas Gresham mercer, merchant, and the greatest financier of his day, 'civic hero' of Heywood's *If You Know Not Me You Know Nobody*, Part 2 (1964).

Plate 7   The lemon tree pelican device in the 1616 Lord Mayor's show designed by Anthony Munday. The lemon tree is a pun on the name of the Lord Mayor, John Leman of the Fishmongers' Company. The symbol of the pelican, representing tragic self-sacrifice as it tears open its own breast to nourish its young with its heart's-blood, also figures in the second part of Thomas Heywood's *Edward IV* (*c.* 1599).

circuit of bourgeois London, never really admit that there may be a
world elsewhere. Fundamentally parodic, they limit and scale down
an original which, for all its absurdity, nevertheless appealed
cunningly and obviously successfully to a considerable section of its
London audience.

Heywood wrote *The Foure Prentises of London, with the Conquest of
Jerusalem* for the Red Bull Theatre, about 1600. This is the comedy
Beaumont was mocking when he contrived the adventures of Ralph
and, at first sight, it seems almost as ludicrous as its imitation. In the
printed version, Heywood's play is dedicated to 'the Honest and
High-spirited Prentises, the Readers', and one quickly sees why. The
basic situation is gloriously absurd. The Earl of Boulogne, deposed
from his lands in France, has fled to the London of William the
Conqueror. There, he apprentices his four sons to four different
trades. Godfrey, the eldest, is bound to a mercer, Guy to a goldsmith,
Charles to a haberdasher, and Eustace (the youngest) to a grocer.
Heywood did not select these occupations idly: they were four of the
most powerful livery companies in the City, the ones which tended to
attract ambitious men who meant to rise. At the beginning of the play,
Godfrey makes it gratifyingly clear that he regards apprenticeship
as no disgrace:

> I prayse that Citty which made Princes Trades-men;
> Where that man, noble, or ignoble borne,
> That would not practise some mechanicke skill,
> Which might support his state in penury,
> Should die the death; not sufferd like a drone,
> To sucke the honey from the publicke Hive.
> I hold it no disparage to my birth,
> Though I be borne an Earle, to have the skill
> And the full knowledge of the *Mercers* trade.
> And were I now to be create a new,
> It should not grieve me to have spent my time
> The secrets of so rich a Trade to know,
> By which advantage and great profits grow.[20]

When one reflects upon the number of younger sons of the gentry
who were forced, by the laws of primogeniture, to step down socially
by binding themselves as apprentices to a trade – and upon the
burning contemporary issue of whether association with a trade
cancelled out original gentility – it becomes obvious what Heywood

---

[20] *The Foure Prentises of London*, in Shepherd, II, pp. 169–70.

was doing. It also becomes clear why the City magistrates had difficulty in keeping apprentices away from the public theatres.

Satisfied though they claim to be with their respective trades, the four noble brothers forget about their shops and their indentures when they hear the call for soldiers to enlist for the holy war in Jerusalem. Their fortunes are initially unhappy. The ship in which they try to leave England is wrecked on Goodwin sands. It's an extremely peculiar shipwreck, because one brother is washed up on the coast of France, one off Boulogne, a third in Ireland, and the fourth somewhere near Venice. The rest of *The Foure Prentises of London* is about the glamorous adventures of the four as they make their way through the world to converge at last upon Jerusalem. Each one believes that all the others have been drowned, with the result that, despite a number of (usually belligerent) encounters, they are all incapable of recognizing one another until the end. In Act v, the brothers perform terrific feats against the infidel, are personally responsible for the conquest of Jerusalem, and finally recognize each other, in a fine, staccato scene: 'My brother, Eustace!' 'Godfrey! Guy! And Charles!' (*All*: 'Brothers!') For King Robert of Normandy, who happens to be standing by, 'this accident breeds wonders in my thoughts'. As well it might. Robert proceeds to ask the predictable rhetorical question:

> Were ye the foure yong *London* Prentises,
> That in the ships were wrackt on *Goodwins* sands?
> Were said to have perisht then of no repute?
> Now come the least of you to leade an Hoast,
> And to be found the sonnes to a great Duke?[21]

After this, all four brothers go off to become kings – with the exception of Godfrey, the eldest, who piously refuses the throne of Jerusalem on the grounds that he will not wear a crown of gold where Christ wore one of thorns.

To anatomize a play like *The Foure Prentises of London* may seem like racking a butterfly. Yet the comedy is not quite as simple as it pretends. Steven Smith has argued that the London apprentices of the late sixteenth and early seventeenth centuries regarded themselves and were regarded by others as forming a definable subculture. They came from a great variety of social backgrounds, and the masters that they served differed enormously in wealth and

---

[21] *Ibid.*, p. 239.

status. All of them, however, shared the common experience of being adolescents uprooted from their own homes and uncertain, as yet, of their place in the world. As such, they needed the support of a group. They also needed, as individuals, to experiment with different roles.[22]

Drama, particularly comedy deriving from the life of their own city of London, was ideally suited to further such experimentation. Psychologically, Heywood's play is cunningly contrived to appeal to the clannishness of the apprentices: their need to see themselves as a coherent, separate society within the City, one with its own ethos and rules. It also encourages their impulse towards individuation, towards realizations of the self in various, fictional forms which might foreshadow an adult reality. Not many of the apprentices in Heywood's audience, needless to say, were the sons of exiled earls. Nonetheless, the dramatist has created a situation which many of the members of his original audience could recognize as a heightened, a fantasized version, of their own. This, of course, is why, as the brothers gradually battle their way to the top, they continue to bear the arms not of their own, noble family, but of the livery company to which each belongs. Their fellow apprentices, too, back in London, are continually in their thoughts. In *Henry V*, the preceding year, Shakespeare's Westmoreland before the battle of Agincourt had wished, 'O that we now had here / But one ten thousand of those men in England / That do no work to-day' (iv.3.16–18). Brother Eustace, in Heywood's play, produces an interesting variation on the words:

> Oh that I had with mee
> As many good lads, honest Prentises,
> From *Eastcheape*, *Canwicke-street*, and *London-stone*,
> To ende this Battle, as could wish themselves
> Under my conduct if they knew mee heere.[23]

The topographical particularity is striking, but so is the sense of social community: a brotherhood of young men, half imaginary, half real, among whom Eustace is a natural leader and whom he also represents in his glorious and highly improbable progress towards the Sicilian crown.

It is surely right, too, in reading *The Foure Prentises of London*, to remember what Foster says in *The Politics of Stability* about the curious mingling of the spiritual and the material in the ethos of the City as

---

[22] Steven R. Smith, 'The London apprentices as seventeenth-century adolescents', *Past and Present* 61 (November 1973), pp. 149–61.   [23] *The Foure Prentises of London*, p. 192.

the London guilds, in effect, rescue the great Christian citadel of Jerusalem from the unbeliever. Heywood is by no means uncritical. The four brothers are often foolishly emulous and quarrelsome in ways that detract from their achievements and clearly reflect the riots and brawls in which the London apprentices all too frequently indulged. Whatever their other merits, these young men have not yet learned the civic virtues of temperance and patience, and this fact matters. Essentially, however, the comedy is concerned to present a considerable section of its contemporary audience with an image of its own state and aspirations: its characteristically adolescent poise between family ties recently slackened, a youth group with which it identified, and an adult world of individual achievement towards which it looked. Drama allowed the London apprentices a vision of themselves that was at once glamorized and anchored firmly in their own urban reality. When Beaumont made the apprentice Ralph leave his place in the audience to become an actor in 'The Knight of the Burning Pestle', he was setting up a parody of Heywood's play. He was also, however, giving a literal form to its intentions, and to the relationship with the younger members of the audience which *The Foure Prentises of London* implies.

The Foure Prentises of London was not the only London comedy of which George and Nell approved. George also claimed to like 'The legend of Whittington', 'The life and death of Sir Thomas Gresham, with the building of the Royal Exchange', and 'The story of Queen Eleanor, with the rearing of London Bridge upon woolsacks'. The first and third of these plays are lost. 'The life and death of Thomas Gresham', on the other hand, is almost certainly the same as Part II of Heywood's *If You Know Not Me You Know Nobody*, of 1605. Like the two-part *Edward IV*, this was a kind of history play, but its affinities were with comedy rather than tragedy, and its emphasis on the City was both more exclusive and, in a curious way, more ambiguous. Part I of *If You Know Not Me* is sub-titled 'The troubles of Queen Elizabeth'. It deals, for the most part, with the Marian persecutions and with the ill-treatment of Elizabeth at her sister's hands. In the person of Thomas Gresham, who prevents the warrant for Elizabeth's execution from being shuffled in among other state papers which Philip of Spain is about to sign, the City saves the life of its future queen. The play ends with Elizabeth's coronation procession, and her ceremonial encounter with the Lord Mayor, who presents her with a Bible and a purse as London's characteristic gifts. Part II, however, displaces Elizabeth from the centre of the stage. Her function now is to christen Gresham's great, new civic building, the Royal Exchange, to make the builder a knight, and to defeat the Armada at the end, with the help of the City's cash. Essentially, this is Gresham's play.

At the beginning of Part II, this future civic hero is an extremely imperfect character. He is touchy, quarrelsome, constantly embroiled in law suits and squabbles with his neighbours, high-handed and impatient. Even his financial policies are somewhat dubious. Gresham has kept back for his own use the inheritance which properly belongs to a nephew, and has to be tricked out of it. In the course of the comedy, however, this man who was born a country yeoman gradually takes on the ethos of the City. Spurred on by the saintly Dean of St Paul's, who impresses him with accounts of the City's great benefactors in the past, Gresham abandons his law suits and pours out money on charitable works. His great moment of triumph comes at the feast he gives to celebrate the opening of the Exchange. At this banquet, where he dines the Court as well as the City, Gresham receives a series of highly unpleasant tidings. The ship which was to bring to London portraits of all the kings and queens of England, as ornaments for the new Exchange, has sunk with all its cargo. Prodigal nephew John has committed another outrage. Worst of all, the King of Barbary has died, and his successor sends word that he means to dishonour the agreement made with Gresham whereby the merchant would have a patent for all the sugar in Barbary – while retaining the thirty thousand pounds Gresham paid for that privilege. In the face of these assorted disasters, Gresham remains wholly unruffled. The King of Barbary has sent him a pair of embroidered slippers in quittance of his bond, and Gresham is pleased to discover that they fit. He even makes a jest of it: 'You may report, lords, when you come to Court, / You *Gresham* saw a paire of slippers weare, / Cost thirty thousand pound'. Not only does he not wish 'his buildings in his purse', as one guest surmises: he ends the feast by pounding a costly pearl to powder and carousing it to the health of the Queen. 'I doe not this', he points out, 'as prodigall of my wealth; / Rather to show how I esteem that losse / Which cannot be regain'd.[24]

Whatever its superficial similarities, this is not really the patience

---

[24] *2 If You Know Not Me You Know Nobody*, in Shepherd, I, pp. 300–1.

of Dekker and Milddleton's Candido. There is about it, despite Gresham's disclaimer, a suspicious element of extravagance, of *sprezzatura*, which points in another, and conflicting, direction. Here, as in its basically lenient treatment of the witty prodigal, Gresham's unregenerate but entertaining nephew, the second part of *If You Know Not Me* betrays an infidelity to the ethos of the City in favour of the alien gods of comedy. It reminds one of how ingenious even the most dedicated, middle-class dramatists, like Heywood, had to be in order to maintain a rapprochement between the two. Comedy has always loved the witty rogue. But it was only the special circumstances of seventeenth-century London, perhaps, which could impel a dramatist to conceal him in the form of a young merchant who, having ruined himself by being charitable and honest to excess, proceeds to regain his money by employing every ruse, wile, clever deceit and hypocrisy in the book. Brome's character Crazy ends the play as a very wealthy man. At which point, he throws off his disguise, returns everything to his creditors that is in excess of his original loss and, presumably, goes back to being Dr Jekyll after this stunning demonstration of how successful he could be as Mr Hyde. This comedy, *The City Wit* (1630), is interesting on a number of counts, but not least because of the commentary it offers on the perennial need of London comedy, especially those plays written for the public theatres, to reconcile civic morality with fun.

There is no way of knowing what Beaumont's George and Nell would have thought of *The City Wit*. It is interesting, however, that they should avoid mentioning Dekker's *The Shoemaker's Holiday* (1599) among those comedies honouring the City of which they approve. Like Gresham or Dick Whittington, Simon Eyre was an historical figure, a man who rose from humble beginnings as a shoemaker to be Lord Mayor of London. Dekker's comedy is a chronicle of the achievements of one of the City's heroes, a celebration of a famous success story. No flesh and blood Lord Mayor, however, no alderman or member of London's Common Council could really feel happy about this play, despite its ostensible magnification of civic deeds and values. Comedy is a dangerous ally, likely without warning to desert the proprieties it is supposed to extol in favour of a rival ethos that is older and more universal than any city. This is what threatens to happen all the time in Dekker's play.

Eyre may be a successful businessman, dedicated to his guild, to London, and to the apprentices who work in his own shop. He

combines these civic virtues with an unbridled individualism, a
sensuous abandon, which serves to associate him with comic heroes
reaching back all the way to Aristophanes, but which had no part in
the composition of any Elizabethan Lord Mayor. Eyre is clever.
Indeed, Dekker insists that his phenomenal rise in the City was
inaugurated by way of a distinctly shady business deal involving his
false impersonation of an alderman. It was just the kind of use of the
theatre in real life that the City fathers deplored and feared: the
techniques of the stage used in the ordinary world as agents of deceit..
A master of rhetoric and highly coloured language, Eyre becomes in
Dekker's comedy something he was not at all in Deloney's *The Gentle
Craft*: a kind of comic Tamburlaine, whose extraordinary and
impatient verbal style not only characterizes him, but is the source of
his power. He collects words as he collects money, and vitalizes both
in a fashion that is essentially amoral.

Dekker has really contrived a complex balancing act in *The
Shoemaker's Holiday*. Eyre is a far more traditional comic hero than
either the patient Candido or the four loyal apprentices in Heywood's
play. In him, the magnificence and love of excess only implied in
Gresham are unequivocal and open. Eyre possesses the immemorial
comic traits of duplicity, individualism, sensuality, and a passion for
food and drink. (At the end of the comedy, he insists upon feasting all
the apprentices of London at his own expense.) The historical Simon
Eyre, as Deloney faithfully reported, had prudently changed midway
in his career from the shoemakers' to the mercers' guild. There was
good reason for this. The cordwainers may have been surrounded by
all the mythology appertaining to 'the gentle craft'. In fact, they
were never included among the twelve powerful guilds which
dominated London. It was normal practice for an ambitious man to
make this kind of switch at a certain stage in his rise to power.
Dekker's Eyre, however, does not. This is because the comedy wishes
to make it clear that Eyre owes his good fortune mainly to himself, not
to his livery company or his associates.

A man who insists upon questioning and breaking down the
ordinary limits of existence, Simon Eyre can be contained only with
difficulty within a City which Dekker has gone out of his way to
identify as sixteenth-century London. The historical Eyre lived in the
fifteenth century. But of the numerous London landmarks actually
mentioned in the play – and at moments it reads almost like a
dramatized *London A to Z* – the majority did not exist in that older

City.[25] Dekker, unlike Deloney in his source, has insisted upon their anachronistic introduction. In doing so, he forced his contemporary audience to experience, simultaneously, the London they themselves knew and, in control of this recognizable City, an over-life-size comic hero whom they did not. At the end of *Eastward Ho!*, the actors pretend that the theatre audience is 'the multitude…gatherd together, to view our comming out at the *Counter*. See, if the streets and the Fronts of the Houses be not stucke with People, and the Windowes fild with Ladies, as on the solemne day of the *Pageant*!'[26] The lines make explicit and specific a situation implied at the end of all these London comedies, as the world of the play gives way to that of the audience from which it was derived. One wonders what that original audience took away from Dekker's *The Shoemaker's Holiday*. Certainly, its particular blend of fantasy and realism was by no means simple or unconsidered. Nor was it a mean feat to palm off as a civic hero – sheriff, alderman, and finally Lord Mayor – a madcap individualist who, in many ways, embodied everything that the City officially deplored.

[25] W. K. Chandler, 'The topography of Dekker's *The Shoemaker's Holiday*', *Studies in Philology* 26 (1929), 499–504.   [26] *Eastward Ho!*, Epilogus 1–5.

CHAPTER 15

Comic London

In the second act of Shakespeare's *As You Like It*, Orlando, made desperate by his own hunger and that of his servant Adam, intrudes upon the rural banquet in Arden with drawn sword. Courteously, Duke Senior requests an explanation of conduct so extreme: 'Art thou thus bolden'd, man, by thy distress? / Or else a rude despiser of good manners, / That in civility thou seem'st so empty?' (II.7.91–3) For the young Orlando, kept 'rustically at home' (I.1.7) by Oliver, his envious elder brother, in a condition he likens to 'the stalling of an ox' (I.1.10–11), the idea of being thought uncivil is particularly painful: 'The thorny point / Of bare distress hath ta'en from me the show / Of smooth civility; yet am I inland bred, / And know some nurture' (II.7.94–7). The excuse paves the way for Orlando's acceptance in this forest society and, while he goes to fetch Adam to the interrupted feast, Duke Senior points out to his fellows in exile that 'This wide and universal theatre / Presents more woeful pageants than the scene / Wherein we play in', provoking Jaques to assert that 'All the world's a stage / And all the men and women merely players' (II.7.137–40).

Unlike most previous expositors of this topos, Jaques refuses to categorize the drama of human life as either comic or tragic. It is a 'strange, eventful history' (II.7.164), focussed, moreover, upon a single performer. Within two lines, 'all the men and women' have been reduced to 'one man, in his time'. The seven parts he plays are crammed with particularities: the school-boy's satchel and his 'shining morning face', or the 'fair round belly' of the justice, 'with good capon lin'd'. Jaques' description is so wonderfully rich in detail, that one almost omits to notice how singularly unlocalized it is in terms of time and place. Do the various acts of this play occur in the country or the city, at court or (perhaps) a provincial town? In England, or somewhere else? And just exactly what are we to understand as their moment of historical time?

Approximately seven years after *As You Like It*, a prose play by Edward Sharpham called *The Fleir* was performed by the children of the Queen's Revels at Blackfriars. It too has a malcontent figure, the exiled duke Antifront disguised under the name 'Fleir', who explores the topos of human life as a stage play:

The Cittie is like a Commodie, both in partes and in apparell, and your Gallants are the Actors: for hee that yesterday played the Gentleman, nowe playes the Begger; shee that played the Wayting-woman, nowe playes the Queane; hee that played the married-man, nowe playes the Cuckolde; and shee that played the Ladie, nowe playes the Painter. Then for their apparell, they have change too: for shee that wore the Petticote, now weares the Breech; hee that wore the Coxcombe, nowe weares the feather; the Gentleman that wore the long Sworde, now weares the short Hanger; and hee that could scarce get Velvet for his Cape, has nowe linde his Cloake throughout with it.[1]

This has nothing like the imaginative richness of Shakespeare. On the other hand, we know exactly where we are: in London, among a throng of men and women, in the first decade of the seventeenth century.

Changes in fashion – the fall from favour of the long sword, the vogue for foolish feathers worn in the hat – and what is almost certainly an allusion to Moll Frith, Middleton and Dekker's 'roaring girl', arraigned by the Consistory Court in 1605 for various offences, including the assumption of masculine attire, all locate us in space and time. Prostitution, and the ageing society beauty's pot of rouge, are specifically urban phenomena. But Fleir even gives such apparently universal human experiences as the vicissitudes of fortune an identifiably contemporary and civic form. Jacobean London, socially and financially mobile, was the one place in England where a man might well half-starve himself in order to present a plausible appearance in a short velvet cape, and obtain (if he was skilful) advancement so great that he could walk thereafter, like Middleton's Andrew Lethe (formerly the humble Andrew Gruel) in *Michaelmas Term*, 'wrapt in silk and silver'.[2] It was also the place where the

[1] Edward Sharpham, *The Fleir* II, lines 135–49, ed. Hunild Nibbe, in W. Bang, gen. ed., n.s., H. de Vocht, gen. ed. *Materialien zur kunde des älteren englischen Dramas* (London, 1912).
[2] Thomas Middleton, *Michaelmas Term*, ed. Richard Levin (London, 1967), Induction, line 32.

wealthy could be ruined – as both fact and city comedy attest – more expeditiously than anywhere else in His Majesty's kingdom.

Shakespeare's Jaques had talked vaguely about a 'strange, eventful history', performed on what Calderón called 'the great stage of the world'. Fleir, by contrast, evokes the very time and city of the audience he addresses. He reminds his listeners, moreover, that, like the play they are watching – which, as it happens, is set in London and contains multiple disguises, two of them trans-sexual, and some abrupt reversals of fortune – the quality of their own lives is essentially that of comedy. The speech acts as a useful reminder of just how individual and aberrant Shakespeare was in choosing, for the most part, to divorce his comedy from the contemporary city, rejecting a natural affinity which not only Fleir (and Sharpham) but almost all comic dramatists from Aristophanes onwards have been happy to exploit. Significantly, not even Shakespeare can obliterate the association completely. Even *As You Like It*, while confining itself officially to the country and Duke Frederick's court, seems to be continually fighting off a shadowy London, clamouring for inclusion. Duke Senior finds himself describing Arden's deer as 'native burghers of this desert city' (II.1.23); Jaques cannot resist turning the wounded stag into a bankrupt cruelly ignored by 'fat and greasy citizens' (II.1.55); and the Hymen who joins the hands of the lovers at the end is 'god of every town' (v.4.146). Language itself conspires against the illusion of Arden's rural self-sufficiency: the word 'civility', so crucial in that first interchange between Orlando and the Duke, derives from the Latin *civis* – having to do originally with the free, but subsequently with the *civilized*, the sophisticated inhabitants of a city.

In a book published in 1974, *The Fall of Public Man*, the sociologist Richard Sennett argues that

There are probably as many different ways of conceiving what a city is as there are cities. A simple definition therefore has its attractions. The simplest is that a city is a human settlement in which strangers are likely to meet. For this definition to hold true, the settlement has to have a large, heterogeneous population; the population has to be packed together rather densely; market exchanges among the population must make this dense, diverse mass interact. In this milieu of strangers whose lives touch there is a problem of audience akin to the problem of audience an actor faces in the theater.[3]

---

[3] Richard Sennett, *The Fall of Public Man* (Cambridge, 1974), p. 39. Sennett's *The Conscience of the Eye: The Design and Social Life of Cities* (London, 1991), which appeared after this essay was written, also bears upon it in a number of ways.

In a milieu of strangers, Sennett goes on to say, the people who witness each other's actions, declarations and professions usually have no knowledge of the other person's history. The knowledge on which belief can be based is confined to the frame of the immediate situation – on how an individual talks, dresses, moves, gestures, listens, within it. Just as the stage-player must arouse belief in a character before an audience which begins the play knowing nothing about that character, so the city-dweller is constantly enacting him or herself in public and, at the same time, attempting to interpret the self-performance offered by strangers. This is a necessity of city life. And, because the scenario of the great city is principally the search for gain and reputations, the actor will always be tempted to falsify rather than reveal. That is why, for Rousseau, the city of Paris and the theatre became linked as agents of moral disaster: twinned and inter-dependent places in which people perform, and their contact with natural virtue and sincerity is lost. It is also likely to explain why Elizabethan magistrates should have gone on trying (unsuccessfully, of course) to enforce the sumptuary laws in London long after the rest of England had ceased to worry that the way an individual dressed might create a seriously misleading idea of his or her social status.[4] In *Michaelmas Term*, it is largely Andrew Lethe's clothes which render him and his origins unidentifiable ''Mongst strange eyes / That no more know him than he knows himself".[5]

Rousseau's animus is directed against comedy and tragedy alike. Sennett, in his discussion of urban role-playing, doesn't distinguish between them. It is clear, however, that the urban scenario he describes is essentially that of comedy – and not just because comic dramatists take a special interest in money-making, the minutiae of social behaviour, imposture and deceit, although of course they do. In the palace or great house, tragedy's typical environment, the identity and past history of everyone who counts are usually matters of public knowledge, as indeed they are in a country town. (One remembers the distress of Proust's Aunt Léonie when she sees a dog she can't recognize go by in the streets of Combray.) More important, however, is the fact that Sennett's stranger-filled city has been a virtual prerequisite of comedy since Menander. Even Shakespeare's Arden, sheep-cotes and murmuring streams, palm-trees, lionesses

---

[4] Jeremy Boulton, *Neighbourhood and Society: A London Suburb in the Seventeenth Century* (Cambridge, 1987), p. 147.   [5] Middleton, *Michaelmas Term*, 1.1.148–9.

and goat-girls notwithstanding, is in a behavioural sense urban. Duke Senior is right when he calls the forest a 'desert city'. Wild but populous, filled with people uprooted from their original homes, it is a place where strangers continually meet. Their principal concern, moreover, in these meetings is exactly the one normally associated with the city: self-performance, and the need to interpret correctly the social display of others whose temperaments and past histories are obscure.

Western comedy as a genre begins formally with Aristophanes. City comedy in Sennett's terms does not. Fundamentally, Old Comedy Athens is a town, a place where everybody seems to know everybody else, or at least can recognize them by sight. This is all the more remarkable given the number of country people, farmers like Dikaeopolis in the *Acharnians*, who normally do not reside in Athens although they spend much of their time there. It is true that Aristophanic Athens would not look anything like so cosy if notice were taken of her resident aliens, of her slave population as a group, and of what went on, not just at the Thesmophoria and the fanciful gathering of women in *Lysistrata*, but in almost every house behind the closed doors of the quarters reserved for women. These, however, were areas of urban life about which Aristophanes probably knew very little and which he chose, in any case, to exclude.

The people who count in Old Comedy – meaning adult male citizens, whether fictional or historically real – are perpetually on view. Athenians spent what seems to us an inordinate amount of time in the open air. It was a way of life fostered partly by the climate, but also by the architecture of the city. Athenian public buildings and spaces were magnificent. Private houses, on the other hand, seem to have been small, and minimally furnished. Those belonging to the rich were not much different from those of the poor. Men, at least, got out of them as quickly as possible in the morning, and spent most of the day elsewhere. This is one reason why Bdelycleon's treatment of his father in the *Wasps* – trying to incarcerate him in his house – registers as a measure so extreme. Not that we are allowed a glimpse of the interior of that domestic prison. Aristophanes is perfectly happy to transport his characters to Mt Olympus, or to Hades, to Cloud-Cuckoo-Land, the Acropolis, or into the country. Unity of place troubles him not at all. But although in the *Clouds* we are specifically told that Socrates' pupils are conspicuous for the pastiness of their complexions, the result of unnaturally long hours spent in the indoor gloom of the 'Thinkery', the comedy itself unfolds, predictably, in the open air.

Greek tragic writers did occasionally avail themselves of an ambiguous device for depicting interior scenes. The tableau (usually one of carnage) presented on the *ekkyklema*, a kind of trolley on wheels, pushed out through the central doors of the stage wall, is something the audience is supposed to imagine as being still indoors, yet (as Oliver Taplin has pointed out), as the scene progresses, 'the indoor/outdoor distinction tends to be neglected'.[6] In effect, the characteristic Greek bias towards the open air begins to re-assert itself. There are one or two moments in Aristophanes – Strepsiades and his son asleep in their beds on a cold night at the beginning of the *Clouds*, or the arraignment of the two dogs in the *Wasps* – which modern readers are likely to find ambiguous: are we indoors or out? It seems unlikely, however, that Greek audiences thought the question worth asking.[7] Certainly the tragic *ekkyklema*, whenever Aristophanes chooses to look at it, becomes hilarious. 'Very well', the fictional Euripides in the *Acharnians* says impatiently from within, 'I'll have myself wheeled out; I've no time to get down'.[8] Tragedy's tentative gesture towards interior space becomes, in Old Comedy, simply the lazy man's way of leaving his house quickly in response to a summons from outside.

In Old Comedy, the *skene* had sometimes been required (as here) to imitate a particular house front, although by no means necessarily throughout the play. Not until the time of Menander, did the fixed and unlocalized city street featuring two or more opposite or adjoining houses became standard, something to be dispensed with only as a conscious violation of what audiences now regarded as the norm. The city which contains this street is still, in many of the surviving New Comedy texts, Athens, but her identifying public monuments have disappeared. The street on one side of the stage is assumed now to lead to the forum or market of a generalized city, on the other towards the country or the harbour. Neither Menander, nor Plautus and Terence later, ever allow us *inside* their stage houses. We are kept in the street. But what we are asked to imagine as happening behind their closed doors, all those arguments and

---

[6] Oliver Taplin, *Greek Tragedy in Action* (London, 1978), p. 12.
[7] K. J. Dover, *Aristophanic Comedy* (London, 1972), p. 106.
[8] Aristophanes, *Acharnians*, ed. Alan Sommerstein (Warminster, 1980), line 409.

misunderstandings, the seductions, births of children, business deals and deceits, has an importance, now, alien to Old Comedy. The plays of Menander, Plautus and Terence continually gesture, as those of Aristophanes had not, towards the private and the hidden. Not infrequently, in Greek and Roman New Comedy, our uncertainty, shared with many of the characters, as to just what is going on indoors forms the basis of plot, as it does (say) over the issue of which room Philocomasium is in at a given moment in the *Miles Gloriosus*, or what is happening in Terence's *Hecyra* at the sickbed of Philumena. Philocleon in Aristophanes' *Wasps* had been passionate to get out of his house and into the street, but in Plautus' *Amphitruo* and *Mostellaria*, or in the *Eunuchus* of Terence, characters who have been excluded, like the audience, from access to a house spend most of their time in frenzied efforts to get in.

Profound social and political changes underlie this new emphasis on interior space. The streets of Hellenistic Athens had become places where strangers met. As public life, moreover, made fewer and fewer demands upon members of the middle classes, domestic life seems to have become more luxurious and complex. The houses of the rich, filled now with beautiful but unnecessary objects, perfume bottles and Tanagra figurines, began to look very different from those of the poor. In the *Mostellaria* of Plautus, a Roman adaptation of a lost Greek original, the concern of Theopropides with the special features of the desirable Athenian residence he thinks he is acquiring, unthinkable in Aristophanes, is entirely explicable in Hellenistic terms. So is the clear distinction drawn in this and other New Comedies between life in the country and in the city. In Aristophanes, the two places had been distinct but interactive, both socially and in terms of staging. But in New Comedy, the city becomes synonymous with luxury and sophistication, the country an invisible place of tedium and strange, old-fashioned ways, from which restive young men and their clever slaves escape in search of the pleasures and freedom of the town.

In adapting his Greek originals for a Roman audience, Plautus changed the names of characters, but not those of the Hellenistic cities in which they were set. The result was to distance and further generalize an urban locale recognizable now neither as Athens, a town most members of Plautus' audience had never seen, nor really as contemporary Rome. Latin comedy inhabits Melania, one of Italo Calvino's invisible cities, a place whose history is only that of the play itself, and whose single visible street runs through a metropolis that cannot be mapped. In some of these plays, moreover, Plautus betrays a most un-Greek hankering towards the actual staging of indoor scenes. Courtesans perform the intimate rituals of the dressing table, or revellers (with equal improbability) lie down on dining couches in the middle of the public street. This is different from the occasional indoor/outdoor ambiguity in Aristophanes. The text makes it plain that these Plautine characters are located physically in a public thoroughfare – slaves come and go with furniture and provisions from the house – but equally plain that what is occurring could only happen plausibly within.

Appropriately enough, two such moments occur in the *Mostellaria*, the one Roman comedy in which the urban house comes to function symbolically, not merely as a theatrical fixture. Almost certainly, Plautus added to his Greek original that long soliloquy in which the prodigal compares his own life to a dwelling, well-built by its maker, generally admired, but subsequently allowed by its slovenly owner to fall into disrepair: storm-damaged tiles and gutters not replaced, timbers rotting in the rain, walls finally caving in.[9] Such a detailed (almost Jungian) equation of domestic house with self is unprecedented in classical comedy. It is still, however, the exterior fabric of the house, and of his life, upon which Philolaches concentrates, not the devastation of what lies within. For that, one must turn to Thomas Heywood's London comedy *The English Traveller* of 1625, an adaptation in part of the *Mostellaria*, where the corresponding lament encompasses the ruin of 'Chambers well contriv'd', 'Roomes concealed, / H[u]ng] with the costliest hangings', 'Emblems and beautious Symbols pictured round', reflecting both an interest in the inner life of the prodigal alien to Greek and Roman comedy, and an equally alien bias towards the representation of indoor scenes.[10]

For the authors of the mediaeval mystery cycles, men prepared to represent the entire history of the world, from Creation to Last Judgement, on a few bare boards, there was never any question of

---

[9] For a discussion of the staging of 'interior' scenes, see W. Beare, *The Roman Stage* (London, 1950), Appendix F, pp. 279–83. Also George E. Duckworth, *The Nature of Roman Comedy: A Study in Popular Entertainment* (Princeton, 1952), pp. 126–7, and Elinor Winsor Leach, 'De exemplo meo ipseo aedificatio: an organizing idea in the *Mostellaria*', *Hermes* 97 (1969), 318–32.

[10] Thomas Heywood, *The English Traveller*, in *The Dramatic Works of Thomas Heywood*, 6 vols. (New York, 1964 repr. from 1874), IV, p. 18.

avoiding interior, let alone country scenes. Confidently, they followed where their biblical narrative led: from Eden to the wilderness, through the doors of palaces, temples, and private houses, into and out of Jerusalem's crowded streets. Noah and his family find it natural to build a stage ark, wrangle and debate around it, and then remain visible to the audience while speaking from within its sealed-up enclosure. This kind of indoor/outdoor flexibility, an insistence that private and public interiors should not only be talked about but seen, was inherited by the Elizabethan and Jacobean theatre. The stricter imitations of Plautus and Terence – Udall's *Jack Jugeler* (1555), for instance, or *Ralph Royster Doyster* (1552) – do for a time try to restrict action to the single, unchanging city street. But the strength of the native tradition was too strong. Not even Ben Jonson, at his most prescriptively classical, ever tried to challenge it.

One of the functions of the medieval guild cycles was to fabricate a sense of civic identity: in a sense to ruralize a large town by bringing most of its members together, whether as participants or audience, in a single, shared enterprise.[11] It was possible to do this in fourteenth-century York and Chester, Coventry or Norwich, but not (as it seems), even at that date, in London: a city already different from any other in England, where the decentralization of urban social structures characteristic of the later middle ages had occurred extremely early.[12] The 'gret pley from the begynnyng of the worlde', London's nearest equivalent to the Corpus Christi cycles, performed over eight days at Skinners' Well in 1409, was unlike its provincial equivalents in several respects: it had no connection with Corpus Christi, it was presented by the city's parish clerks, as opposed to being a joint enterprise of its guilds, its audience consisted of 'the most parte of the lordes and gentylles of Ynglond', on occasion including the king and queen, and it took place not in London itself, but north of the city, in the neighbouring county of Middlesex.[13] As such, it made no pretence to unify a metropolis already too large and diverse to function, even on special occasions, as a community.

---

[11] Mervyn James, 'Ritual, drama and social body in the late mediaeval English town', in *Society, Politics and Culture: Studies in Early Modern England* (Cambridge, 1986), pp. 16–47.

[12] Frank Freeman Foster, *The Politics of Stability: A Portrait of the Rulers in Elizabethan London* (London, 1977), p. 35.

[13] E. K. Chambers, *The Mediaeval Stage* (Oxford, 1903), II, pp. 118–19. Also see Ian Lancashire, *Dramatic Texts and Records of Britain: A Chronological Topography to 1558* (Cambridge, 1984), pp. 112–14, and the account in John Stow, *A Survey of London*, ed. Charles Kingsford (Oxford, 1980), I, p. 93; II, p. 31.

No text of these plays survives. Were the parish clerks ever tempted to superimpose London on Jerusalem, as Lodge and Greene were to do in *A Looking Glass For London and England* (1590)? Certainly, London places and landmarks appear comparatively early in moral plays devised for audiences in the city. By the beginning of the sixteenth century, scattered references like the one to the Marshalsea in the fifteenth-century *Mind, Will and Understanding* have significantly increased. Moral interludes which remain fancifully abstract in their choice of characters' personal names, nonetheless allow these characters to talk familiarly about Newgate and Tyburn, Holborn, Westminster, Ludgate, and St Giles in the Fields. Like the Acropolis, the sea-port of Piraeus, or the Agora in Aristophanes, these localities are symbolic as well as real. All, however, in keeping with the didactic nature of the plays themselves, either are or conspicuously lead to places associated with punishment, imprisonment, or the processes of law. In later Elizabethan and in Jacobean comedies, these sinister names continue to figure, but as part now of an infinitely more complex and various topography: a topography reflecting not only the way individual dramatists interpreted the city, but far-reaching changes in the character of London itself. The result is something new in the history of drama.

No other city – not even Aristophanic Athens, certainly not its New Comedy equivalents, or the Renaissance Italian cities dramatized by Machiavelli and his contemporaries – had ever prompted topographical attention of this kind. Comic London is a city experienced both indoors and out, in public places like St Paul's or the Royal Exchange, but also in particular districts within and beyond the walls, in the rough and tumble of taverns actually frequented by members of the audience, and in the intimacy of private houses standing in named, familiar streets. Aristophanes refuses to indicate just where one might find the domestic dwellings from which his fictional characters (Praxagora and Philocleon), or even living contemporaries like Socrates and Euripides, emerge. London, however, in the late sixteenth and early seventeenth centuries, is a place which dramatists seek to present simultaneously in detail and (for a while, at least) as a whole.

That this should have happened has a good deal to do with the special problems and requirements of life in this city at the end of Elizabeth's reign, when London comedy begins to be written. During the sixteenth century, the population of London had roughly trebled, the most spectacular expansion occurring between 1570 and 1600, when it may have leapt to about 200,000. By 1650, with a population of some 375,000, London equalled any city on the Continent in size and was well on its way to becoming the largest city of Europe.[14] Yet between 1570 and 1650, a comparatively low birth rate coupled with appalling mortality figures meant that London's population ought in fact to have *declined*. Immigration from other parts of England and from the Continent was entirely responsible for the population explosion in the capital.[15] This city was packed, often dangerously, with strangers, people whose principal obligations were to themselves: 'a wood', as the seventeenth-century author of *The Art of Living in London* (1642) put it, 'where there is as many briers as people, everyone as ready to catch hold of your fleece as yourself'.[16] Not by accident does the first London comedy we possess, Robert Wilson's *The Three Ladies of London* (1581), begin with the chance encounter of travellers from different parts of England, just outside the city where they intend to make their fortunes, by fair means or foul.

Royal proclamations and other measures designed to stem the human tide flowing into the metropolis begin to appear late in Elizabeth's reign. They were unavailing. 'Soon London will be all England', King James opined despairingly.[17] Apprentices, journeymen looking for work, gentry who acquired the habit of abandoning their country estates for most of the year in favour of lodgings in town, foreign Protestants fleeing religious persecution, the rural poor, students destined for one of the inns of court, gentlemen with legal business to transact, poor scholars like those in the Parnassus Plays, searching for patrons and employment, aspirants to positions at court, and adventurers of all descriptions poured into (and out of) a city which was still contained under Elizabeth within little more than one square mile. It was possible to walk from the Tower at the eastern

---

[14] See Roger Finlay and Beatrice Shearer, 'Population growth and suburban expansion', in *The Making of the Metropolis 1500–1700* (London, 1986), pp. 37–57. Their calculations have been questioned by Vanessa Harding, 'The population of London 1500–1700: a review of the published evidence', *The London Journal* 15, no. 2 (1990). She suggests, however, that although actual figures may be considerably lower than Finlay and Shearer maintain, London in fact grew more rapidly at the end of the sixteenth century than they recognized.

[15] Steve Rappaport, *Worlds Within Worlds: Structures of Life in Sixteenth Century London* (Cambridge, 1989), pp. 61–86.

[16] Henry Peacham, *The Art of Living in London*, in *The Complete Gentleman, The Truth of Our Times and The Art of Living in London*, ed. Virgil B. Heltzel (Ithaca, 1962), p. 244.

[17] Quoted by E. A. Wrigley, 'A simple model of London's importance in changing English society and economy 1650–1750', in P. Abrams and E. A. Wrigley, eds., *Towns in Societies. Essays in Economic History and Economic Sociology* (Cambridge, 1978), pp. 215–43.

end to Ludgate just past St Paul's at the western boundary in about half an hour.[18] John Stow, when he compiled his great *Survey* of London in the 1590s, was an old man, but he was nonetheless able to perambulate the city's twenty-six wards and liberties, into which the bulk of the population at this time was crammed, street by street.

Although increasingly unlikely, after the middle of the sixteenth century, to come together in the kind of shared recreation once provided by traditional festivals such as May Day, Midsummer watches, or church ales, Londoners obviously did manage to establish and maintain family and neighbourhood, as well as business ties.[19] Jeremy Boulton has analysed the pattern of such relationships in his study of marriages and friendships in the seventeenth-century parish of St Saviour's, Southwark. The tendency for apprentices all over the city to band together, and for freemen of the same livery company to cluster in one residential district must have helped too, although in the seventeenth century occupational zoning was beginning to break down.[20] The inhabitants of large cities, moreover, will be as curious about the doings of their neighbours as those who live in small towns, though their actual acquaintance with them is slight. Ben Jonson seizes on the dramatic potential of this in *The Alchemist*, when Lovewit is showered with information from the people in adjoining houses as to what has been going on in his own. Even the horrible Yellow-hammers in Middleton's *A Chaste Maid in Cheapside* (1613) observe glumly after driving their daughter (as it seems) to her death: 'All the whole street will hate us.'[21] Yet a large proportion of London's shifting and transient population, living for the most part in rented lodgings, must have felt singularly isolated. The assurance offered to Bella Franca, recently arrived in the city from abroad in Heywood's *The Foure Prentises of London* (1600) – she complains because her brothers insist on going off and leaving her 'midst a world of strangers' – is the feeblest of bad jokes: 'Why, sister, / Can you be left alone 'mongst multitudes? / *London* is full of people every where'.[22]

It is in the nature of life in a great city that it constantly impels

---

[18] Rappaport, *Worlds Within Worlds*, p. 64.

[19] See Peter Burke, 'Popular culture and seventeenth-century London', *The London Journal* 3 (1977), 143–62 and Ian W. Archer, *The Pursuit of Stability: Social Relations in Elizabethan London* (Cambridge, 1991), pp. 93–4.   [20] Boulton, *Neighbourhood and Society*, p. 61.

[21] Middleton, *A Chaste Maid in Cheapside*, ed. Alan Brissenden (London, 1968), v.2.108.

[22] Heywood, *The Four Prentises of London*, in *The Dramatic Works of Thomas Heywood*, ii, pp. 173, 5.

people out of a small neighbourhood into the metropolis at large. Here, twentieth-century sociologists like to talk about the 'urban image': that highly selective and symbolic mental map which people develop in order to understand and find their way about in an environment which is too complex to contend with in its entirety.[23] Such maps almost invariably rely on five components: paths, nodes – places where strategic navigational decisions have to be made; edges – rivers or other barriers impeding movement – landmarks, and areas – districts with an identifiable, homogenous character. Although no two individuals will imagine a particular city in exactly the same way, there is likely to be a degree of accord as to its most significant and central places: places which everyone, unless they are very recent arrivals, is likely to have in common.

In London comedies written at or just after the turn into the seventeenth century, this urban image is at its most manageable and cohesive. Public theatre plays like Haughton's *Englishmen For My Money* (1597), Dekker's *The Shoemaker's Holiday* (1599), Heywood's *The Foure Prentises of London*, *If You Know Not Me, You Know Nobody* (1604), or the first part of *Edward IV* (1599), repeatedly invoke the same landmarks and thoroughfares: St Paul's, Leadenhall, the Guildhall, the Royal Exchange and London Stone, Fleet Street, London Bridge, Bedlam and the various Counters, and above all Cheapside, with its conduits and cross, and the streets in its vicinity: Cornhill, Lombard Street, Tower Street, Fenchurch Street, Gracious Street, Canwick Street and Crutched Friars. People can easily lose each other in this London – when Ralph's wife Jane, in *The Shoemaker's Holiday*, quarrels with Eyre's wife and leaves the shop in Tower Street, she disappears as effectively as Aemilia, in *The Comedy of Errors*, does in the wide spaces of the Mediterranean – but it is far more difficult for them to lose their way. There was to be no effective street map of London until 1676, but most characters in these plays manage cheerfully enough without. Even a country pedlar like Tawny-coat in *If You Know Not Me*, visiting town to repay money owing to his wholesaler, can find the 'Stocks' meat market on the east of Cheapside, where Cornhill meets the Poultry, without difficulty, and manoeuvre from there: 'I, sure, 'tis in this lane: I turned on the right hand, coming from the Stockes... theres the Windmill; theres the Dogs head in the pot; and heres the Fryer whipping the Nunnes

[23] D. J. Walmsley, *Urban Living: The Individual in the City* (London, 1988), pp. 12, 36–7, 62.

arse. Tis hereabout sure.'[24] You have to be an outsider who is also an idiot, like Jonson's Bartholomew Cokes, not to be able to use paths, nodes, shop and tavern signs in this way.

Although by no means unaware of London's outskirts and environs, popular plays like these are centripetal. The reassuringly familiar city they honour is essentially the one defined by Queen Elizabeth's progress on the day before her coronation, from Fenchurch Street along Gracious Street, Cornhill and the great artery of Cheapside to St Paul's and Temple Bar – a route followed almost exactly on the occasion of his royal entry in 1604 by King James, and subsequently reaffirmed by the annual, and increasingly elaborate, Lord Mayor's Shows. In those Jacobean civic pageants, a number of which were to be written by Dekker and Heywood themselves, London is frequently personified as a female figure, by implication something to which an individual can relate. The Shows maintain this fiction straight up to the point of their suppression at the outbreak of the Civil War. By then, however, actual London had for some time looked very different.

In mocking plays like *The Foure Prentises of London* or *If You Know Not Me*, Beaumont in *The Knight of the Burning Pestle* (1607) and (to a lesser extent) Chapman, Jonson and Marston in *Eastward Ho!* (1605) had also travestied their topography: their tendency to produce a litany of linked street and district names. Middleton, although like Dekker and Heywood he later provided texts for the Lord Mayor's Shows, subverts in *A Chaste Maid in Cheapside* of 1613 exactly that mercantile centre – 'the heart of the city', as Sir Walter Whorehound calls it – which so many of the earlier London plays had celebrated.[25] Neither the establishment of the Yellowhammers, in Goldsmith's Row, nor that of the Allwits, within sight of Pissing Conduit in Cheap, is exactly a credit to the district. The chaste maid of the title, Moll Yellowhammer, is an anomaly in the area, from which, indeed, she spends most of the play vainly trying to escape: through its streets, over its roofs, or along the Thames.

---

[24] Heywood, *If You Know Not Me, You Know Nobody*, in *The Dramatic Works of Thomas Heywood*, I, p. 282. In the fourth act of William Haughton's *Englishmen For My Money* (1598), three unwelcome foreign suitors trying to reach the house of their prospective father-in-law in ·Crutched Friars on a dark night, are tricked and humiliated because of their imperfect knowledge of London topography. All three, together with a drunken clown, have to be rescued at last by the bellman on his rounds, in Fenchurch Street.

[25] Middleton, *A Chaste Maid in Cheapside*, 1.1.92.

In one form or another, escape from the traditional centre of London comes to loom increasingly large in comedies written under the Stuarts. Sometimes it involves nothing more than a day's outing for citizens: up the river to Brainford, as in *Westward Ho!* (1604), along the road to Ware in *Northward Ho!* (1605) or, in *The Roaring Girl* (?1607) a duck shooting expedition to Hogsdon's Parlous Pond. Going to the theatre, of course, had usually involved Londoners in a kind of escape from official city limits. But as the century proceeded, they needed to go further and further, in a city largely devoid of private gardens, simply to breathe fresh air. Even in the 1590s, Stow was complaining that the open fields beyond the walls where he had walked as a boy had become covered with buildings. Whereas Londoners used to endow hospitals and other civic monuments, they now spent their money on fashionable summer houses, in effect weekend cottages, often constructed (greatly to Stow's disgust) as little follies with towers, turrets and chimney-tops, 'like Midsommer Pageantes'.[26] In *Westward Ho!* of 1604, the acquisition of one of these houses is said to have bankrupted the protagonist, while in *Northward Ho!*, in the following year, a summer house in Moorfields serves as a convenient place for its owner to be cuckolded. Dramatists were not slow to exploit the potentialities of such places for sexual licence and intrigue.

Ultimately more consequential, however, was the large-scale building which went on both to the north and west of the city throughout the seventeenth century. By the end of Charles I's reign, in a striking reversal of the situation which had obtained for centuries, there were actually more people living outside the twenty-six wards, in greater London, than within.[27] This was no longer a city which comedy could pretend to unify. 'O London', a character exclaims in *A Match at Midnight*, written in 1622, 'Thou labyrinth that puzzleth strictest search.'[28] No Jacobean or Caroline dramatist displays a knowledge of that labyrinth, in all its bewildering ramifications, equal to that of Ben Jonson – a Londoner all his long life. Yet the London he presents in his mature plays is a curiously discontinuous city, at least by comparison with earlier comedies, a place apprehended in snatches, usually from one fixed and (*Bartholomew Fair* apart) primarily indoor locale. The *Mostellaria* of Plautus lies behind

[26] Stow, *Survey* II.78.   [27] Rappaport, *Worlds Within Worlds*, p. 62.
[28] W. R. London, *A Match at Midnight*, in Dodsley's *Old English Plays*, rev. edn W. Carew
Hazlitt, 15 vols. (London, 1874–6), XIII, p. 17.

The Alchemist, but it is the two small scenes in the street outside Lovewit's house, at the beginings of Acts III and V, which now seem theatrically a bit aberrant, not the presentation of interior space: empty rooms, visible or (like Subtle's laboratory) unseen, contain virtually all of the play.

In *The Alchemist*, Captain Face still trawls wide, and particularized, areas of London in search of prey to lure back to the house in Blackfriars. It was becoming possible, however, in the second decade of the seventeenth century, to write London comedy containing a minimum of such topographical reference, and without even specifying the location of the one or two town houses in which almost all the action takes place. The gentry experience of London, not the citizens', usually informs such plays. The traditional places of the city, Poultry, or the Cheap, are of little interest to characters whose servants do their shopping for them, or for whom merchandise is brought to the house: a space more intimate and finely graded, whose organization reflects the structures of social authority. Insofar as topography interests Fletcher, for instance, in his six London comedies, it is that of the town house interior. In *The Scornful Lady* of 1613, we are made aware of an entire building: kitchens, gallery, bedchambers, private chapel, and that cold if pretty reception hall in which the lady bids her suitor speak 'hastily and plainely', while she orders her attendant to 'make a good fire above', and prepares to withdraw to the warmth and privacy of the chamber upstairs.[29] The whole action of Shirley's *The Lady of Pleasure*, some years later, takes place indoors, in one or the other of two houses in the fashionable Strand. This is the archetypal New Comedy setting, except that here the stage locale of Menander and Plautus has been turned inside out. Shirley's two houses stand neither opposite each other, nor side by side. But, as neither exterior is ever implied, let alone seen, such lack of proximity doesn't matter. The Strand may be named; the street is out of bounds. What Shirley focusses on is a series of interiors, carefully graded, from the relatively public to the intensely private: various reception rooms receding to withdrawing room, to the dangerous intimacy of the closet, the one place in the house where you are, or ought to be, alone.

Fletcher's and Shirley's own temperaments and social backgrounds were obviously responsible in part for the way they chose to depict

---

[29] John Fletcher, *The Scornful Lady*, ed. Cyrus Hoy, in *The Dramatic Works in the Beaumont and Fletcher Canon*, gen. ed. Fredson Bowers, vol. II (Cambridge, 1970), I.I.77, 85.

London. Yet their preference for the private, their neglect of the old public places of the city can also be set within a wider frame. Although the Lord Mayor's Show continued to wind its way along the traditional route during the last years of James's reign, and under Charles, this time-honoured area of London had now lost much of its centrality and significance. Its royal associations, for one thing, had lapsed. King James, unlike his predecessors, disliked both progresses and crowds. During twenty-two years of rule, he made only three ceremonial entries into the city. His son Charles refused to make any at all, apart from one grudging appearance in 1638 when he was obliged to accompany his mother-in-law, the Dowager Queen of France, through the city to her lodgings in St James's Palace.[30] He rode then in a closed carriage, along a route which the account of the procession by Jean Puget de la Serre published in the following year disdains to notice until it reaches the now fashionable West End: a locality which, in the urban images most Londoners were constructing during the 1630s, had become equally or more important than the old civic centre around the Cheap.[31]

It has been estimated that whereas in 1600 two-thirds of London's adult men were citizens – members of one of the livery companies – by 1640 citizens accounted for only half the adult male population.[32] Considerably before that, the gentrification of the metropolis had altered its topographical form. In carefully planned areas, mostly to the west of the old city, the rich and the poor no longer lived, as they traditionally had in London, in randomly adjacent buildings. Everyone who acquired, or lodged in, one of Inigo Jones's elegant new houses in Covent Garden was, or at least was supposed to be, genteel. The rest of London had to be content to come and look. 'Dwell they all here abouts?', a countryman asks, observing the throng around him, in a play by Thomas Nabbes acted in 1632. 'I scarce thinke they are all of one Parish', he is informed, 'neither doe they goe to one Church. They come onely for an evening recreation to see COVENT-GARDEN'.[33]

Late Jacobean and Caroline comedy seizes the dramatic possibili-

[30] R. Malcolm Smuts, 'Public ceremony and royal charisma: the English royal entry in London 1485–1642', in *The First Modern Society*, ed. Beier, Cannadine, Rosenheim (Cambridge, 1989), pp. 82–93.

[31] See Emrys Jones, 'The first West End comedies', in *Proceedings of the British Academy 72* (1983), 215–52.   [32] Boulton, *Neighbourhood and Society*, p. 151.

[33] Thomas Nabbes, *Covent Garden*, in *The Works of Thomas Nabbes*, ed. S. H. Bullen, 2 vols. (New York, repr. 1964), I, p. 8.

ties of this, the compartmentalizing, the increasing fragmentation of the early seventeenth-century city. Earlier London plays which incorporated a place name in their titles – *The Fair Maid of the Exchange* (1602), *The Widow of Watling Street* (1606), *The Black Dog of Newgate* (1603), *Ram Alley* (1608), or *The Old Joiner of Aldgate* (1603) – had pointed towards the traditional centre or its defining edges. But in the 1630s plays spring up with titles like *Hyde Park* (1632), *The New Exchange* (1635), *The Sparagus Garden* (1635), *Holland's Leaguer* (1631), or *Totenham-Court* (1634). The Asparagus Garden, and Holland's Leaguer, a high-class brothel, were located across the river in Southwark; the other places in, or just beyond, the West End. The audience for whom Brome, Shirley, Nabbes and Marmion wrote these plays was, like the majority of their characters, 'town' as opposed to 'city': drawn from a gentry group present in London either permanently or for the 'season'.

In some of these comedies, the place named in the title is visited for only a few, central scenes. In others, it dominates the whole play. All, however, are distinguished by a desire, rare in earlier comedy, to evoke locality as opposed to district – not only its character, activities and inhabitants but its visual appearance – with a realism that verges on the photographic. London has become 'all England', as James put it, in a new and different sense: a concatenation of unlike and different places, tempting the writer to specialize. Audiences sitting at the Cockpit in Drury Lane were being encouraged now to 'see' Covent Garden. Plays of this kind were not directed exclusively at the gentry. Thomas Jordan's *The Walks of Islington and Hogsdon, with The Humours of Wood Street Counter* (1641), the topographically meticulous account of a pub crawl in the northern suburbs which eventually lands most of its participants in jail, ran for a staggering nineteen consecutive days in 1641 at The Red Bull, the most low-brow of London's theatres. Most, however, were. All share an attitude towards the theatrical representation of place akin to that of certain late Jacobean and Caroline court masques.

Although Inigo Jones had begun to experiment with changeable scenery as early as 1605, in the royal entertainments at Oxford, it was not until the 1620s that painted representations of London landmarks (Somerset House, St Paul's, or the banqueting house at Whitehall itself) began to appear in his masques. In 1632, *Albion's Triumph* apparently displayed, even more ambitiously, 'a landscipt in which was a prospect of the King's palace of Whitehall and part of the city

Plate 8 'Sceane with London farr off', from Davenant's masque *Britannia Triumphans*.

of London seen afar off'.[34] A drawing still survives for the Davenant/Jones masque *Britannia Triumphans* of 1638, showing 'English houses with London and the Thames afar off'. Significantly, it places St Paul's in the exact centre of the prospect, partly (no doubt) because of the topicality at the time of its restoration, but also suggesting how far the urban image had now drifted to the west – as well as implying that the city was now too large to be seen whole, except from afar.

Despite the existence of one Inigo Jones drawing, dated 1639, and apparently showing the Cockpit in Drury Lane temporarily equipped with back shutters and painted flats, no agreement has been reached as to the use of changeable scenery in London playhouses before the Restoration.[35] Yet several prologues during the 1630s seem to refer to such an innovation, while one London comedy written in this decade, Thomas Nabbes' *Covent Garden*, makes sense only as a re-hash

[34] Texts and sketch for the prospect of London in *Britannia Triumphans* in Stephen Orgel and Roy Strong, *Inigo Jones: The Theatre of the Stuart Court*, 2 vols. (London, 1973), II, pp. 457, 670–1.

[35] See Allardyce Nicoll, *Stuart Masques and the Renaissance Stage* (London, 1937), Richard Southern, *Changeable Scenery: Its Origin and Development in the British Theatre* (London, 1952), Kenneth Richards, 'Changeable scenery on the Caroline stage', in *Theatre Notebook* 23 (1968), 6–20.

of Brome's *Covent Garden Weeded* in the preceding year, this time equipped with painted scenes. Nabbes' play contains meticulous stage directions instructing characters to enter or exit by the 'balcone', or by the 'right', 'left' or 'middle scaene'. The country clearly lies to the right of the stage, the tavern to the left, while Sir Generous Worthy's house stands in the centre. This, however, by no means implies a return to the fixed, New Comedy street. Nabbes continues to use English flexible staging, showing us the interior of the tavern and the house as freely as the piazza. Characters at one point even walk through the middle scene from a first into a second room. He gives every appearance of mapping his stage in this way because he had at his disposal movable flats and shutters carrying painted representations of the principal localities in the play.

Staging of this kind, a logical development of Caroline place realism, would have to wait until the Restoration to come into its own. Certainly, the kind of relationship which *Totenham-Court* (1633), Nabbes' next comedy, has to the distant prospect of London in *Britannia Triumphans* is more typical of the 1630s. Here, in a striking inversion of the situation at the beginning of *A Midsummer Night's Dream*, a young woman whose family opposes her choice, flees with her lover from the country to the city. The pair get within sound of London, in whose vastness they hope to vanish and elude pursuit – 'Sure I heare / The Bridges *Cattaracts*, and such like murmures / As night and sleepe yeeld from a populous number' – but then lose each other in the early morning mist.[36] They are, in fact, in Marylebone deer park, a place invaded as the morning wears on by a stream of people who have walked out from the city to take the air: citizens and their wives, gallants, courtiers, and young gentlemen from the inns of court. In this Arden on the outskirts of London, even the natives are street-wise. The milkmaid Cicily, far more sophisticated than Shakespeare's Audrey, knows immediately that at this hour a bedraggled young lady in a satin gown spells whore. When the heroine, Bellamie, apparently dies at the very suggestion, Cicily changes her mind – only to begin worrying, as no one in Arden ever does, about what a Middlesex jury is likely to conclude: 'I were in danger, having no witnesse to purge the suspition of being her murderesse.'[37] As for the three young deer found truly dead in the park at sunrise, they are briskly explained, and equally briskly

[36] Nabbes, *Totenham-Court*, in *The Works of Thomas Nabbes*, I, p. 101.
[37] Nabbes, *Totenham-Court*, p. 101.

despatched to city markets, without moralizing: 'Some Cuckolds curre (for I saw him run towards *London*)' has pulled them down.[38] One victim goes to 'a longing Lady in the strand', another to a feast at Barber-Surgeons hall, and the fawn to a poor poet in the city, so that he can lament its fate in a poem dedicated to his patron.

Totenham-Court is a play oddly suspended between *As You Like It* and the comedy of the Restoration. Henry VIII, who had created both Hyde Park and St James's as places to indulge his own passion for the chase, found it necessary to restrain other Londoners from hunting within an area from St Giles to Islington, Hornsey and Hampstead and back through Marylebone to Westminster. Yet even in the mid-sixteenth century, members of the Citizens' Hunt had still been able to disport themselves without going very far from their own homes. John Stow records a meet on 18 September 1562 when

the Lord Mayor, Harpur, the Aldermen and divers worshipful persons, rid to the Conduit-Head before dinner. They hunted the hare and killed her and thence to dine at the Conduit-Head. The chamberlain gave them good cheer, and after dinner they hunted the fox. There was a great cry for a mile, then the hounds killed him at St Giles; great hallooing at his death, and blowing of horns; and then the Lord Mayor and all his company rode through London to his place in Lombard Street.[39]

By the beginning of the seventeenth century, such an outing was no longer possible. Even King James, whose passion for the chase was almost pathological, had taken to indulging it in places considerably removed from London.

The other, smaller parks and pleasure gardens which sprang up in central London – Spring Gardens or the Mulberry Gardens – were not, like Hyde Park and St James's, originally royal game preserves. Yet around all of them there clung associations of the hunt, associations with a rich future in comedy. It was not until the Restoration that the purposeful movement of characters between the town-house interior and the public, erotically dangerous but exciting world of the park became a common structural feature of comedies set in London. Apart from the very special case of Shadwell's *The Squire of Alsatia* in 1668, every surviving Restoration play title referring to a specific part of London was to fix on one of its public gardens or parks: *Love in a Wood, or St James's Park* (1671), *Greenwich Park* (1691), *The Mall* (1674), *The Mulberry Garden* (1668).

---

[38] Nabbes, *Totenham-Court*, p. 111.
[39] Stow, *Survey of London*, ed. and extended by John Strype (London, 1720), I, p. 62.

In those Restoration plays which are set in the London of the theatre audience, the park or pleasure garden is the place where the city is most obviously like a comedy. Ladies go there masked and often illicitly, as they did in real life, to mingle with a crowd of fiercely observant people, everyone concerned to read the meaning of the dress, gestures, movements, declarations and pairings of everyone else. What in the drawing room can be stifled or concealed, tends to break out here, in what is really a miniature Spenserian forest of the passions. In play after play, the park, or public garden, plainly identifiable because actually painted on the stage flats, is the place where assignations are made, where marriages break down, and where people inadvertently betray feelings they have normally been able to control – as Mrs Marwood and Mrs Fainall do in Congreve's *The Way of the World* (1700), when, walking together in St James's Park, they are led to speak of Mirabell.

Jonsonian comedy (in particular *Epicoene* and *The Devil is an Ass*), may be a source for many aspects of Restoration comedy, but it was Shakespeare who pointed towards the park. If *As You Like It* had within it the germs of city comedy, *The Man of Mode* (1676) and *The Way of the World* are London plays with the green place showing through. In the restricted gentry circles of such plays, strangers do not normally meet, or if they do so much is understood between them in terms of background and behaviour that they seem to be operating in a kind of village within the city. The park serves to inject uncertainty and danger. Pervading all such scenes is the idea of the hunt, except that now hunter and hunted are members of the same species. Bullies and ruffians, swaggerers and drunks occasionally invade these places, but they are never the real danger. Tom Brown, in *Amusements Serious and Comical*, published in 1700, the year of *The Way of the World*, was only half in jest when he observed: 'The ladies that have an inclination to be private take delight in the close walks of Spring Gardens, where both sexes meet and mutually serve one another as guides to lose their way; and the windings and turnings in the little wildernesses are so intricate that the most experienced mothers have often lost themselves in looking for their daughters.'[40]

Restoration plays are of the city without really being city comedies. City comedy as discussed in this essay is a brief and unique phenomenon in European culture, born of the confluence of a rich

---

[40] Tom Brown, *Amusements Serious and Comical*, ed. Arthur L. Hayward (London, 1927), p. 40.

classical tradition and the explosive development of a wealthy, increasingly frightening urban centre. Fragmented during the first half of the seventeenth century into a comedy either of localities or of interior space, it narrows further at the Restoration, no longer attempting to grapple with the city as a whole or with its diversity. London had become too huge for comedy, too sprawling indeed for its inhabitants. A foreign visitor in 1690 remarked that most Londoners now were familiar with about one-quarter of the city's streets. Outside the confines of Restoration comedy, felt as a pressure excluded for the sake of a privileged audience, stretches that labyrinth of which the park maze is a minute simulacrum. That is the London we recognize today as 01 breaks down into 071 and 081 and even the taxi drivers – who are no longer required to pass an examination, but have the city mapped on computers – nevertheless get lost. It is the expanding chaotic place that Harold Pinter, our contemporary John Stow, describes as no man's land:

I was standing on a street corner. A car drew up. It was him. He asked me the way to Bolsover Street. I told him Bolsover Street was in the middle of an intricate one-way system. It was a one-way system easy enough to get into. The only trouble was that, once in, you couldn't get out. I told him his best bet, if he really wanted to get to Bolsover Street, was to take the first left, first right, second right, third on the left, keep his eye open for a hardware shop, go right round the square, keeping to the inside lane, take the second Mews on the right and then stop... He's got the Post Office Tower in his vision the whole time. All he's got to do is to reverse into the underground car park, change gear, go straight on, and he'll find himself in Bolsover Street with no trouble at all. I did warn him, though, that he'd still be faced with the problem, having found Bolsover Street, of losing it. I told him I knew one or two people who'd been wandering up and down Bolsover Street for years... I told him that probably the best thing he could do was to forget the whole idea of getting to Bolsover Street. I remember saying to him: This trip you've got in mind, drop it, it could prove fatal. But he said he had to deliver a parcel.[41]

[41] Harold Pinter, *No Man's Land* (London, 1975), p. 62.

CHAPTER 16

Parks and Ardens (1992)

In 1702, a play called *The Comical Gallant: Or, The Amours of Sir John Falstaffe* was performed at the Theatre Royal, Drury Lane. Its author, John Dennis, later claimed that because the actor entrusted with Falstaff failed to please, the audience 'fell from disliking the Action to disapproving the Play'.[1] Certainly, *The Comical Gallant* did not dislodge *The Merry Wives of Windsor* from the repertory. Shakespeare's comedy, un-adapted, had been one of the first plays performed after the Restoration. Revivals were frequent, and in 1704 Dennis had the humiliating experience of seeing Shakespeare's original, rather than his own 'improved' version, presented at court with a glittering cast that included Betterton, Mrs Bracegirdle and Mrs Barry. Yet he had worked hard to accommodate *The Merry Wives* to contemporary taste. Jeremy Collier's strictures in *A Short View* of 1698 clearly lie behind this Fenton's revelation to Master Page that he and Ann have not availed themselves (as they do in Shakespeare) of the confusion at Herne's oak to steal a marriage: having 'truly considered of the terrible consequences which attend the just displeasure of a Parent'.[2] Shakespeare had reserved Windsor Park as a setting until this final, nocturnal scene. Dennis insists that his play should not only end but begin in the park. Moreover, as the assembled characters cross and re-cross the stage in Act 1, greeting one another, scheming, exchanging confidences and billets-doux or, in the case of Ann Page, slipping away from her mother to snatch a meeting with Fenton, it becomes apparent that what Dennis really has in mind is not Windsor but London's St James's Park: the Mall, to be precise, shortly before mid-day, the time of the pre-dinner promenade.

---

[1] John Dennis, 'The epistle dedicatory' to *The Comical Gallant: Or, The Amours of Sir John Falstaffe*, Cornmarket Shakespeare Series, vol. 42 (London, 1969).　　[2] *Ibid.*, p. 48.

In his softened and more cautious way, Dennis was following the example of a great many late seventeenth-century dramatists in gravitating to the Mall. By 1702, park scenes had for decades been a staple of comedies set in contemporary London. Several of them, indeed, had contrasted St James in its fashionable daylight hours with the same place seen at night: *The Mall: Or, The Modish Lovers*, for instance, of 1674, probably the work of John Dover, or Southerne's *The Wives' Excuse* (1691) and *The Maid's Last Prayer* (1693). If Wycherley's character Ranger, in *Love in a Wood: Or, St James's Park* (1672), can be trusted, 'the new-fashioned caterwauling', 'this midnight coursing in the Park' as he calls it, was à la mode by the early 1670s.[3] A risky activity, associated with the illegal pleasures (and dangers) of actual deer coursing after dark, it had been anticipated in the nocturnal park of *The Merry Wives of Windsor* – the first such scene, so far as I can tell, in English drama.[4] For Shakespeare's Windsor Park, where the younger generation deceives the old, and the heiress elopes with a libertine of 'riots past' and 'wild societies' is an oddly Restoration place.[5] Hence the anxiety it caused Dennis in 1702. Struggling to distance himself from the venery associated with parks, he omitted not only the clandestine marriage and all reference to Fenton's rakish reputation, but those shaggy-thighed satyrs originally involved in the hunting of Falstaff. Dennis's night park is more decorous than Shakespeare's. Partly for this reason, it brings into focus a real affinity between *The Merry Wives* and the urbane, tough-minded comedy of dramatists like Wycherley and Southerne – an affinity all the more surprising because of the rustic, Warwickshire roots of this, as of Shakespeare's three other parkland plays.

What was the landscape of Shakespeare's boyhood? One haunted, I want to suggest, by the ghost of the Forest of Arden. In the thirteenth song of *Poly-Olbion*, published in 1612, Michael Drayton – himself a Warwickshire man – gave that ghost a voice: a lament for its destruction at the hands of those 'gripple wretch[es]' who spoiled

---

[3] Sir William Wycherley, *Love in a Wood: Or, St James's Park*, in *The Plays of William Wycherley*, ed. Peter Holland (Cambridge, 1981), II.1.2–3.

[4] Hunting game (except for hares) at night had been illegal since the late sixteenth century. See P. B. Munsche, *Gentlemen and Poachers: The English Game Laws 1671–1831* (Cambridge, 1981), pp. 175–6. The Game Act of 1671 excluded deer – now regarded as a gentleman's private property and so covered by Common Law – from its protection, while effectively restricting the right to hunt game to the landed gentry.

[5] III.4.8. Subsequent references to works by Shakespeare have been incorporated in the text.

'my tall and goodly woods, and did my grounds inclose'.[6] Drayton's claim that Arden was once the greatest forest in Britain is often dismissed as antiquarian fantasy, sparked off by Camden's revelation that '*Arden* among the ancient Britans and Gaules signified a *wood*'.[7] A twelfth-century document, however, decisively supports Drayton. Colossal, on the scale of the greater French forests, Arden once covered Warwickshire and spilled over into Worcestershire and Staffordshire. It seems never to have been Crown property – protected by royal Forest as opposed to Common Law – and that, of course, was its undoing. Patchily but steadily, it was felled, cleared and cultivated, especially to the south of the Avon where the soil was more fertile.[8] Leland, writing in the reign of Henry VIII, observed that only the wooded country north of the river was still known as 'Arden'. It comprised the larger part of the shire, but by 1586 Camden, while recording the same division between felden (or fields) and wooded country, found that 'Arden', as a territorial name, had fallen into disuse. The part north of the Avon, 'much larger in compasse than the *Feldon*,...is for the most part thicke set with woods, and yet not without pastures, corn-fields, and sundry mines of Iron: This part, as it is at this day called *Woodland*, so also was in old time knowen by a more ancient name *Arden*...'[9]

Like Drayton's, Shakespeare's Forest of Arden in *As You Like It* has often been described as imaginary: a purely 'mythic and hypothetical' setting, as one critic puts it.[10] It is true that palm trees and olives, not to mention lionesses, are scarcely Warwickshire products. On the other hand, when Shakespeare, a man born and bred on the north side of the Avon, confronted the Forest of Arden in his source, Lodge's *Rosalynde*, considerably more than just his mother's surname, or the French Ardennes intended by Lodge, must have sprung to mind. Shakespeare's Forest of Arden is the shifting and contradictory

---

[6] Michael Drayton, *Poly-Olbion*, in *The Works of Michael Drayton*, IV, ed. J. William Hebel (Oxford, 1933), p. 276.

[7] William Camden, *Britain, or a Chorographicall Description of the Most Flourishing Kingdomes England, Scotland, and Ireland, and the Ilands Adjoyning...* (English trans. of the 1586 edn, London, 1610), p. 565. See also the seven Warwickshire volumes of *The Victoria County History*, II (London, 1908), pp. 287–8.

[8] Oliver Rackham, *Ancient Woodland: Its History, Vegetation and Uses in England* (London, 1980), pp. 127, 175–82. See also Leonard Cantor, 'Forest, chases, parks and warrens', in *The English Mediaeval Landscape*, ed. L. Cantor (London, 1982), pp. 80–1.

[9] Camden, *Britain*, p. 565.

[10] David Young, *The Heart's Forest: A Study of Shakespeare's Pastoral Plays* (New Haven, 1972), p. 42. For an attempt to redress this view, see A. Stuart Daly, 'Where are the woods in *As You Like It*?' *Shakespeare Quarterly* 34 (1983), 172–80.

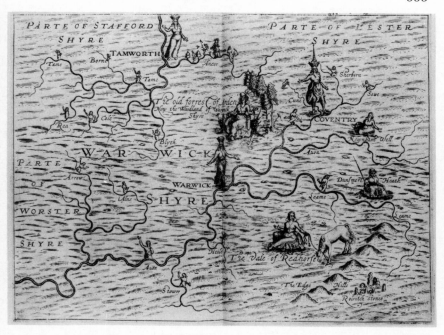

Plate 9   A map of Warwickshire showing 'The old forrest of Arden', from Michael Drayton's *Poly-Olbion* (1612).

place it is because, unlike Lodge's, it compounds the fantastic with something native, real and intimately known. An 'uncouth forest' (II.6.6), a 'desert inaccessible, / Under the shade of melancholy boughs' (II.7.110–11), Arden presents itself initially to Orlando and Adam as untouched woodland. Wandering about helplessly, both nearly starve to death in a place apparently devoid of any settled human habitation. When Orlando fortunately stumbles upon Duke Senior and his fellow outlaws, he is anxious to know if they have ever been 'where bells have knoll'd to church' (II.7.114). And yet Arden is not only where William says he was born, the place he, Audrey, Corin, Silvius and Phebe call home, Touchstone has no difficulty in rustling up Sir Oliver Martext, 'the vicar of the next village' (III.43–4), and a chapel, when 'wedlock would be nibbling' (III.3.80–1).

Shakespeare's Arden, unlike that of Lodge, has experienced enclosure. In the source, Rosalynde and Aliena first encounter Coridon and Montanus sitting side by side 'in a faire valley', their two flocks of sheep feeding around them on common pasture.[11] As they talk, it becomes clear that Coridon is a tenant farmer who, as well as tending his 'landlord's' sheep on the common, supports himself by tilling arable land belonging to the cottage he rents. The landlord has now decided to sell, terminating the lease-hold. When Rosalynde and Aliena offer to buy both sheep and farm, Coridon gladly agrees to share the cottage he previously enjoyed alone, and relinquish to them the task of escorting sheep to the common. The position of Shakespeare's Corin is very different. A wage-earner, not a tenant, he is not only unable to 'shear the fleeces that I graze' (II.4.79) – the grazing itself – or 'bounds of feed' (II.4.83) – is up for sale too, along with the flock and the cottage. There is no 'landlord' in the case, only a churlish 'master' in whose cottage Corin, the labourer, is allowed a bed. Because this master is currently away, as Corin explains to Rosalind and Celia, there is almost nothing in this house on the 'skirts' (III.2.336) or 'purlieus' (IV.3.77) – Shakespeare uses the technical word for a cleared space on the edge of a forest – of Arden 'that you will feed on' (II.4.86), although he proposes to make them as welcome as he can.

Enclosure in Arden, unprotected as it was by Forest law, had begun early. Coridon's slide from tenant to hired man was a more recent phenomenon. In his study of 'Economic and Social Change in the Forest of Arden: 1530–1649', the agrarian historian V. H. T. Skipp identifies a steady rise there towards the end of the sixteenth century in the number of landless labourers, proportions of about twenty per cent already registering in one parish by 1605.[12] It would be more than forty per cent by the middle of the century. The change seems to have been linked to Arden's gradual abandonment of its traditional pastoral economy, based on sheep and cattle, in favour of those 'green corn-field[s]' and 'acres of the rye' (V.3.18.22) characteristic of the other side of the river. And Shakespeare's play faithfully reflects it.

In their sylvan exile, Duke Senior and his court subsist on fallow deer – 'poor *dappled* fools' (II.1.22) – an imported species, associated primarily with parks, where they tended to be kept at least as much to supply venison for the table as for sport. The wild red deer, the

---

[11] Thomas Lodge, 'Rosalynde', in *Narrative and Dramatic Sources of Shakespeare's Plays*, ed. Geoffrey Bullough, II (London, 1958), p. 182.

[12] V. H. T. Skipp, 'Economic and social change in the Forest of Arden', in *Agriculture History Review* 18 (suppl.) (1970), 84–111.

hart, from time immemorial the noblest of quarries, which Drayton depicts being hunted 'at force'[13] (that is, with hounds) through the spacious tracts of an older Arden, makes only a distant appearance in *As You Like It*, by way of Touchstone's parodic verses: 'If a hart do lack a hind, / Let him seek out Rosalind' (III.2.101–2). Warwickshire from medieval times had been particularly rich in parks and, of those established before the sixteenth century, fifty out of fifty-two were located north of the river.[14] Charlecote Park, bifurcated by the Avon, may not have been enclosed and stocked with deer in time for the young Shakespeare, 'much given to all unluckinesse in stealing venison', according to Richard Davies in 1695, to have chosen it as the scene of his depredations.[15] There were plenty of others in the vicinity, including (of course) Kenilworth, greatly enlarged by the Earl of Leicester, where Queen Elizabeth in 1575 had spent more time slaughtering deer than attending to the ingenious shows and entertainments with which these ceremonial hunts were entwined. Shakespeare may or may not, like his own Falstaff in *The Merry Wives*, actually have beaten keepers, killed deer, broken open a lodge, and then (as the legend has it) been obliged to flee Warwickshire and become England's greatest dramatist. But parks, during the 1590s, when he was still close to his Warwickshire youth, do seem to have been much on his mind.

I can find only one allusion to a park in Shakespeare's Jacobean work. The Queen, in *Cymbeline*, imagines all Britain as 'Neptune's park, ribb'd and pal'd in / With oaks unscalable and roaring waters' (III.1.19–20). The image is accurate, and ought never (though it often is) to be emended. In 1611, Arthur Standish, in *The Commons Complaint*, the first recorded book on English forestry, three slightly different versions of which, all dedicated to King James, appeared in 1611, 1613 and 1615, extended particular approval to park owners who reinforced their enclosures, whether hedge or the more usual cleft stakes, with living timber trees, a barrier of ash or oak, allowed to grow to full maturity, and 'once made, never to be made againe'.[16] The *Cymbeline* passage set aside, all Shakespeare's other park references or settings are Elizabethan: Talbot's dismayed exclama-

---

[13] Drayton, *Poly-Olbion* p. 278. [14] Cantor, 'Forest, chases, parks and warrens', p. 80.
[15] Sir Edmund Chambers, *William Shakespeare: A Study of Facts and Problems*, 2 vols. (Oxford, 1930), I, pp. 18–21, II, pp. 255–7.
[16] Arthur Standish, *The Commons Complaint* (London, 1615), D3.

tion in *1 Henry VI*, 'How are we park'd and bounded in a pale, / A little herd of England's timorous deer, / Maz'd with a yelping kennel of French curs!' (IV.2.45–7), Venus' unsuccessful attempt, in *Venus and Adonis*, to transform her body into a park, encircled by an 'ivory pale' (230), where Adonis might erotically and safely browse, or the complaint of Adriana in *The Comedy of Errors* about her husband's infidelities – 'too unruly deer, he breaks the pale, / And feeds from home' (II.1.100–1). Other instances, literal rather than metaphoric, conjure up a shadowy park setting, just out of sight: Hotspur's park in *1 Henry IV* in which the crop-eared roan awaits his master, or Petruchio's in *The Taming of the Shrew*, where the servants ought to be lined up to welcome Kate. Editors of *The Merchant of Venice* usually indicate that Lorenzo and Jessica listen to music, just before Portia's return, in the open air of a garden or 'avenue before the house'. Judging from the fact that she and Nerissa left for Venice by coach from 'the park-gate' (III.4.83), Shakespeare may well, in an interesting anticipation of *The Merry Wives*, have imagined, without specifying, a night park.

Far more concretely realized are the paired park scenes of *3 Henry VI*. At the beginning of Act III, King Henry, fleeing from the battle of Towton, is taken prisoner by 'keepers' concealed in a thicket beside the 'laund' (or open space) of what editors usually designate as a 'forest', but which must, given the vocabulary used, be a park. Armed with crossbows, they are out 'culling the principal of all the deer' (III.1.4), but succeed in bringing down a different kind of royal stag. The scene has a carefully constructed obverse in Act IV, when the imprisoned Edward IV manages to escape from the Bishop of York's custody while walking in his park, despite the efforts of the 'huntsman' accompanying him. There is no indication in Shakespeare's sources that Henry was taken prisoner in either a forest or a park. For his rival's evasion of captivity, there is only Hall's testimony that because Edward 'spake ever fayre to the Archebishop and the other kepers', he had liberty to go hunting, and one day met 'on a playne' with such a large body of his friends that 'neither his kepers woud nor once durst, move him to retorne to prison agayn'.[17] Shakespeare has availed himself of the suggestive word 'keper' to turn Hall's aristocratic gaolers into the single 'huntsman' responsible for showing Edward 'where lies the game' (IV.5.14). He also turns

[17] Edward Hall, *The Union of the Two Noble and Illustre Famelies of Lancaster and York* (London, 1550), 'The viii yere of Kyng Edward the iiii', fol. xiiij^r.

Hall's 'playne' into an enclosed park, at the 'corner' (IV.5.19) of which Edward's horse stands ready. Across the space of nearly two acts, Lancaster's capture and York's escape are counter-balanced structurally by way of their shared parkland setting.

The park in *Titus Andronicus* seems also to have been Shakespeare's invention. The hunt, with 'horn and hound', of 'the panther and the hart' (I.1.494, 493) in Act II is usually said to take place, quite simply, in a forest. Richard Marienstras, in his 1981 essay, 'The Forest, Hunting and Sacrifice in *Titus Andronicus*', makes much of it as 'a place predestined by nature to the release of savagery'.[18] That is partly true. But it is also true that, like Arden later, this forest keeps shifting its character and identity. 'The woods are ruthless, dreadful, deaf, and dull' (II.1.128), as Aaron says, but they are also – and not just in Tamora's imagination – 'green' (II.2.2), a 'pleasant chase' (II.3.255), full of bird-song, 'cheerful sun' (II.3.13), and of wide and spacious 'walks' where 'the lovely Roman ladies' (II.1.113–14) can saunter at their ease, like those fifteenth-century Flemish beauties in the Victoria and Albert Museum's Chatsworth tapestries, while the hunt goes on around them. Tamora's two contrasting vignettes of the particular spot that is at one moment a *locus amoenus* and, in the next, a 'barren, detested vale' (II.3.93), merely polarize a general ambiguity, one reflected in the different terms used to describe the scene of the hunt: 'woods' and 'forest', but also (on two occasions) 'chase' – a small, managed forest in private hands – equipped, in this instance, on 'the north side' with a keeper's lodge (II.3.254–5). Finally, Marcus tells his brother Titus that he found the raped and mutilated Lavinia, straying, 'as doth the deer / That hath receiv'd some unrecuring wound', 'in the park' (III.1.88–90).

T. J. B. Spencer once remarked of *Titus* that Shakespeare seemed determined to include in it all the political institutions Rome ever had, not so much to get Roman history right, as to get it all in.[19] That impulse also seems to lie behind the hunt in this play and its setting. Titus' proposal to the emperor and his bride, 'Tomorrow... / To hunt the panther and the hart with me' (I.1.492–3), is startling, especially when surrounded, as it almost immediately is, with ceremonial detail – the horn call when hounds were uncoupled, the

[18] Richard Marienstras, *New Perspectives on the Shakespearean World*, trans. Janet Lloyd (Cambridge, 1981), p. 44.
[19] T. J. B. Spencer, 'Shakespeare and the Elizabethan Romans' in *Shakespeare Survey 10* (1957), p. 32.

baying of what the stage directions suggest must have been real dogs, the different 'horns in a peal' described in Gascoigne's *Noble Arte of Venerie* of 1575 as appropriate to call 'a companie in the morning' – all things associated specifically with the singling out and hunting, *par force des chiens*, of the red deer stag.[20] Shakespeare must have been aware that panthers are as impossible in Italy as lions in Arden, unless (of course) someone imports them, like those Elizabethan lions languishing in the Tower of London, for a purpose. Certainly a 'solemn hunting' (II.I.112), as this one is said to be, is implausible with both the panther and the hart as intended and simultaneous quarry. Or at least it is in a forest or chase. The enclosed park is a different matter.

At this point, the vexed issue of Shakespeare's 'small *Latine*, and lesse *Greeke*' becomes more than usually troublesome. Like the fallow deer with which they became so closely associated, parks were of eastern origin. Persia in particular was renowned for them. *Pairidaeza*, the Old Persian word for park – it means to 'shape' or 'mould around' – was first Hellenized by Xenophon, in the *Anabasis*, when he wrote about the great royal *paradeisos* of Cyrus, full of wild animals.[21] This Greek word was destined to become complexly entwined with the ancient Hebrew *pardes* and end up signifying both heaven and the garden of Eden. Meanwhile, according to Quintus Curtius, Alexander the Great, entering a great walled park in the heart of Asia which had not been touched for four generations, ordered all the beasts to be driven from their cover, and despatched single-handed the huge lion that attacked him. It was largely as a result of Alexander's progress through Persia that parks, enclosing beasts of various kinds, soon began to appear all over the Mediterranean.[22] Some were really menageries. Varro writes admiringly of the park belonging to the Roman orator Hortensius, where guests banqueting on an artfully raised triclinium watched a slave, dressed up as Orpheus, with a long floating robe, gather stags, wild boar, and a multitude of other quadrupeds around him with the music of his lyre.[23] This wonderful spectacle, Varro claimed, could be compared

[20] Hereward T. Price discusses the hunting music, and its precision, in 'The authorship of *Titus Andronicus*', in *The Journal of English and Germanic Philology* 42 (1943), 61.

[21] A. Bartlett Giametti, *The Earthly Paradise and the Renaissance Epic* (Princeton, 1966), pp. 11–15.

[22] Russell Meiggs, *Trees and Timber in the Ancient Mediterranean* (Oxford, 1982), p. 272.

[23] Jacques Aymard, *Essai sur les Chasses Romaines, des origines à la fin du siècle des Antonins* (Paris, 1951), Bibliotheque des Ecoles Françaises d'Athènes et de Rome, p. 71.

only to the great *venationes*, the hunts and other displays of the Roman circus, or at least to those which did not include African animals. They, according to Livy, had first appeared in the year 186 BC, in the form of a combat of lions and panthers.

In his *Historie of the Foure-Footed Beastes* (1607), Edward Topsell, assembling information from a wide range of classical and other sources, asserts that although the senators of Rome 'in auncient time' wisely forbade anyone to import panthers, the needs of the circus soon prevailed: Pompey the Great, we are told, brought in four hundred and ten of them, and Augustus four hundred and twenty.[24] These figures sound exaggerated, but there can be no doubt that panthers did feature prominently in the gory spectacles of the Roman circus, especially under the empire, and that a variety of other victims – including stags – were often hunted in the arena with them at the same time. In the most elaborate, moreover, of these *venationes* – they were known as *silvae* – the amphitheatre, at enormous expense, was landscaped: provided with trees and rocks, thickets, running streams, and artificial hills, so that the Roman crowd seemed to be looking down at a real forest or, given its protective barriers and circular shape, upon an enclosed park.[25] Some emperors – Nero, Caracalla – actually entered it themselves to display their prowess. I don't know whether Shakespeare had read or heard about the Roman *silvae* in Calpurnius and later Roman authors, but the mixed nature of the hunt, including the slaughter of human participants, in *Titus* eerily resembles them.

Tamora's son Demetrius assumes a shared experience of ordinary deer-stealing among Chiron, Aaron and himself: 'What, hast not thou full often strook a doe, / And borne her cleanly by the keeper's nose? (II.1.93–4). But when he reminds Chiron that 'we hunt not, we, with horse nor hound, / But hope to pluck a dainty doe to ground' (II.2.25–6), he has ceased to be the human hunter and become the hound, one of those masterless 'whelps, fell curs of bloody kind' (II.3.281) that Saturninus, speaking more truly than he knows, later accuses of having murdered Bassianus. Lavinia, in Act II, describes Tamora as a tiger, but the honey-tongued and treacherous conciliatress of the play's first scene is more concretely emblematized by that panther Aaron persuades Titus' sons they can surprise fast asleep in the bottom of a pit. 'As a Lyon doeth in most thinges imitate and

[24] Edward Topsell, *The Historie of the Foure-Footed Beastes* (London, 1607), p. 583.
[25] Aymard, *Essai sur les Chasses Romaines* pp. 189–96, 354.

resemble the very nature of man', Topsell misogynistically recorded, 'so after the very selfe-same manner doth the panther of a Woman, for it is a fraudulent though a beautiful beast'.[26] Panthers in the wild, as Topsell also records (following Oppian) were taken in pit-fall traps, baited with carrion; this 'subtile hole' (II.3.198), its mouth 'covered with rude-growing briers' (II.3.199), is the place to which two young men, lured by the panther, come unsuspectingly and, when they have fallen helplessly into its depths, discover human carrion.

The 'loathsome pit' (II.3.176) in *Titus*, a 'fell devouring receptacle, / As hateful as [Cocytus'] misty mouth' (II.3.235-6), was already complicated enough before the Freudians got hold of it. A natural cavity, a trap, a grave, hell-mouth, the entrance to the underworld, it also provokes thoughts of a Warwickshire saltory, or deer-leap: an excavation, usually combined with a steep bank, which allowed wild deer to enter a park through a gap in its palings, but not to get out again. Edward Ravenscroft, adapting Shakespeare's tragedy in 1686, rejected all these associations. He turned it into an ice-house. Unlike Dennis's *Comical Gallant*, Ravenscroft's *Titus* was a theatrical success. Establishing itself in the repertory as 'a Stock-Play', it not only replaced the original, but continued to be performed well into the eighteenth century.[27] One reason for its acceptability may have been the drastic – and revealing – measures Ravenscroft had taken when confronted with the peculiarities of Shakespeare's hunt and its locale. The hunt he abolished entirely; the ambiguous forest he transformed unequivocally into a park, or pleasure garden.

'Come *Tamora*', Ravenscroft's Saturninus says near the end of Act I,

> this is a day of Triumph,
> All Pleasures of the *Banii* shall delight thee,
> Where every Sense is exquisitely touch'd,
> Pleasures that not the World affords,
> And yet is only known to Roman Lords.[28]

I owe to Jeremy Maule the suggestion that 'Banii' represents Ravenscroft's attempt to Latinize the famous sixteenth-century Bagnaia Gardens attached to the Villa Lante, outside Rome near Viterbo. He may have visited them himself, as John Evelyn did. But

---

[26] Topsell, *The Historie* pp. 581-2.
[27] Edward Ravenscroft, 'To the reader', *Titus Andronicus: Or The Rape of Lavinia* (London, 1969), Cornmarket Shakespeare Series, vol. 71.   [28] *Ibid.*, p. 15.

although the same dreadful things happen in Ravenscroft's Banii Gardens as had in Shakespeare's ruthless woods, they are everywhere coloured by suggestions of a place closer to home. Whatever may have been painted on the stage shutters, this scene of public promenade, but also of 'close walks' and 'private Groves', 'Grottoes', and retreats for lovers, where 'none may hear / Their Amorous talk', is again (like Dennis's Windsor Park) really London's St James's.[29]

In his poem, 'On St James's Park, As Lately Improved By His Majesty', published in 1661, Edmund Waller had paid particular attention to the marvel of the royal ice-houses: those 'deep caves', 'Winter's dark prison', whose 'harvest of cold months laid up, / Gives a fresh coolness to the royal cup'.[30] There was, as it happens, an ice-house in the Bagnaia Gardens. Its presence is clearly visible in an engraving of 1612–14, from the *Antiquae urbis splendor Roma*.[31] One needs, however, to remember that although common in Italy, and beginning to appear in France, ice-houses (as opposed to rudimentary snow conserves of the kind King James had at Greenwich Park and Hampton Court) were unknown in Britain until John Rose in October 1660 constructed the ones in St James's Park on the model of those recently introduced at Versailles.[32] Ice-houses were sufficiently novel and also rare for the Royal Society to hold a special meeting on the subject in 1662, at which Robert Boyle gave a paper incorporating some of the observations made by Evelyn during his travels in Italy, and for Charles II in February 1664 to swear in one Simon Menselli (significantly, an Italian) in a newly created post as 'Yeoman of O[u]r Snowe and Ice'. For London audiences, it would have been these celebrated ice-houses in St James's Park, presided over by Menselli and his successors, with which Ravenscroft endowed Saturninus:

> on the more Remoter parts
> Dark Caves and Vaults, where water crusted Lyes
> In ice, all the hot season of the year.

---

[29] *Ibid.*, pp. 17–18.

[30] Edmund Waller, 'On St James's Park as lately improved by his majesty', in *The Works of Edward Waller Esq. in Verse and Prose* (London, 1729), p. 208.

[31] The engraving by G. Lauro, showing the ice-house, is reproduced by Bruno Adorni in his essay, 'The Villa Lante at Bagnaia', in *The History of Garden Design: The Western Tradition from the Renaissance to the Present Day*, ed. Monique Mosser and Georges Tessot (London, 1991), p. 92.

[32] Sylvia Beamon and Susan Roaf, *The Ice-Houses of Britain* (New York, 1991), pp. 12–19, 34.

> As Chrystillin, and firm as when
> 'Twas taken from the Winter's frost.[33]

It is to the deepest and most gloomy of these vaults, now containing the body of Bassianus, that the sons of Titus are decoyed. The attraction is not a panther, but what Quintus calls the 'pleasant Secret' of an anonymous letter:

> Quintus, as soon as this comes to your hands, find out your Brother Martius, Bring him with you into the Banii Gardens, and attend a while at the Mouth of the Vault which is called the Serpents-Den, where once the mighty Snake was found: Your Expectations shall be rewarded with the company of two Ladies, Young, and in our own opinions not unhandsome, whose sight shall not displease you; Love gives the Invitation, and we believe you both Gallant Enough to know how to use it, and to conceal our favours.[34]

Here, and for several ensuing lines of dialogue, as the deluded brothers await 'these kind and Loving ones', Ravenscroft begins to write Restoration comedy: the kind of play – *The Mall*, or Southerne's *The Maid's Last Prayer* are examples – in which one or two men are lured into St James's Park by a note (usually deceptive) of assignation.

Waller's encomium on St James's Park, a 'Paradise', as he calls it, another Eden, presided over by a benevolent shepherd king, had dealt entirely with its daylight hours and cheerful, public pursuits: 'the lovers walking in that amorous shade; / The Gallants dancing by the river's side; / They bathe in summer, and in winter slide'.[35] A decade later, in 1672, Rochester revisited the place, in his nocturnal 'A Ramble in St James's Park', and saw something very different: an 'all-sin-sheltring Grove', where every imitative branch does twine / In some lov'd fold of Aretine / And nightly now beneath their shade / Are Buggeries, Rapes and Incests made'.[36] Ravenscroft has managed to invoke both Waller's *paradeisos* and Rochester's surreal landscape of violence and lust, translating Shakespeare's ambivalent forest into an equally ambiguous but recognizable contemporary place.

Titus, *The Merry Wives*, and *3 Henry VI* were all adapted in the later seventeenth century or early in the eighteenth. (Crowne's version of

---

[33] Ravenscroft, 'To the reader', pp. 17–18.   [34] *Ibid.*, p. 23.
[35] Waller, 'On St James's Park, p. 207.
[36] John Wilmot, Earl of Rochester, 'A ramble in St James's Park', in *The Poems of John Wilmot, Earl of Rochester*, ed. Keith Walker (London, 1984), p. 64.

the last, *The Misery of Civil War*, of 1680, omitted the scenes of Henry's capture and Edward's escape.) *Love's Labour's Lost* – the fourth and last of Shakespeare's parkland plays that I want to discuss – remained untouched until 1762. Nor, although it appears (together with *As You Like It*) in the long list of works, formerly the property of Shakespeare's company at Blackfriars, that were 'allowed' to the King's Company at Drury Lane in January 1669, does it seem to have been performed after the Restoration. That, given its intransigently Elizabethan wit, combined with a plotlessness exceeding even that of *As You Like It*, is understandable. More surprising is the fact that this play, available only as a text for reading, should have exercised such an influence on the best comedies of the period: an influence, as I believe, far more profound than that of Fletcher or Shirley, whose comedies were frequently revived, and rivalled only by that of Jonson.

Love's Labour's Lost is usually said by its editors to be set entirely in the royal park of Navarre. That is not strictly true, although the unlocalized staging of Shakespeare's theatre must have blurred this fact. The anonymous author of *The Students* in 1762, however, who had experienced the comedy only on the printed page, displayed a rare flash of intelligence when he discriminated, in the scene headings of his version, between 'the fields' and 'the park'. The tents in which Shakespeare's Navarre lodges the Princess and her ladies stand in 'the wide fields' (1.1.93), somewhere close to that manor-house, the King's silent and 'un-peopled' court, whose gates they cannot enter. The park, abutting, as Armado tells us, on the manor's 'curious-knotted' garden (1.1.245–6), is a place slightly but significantly different. The women enter it for the hunt and then, at the end of Act IV, are escorted back to their tents ('from the park let us conduct them thither', IV.3.371) by men whose vows of asceticism and study have crumbled ignominiously in the parkland setting. It is a populous place, not only in terms of the deer, and the foresters in the 'lodge' who look after them, but because a variety of people like to walk there – the King and his three 'book-mates', Armado giving his melancholy some fresh air, Costard in amorous pursuit of Jaquenetta, or local villagers, the schoolmaster Holofernes and Nathaniel the curate, lost in erudite discourse.

The hunt arranged to divert a somewhat reluctant Princess is of the 'bow and stable', as opposed to *par force*, variety most often associated in the Tudor period with parks. As Queen Elizabeth did so often, she stands in an appointed place, armed with a cross-bow, while the deer are driven past, and her success is greeted by the shouts of assembled spectators. Meanwhile, Berowne is observing gloomily that while the King hunts deer, 'I am coursing myself', caught in a 'toil' of love he likens to the one set up in the park, the deer-haye forcing the animals towards the waiting archers (IV.3.1–3). This particular version of the Actaeon image (later elaborated by Orsino in *Twelfth Night*, in the context of a *par force* chase), in which the lover is both quarry and hound, is altogether more complicated than the brutally simple intention of Chiron and Demetrius in *Titus* to 'pluck down a dainty doe'. It links back, indeed, to the courtly love poetry of the fourteenth century, to Hesdin and the great *Jagd* of Hadamar – in which named hounds, sometimes in fell pursuit of the lover to whom they belong, are aspects of his self, or of his relationship with the lady. But it also looks forward to the Restoration.

It was once a critical fashion to assail even the best Restoration comedy for its supposed dullness and triviality, and to instance its repetitive imagery of the sexual hunt. This imagery is not, in fact, either as monotonous or as fatuous as was claimed – although it could be used to signal either the inappropriateness of the love chase to the old (Sir Oliver Cockwood and Sir Joslin Jolly in Etherege's *She Wou'd If She Cou'd* (1668), for instance) or the habituated response of fashionable young philanderers before they fall under the spell of a genuinely witty and interesting woman. Although usually, it is by no means invariably the language of men. Crowne's heroine Christina in *The Country Wit* (1675) intends to pursue the outrageous Ramble to his lodging 'And hunt him dry-foot thence: – would odds were laid me, / I did not rouse my wild, outlying buck / This hour, and catch him brousing on some common …',[37] and Farquhar's Lucinda in *Love and a Bottle* (1698), catching sight of the aptly named Roebuck, in one of the walks of Lincoln's-Inn Fields, goes in pursuit, thinking 'He may afford us some sport.'[38] A great many of these hunting images appear in scenes set in London's St James's Park, which did as it happens still contain deer. Even when they do not, the presence of that park still tends to be felt behind them, as a focus of daily life in town.

[37] John Crowne, *The Country Wit*, in *The Comedies of John Crowne*, ed. B. J. McMullin (New York, 1984), (*The Renaissance Imagination*, gen. ed. Stephen Orgel), 1.1.317–19.
[38] George Farquhar, *Love and a Bottle*, in *The Works of George Farquhar*, ed. Shirley Strum Kenny, 1 (Oxford, 1988), 1.1.130.

Although Shirley's *Hyde Park* of 1632 was revived after the Restoration – Pepys saw it in 1668, apparently with live horses – and although a scattering of comedies visit the New Spring Gardens in Lambeth, Lincoln's-Inn Fields, or Greenwich Park, St James's was overwhelmingly the preferred park setting. (The Mulberry Gardens, used by Newcastle, Sedley and Etherege, on the site of what is now Buckingham Palace, were merely an extension of it.) St James's was not, in fact, any more fashionable or more frequented than Hyde Park in the period. The latter, however, although much mentioned in comedy, had become useless as a dramatic setting, for the simple reason that the 'done' thing there after 1660 was for people to sit in a coach, equipped with footmen and six Flanders mares, and ride round and round in up to twelve concentric and very dusty circles, each revolving in the opposite direction to the one flanking it. This was called 'The Ring' or 'Tour', and apart from being unstageable, it reduced conversation outside the cramped confines of each coach to what Etherege's Harriet in *The Man of Mode* (1676) dismisses contemptuously as 'the formal bows, the affected smiles, the silly by-words, and amorous tweers, in passing'.[39] Some signals could be given in the Ring: Charles II and the Duchess of Castlemaine formally greeting one another, as Pepys noted, at each revolution, or (on a different occasion) the Duchess expressing her superiority to the whole gilded and competitive show by allowing herself to be carried round fast asleep, with her mouth open. According to Stanmore in Shadwell's *A True Widow* (1678), Restoration Hyde Park had even invented a 'new method' of making love 'without speaking': 'your side glass let down hastily, when the party goes by, is very passionate. If she side *glass* you again, for that's the new word, ply her next day with a *billet doux* and you have her sure'.[40] It all depended, as Stanmore's interlocutor points out, on the two coaches *not* circulating in the same direction.

Etherege's Harriet, however, walking – as was the custom – in St James's Park at 'high Mall', the second of the two fashionable times to be seen there, after the play and the Ring, observes that 'here one meets with a little conversation now and then'.[41] 'These conversations', her escort replies, 'have been fatal to some of your sex'. But

---

[39] Sir George Etherege, *The Man of Mode*, in *The Plays of Sir George Etherege*, ed. Michael Cordner (Cambridge, 1982), III.3.49–51.
[40] Thomas Shadwell, *A True Widow*, in *The Complete Works of Thomas Shadwell*, ed. Montague Summers, III (London, 1927), p. 290.   [41] Etherege, *The Man of Mode* III.3.49–51.

Harriet likes to live dangerously. A moment later the park brings her face to face with Dorimant, the charismatic libertine of whom her mother is so terrified. Harriet has already seen and been fascinated by him at a distance. The Mall allows not only an introduction, but a tensely consequential crossing of verbal swords that she could have engineered nowhere else. It is also the arena Dorimant finds essential when he wants to quarrel with his mistress Mrs Loveit, later in the same scene, severing their relations before the eyes of the whole town, and where she, at least briefly, is able to humiliate him.

'The hours of *Park-walking* are times of perfect *Carnival* to the Women', Sir Harry Peerabout later observed in an anonymous play of 1733 called *St James's Park* and actually performed there 'Every Fine Day Between the Hours of Twelve and Two, During this Season':

> She that wou'd not admit the Visits of a Man without his being introduced by some Relation or intimate Friend, makes no scruple here to commence acquaintance at first sight; readily answers to any question shall be asked of her; values herself on being brisk at Repartee; and to have put him to it (as they call it) leaves a pleasure upon her Face for the whole day. In short, no Freedoms that can be taken here, are reckon'd indecent: All passes for Rallery, and harmless Gallantry.[42]

Almost half a century separates this passage from *The Man of Mode*, reflected not only in the later dinner hour and consequent advancement in the time of the morning promenade, but in the stiff response Peerabout's report of these manners elicits from Truelove: 'I should be sorry my Wife or Daughter were practis'd in them. But do any Women of real Honour take these Liberties?' The answer now, even from a Peerabout, is 'No'. It would have been 'Yes' before 1700, and not only in London's St James's. Peerabout's account of raillery and repartee on slight acquaintance, bold skirmishes of wit in which women amuse themselves by putting down their male opponents, could also be a description of the Princess of France and her ladies, their mocking merriment at masculine expense, in that other royal park of Navarre.

Like Hyde Park, St James's had been acquired and paled in by Henry VIII. He used it for hunting, as did Elizabeth.[43] Originally

---

[42] *St James's Park* (London, 1733), p. 3.
[43] For Henry VIII's 'mania' for hunting in parks, see Oliver Rackham *Trees and Woodland in the British Landscape* (rev. edn, London, 1990), p. 158 and 'The King's Deer' [Nonsuch

restricted to the royal family – St James's Palace was incorporated in the grounds – it came under James I to be a place where other people, initially those attached to the court, came to stroll in the fresh air and admire not only the deer but the king's growing and expensive menagerie of wild animals. (The board of the elephant alone cost £273 a year, and that was exclusive of the gallon of wine a day his keepers said he required from September to April.)[44] Already fashionable under Charles I, St James's continued to be frequented by Cromwell and his courtiers during the Commonwealth, and so escaped being sold off with the other royal parks. But it was only after the Restoration that it came into its own. Extensively re-designed and planted by Andrew Mollet, 'Master of His Majesty of England's Gardens in His Park of St James' – two copies of his book, *The Garden of Pleasure*, one with diagrams of the park, survive – this was the place where Charles II liked to exercise (and tended to lose) his spaniels, where he fed the ducks and played pall-mall, a form of croquet, on an avenue covered with powdered cockle-shells. Around him, Londoners with any social pretensions thronged to bask in the presence of this strikingly informal king and, even when he was only symbolically there, to see and be seen, to observe the follies of others and commit their own.

Thanks to the efforts of Mollet, the park was wonderfully diverse.[45] Dominating it were the new canal, nearly half a mile long and one hundred feet wide, that extended down the middle, with an avenue of trees on each side, and the upper and lower Mall, the place of public promenade. But there was also a multitude of lesser walks, some of them named – the Green Walk, or Birdcage Walk, featuring some of the inmates of the royal zoo – others anonymous alleys or

Palace Centenary Celebrations], which the author has kindly allowed me to read in typescript. See also E. P. Shirley, *Some Account of English Deer Parks* (London, 1867), A. S. Barrow ('Sabretache'), *Monarchy and the Chase* (London, 1948), and Susan Lasdun *The English Park: Royal, Private and Public* (London, 1991).

Edward Hall's account (*The Union of the Two Noble and Mystic Families of Lancaster and York*, fol. iiii) of the festivities following Henry VIII's coronation ('The first yere of Kyng Henry the viii') includes a description of the 'faire house' erected in the Palace of Westminster, into which was brought a pageant in the form of a deer-park, 'paled with pales of White and Grene, wherein wer certain Fallowe Dere'. When its doors were opened, the deer 'ranne out therof into the Palaice, the greye hounds were lette slippe and killed the Dere: the whiche Dere so killed, were presented to the Quene and the Ladies' by Diana's knights.

[44] Jacob Larwood, *The Story of the London Parks, vol.* II (London, 1881), p. 72.
[45] Andrew Mollet, *The Garden of Pleasure* (London, 1670), pp. 11–12. For the complicated history of this rare, posthumously published volume, see Blanche Henrey, *British Botanical and Horticultural History Before 1800* (London, 1975), pp. 198–203, 259.

Plate 10   An engraving by Kip showing St James's Palace and part of St James's Park, with the London skyline, from *Britannia Illustrata* (1707).

cross-walks lined with dwarf fruit-trees and leading to arbours or, in some cases, into what Mollet calls the 'wild Wood' at one end of the park and the artificial wilderness he had created at the other. Couples with something other than the promenade on their minds tended to arrange assignations in remote and specific areas: on the Duckpond side, or at the mysteriously named Rosamond's Pond. The latter, at the west end of the park, had existed for centuries, but it was Mollet who surrounded it with trees and also constructed an artificial mount in the vicinity. An evening rendezvous at Rosamund's Pond, whether proposed or merely accepted by a woman, was usually regarded as tantamount to sexual surrender, something which might take place there and then. Not that Rosamond's Pond had a monopoly on such scenes. Courtall and Mrs Wouldbee, in Dover's *The Mall*, are on 'the Duck-pond side' when she tells him, 'Sir, you have prevail'd, and overcome, but methinks this Bench is a very undecent place'. 'Oh Madam!', Courtall replies, 'There has been many a worse shift made'.[46] *Exeunt*, hand in hand.

[46] John Dover, *The Mall: Or, The Modish Lovers*, in *The Dramatic Works of John Dryden*, ed. George Saintsbury, VIII (London, 1882), p. 537.

Plate 11 A detail from the engraving by Kip of St James's Palace and part of St James's Park from *Britannia Illustrata* (1707). Deer can be seen in the distance and, in the foreground on the right, gentlemen playing pall-mall on the cockle-shell walk.

It was, however, as a setting for the chase, rather than for consummation, that St James's usually figured in comedy of the period. Women sometimes go there to spy upon and pursue erring lovers or husbands, as Lydia and Amanda do in Cibber's *Love's Last Shift* (1696) and Wycherley's *Love in A Wood*. Witty young heroines, cooped up at home by watchful parents or guardians, escape and range freely over the park in order to flush out and attract a young man to their taste. The young men themselves are the most habitual hunters. 'Yes faith, we have had many a fair course in this paddock', Freeman tells Ariana and Gatty in *She Wou'd If She Cou'd*, 'have been very well fleshed, and dare boldly fasten'.[47] Such predators often refer to their quarry as though they were female deer: 'does', a word that could mean 'prostitutes', but was also used of young women presumed to be respectable.[48] Because upper-class women, as well as whores, tended to wear vizard masks in the park, unless they were displaying themselves in the Mall, or were properly escorted, the chase often began with considerable uncertainty on the man's part as to the social standing, as well as identity, of the moving target. It was even possible to make the catastrophic mistake of pursuing one's own wife. The kind of embarrassment suffered by Navarre and his friends in *Love's Labour's Lost*, when the women mask and exchange love-tokens, and each man plays court to the wrong girl, is endemic in the park scenes of Restoration comedy.

But it is not only the masking and hunting in *Love's Labour's Lost*, its park setting and wittily realistic women, that make Shakespeare's play seem so uncannily to foreshadow those of a later period. As its title indicates, this is a work which concludes with the separation of people in love, with partings rather than marriage, and the reason is not to be found on the level of plot. The initial impediment – that league of study binding Navarre and his friends to shun female company for three years – crumbles midway through the comedy. What still holds Navarre and the Princess of France, Berowne, Rosaline, and the other two couples apart in Act v is not so much broken vows as attitudes of mind: chief among them, on the women's part, a deep distrust of the men's ability to sustain their love within

---

[47] Etherege, *She Would If She Could*, II.1.105–7.

[48] Sir Mannerly Shallow, the rustic fool in Crowne's *The Country Wit*, finds London's Whetstone Park, now built over, and notorious for its brothels, puzzling because devoid of grass and deer. 'I...spoke for a pasty; and they told me the strangest thing, they said their rooms were full of cold pasties, so big two people might sleep in one, and that if I had a mind to a doe, they would put me in a pasty, and put a doe to me' (III.4.107–10).

Plate 12   Ladies and gentlemen taking the air in St James's Park with a troop of horse guards on the left and, in the centre distance, the end of the Pall Mall court. From a view by Kip in the Crace Collection. Detail from a view by Kip in the Crace Collection.

marriage. That is why, in the final moments, they impose on their suitors penances designed to test the strength of their commitment and, in the case of Berowne, sent to jest a twelvemonth in a hospital, the validity of an accustomed social manner. Whether the men will return to claim their ladies at the end of the stipulated year of trial and waiting is unknown: something as much outside the limits of the play as the question of whether Etherege's Dorimant will survive his month of exile among the bucolic horrors of Hampshire and marry Harriet, or will flee after a fortnight, back to London and his bachelor life.

The ending of *Love's Labour's Lost* is unique in its period and, so far as I know, in English comedy generally before the Restoration. But between 1667 and 1700 versions of it turn up over and over again in plays by very different authors. In some comedies, the test is contained within the action. The man either passes it, or he fails. In the latter eventuality, if the woman accepts him, she does so with a measure of cynicism. In a number of plays, however, the ending is left open, as it is in *Love's Labour's Lost*. The woman turns aside the proposal of marriage finally elicited from the man she loves, for a definite or indefinite period. This is what not only Etherege's Harriet, but his Ariana and Gatty, for instance, do in *She Wou'd If She Cou'd*, Miranda and Clarinda in Shadwell's *The Virtuoso* (1676), Mrs Sightly in Southerne's *The Wives' Excuse*, and Araminta in Congreve's *The Old Batchelour* (1693). A test, as the Princess of France puts it in *Love's Labour's Lost*, of whether an 'offer made in heat of blood' will 'bear this trial, and last love' (v.2.803), it can even (as in the Congreve and Southerne) suggest an impasse never to be broken.

Wellvile, in *The Wives' Excuse*, has been Mrs Sightly's passionate, jealous but 'Platonick lover' for seven years. At the end, he offers to give up what he values most, 'my liberty'. Sightly, however, although she loves him, turns aside his proposal: 'This is too sudden to be serious.'[49] In the concluding moments of *The Old Batchelour*, when Bellmour and Belinda have agreed to marry, Araminta evades Vainlove's 'May I presume to hope so great a Blessing?' 'We had better', she tells him, 'take the Advantage of a little of our Friends Experience first.'[50] Bellmour's response to this – 'O my Conscience,

[49] Thomas Southerne, *The Wives' Excuse*, in *The Works of Thomas Southerne*, ed. Robert Jordan and Harold Love, 1 (Oxford, 1988), v.3.294.
[50] William Congreve, *The Old Batchelour*, in *The Plays of William Congreve*, ed. Herbert Davis (Chicago, 1967), v.2.172–6.

she dares not consent, for fear he shou'd recant' – is shrewd. Throughout the comedy, Vainlove has suffered agonies of desire for Araminta, but retreated in disgust as soon as he thought she might allow herself to be captured: 'I stumble ore the Game I would pursue. – 'Tis dull and unnatural to have a Hare run full in the Hounds Mouth; and would distaste the keenest Hunter'.[51] Like Laelaps, the miraculous hound given by Minos to Procris, which never failed to pull down its prey – until it had the misfortune to meet up with an equally miraculous hare, which could never be caught – Wellvile and Vainlove seem forever frozen in pursuit, the distance between them and Sightly and Araminta impossible for either side to diminish. A situation frequently debated in those Restoration love poems which argue for and against 'fruition', it also reaches back to Hadamar's medieval *Jagd*, in which the lover, hunting in a park with fifty allegorical hounds, finds himself quite unable, when he has the deer at bay, to unleash the one called 'Consummation', but lets his quarry escape, to be once more and endlessly pursued.[52]

In 1762, the anonymous adapter of *Love's Labour's Lost* permitted the Princess to enter Navarre's park accompanied by a forester, but not to be so unlady-like as to shoot anything. He also closed Shakespeare's ending. Although the women try in the final moments to exact the year of trial and penance, Biron needs only to break into the 'Have at you then, affections men at arms' speech, from Act IV of Shakespeare's play, for them to abandon the whole idea. 'My liege', Biron complacently points out, 'you see how / Woman yields, when woo'd in proper terms.'[53] And as they all leave for France to get married, Biron neatly inverts the words of his Shakespearean original: 'Our wooing now doth end like an old play; / Jack hath his Jill; these ladies courtesie / Hath nobly made our sport a Comedy'. Imbecile though it is, *The Students* is nonetheless indicative of its period in its nervousness about truly independent and witty women, its rejection not only of the love chase, but of any suggestion that comedy need not end in marriage, and on male terms. I have been arguing not only for Shakespeare's special Elizabethan interest in parks, but for suggestive

---

[51] *Ibid.*, IV.1.175–80.
[52] For an account of this and related poems, see *The Stag of Love: The Chase in Mediaeval Literature*, by Marcelle Thiebaux (Ithaca, 1974). Also, for the symbolism of the hunt, see John Cummins, *The Hound and the Hawk: The Art of Medieval Hunting* (London, 1988), esp. pp. 68–83.
[53] *The Students: A Comedy altered from Shakespeare's Love's Labour's Lost and Adapted to the Stage* (London, 1969) (Cornmarket Shakespeare Series, vol. 33), pp. 74, 78.

links between the ones in *The Merry Wives*, *Titus Andronicus* and *Love's Labour's Lost*, and those in some of the best comedies of the later seventeenth century: links which the three adaptations, by Dennis, Ravenscroft and the author of *The Students*, help (in their several ways) to define. In the course of the eighteenth century, that association was eroded, and so was a whole rigorous and sexually candid tradition of English comedy which had managed, in certain fundamental respects, to overleap the eighteen years of the theatre's interregnum.

Although St James's (like Hyde Park) remained for some time fashionable, its appeal was gradually superseded by that of Vauxhall Gardens and the more various but theatrically not very assimilable entertainments in which it specialized. Fielding's Amelia, in 1751, takes the air in St James's, but sees in Vauxhall the true *paradeisos*: fancying herself, on her first visit, 'in those blissful Mansions which we hope to enjoy hereafter'.[54] The transfer, under William and Mary, of the royal residence to Kensington (at least one park play, Leigh's *Kensington Gardens* of 1719 attempted to follow them) also diminished the centrality of St James's. Most important of all, however, was what registers increasingly in eighteenth-century comedy as a real change and diminution in the comedic value of the park: one in which the imagery of the hunt was eventually to become obsolete. Already, in Steele's *The Lying Lover* of 1704, an assignation at Rosamond's Pond has entirely lost its sexual implications. The anonymous author of *St James's Park*, in 1733, does almost nothing with an enormous cast of characters clearly intended to mirror his actual outdoor audience but have them walk up and down the Mall slandering each other. Some of the dialogue, genuinely funny, looks forward to Sheridan's *The School For Scandal* (1777). Nonetheless, when five of them decide to march abreast down the Mall and 'as Congreve says, *Laugh at the great Vulgar and the Small*... Sneer all the Men we meet that are Strangers to us, out of Countenance. And jostle all the Women', it is impossible not to remember that in *The Way of the World* (1700) these were the very minor voices of Petulant and Witwoud, whose proposal to do just this Mirabell treated with contempt.[55] Certainly St James's Park in Congreve's play, that miniature forest of the passions, of dangerous *éclaircissements* between the sexes, and snatched private meetings, had been, as it was in so

---

[54] Henry Fielding, *Amelia*, ed. Martin C. Battestin (Wesleyan edition of the Works of Henry Fielding) (Oxford, 1983), p. 395.   [55] *St James's Park*, p. 17.

many late seventeenth-century comedies, the scene of something far more consequential than mere backbiting.

To talk about the declining fortunes of London's parks in eighteenth-century literature would require another essay. I want only to suggest that the risk and potential anarchy of parks becomes increasingly prominent in novels of the period, and is associated there with a more timorous kind of heroine. Amelia's Vauxhall paradise rapidly turns nasty, even though she has two male friends with her, as a young rake forces his way into a place opposite her at table and gazes 'in a Manner with which Modesty can neither look, nor bear to be looked at'.[56] Fanny Burney's Evelina and her two companions have to be rescued, again at Vauxhall, from an insolent ring of bullies, 'laughing immoderately'.[57] Earlier comedy heroines had, on occasion, positively invited this kind of situation. Fiorella and Violante, for instance, in Mountfort's *Greenwich Park*, coolly approach and 'rally' with a group of blustering strangers, summoning assistance only when the men, no match for them verbally, resort to violence.[58] The later women, far from relishing such encounters, are terrified even by pale equivalents, and tremulously grateful to the noble gentlemen who spring to their aid.

No longer fashionable, London's parks, like those of almost all great cities, are now dangerous by day and can be deadly at night. Individuals, outside the special fraternity of dog-walkers and pram-pushers, tend to think twice about striking up an acquaintance with strangers. Sociologists and psychiatrists produce complicated studies of why normal behaviour patterns should alter so radically within the gates of these public places. And parks have taken on a new and sinister lease of life as the setting for plays. Not even Rochester thought to list infanticide among the nocturnal crimes of St James's, but in Edward Bond's *Saved* youths stone a baby to death in its pram, in a park 'at closing time'.[59] The London taxi-driver in Pinter's *Victoria Station*, whose cab has gravitated to the side of an unidentified 'dark park', is possibly mad; his woman passenger, silent and invisible on the back seat, seems to be dead.[60] When, in Pinter's *Old Times* (1971), Kate imagines a 'walk across the park', Anna shudders

---

[56] *Amelia*, p. 396.

[57] Fanny Burney, *Evelina: Or, The History of a Young Lady's Entrance into the World*, ed. Edward A. Bloom (London, 1986), p. 195.

[58] William Mountford, *Greenwich Park*, ed. Paul W. Miller (Scholars' Facsimiles and Reprints) (New York, 1977), p. 4.   [59] Edward Bond, *Saved* (London, 1965), scene 6.

[60] Harold Pinter, *Victoria Station*, in *Other Places: Three Plays* (London, 1982), p. 51.

away from the memory: 'The park is dirty at night, all sorts of horrible people, men hiding behind trees and women with terrible voices, they scream at you as you go past, and people come out suddenly from behind trees and bushes and there are shadows everywhere...'[61] I want to end, however, with a different contemporary play: *Der Park* by Botho Strauss, an adaptation of Shakespeare's *A Midsummer Night's Dream*, first published in Germany in 1983, and recently performed at the Crucible Theatre, Sheffield.

Although Puck's wanderings, in Shakespeare, had taken him 'over park, over pale' (II.1.4) in Titania's service, the 'palace wood, a mile without the town' (1.2.101–2) appeared to be the equivalent of a royal forest. There is a forester in charge (IV.1.103), but no hint of any other human habitation, let alone of the sheep and goats pastured in Arden. Duke Theseus hunts there. Other people enter the wood on May Morning, or for special reasons such as an elopement, or the need to rehearse a play. Even the fairies are transients. When, in 1692, someone – possibly Betterton – turned Shakespeare's comedy into *The Fairy Queen*, a spectacular opera with music by Purcell, this forest setting survived for only one act. Titania then commands that everything should be transformed into Fairy-land: something which turns out to mean an enormous paradisal park, with grottoes, arbours, tree-lined avenues and delightful walks, a lake, a pretend forest, and a river with swans.

The park of *The Fairy Queen*, its different aspects revealed and changed through the use of movable scenes, stands in a fluid but organic relationship to the palace of Duke Theseus, where the opera ends. In the Strauss play, it has become a municipal green space paled in by an un-named city. Here, the stage is dominated by a large elder bush, its leafless twigs festooned with 'bits of paper, beer cans, tights, a shoe, a broken cassette-recorder with its tape flapping about, etc.'[62] Animal noises emanate from the cages of a sleazy circus. In the foreground: a shallow pit filled with dirty sand. Into this dispiriting setting, from some beautiful other planet 'where the wild thyme blows', comes Oberon, hunting Titania, his 'usual quarry', but also benevolently intent on teaching human beings how to make the most of the divine gift of sexuality. His project fails. The play's version of love in idleness only makes its quartet of young lovers more faithless and petty, while turning Titania into a bestial Pasiphaë. The

[61] Pinter, *Old Times* (London, 1971), pp. 43–4.
[62] Botho Strauss, *The Park*, trans. Tinch Minter and Anthony Vives (Sheffield, 1988), p. 7.

changeling boy, now a black park attendant, for whose sexual favours a gay sculptor called Cyprian (alias Puck) once competed with Titania, brutally murders Cyprian. Victimized and be-fouled by packs of young people who rove aimlessly through the park, the immortals gradually forget those talismanic Shakespearean lines about the 'bank where the wild thyme blows': the memory of which might enable them to return to their extraterrestrial paradise. They too are trapped, at the end, in a world epitomized by the litter-strewn city park and its elder bush, 'so dirty, sick and bare': a place from which wit and elegance have vanished as completely as the deer.

Index